THE ANATOMY OF MADNESS

Essays in the History of Psychiatry

VOLUME I

THE ANATOMY OF MADNESS

Essays in the History of Psychiatry

VOLUME I

People and Ideas

EDITED BY

W.F. Bynum, Roy Porter,
and Michael Shepherd

Tavistock Publications

LONDON AND NEW YORK

First published in 1985 by
Tavistock Publications Ltd
11 New Fetter Lane, London EC4P 4EE
Published in the USA by
Tavistock Publications
in association with Methuen, Inc.
29 West 35th Street, New York, NY 10001

© 1985 W.F. Bynum, Roy Porter, and Michael Shepherd

Typeset by Graphicraft Typesetters Ltd, Hong Kong
Printed in Great Britain at
the University Press, Cambridge

British Library Cataloguing in Publication Data

The Anatomy of madness: essays in the history of psychiatry.
    1. Psychiatry—History
I. Title II. Porter, Roy, 1946– III. Bynum,
    W.F. IV. Shepherd, Michael, 1923–
        616.89'009   RC438

ISBN 0–422–79430–9 (V. 1)
ISBN 0–422–79440–6 (V. 2)
ISBN 0–422–60350–3 (Set)

Library of Congress Cataloging in Publication Data

Main entry under title:
The Anatomy of madness.

'Most of the papers in these volumes arose from a seminar series
on the history of psychiatry and a one-day seminar on the same
theme held at the Wellcome Institute for the History of
Medicine, London, during the academic year 1982–83'—
Acknowledgements.
Includes bibliographies and indexes.
Contents: v. 1. People and ideas v. 2. Institutions and society.
    1. Psychiatry—Europe—History—Addresses, essays,
lectures. 2. Psychiatric hospitals—Europe—History—Addresses,
essays, lectures. I. Bynum, W.F.
    (William F.), 1943– II. Porter, Roy,
    1946– III. Shepherd, Michael, 1923–
IV. Wellcome Institute for the History of Medicine.
RC450.A1A53 1985   362.2'094   85–9824

ISBN 0–422–79430–9 (V. 1)
ISBN 0–422–79440–6 (V. 2)
ISBN 0–422–60350–3 (Set)

Contents

Contents of companion volume
Volume II
Institutions and Society

Contributors

G.E. BERRIOS, MA (Oxon); MD; FRCPsych; DPM, is consultant Psychiatrist to Addenbrooke's Hospital, Cambridge and University Lecturer in Psychiatry. He is also Director of Medical Studies and Fellow of Robinson College, Cambridge. He trained as a psychiatrist in Oxford and was a Wellcome Scholar at Corpus Christi College, where he read Psychology and Philosophy, and later obtained the Oxford Diploma in the History and Philosophy of Science. Before moving to Cambridge in 1977 he was a lecturer in psychiatry at Leeds University. His special interests include the psychiatric complications of endocrinological and neurological disease, and the psychopathology of dementia and transient psychoses. He has published widely on these subjects and also on the historical and conceptual aspects of neuropsychiatry. He is the main editor of *Treatments and Management in Adult Psychiatry*.

THEODORE M. BROWN was trained in the History of Science at Princeton University and in the History of Medicine at Johns Hopkins. He also studied at Cambridge University. Since 1977 he has taught at the University of Rochester (USA), where he is Associate Professor of History and of Preventive Medicine and where, in 1981, he studied with the Medical-Psychiatric Liaison Group. His initial research and publication is in seventeenth- and eighteenth-century science and medicine. In addition to numerous articles, in 1981 he published *The Mechanical Philosophy and the 'Animal Œconomy': A Study in the Development of English Physiology in the Seventeenth and Eighteenth Century*. In recent years, he has become increasingly interested in the history of the behavioural sciences, particularly in twentieth-century American medicine. Brown serves on the editorial board of *Medical History*.

JANET BROWNE is Associate Editor of the *Correspondence of Charles Darwin*. Previously she was a Wellcome Fellow at the Wellcome Institute for the History of Medicine and then Research Assistant to the Unit for the History of Medicine at University College London, where she worked on Darwin and the history of physiognomy; she also edited, with W.F. Bynum and Roy Porter, *Dictionary of the History of Science*. Since 1983 she has been an Honorary Lecturer at the Unit for the History of Medicine, University College.

W.F. BYNUM is Head of the joint Academic Unit for the History of Medicine at the Wellcome Institute for the History of Medicine and University College London. He is the editor (with Roy Porter and E.J. Browne) of *A Dictionary of the History of Science*, and the author of a number of articles on the history of psychiatry. His study of the relationship between basic science and clinical medicine in the nineteenth century will be published by Cambridge University Press.

ANTHONY CLARE is Professor and Head of Department of Psychological Medicine, St Bartholomew's Hospital Medical College. He qualified in medicine in Dublin, and was Senior Registrar and Deputy Director at the General Practice Research Unit, Institute of Psychiatry, London from 1975 to 1983. He is the author of many papers on premenstrual tension, alcohol abuse, psychiatric aspects of general practice, and controversial issues in psychiatry. His books include *Psychiatry in Dissent*; *Let's Talk About Me*, a critical view of the current psychotherapies; and *In The Psychiatrist's Chair*, a collection of in-depth interviews broadcast by the BBC. He is a regular broadcaster.

IAN DOWBIGGIN is a PhD candidate in history at the University of Rochester (NY) currently writing his doctoral dissertation on nineteenth-century French psychiatry, provisionally titled 'The Professional and Cultural Dimensions of Psychopathology in France 1840–1890'. He received his MA at the Institute for the History and Philosophy of Science and Technology at the University of Toronto, where his master's thesis was on the psychiatric issues characterizing the collaboration between Sigmund Freud and Carl Jung from 1906 to 1913.

JOHN FORRESTER has studied the history of psychoanalysis for some years. He is the author of *Language and the Origins of Psychoanalysis* and numerous articles. He is editor and co-translator of the Seminars I and II of Jacques Lacan, soon to be published. His forthcoming books include *The Dream of Psychoanalysis* and *Lying, Gambling and Other Paradoxes*. He is Lecturer in the History and Philosophy of Science, University of Cambridge.

MICHAEL NEVE is lecturer in the history of medicine at University College London and at the Wellcome Institute for the History of Medicine.

His PhD thesis was on the history of science and scientific institutions in provincial England in the early nineteenth century, and he has published articles on the history of geology and on the social organization of science in early Victorian England. He is currently studying the history of psychiatry in a broad historical context, with particular reference to the place of degenerationist ideas in the late nineteenth-century European historical and cultural context.

ROY PORTER is Senior Lecturer at the Wellcome Institute for the History of Medicine, London. After working early on the history of the earth sciences, and writing *The Making of Geology*, he has subsequently researched in parallel into social history (*English Society in the Eighteenth Century*), and the social dimensions of the history of medicine. He is currently working on the early history of psychiatry in Britain, on quackery and on the lay experience of illness and doctors.

M.A. SCREECH, BA (London), MA (Oxon), DLitt (Birmingham), DLitt (London), FBA; Senior Research Fellow, All Souls College, Oxford. Born in Plymouth, he studied at Sutton High School, Plymouth and University College London, returning to UCL after service in Intelligence (Far East), and graduating in French in 1950. After lecturing in Birmingham, with periods in Canada and the USA, he returned to UCL in 1961 as reader, then professor. From 1971 to 1984 he was Fielden Professor of French Language and Literature, lecturing frequently in continental Europe and North America (including a year as Johnson Professor at Madison, Wisconsin). His published works include studies and editions of Rabelais, books on Marot, the poet Du Bellay, and the Biblical scholar, Lefèvre d'Etaples; a book on Erasmus's religion, *Ecstasy and the Praise of Folly*, and *Montaigne and Melancholy*, an exploration of the role of melancholy ecstasy in Montaigne's life and writings. He continues to work on the history of ideas. In 1956, he married Anne Reeve; they are collaborating together in a critical edition of Erasmus's *Annotationes in Novum Testamentum*.

ANDREW SCULL, Professor of Sociology at the University of California, San Diego, was educated at Balliol College, Oxford and at Princeton University. At various times during the past decade, he has held fellowships from the Guggenheim Foundation, the American Council of Learned Societies, and the Shelby Cullom Davis Center for Historical Studies at Princeton University. His books include *Decarceration; Museums of Madness; Madhouses, Mad-doctors and Madmen; Social Control and the State;* and *Durkheim and the Law*. In addition he has contributed numerous articles and review essays to leading journals in sociology, history, psychiatry, and law.

MICHAEL SHEPHERD is Professor of Epidemiological Psychiatry and Honorary Director, General Practice Research Unit at the Institute of Psychiatry, University of London. He is the author of several monographs and many research papers; a bibliography of his publications may be found in a volume of his selected papers, *The Psychosocial Matrix of Psychiatry*. In 1970 he founded the distinguished journal *Psychological Medicine*, which he still edits. He is also general editor of the multivolume *Handbook of Psychiatry*.

J.P. WILLIAMS is a member of the Wellcome Unit for the History of Medicine, Cambridge. After studying science and history of science, with a dissertation on the educational philosophy of William Whewell, he did a PhD in history on the subject of Victorian psychical research. Currently he is teaching courses in Cambridge University in the history of medicine, and researching and writing on the responses to the Victorian women's movement, especially those for women's medical training and higher education.

Acknowledgements

MOST OF THE papers in these volumes arose from a seminar series on the history of psychiatry and a one-day seminar on the same theme held at the Wellcome Institute for the History of Medicine, London, during the academic year 1982–83. The editors wish to express their gratitude to the Wellcome Trustees for providing facilities for these meetings and for providing funds to meet research expenses. We also wish to put on record our deep thanks to the staff of Tavistock Publications, in particular its chief editor, Gill Davies, for the exemplary interest and courtesy, enthusiasm and efficiency which we have received from them during the putting of these volumes through the press.

Introduction

IN RECENT YEARS, the challenge of interpreting the history of madness in its relation to the emergence of psychiatry has assumed fresh urgency yet also new difficulty.[1] This is a situation which has been brought about by a conjuncture of anxieties and advances, both in debates about psychiatry and in the practice of history.

On the one hand, the antipsychiatry movement, spearheaded by R.D. Laing's and Thomas Szasz's exposés of the 'myth of mental illness', helped to precipitate what Charles Rosenberg has called a 'crisis of psychiatric legitimacy', thereby forcing scholars to delve back into the past for the roots of the present crisis, and in search of the possibilities of alternative psychotherapeutics.[2] At the same time, but rather more generally, the mounting critique of 'welfarism' and of today's 'caring professions' (more aptly termed 'disabling', according to Ivan Illich)[3] has reopened for historical interpretation the meaning of the rise of professional mental health-care services and of the modern mental hospital – developments traditionally hailed as milestones in the march of humane progress out of the 'dark ages' of unreformed Bedlam and all its horrors. And, not least, capping these rethinkings, the recent introduction of policies of 'decarcerating' mental patients has thrown into doubt that keystone institution, the asylum, sending historians back to re-examine its 'discovery' and rationale, and the socio-politics of its rise to centrality.[4]

On the other hand, today's trends in history-writing itself have also shed new light on madness. The 'new social history' – with its commitment to viewing society 'from below' – has diverted social historians from the traditional Fabian favourites of scandals and enquiries, reformers and legislation, pointing them instead towards the heartlands of personal experience: the family, sex and marriage, the politics of household and community pressures, vernacular culture and its struggles with elite power.[5] In these contexts, discovering how madness appeared, not only to doctors, magistrates, and bureaucrats, but within the knotted skeins of personal and social relations, has become a major challenge, taken up in the brilliant reconstructions of scholars such as Michael MacDonald, whose pioneering *Mystical Bedlam* resurrected the social experiences of 'troubled souls' in seventeenth-century English rural settlements.[6] Moreover the new-wave history has been emphatically evangelical in insisting there can be no such animal as social history with the politics left out. The history of madness is now self-consciously being written not just as the history of disease or affliction, but as the story of power relationships – paternalistic, legal, institutional, therapeutic, commercial. Psychiatric power, so long medicalized and normalized, masked and idealized, is itself being laid bare.

Focusing on the politics of madness in times past, historians have been repudiating many time-honoured readings of the subject. Open almost any book published within the last decade tackling the history of what Scull terms 'madhouses, mad-doctors and madmen', and you are almost sure to find it prefaced with a blistering critique of the so-called received or dominant 'line'. Mainline histories of psychiatry and the mental health movement – for example, the works of Zilboorg, Alexander and Selesnick, or Kathleen Jones – are now accused of committing the crimes of Whiggishness, presentism, and scientism, and found guilty of being 'in-house jobs', written by or on behalf of the psychiatric profession, and providing legitimations for entrenched psychiatric orthodoxies.[7] In thus making the past collude in the purposes of the present, traditional histories offered visions of a meliorist psychiatric trinity: science, humanity, and policy; of advance from brutal madhouses like unreformed Bedlam, through humane lunatic asylums, up to scientific mental hospitals; of breakthroughs in science such as David Ferrier's researches into brain localization; and they have presented dramatic tableaux starring reforming heroes, such as Pinel striking the chains off the insane in the Bicêtre. But all such readings are now accused – almost ritualistically – of being uncritical and even mystifying.

By contrast, the 'Young Turks' amongst the scholars, mobilizing what the late Peter Sedgwick dubbed an 'anti-history of psychiatry', offer iconoclasm.[8] Teleological and 'tunnel' history are out. Practitioners, theories, and movements are to be rated not according to their place in the current psychiatric pantheon, but critically and neutrally, in historical context. Thus anachronism must be avoided; the ideas and intentions of the past must be understood on their own terms. And neither must the dynamo of revaluation halt there. For the new history does not simply take the past at its own word (surely a sound psychoanalytical maxim). Hidden interests and latent social functions must also be teased out; Clio too must read between the lines, and the right of historical actors to be their own mystagogues must be challenged. For instance, Victorian superintendents portrayed their asylums as havens in a heartless world; and their word has often been accepted. But the new history is also sensitive to how asylums could additionally serve functions of 'social control'[9] – indeed, frequently, also of *gender* control – all the more potent, even sinister, in view of their benign fronts of care and protection. In a similar way, Foucault and his followers have argued that the much trumpeted 'moral therapy' of Pinel, Tuke, and Chiarugi should be seen not, as customarily, as the freeing of the insane from the obscene terrors of whips, chains, and manacles, but rather as the imposition of more subtly terrifying 'mind-forged manacles' of guilt and self-control.[10] Liberation from the racking of the body merely meant new tortures for the mind.

If it is the sin of Whiggery to believe in the myth of progress,[11] then this onslaught on Whig history of psychiatry may readily become Whiggish itself, if it complacently asserts its own superiority. So is our historiography advancing? Now, few will dispute that the waves of fresh empirical research and massive conceptual reorientation appearing over the last twenty years, much of it stemming from the breathtaking iconoclasm of the late Michel Foucault,[12] have proved stimulating, even intoxicating. So many of our old cast-iron certainties have been toppled into the melting pot of revaluation. Take for example, what was traditionally billed as the opening chapter in the foundation of psychiatry, the 'recognition' of sixteenth-century pioneers such as Johannes Wier and Reginald Scot that 'witches' and 'demoniacs' were not after all genuinely possessed by the devil, but rather were mentally sick; they were in need not of the faggot but of medication. Yet even this hallowed reading of what seems like a salutary breakthrough from ecclesiastical persecution into medical tolerance has been dynamited, above all by Thomas Szasz, who argues that the alleged mental illness of the possessed was all a myth.[13] For their part, feminists have contended that the psychiatric 'exposure' of witchcraft amounted in reality to a typical patriarchal tactic for neutralizing a bastion of female power.[14] And radical historians have argued that the true significance of the shift lay not in any mercy towards 'witches' but in territorial imperialism by the emergent medical profession against the Church and people. The medicalization and psychiatrization of witchcraft thus involved an elite onslaught against popular culture (one, MacDonald suggests, whose therapeutic implications for the disturbed were wholly retrograde).[15] Moreover, as Szasz and others have stressed, in the ending of witchhunts against witches lay the beginnings of witchhunts against the poor at large.

Or, to take another example of how the old saga of psychiatry has been turned upside down by the new historiography: Freud's flash of recognition that the tales of childhood sexual assault and rape recounted by hysterical female clients were not genuine memories at all but instead wish-fulfilling fantasies. This has traditionally been regarded as the great 'Eureka-episode' in the formation of the psychoanalytic paradigm of the unconscious, of infantile sexuality, of the submerged and Protean powers of desire and repression, of the relations between neurosis and hysteria. Freud certainly regarded it as such. But new critical interrogations of the early Freud, for example the work of Jeffrey Masson, are challenging this reading, arguing that Freud was, by contrast, guilty in this instance of certain dubious acts of screening and intellectual bad faith: the truth – that these clients had indeed been assaulted – was for complex professional causes inconvenient, or perhaps for personal reasons too uncomfortable, for Freud to bear; it required to be mystified.[16]

And then, to bore into the very core of the problem, the new historiography insistently poses the question: is there any such natural object as 'madness' at all? Few would deny that when the historical demographer confronts Bills of Mortality, he is dealing with a real natural object (death).

Is the historian of insanity treating something equivalent? Or is he more like the student of religious heresy, probing what are essentially relativistic cultural constructs? Today's scholarship is sceptical whether any such unambiguous substratum of madness is accessible to historians. Hence, it is argued, our histories must be about something other than the pathos of the mad and the sad, or how monomaniacs or schizophrenics were diagnosed, cared for or cured. They must fundamentally confront what Szasz has termed 'the manufacture of madness' itself,[17] the labelling of the disturbed in the first place, and the social system within which such stigma operates. Szasz's phrase, perhaps unfortunately, carries suggestions of conspiracy; yet sensitive historical and sociological scholarship over the last two decades has performed valuable service in making us aware how far the recognition and interpretation of mental illness, indeed its whole meaning, are culture-bound, and change profoundly from epoch to epoch, in ways inexplicable unless viewed within wider contexts of shifting power relations, social pressures, and ideological interests.

The danger of course is that today's radicalism rapidly ossifies into tomorrow's dogma. New certainties may supplant the old, which are, however, no less monolithic, impervious to criticism, and subservient to current causes (albeit *ours*, not *theirs*). It is wholly a gain that the old dogmas have been challenged. For these were vitiated by a fundamental flaw: they were not built upon large foundations of empirical research. There are, indeed, precious few investigations into the history of madness and psychiatry published more than thirty years ago which, in conscience, one would seriously miss. Recent revisionist history is on the whole more thoroughly researched. Yet that is no reason for complacency. The late Michel Foucault's *La Folie et la déraison* (translated and abridged as *Madness and Civilization*) is a truly magisterial work. But it would be a mistake to assume that on many topics its roots in historical evidence are very secure, as Eric Midelfort, Peter Sedgwick, and others have already pointed out.[18] Hence, for our generation to bandy around slogans like 'the ship of fools', 'the great confinement', 'the medicalization of madness', or 'the discovery of the asylum', would be no advance on chanting the ancient war-cries of the march of scientific psychiatry.

The work of criticism has thus been launched. What hasn't, to anything like the same degree, is the labour of actually *finding out*. We remain simply very ignorant about most aspects of 'madhouses, mad-doctors and mad-men'. And it is important that this research agenda should not be thought of as just a routine filling-in job, humdrum painting-by-numbers now that the main lines have been blocked in. Rather there must be energetic dialogue between research, in many cases in absolutely virgin fields, and conceptual renewal. Examine many departments of the history of insanity, and it becomes abundantly clear on what slim foundations our sweeping gener-alizations rest. There have been heated debates, for instance, over how to interpret the Tukes's 'moral therapy' at the York Retreat: was it really a new awakening of reason and kindness, or was it rather a devilish twist of the screw of psychological torture?[19] But interpreters of Tukean moral therapy have relied almost wholly upon the testimony of a single key propaganda document, Samuel Tuke's *Description of the Retreat* (1813), for no investigation of how moral therapy actually worked at the Retreat, drawing on the ample archive of case books, has ever been published. This situation has now been rectified by Anne Digby, in a paper in the companion volume and in a new monograph, and the results are challenging.[20] One trusts that as a consequence premature construals of the Retreat will wither away. Such hopes may be over-optimistic, however, since in the case of Bedlam (as Patricia Allderidge points out in the companion volume) careless assertions continue to be repeated and embellished, full of elementary errors and misconceptions, which recourse to the archives would instantly scotch. The folklore of 'scandalous Bedlam' seems too psychologically convenient to be abandoned.

Our aim, therefore, in planning these twin volumes, has been to marshal a wide-ranging body of unpublished research-in-depth covering key topics in the history of 'madhouses, mad-doctors and madmen'. These meaty and varied explorations by scholars employing distinctive methods should prove both a stimulus and an irritant. Rather like the obsolete medical therapy of the 'issue' (an incision kept open to facilitate the beneficial formation of pus), these volumes will, we trust, prevent old wounds in the history of psychiatry from closing prematurely, leaving only cosmetically smooth scar tissue. More blood yet remains to be let.

The mix of depth, detail, and diversity to be found here reveals a complex historical fabric, and raises again and again the problems historians must face in relating intentions to outcomes, science to ideology, knowledge to control, and the overt to the latent functions of actions and institutions. The authors remind us of the dangers of generalizing prematurely – of speaking, for instance, of *the* asylum as if asylums came like Model T Fords. Instead, they probe the distinctions between asylums large and small, public and private, between eighteenth- and nineteenth-century prototypes, between English experiences and those in Sweden or Italy (as explored by Qvarsell and Tagliavini in the companion volume). This stress on complexity is not a blank cheque for historiographical nihilism or mindless empiricism. It merely reminds us that (*pace* Lytton Strachey) ignorance remains a dubious basis for generalizations, and that in many fields ignorance is precisely the state of the art.

These two volumes thus make no pretence to being an answer book, or a textbook overview of 'madhouses, mad-doctors and madmen'. Rather they offer a kind of dispatch from the front, reporting on many of the key areas where enquiry – empirical and conceptual – is currently progressing. The balance lies with the British scene, though the 'Introduction' to the companion volume offers a substantial comparison between developments in the Old World and the New.[21] These essays toe no uniform methodological party line, and there has been no editorial 'whip'. We have opted for breadth, believing that catholicity of method, viewpoint, and perhaps especially time-span, are all eye-opening. This last point is important. Social history nowadays all too readily bunches itself around the Victorian epoch. It has been the almost axiomatic assumption of scholars such as Foucault, Scull, and Donnelly[22] that the decades of the nineteenth century formed the turning-points in the history of managing the mad; a view which is reinforced by the tempting assumption that before industrialization, before the Victorian administrative state, before the age of the masses – or, alternatively, way back in the 'world we have lost' – madness was just some protean phenomenon allowed its 'head', permitted to go its own way. Without an eye to the *longue durée*, many studies will miss the tenacity of traditional modes of reasoning about madness – such as Christian ones – which the historian ignores at his peril.

Furthermore, we must also avoid seeing the saga of 'madhouses, mad-doctors and madmen' as if it were – as certain Foucaultians and antipsychiatrists hint – nothing other than a dire tale of irresistible penetration by the psychiatric gaze, relentless steps in the formation of what the Castels have denounced as the 'psychiatric society'.[23] Understanding the alchemy of how psychiatric *savoir* becomes psychotherapeutic *pouvoir* is of course crucial, and it watermarks these essays. But the authors recognize that other gazes apart from the psychiatrist's have also been influential. In his evaluation of Christian madness, Screech looks at being out of one's mind as the Church saw it. Several of the essays touch on, and Neve and Bynum's 'Hamlet on the couch' closely explores, the enigma of literary responses to madness (an important field, for it is one in which arguably life mimics art).[24] In the companion volume, Eigen explores courtroom and jurisprudential notions of what constitutes madness (another *professional* gaze certainly, but, as Roger Smith has stressed in *Trial by Medicine*,[25] one perhaps incommensurable with that of psychiatry). Porter's essay on Samuel Johnson's 'vile melancholy', and Bynum's on 'The Nervous Patient' both probe sufferers' own experiences of mental disturbance – experiences which we mustn't naively expect to be 'uncontaminated', since they are mediated through the words, if not the pen, of medical authority.[26] In a somewhat parallel case, Clare ponders how far we can recover the patient-on-couch from the Holmesian detective thrillers which are Freud's published case studies – a theme recently explored in D.M. Thomas' novel, *The White Hotel*. Still another essay, Janet Browne's, tosses a further spanner into the works of psychiatric reality, with her picture of a great scientist, Charles Darwin, trying, through the use of photographs, literally to identify madness in the same way as a great psychiatrist had: and failing!

So current doubts about the caring professions and their latent potential for 'social control' can readily lead us to an anti-history of psychiatry, viewing the history of madness as a series of quasi-conspiratorial 'imperialistic' actions launched by psychiatry against its clients. This view, consonant with recent trends in the radical sociology of the professions, certainly offers powerful insights. Yet we hope that the catholic diversity of these essays will also guard against 'single vision', whether old or new.

Modern iconoclasm about the history of madness and psychiatry stems from Michel Foucault.[27] The strength of Foucault's analysis of the shifting construction of 'humanity' as both subject and object of the discourse of the human sciences over the last five centuries arises from his presentation of the problem of 'man' as embodying a double face.[28]

On the one hand, man has entered into the field of discourse as *subject*, being conceptualized in successive historical epochs as the microcosmic key to a forest of symbols, as the focus of exchange relations, as the generator of language, and then as the bearer of a biohistory. Finally, as Foucault elegizes, this enticing 'anthropology' became erased from the Rhodian shore at the twilight of the nineteenth century through the heroic nihilism of Nietzsche and the dissolution of identity in Freud's formulation – significantly for our purposes – of the unconscious and the fragmented psyche.

And yet the verso of this honourable anthropology of man viewed as the site of personality, will, and meaning has been a different kind of 'visibility' for man, regarded as the *object* of the scientific gaze. Here man becomes conscripted within discourses of knowledge and manipulated by disciplines at the service of paternalistic control and the bureaucratic state. Reversing the Enlightenment's credal linking of the advancement of learning with human emancipation, Foucault has argued how the appearance of discourses whose object was insanity was coterminous with the administrative policing of dissent and the penalizing of deviance. Not all will endorse his seemingly fatalistic recension of the Fall, the poisoned fruit of the tree of knowledge, whereby from the reign of Louis XIV, Reason, in cahoots with Absolutism, proved so tyrannical yet so vulnerable that it could not bear the rebuke of its opposite, Unreason, and needed to shut it up in the 'Great Confinement'. We can readily agree with him, however, that to understand insanity, we need to consider *both* the free power of madness as an existential moment of the human condition, *and* also its inscription within the disciplines of nosology, pathology, and therapeutics.[29]

And this duality is somewhat reflected in the way our pair of volumes has been thematically carved up: this one exploring madness as a personal reality and as represented in the 'anthropologies' of psychiatric theories; the other, examining the institutions – private and public, formal and informal – for which madness was the *raison d'être*.

Of course the split is artificial. Yet even this division of intellectual labour between the two volumes, *ad hoc* though it is, may itself serve a useful cautionary purpose. For when dealing with amorphous tendencies such as the 'manufacture of madness' or the 'psychiatrization of society', we all too readily lean lazily on the jargon of social holism, invoking often tautologous social 'demands', 'functions', 'responses'. The coming of the asylum, for example, is facilely predicated (as Scull rightly complains)[30] upon alleged procrustean 'needs' created by forces such as urbanization or industrializa-

tion, without sufficient exploration of tangible social and ideological media-
tions. But things were more complicated. It is easy to write as if there had
been a homogeneous 'asylum movement'. Yet in his admirable *The Prerogative of Asylumdom*, D.J. Mellett has traced the heavy swell of doubt and
discord over asylums as the mainstay of treating the mad, voiced both *within*
the Victorian psychiatric profession itself, and between it and other vocal
lobbies.[31] We hope that by drawing attention to a distinction here, with one
volume looking at individuals and their belief-systems, and the other
investigating public institutions in the contexts of society and politics, we
may provide a reminder of that great historical truth that men make their
own history, but not under circumstances of their own choosing.

The essays in this volume explore key issues about insanity and how it was
conceptualized. The remainder of this introduction situates these contributions in context of the wider problems raised by current research.

   Though once popular, quests for origins, roots, and founding fathers are
now reckoned antediluvian amongst intellectual historians. Foucault has
suggested that there was no 'psychology' before the nineteenth century;[32]
and the virtue of this otherwise extravagant view surely lies in the desire to
avoid the red herring of 'origin hunting'; for, as Sylvana Tomaselli has
recently suggested, otherwise one becomes bogged down in futile priority
disputes and in reliving Oedipal conflicts about contested parentages.[33] The
old debate as to who was real father of psychiatry (was it Descartes or
Burton? Paracelsus or Ficino? Aristotle or Democritus?) is evidently sterile.
Yet it would also be evasive to write as if significant transformations never
had occurred, as if no importance lay in the fact that the term 'psychology'
came into use in the eighteenth century, as if William Cullen hadn't
formulated the category 'neurosis' – though, as Lopez Piñero stresses, not
with today's meaning.[34] Similarly, it would be evasive to acknowledge that
such shifts had occurred, yet to suppose they had done so – as Foucault's
approach seems to imply – via inscrutable epistemological ruptures.

   Indeed, two orthodoxies run deeply entrenched through the scholarship,
nudging us towards particular readings of how the modern psycho-sciences
actually did take shape. One concerns what they superseded, the other what
precipitated them; or, in other words, one is about the relations of insanity
and psychiatry first with Christianity and then subsequently with secularization; the other is about their links to the scientific revolution, and the
renderings of mind postulated by the mechanical philosophy.

   When physicians came to survey the annals of insanity, they were confident that much of what had traditionally passed – and still did pass – for
religious ecstasy and inspiration involved nothing other than travesties of
true Christianity produced by disease – religious melancholy, megalomania,
and of course enthusiasm, deluded prophesying, or epilepsy.[35] And they
regarded as the greatest leap forward their speciality had ever made the view,
gaining ground amongst doctors from the late Renaissance, that witchcraft

and 'possession' were not, after all, authentic acts of the devil, but rather symptomatic of bodily or mental disease. The ending of this confusion, whereby afflictions whose province was properly physic had been rescued from the clutches of the clergy, was, it seemed, the first great triumph for psychological medicine. Many historians of psychiatry, notably Alexander and Selesnick, and Zilboorg, have endorsed this view.[36] Chastened by Szasz's warnings against slapping retrospective psychiatric diagnoses upon the deviant dead, we can, however, no longer regard these events as bathed in such a roseate glow; but neither can we avoid confronting the issue of how madness was actually construed within the Christian religion. And what Screech demonstrates in his essay in this volume is that posing the matter antithetically (were certain kinds of religious manifestations *mad*? or were they *divine*?) is anachronistic and misleading.[37] For theological traditions stretching right back to the Bible, reiterated within scholasticism, and then elaborated with playful energy by Renaissance Christian humanists such as Erasmus, argued that the proper goal of the Christian did indeed lie in achieving a divine madness, an utter other-worldliness. To go out of your senses, to be ravished in ecstasy (literally: standing out of yourself) was the believer's true release from the snares of shallow worldly wisdom within this vale of tears. As Screech provocatively puts it, 'Madness and Christianity go hand in hand.'

Rather in parallel to the fêting of melancholy genius,[38] this Christian celebration of divine madness, this praise of folly, continued to resonate down the ages, explicitly in both mainstream and heterodox theology, but no less conspicuously in Tolstoy's and Dostoievsky's incarnations of the holy fool, and surfacing also in mutated forms as the rescuing of the transcendental.[39] For example, as Williams shows below, Victorian psychological investigators such as Frederick Myers and Edmund Gurney systematically explored alleged 'psychic phenomena' such as the possession of a spiritualist medium, the trance of a hypnotic subject, or the seeing of a ghost, in the hope of gratifying their longings for proofs of a higher, numinal plane of existence – call it the spirit world, the immortality of the soul, or what you will.[40]

Of course, by the late Victorian age intellectual priorities amongst the leading lights of the Society for Psychical Research were quite different from those of Erasmus' circle. It was the hope of certain Victorians that psychology might authenticate the soul, whereas three centuries earlier the patent truths of Christianity had obviated the need for the auxiliary of psychology at all, since abnormal mental states were understood as typifying the varieties of religious experience. And the paradox, as the irresistible allusion to William James makes plain, is that by the age of James, as his own case amply proves, the analytical edge of the psychiatric temper, honed on distrust and scepticism, was rendering psychic 'phenomena' (e.g. hypnotic trances, automatism, multiple personality) more credible as symptoms of mental pathology than as proofs of the reality of spirits.[41] Psychiatry might demonstrate that something beyond the normal rational mind did indeed exist, but that something was not, however, the kind of soul that was being sought.

This dilemma, generated by the equivocal project of recruiting psychology to shore up belief in the transcendental, also appears in psychiatry's brushes with imaginative literature, where it has likewise proved a mixed blessing. The pioneering of psychological criticism by Romantics such as Coleridge proved in many ways a great advance over the formal, textual, and rhetorical rules of taste previously canonical. But in the hands of nineteenth-century alienists (suggest Bynum and Neve below in their 'Hamlet on the Couch'), psychological criticism boiled down to the remorseless extension of diagnostic categories to fictional characters (was Hamlet paranoid? was Shakespeare a great psychiatrist?) All too often the result showed crass insensitivity to the subtle mysteries of creativity, and an ingrained fear of the imagination, paralleling that perverse *fin-de-siècle* desire to demonstrate that genius was essentially a species of disease, and heralding some of the more banal excesses of Freudian psycho-biography and subsequent psycho-history.[42]

This raises perhaps the cardinal issue surrounding the functions of the emerging psychiatric disciplines: did their main thrust lie in the *stigmatization* of the 'abnormal' by psychiatric means? Or were they mainly instrumental in *legitimating* personality differences in creating tolerance for pluralism in behaviour? This has important bearings in practice. For instance, as Godlee shows in the companion volume, for first-generation Quakers of the seventeenth century, the true disciples of George Fox, violations of socially acceptable behaviour such as faith-healing, or remaining silent or speaking as the Spirit moved, or even Adamic nakedness, were marks of authentic spiritual indwelling.[43] For their descendants by contrast, including those Friends who at the beginning of the nineteenth century ran the York Retreat, suchlike eccentricities had become symptoms of mental disturbance indicating suitable cases for treatment.

Thus religious possession was Janus-faced: it could be regarded as the blessing of the chosen, or as a manifestation of psychopathology. Where the dividing line was to be drawn, and by whom, remained problematic, as the tribulations of individuals demonstrate. In the mid-eighteenth century a clutch of leading English men of letters suffered parallel crises of faith and personality. William Cowper, juvenile versifier and later eminent poet, had had a childhood religious indoctrination which left him convinced of his own ineradicable sinfulness and predestined damnation. Unable to face his guilt, he sought escape in madness, but actually experienced derangement and depression as the worst of torments.[44] In total contrast, the mystic poet Kit Smart, confined to an asylum, gloried in his own ravings, seeing them as the medium through which the mysteries of creation should be celebrated.[45] His acquaintance, Samuel Johnson, suspected that a different kind of spirit, strong liquor not pentecostal, was the cause of Smart's disturbance, yet disapproved of Smart's being locked up, merely on account of his flights of religious zeal. Johnson noted that Smart wanted everyone to pray with him in public: yet what business could a Christian society have in calling that mad? And yet (as Porter argues in his essay below), from the point of view of his own solemn Anglicanism, Johnson himself was utterly suspicious of those who glamorized madness as a superior or privileged state. For to Johnson the Christian's vocation lay in absolute rational self-command. Any lapse of rational will was an extinguishing of the divine spark. Ironically, then, it was precisely his morbid anxieties about the eclipse of reason in himself that drove Johnson to teeter on the brink of madness.[46]

As the above discussion shows, several essays in this volume thus query interpretations which view religion as in any linear way ceding territory to psychiatry (or, put another way, which see psychiatry as the unlaid ghost of faith). Of course, as Michael MacDonald and others have argued, from the dawn of the Enlightenment psychiatric labels became programmatically used to disqualify those antinomian and 'enthusiastic' modes of popular religious witness which posed threats to propertied and polite society.[47] Yet we must not forget that for a significant minority, 'psychiatry' has been not the quietus of the pilgrimage of grace, but its medium, language, and expression; names such as Paracelsus, George Cheyne, Coleridge, and, looking further afield, Lavater, Reil, and later William James and of course Jung readily suggest themselves.

Thus the fortunes of 'psychiatry' from the early modern period cannot fully be laid at the door of 'secularization', the rationalization of religion, or the 'disenchantment of the mind'. How far then should the scientific revolution bear the credit or blame? Superficially at least, the proposal is plausible. Surely it was one of the triumphs of the new science, especially the spread of atomism, that the Greek doctrines of the elements, humours, and temperaments were proved incapable of offering scientific explanations of distempers, and were thus superseded? Did not this lead eventually to more fruitful doctrines of the natural laws of the mind, a superior epistemology based upon a physiology of sensation in the associationism of Hartley, and even the model of the mind as a machine in Enlightenment materialism? Why else, after all, were so many Enlightenment thinkers aspiring to be the Newton of the mental sciences?

In his paper, Theodore Brown grasps these nettles specifically with regard to the impact of Descartes and Cartesianism.[48] In the paternity suit to reveal the true founding father of the psycho-sciences, the finger has always pointed at Descartes. For didn't the celebrated Cartesian dualism at long last clearly demarcate mind from body? Wasn't it Descartes who thus emanci-pated science from theology, and psychology from general medicine, carving out essential new disciplinary spaces? Or – looking instead through the jaundiced eyes of detractors – didn't Cartesian dualism fatally disorient, dichotomize, and alienate western man, by severing the 'ego' from all connections with anything – except via the sliver of the pineal gland – and postulating it as ontologically alien from body, from nature, from matter, and thus left alone, self-regarding and morbidly introspective?[49]

Yet Brown shows that this is to misunderstand Descartes' own theories. It wasn't the mind/brain which he cordoned off thus but the theological soul. It also completely misjudges the impact of his teachings. For both general and psychological medicine after Descartes, though often couched in Cartesian terms, went on being as thorough-going and common-sensically 'psychosomatic' as they had always been, or indeed, as Lain Entralgo would suggest, clinical medicine necessarily is.[50] The significance of Descartes may lie less in the dualism he supposedly occasioned than in the subsequent enlistment of his name, for extraneous purposes, as hero or bogeyman.

Yet this is not to deny that subsequent centuries saw diverging movements in psychiatry, some militantly physicalist, others programmatically psychical (one notes in passing that these latter, of which moral management and moral therapy are key instances, render the frequently advanced view that it was the eighteenth century which witnessed the 'medicalization of madness' rather peculiar).[51] The division between William Battie and John Monro in the mid-eighteenth century, and that between 'physicalists' such as Thomas Mayo and George Nesse Hill and 'mentalists' such as Andrew Harper and Alexander Crichton at the turn of the nineteenth,[52] hinged on whether madness was at root an organic disease or a psychic disorder – a debate with a long future ahead of it, as has been made clear in Bonnie Blustein's and Michael Clark's analyses of late Victorian debates over mind and brain, psychiatry and neurology in America and Britain.[53]

The eighteenth and nineteenth centuries were times of mounting public concern over madness; indeed according to Foucault they were the epoch when civilization anathematized madness, fearing its anarchic otherness, and cast its victims into asylums. Panic-stricken psychiatrists foretold that the tide of madness was becoming a flood, whipped up by luxury, urbanization, individualism, liberty, and other evils of civilization.[54] Or, putting it into economic terms, the market was generating spare incarcerating capacity through the emergent trade in lunacy,[55] bringing in its wake appropriate rationalizing ideologies of the asylum; or, seeing it in terms of social management, the anxiety-creating logic of capitalism was leaving trails of human casualties, both victims and threats, prompting the institutional fix of the asylum, to the satisfaction of newly professionalizing psychiatric cadres. Indeed, allowing for the melodramatic distortions which drastic precis entails, this resembles the interpretation advanced by Doerner in *Madness and the Bourgeoisie*.[56]

There is indeed much to be said for seeing the history of policy towards the insane during the last couple of centuries as responsive to the phobias of the polite and the propertied. The mad did indeed become nightmares of the normal, just as politicians, magistrates, police, priests, and press conjured up whole tribes of bogeymen and scapegoats in the shape of criminals, paupers, foreigners, atheists or whatever – all liminal cases defining and reinforcing normalcy.[57]

Opinion-formers and policy-makers produced their own phantom *Doppelgänger*, reminders of dangers lurking within, of what would break loose if law and morality broke down. Thus Ruth Harris's essay in the companion volume demonstrates how late nineteenth-century Parisian fears of demoralized, hypnotized, hysterical, or nymphomaniac women reveal male insecurities about precisely what *normal* women – your wife and daughter! – were really like. In a comparable case, P. Fullinwider's recently published analysis of Morton Prince's treatment of 'Miss Beauchamp' argues that the theories of multiple personality and identity fragmentation which late nineteenth-century American psychiatrists applied to their patients make the best sense if seen as projections, disclosing more about the crisis in personal beliefs and professional status of the psychiatrists themselves than about their clients' 'diseases'.[58]

Indeed psychiatrists' tendency to construct models of madness echoing their own phobias is nowhere more powerfully exemplified than in images of deranged women. As Elaine Showalter and others have established,[59] the Victorian psychiatric identikit picture of the neurasthenic or hysterical woman tells us principally about the roles Victorian men had allotted to 'normal' women. Charlotte Mackenzie's essay in the companion volume similarly shows how life in the asylum could prove for late Victorian women both a refuge from, yet also an intensification of, the helplessness which patriarchy enforced in the outside world. Yet, as Bynum suggests in his essay below on the nervous patient, the construct of the neurasthenic lady – delicate, highly strung, too fragile for manual labour, intellectual labour, or even for reproductive labour – could be colluded in by all parties, for it might simultaneously help meet the needs of the insecure husband, of the trapped wife craving breathing space, attention, and the compensatory power that invalidism conferred, and not least those of the assiduous and sometimes insidious figure of the medical attendant.[60] The cases of Emily Dickinson, Alice James, and Virginia Woolf illuminate these intersecting planes of collusion in and rejection of psychiatric stereotypes.[61]

Yet it would ultimately be facile to regard the 'madwoman in the attic', and the disturbed in general, as little other than bogeys of the bourgeoisie, Frankenstein's monsters embodying psychiatrists' phobias. This would, not least, be patronizing to the victims. And we can escape from it, partly because in a few cases we can approach the disturbed through channels other than the verdicts of psychiatrists and the public. The autobiographical *Narrative* of John Perceval has long been available as the deluded visionary's account of what his modern-day editor Gregory Bateson has termed his 'schizophrenia', though the introduction of this intrusive and anachronistic psychiatric label should alert us to the fact that, long before Bateson, Perceval *himself* had also done his own self-editing job, writing after the event (when he had 'recovered his sanity'), and writing polemically on behalf of a cause, that of wrongfully confined lunatics.[62] Nowadays, with the help of Dale Peterson's *A Mad People's History of Madness*,[63] we have become better aware of the wealth of accounts of their afflictions and treatment written by the mentally ill. We must avoid, of course, the trap of automatically privileging the testimony of the mad (not least because most such accounts were written retrospectively); madness, in any case, has no corner on insight. Nevertheless, these neglected writings constitute a significant addition to the archives of insanity, challenging what might otherwise be glib generalizations.

For example, in his essay below analysing Samuel Johnson's fears of incipient madness, Porter shows how Johnson's protracted self-diagnosis of his own 'vile melancholy', recorded in letters, journals, and in contemporary biographers' oral histories, lends no support to certain currently much-touted interpretations. It is often suggested nowadays[64] that the dry rationalism of Latitudinarian Anglicanism and the scientific revolution together exacerbated melancholy and depleted the therapeutic armamentarium in the eighteenth century. Yet, in Johnson's case, it was religious conviction itself, not its absence or mere husk, which was the catalyst, perhaps even the cause, of mental anguish.

Then again it has been argued that madness became significantly more 'medicalized' in the eighteenth century. Yet Johnson's dealings with doctors show that neither Johnson nor his bevy of long-suffering physicians expected that medicine would be of use in treating his moods of dark despair. Thirdly, it has been suggested that the mentally afflicted were treated in a particularly callous fashion during that century which was 'a disaster for the insane', to recall MacDonald's phrase.[65] Yet what scandalized Johnson was just how *fashionable* neurotic complaints had become amongst the polite. Indeed, study of Johnson's melancholy lends support to Nicholas Jewson's view,[66] developed to apply to medicine in general, that the Georgian age was a time when patients – affluent males, that is – were still able to 'prescribe' to their own physicians rather than having to accept medical dominance. If Jewson's model applies to the mentally as well as the physically sick, we must actively pursue the story of madness, and its treatment, from the sufferer's point of view, as well as through the physician's eyes.

But the medical side must be examined as well. For it would be a gross caricature to depict, say, late Victorian psychiatry as if it amounted to little more than male physicians, as guardians of official values, invaliding neurasthenic ladies. Indeed, as Bynum rightly stresses below, *that* element is surprisingly inconspicuous in Britain. Britain produced no Silas Weir Mitchell, no George Beard, but instead a chain of neurologists, from Carpenter and Laycock through to Hughlings Jackson and Ferrier, who were more preoccupied with fundamental research into the nervous system and the brain than with fashionable rest-cures. What may be a divergence of American and British traditions at this point warrants further research.

Thus the medical gaze also needs attention. It would be tempting to paint a caricature canvas of the irresistible rise, from the late eighteenth century onwards, of the psychiatric profession, as 'experts' steadily consolidating their grip over the asylum system, a system which they had a vested interest in extending as much as possible (this cynical reading of the profession would have rung as true to Georgian moralists as to today's radical sociologists). Yet under the microscope, many of these ringing generalizations dissolve like mist at sunrise. We might airily invent slogans about psychiatrists' professional dominance, but our grounds for this would be flimsy, since we possess few extended studies of the authority of early psychiatrists *vis-à-vis* magistrates, Poor Law officers and central government, and those that there are present deeply ambiguous findings. Thus Roger Smith has shown that Victorian psychiatrists got a rough ride as expert witnesses in Victorian murder trials.[67] Few in-depth career studies have yet been published of nineteenth-century asylum superintendents and alienists – even the most distinguished, such as J.C. Prichard and Henry Maudsley, still await their biographer. Andrew Scull's study of John Conolly in this volume is therefore particularly welcome.

Conolly has traditionally been the arch-hero of liberals for pioneering 'non-restraint' during his brief regime at the vast Hanwell public asylum around 1840.[68] Scull's study does not deny Conolly's achievement. But he does stress what a brief – less than four years – and in some respects uncharacteristic interlude that was in Conolly's chequered career, during which he failed as a GP and as an author, and failed to get psychiatry put on the map during his occupancy of the unprestigious medical chair at the recently founded University College, London. Indeed, as Scull shows, Conolly's career actually culminated in his being proprietor, occasionally in legally murky circumstances, of a traditional private lunatic establishment of precisely the kind he had earlier so passionately denounced in print. Conolly – even the articulate and charming Conolly! – remained isolated from his fellow alienists, a man whose career, despite his sprawling books, was surprisingly little occupied with psychiatry as a public discipline. Scull's timely study thus bids us exercise extreme caution before we attribute collective voices or common intentions to the 'psychiatric profession' of Conolly's time for, as Mellett has stressed, psychiatrists' views long remained a babble – disparate, discordant, ambiguous – though as yet not very audible.[69]

The view that medical and scientific engagement with madness in the Victorian era was characterized more by strife, confusion, and cross-purposes than by a united professional front is supported by two further studies in this volume, those by Browne and Williams. One of the prime self-appointed tasks of early Victorian alienists and asylum superintendents was to utilize the new medium of photography – a technology speedily absorbed within the medical profession at large, as Fox and Lawrence have emphasized.[70] Psychiatrists believed that being cheap, easily reproducible and, it seemed, exact copies of reality, photographs could prove invaluable objective diagnostic tools. Things proved, however, more complicated than that, for, as Gilman and Didi-Huberman have recently demonstrated,[71] psychiatric photography actually went on largely reproducing age-old aesthetic and moralistic stereotypes of insanity, rather than snapping the natural faces of the mad. And even the hope of rendering the distinct types of insanity directly and unambiguously 'physiognomically' legible to the eye proved, as Browne shows in her case study, at best dubious.

Wanting to discover how far the insane provided links on the chain between man and beast in the expression of emotion, Charles Darwin obtained from the leading alienist, James Crichton Browne, a collection of photographs of his patients, depicting various categories of disturbance (hypochondria, melancholia, euphoria, etc.). The rich irony was that the physiognomic stigmata of madness which were so plainly decipherable to the alienist remained illegible to Darwin. Before one could 'see the mad', one evidently had to be trained to look; the psychiatric gaze itself thus hinged on a psychology of perception!

This raises the general problem of how the will to believe relates to science as dispassionate enquiry. Here lies the nub of Williams's paper. Examining the attempts of the Society for Psychical Research in the 1880s to adjudicate the truth about the spirit world, he reveals that the organization was riddled by a clamouring host of rival epistemologies, methodologies, and pre-judices.[72] Against this hubbub, Frederick Myers and Edmund Gurney sought to carve out a middle position by advancing their notion of the 'subliminal' self. This affirmed the reality of spiritual events (by postulating what we would call ESP) but located them not 'out there' but in the psyche, in unconscious yet purposive operations of the mind. This middle position, embracing, for example 'telepathy', satisfied their need to believe in a higher realm, while also holding faith with scientific scruples. But their construct of subliminality (a key stage in what Ellenberger has called 'the discovery of the unconscious')[73] satisfied no other party – neither the hard-nosed physiolo-gists, neurologists, and positivists, for whom the idea was metaphysical mumbo-jumbo, nor the spiritualists and theosophists, for whom it was a piece of crass reductionist 'psychologization'.

As this example suggests, the problems of how to construct an adequate science of mental states – both normal and pathological – were still perplexing towards the end of the last century. No agreement had been reached as to whether disturbances should be regarded as organic, or instead merely (or essentially) psychological, or about how mind and body in-teract. Freud's unresolved oscillations between essentially neurological models of mind and functional approaches, underline these dilemmas.[74] Nonetheless, psychiatry actually made progress as a discipline during the nineteenth century, partly through being able to put such fundamental dilemmas on ice.

One of the real triumphs of psychiatry from the age of Pinel and Esquirol through to Griesinger, Krafft-Ebing, and Kraepelin lay in bringing order, clarity, and universality to the basic concepts, indeed the very language of psychopathological practice. Through the early modern period there had been some pool of nomenclature inherited from antiquity (e.g. the polarity between mania and melancholia), but beyond that the principle of *cuius regio, eius psychologia* operated. In England idiosyncratic taxonomies of insanity had blossomed and withered among mad-doctors such as Thomas Arnold,[75] while others, such as John Monro, physician at Bethlem, had dismissed the classifying urge as almost a species of mania itself, or at best wasted labour. Before 1800, there was little common international psychiatric nomenclature and no standardized diagnostics. With Pinel this state of affairs began to change, through systematic clinical observation of disorders, and not least the presentation of extensive quantified evidence.

In his examination below of the terminology of the obsessional disorders, Berrios charts this nineteenth-century process of semantic and conceptual stabilization. But he also demonstrates the rise and supersession of successive 'mappings' of obsessional disorders upon the wider cartography of insanity. For instance, Esquirol's influential formulation of the obsessions as modes of monomania, that is, as intellectual delusions, was superseded from mid-century by the notion, championed by Morel within the larger context of 'degeneration' theory, that they were essentially emotional disturbances, thus falling within the neuroses. Morel's formulations were to provide the framework in which Janet and Freud could later pursue their fundamental researches.

One reason why new taxonomic grids of the varieties of mental illness gained such purchase lies in the fact that, in providing a natural history of clinical signs, they sidestepped some of the more intractable, more philosophical problems of understanding madness. For the new symptomatological classifications tended to be reticent on the aetiology or site of the disorders (were they organic? 'psychological'? 'functional'?), and did not commit themselves to particular therapies, remaining 'instrumental'.

Such questions of course could not be avoided entirely. Indeed, certain schools of psychiatric investigators were keen to pronounce on them. In part this may have been because *ideologically* a great deal lay at stake. The mid-nineteenth-century intellectual milieu, after all, simultaneously offered vast prospects, yet also dire threats, to the emergent profession of psychiatry.[76] On the one hand, as the authority of the churches to pontificate on the nature of man and the human condition underwent challenge, the new perspectives opened up by anthropology, evolutionism, positivism, and parallel movements seemed to cry out for a comprehensive new psychology. This demand was confirmed by growing social bewilderment. As European regimes plunged deeper into mass politics, social unrest, revolutions, and staggering industrial and urban disruptions, the stage lay open for psychiatrists to offer explanations and prophecies for this mysterious and frightening world. Yet massive residual public suspicion of the psychiatrists needed first to be overcome, for to many they seemed part of the problem rather than the providers of solutions. The 'materialist' psychiatric vision of mankind, revealing the low motives and animal nature within, threatened to toll the knell of human dignity, morality, and civilization, as Ruth Harris points out in her essay in the companion volume.[77] Moreover, the role of psychiatrists, in defending criminals with 'insanity pleas' in the courts, attracted great public opprobrium.

In these circumstances, argues Ian Dowbiggin below, examining the French experience, psychiatrists united around a synthetic theory, which satisfied the professional imperatives of positive science while also adjusting to the moralizing temper of the respectable public. This was the theory of neuropathic degeneration.

For in the age of Darwin, psychological explanations of man (seen both as an individual and as a biological and social animal) came to be bundled in with physical and cultural anthropology, racial theory, neurology, biology, craniometry, and morbid anatomy, all held together by the glue of evolutionary development and hereditarianism. Such theories, advanced by psychiatric doctors such as Moreau, Morel, and Magnan in France, Griesinger in Germany and Maudsley in England, could authentically draw on the psychiatric heritage of Pinel and Esquirol while offering popular explanations of soaring criminality, alcoholism, pauperism, venereal diseases, etc., assuaging *haut bourgeois* fears, or at least endorsing their prejudices and pessimism. Psychiatry thus staked its claim to a place in the sun, by identifying the seat of all social ills.

Dowbiggin's paper thus raises key dilemmas threatening the standing of psychiatry: the problems of science and ideology, of elite knowledge and common prejudice. Psychiatry demanded a hearing – in public, in the law courts, in penology, in policy-making – through its claim to be scientific, dispassionate, objective, value-neutral. Yet psychiatric pronouncements in France, and in Europe as a whole in the latter part of the nineteenth century, seem to betray these birthrights, wallowing in an orgy of panic, prejudice, and prophecy. Listen for example to Max Nordau projecting forward, on the basis of contemporary trends, what would be the psyche of the twentieth century:[78]

> 'Modesty and restraint are dead superstitions of the past, and appear only as atavism and among the inhabitants of remote villages. The lust of murder is confronted as a disease and treated by surgical intervention.
>
> The capacity for attention and contemplation has diminished so greatly that instruction at school is at most but two hours a day, and no public amusements, such as theatres, concerts, lectures, etc. last more than half an hour. For that matter, in the curriculum of studies, mental education is almost wholly suppressed, and by far the greater part of the time is reserved for bodily exercises; on the stage only representations of unveiled eroticism and bloody homicides, and to this, flock voluntary victims from all the parts, who aspire to the voluptuousness of dying amid the plaudits of delirious spectators.' [and so forth]

Confronting this, well might we be tempted to respond: psychiatrist, heal thyself! How far the impressive structures of late nineteenth-century psychiatry and neurology were built upon foundations that remained utterly ideological, and which indeed betray personal pathologies, clearly requires attention.

The two papers in this collection which press on, like Nordau, into the twentieth century, into the Freudian revolution, both explicitly take up this self-referential question of the psyche of the psychiatrist. What standing does the discourse Freud formulated actually command? How far are his writings, in particular the casebooks tracing his therapeutic encounters, 'scientific' records carrying an authority distinct from their author? Or how far, on the other hand, are they better regarded, as Steven Marcus would argue, as *literary* texts? Or do they transcend these stilted conventional polarizations, and artfully become a new order of discourse, in which the writing itself becomes part of the therapy?[79] Assessing Freud's own intentions in this regard is peculiarly difficult, for, as always, he was at once the most self-aware, yet also seemingly the most devious of explorers of his own psyche. John Forrester's chapter explores this very question (did Freud understand what he was doing?) through suggesting how the steps in Freud's development of psychoanalytic technique reveal not only a concern to find solutions to the problems of the *patient*'s needs, but that such a concern required him to resolve the dilemma of the threatened authority of the physician-analyst.

Both the general practitioner's bedside manner and the act of the psychotherapeutic hypnotist were, as Freud discovered to his embarrassment, vulnerable in psychiatric encounters; the patient might not respond at all, or might win the initiative. The procedures of psychoanalysis, the talking cure, however, were devised by Freud so as to ensure that the analyst's authority should be impregnable.[80] Freud's rules for forestalling client 'resistance' fall within the high-minded canons of political liberalism – a free contract, free speech – yet they uncannily reproduce the strategies of the traditional game of seduction. Freud himself might well have resisted that analogy, for Forrester hints it was rather near the bone, in view of the tortured personal anxieties, repressed desires, and fear of failure that preoccupied his early years – factors which the long unavailable or censored early correspondence, especially with Wilhelm Fliess, now belatedly dribbling out into the public domain, are beginning to confirm.

What Freud may have kept from himself we may have no clue of. What Freud kept from us we can at least frame informed guesses about – partly with the aid of other witnesses, as provided for example by Karin Obholzer's interviews, late in his life, with the 'Wolf Man'.[81] Indeed, historians might take a leaf out of the psychoanalyst's book and address themselves to those very areas of silence and suppression, not least because Freud wrote so persuasively that we all too readily accredit him as his own historian. Detached reading and reconstruction, suggests Anthony Clare in his essay below, will help dispel the rosy haze.

For what do we really know about the banausic details of Freud's clinical practice? The amount of detailed, day-to-day evidence provided by his own published cases – and how few of these there are! – is extremely slight. And when we scrutinize them in detail, as Clare undertakes for the tale of Little Hans, we become aware how sketchily Freud informs us of what actually was transacted; and how the adroitly manipulated information we do receive seems, when interrogated, to reveal unrigorous practices, vast inferential leaps, and a stampede towards *a prioristic* conclusions hardly compatible with the claims of psychoanalysis to be scientific.

The jolted historian may yet feel some sympathy for Freud's endeavour; for his relentless quest for satisfactory levels of meaning precisely mirrors the voyage of the historian. Yet Freud's own proclivities to render the evidence into epic, his selective destruction of the records of his own life, and the subsequent evasive and obstructionist behaviour of those entrusted with his archives, must all remind us that meaning is worthless unless it respects truth.

Research into the history of madness and psychiatry has made great strides in the last decade, not least in searching for deeper levels of meaning and interpretation, seen from viewpoints other than the present psychiatric point of view. We must beware, however, lest our new interpretations outstrip the evidence for them.

This has been a guiding concern of these volumes. Taken together, the score or so essays printed here do not aim to draw morals from key events in the history of psychiatry, but rather to present a sequence of encounters in which scholars grapple with different kinds of often unfamiliar evidence and ponder the hermeneutic problems clustering at the crossroads where the sufferers and their experiences meet the physicians with their *savoir-pouvoir*. The history of madhouses, mad-doctors, and madmen still needs, above all, opening up on new flanks, further detailed information, continuing pluralism in approaches, and well-informed, concentrated discussion, all of which, we hope, will be stimulated by this collection of original and wide-ranging essays.

Notes

1 For recent evaluations of the state of the art in the history of psychiatry, see A. Scull, 'The Social History of Psychiatry in the Victorian Era', and 'The Discovery of the Asylum Revisited: Lunacy Reform in the New American Republic', in A. Scull, *Madhouses, Mad-doctors and Madmen* (London: Athlone Press, 1981), pp. 5–34, 144–65; Roy Porter, 'Shutting People Up', *Social Studies of Science* 12 (1982): 467–76.

2 For an introduction to the literature see D. Ingleby (ed.), *Critical Psychiatry* (Harmondsworth: Penguin Books, 1980).

3 See for example I. Illich (ed.), *Disabling Professions* (London: Marion Boyars, 1977).

4 A. Scull, *Decarceration* (Englewood Cliffs, NJ: Prentice-Hall, 1977; revised ed., Oxford: Polity Press, 1984).

5 For an introduction see T. Judt, 'A Clown in Regal Purple: Social History and the Historians', *History Workshop Journal* 7 (1979): 66–94; R. Samuel (ed.), *People's History and Socialist Theory* (London: Routledge & Kegan Paul, 1981).

6 M. MacDonald, *Mystical Bedlam* (Cambridge: Cambridge University Press, 1981).

7 G. Zilboorg, *A History of Medical Psychology* (New York: Norton, 1941); F. Alexander and S. Selesnick, *The History of Psychiatry* (London: Allen and Unwin, 1967); K. Jones, *A History of the Mental Health Services* (London:

Routledge & Kegan Paul, 1972). For a defence of these positions see K. Jones, 'Scull's Dilemma', *British Journal of Psychiatry* 141 (1982): 221–26.

8 P. Sedgwick, *Psychopolitics* (London: Pluto Press, 1981).

9 For the meanings of the concept see S. Cohen and A. Scull (eds), *Social Control and the State* (Oxford: Martin Robertson, 1983).

10 M. Foucault, *Madness and Civilisation* (New York: Pantheon Books, Tavistock Publications, 1965).

11 H. Butterfield, *The Whig Interpretation of History* (London: Bell, 1931).

12 See Foucault, *Madness and Civilisation*, and M. Foucault, *The Order of Things* (New York: Pantheon Books, 1965); M. Foucault, *The History of Sexuality* (Harmondsworth: Allen Lane, 1978),Vol. 1, 'Introduction'.

13 T. Szasz, *The Myth of Mental Illness* (London: Paladin, 1972); T. Szasz, *The Myth of Psychotherapy* (New York: Anchor Press, 1978).

14 B. Ehrenreich and D. English, *Witches, Midwives and Nurses* (Old Westbury, NY: Feminist Press, 1973); B. Easlea, *Witch-Hunting, Magic and the New Philosophy* (Brighton: Harvester Press, 1980).

15 MacDonald, *Mystical Bedlam*; M. MacDonald, 'Religion, Social Change and Psychological Healing in England 1600–1800', in W. Sheils (ed.), *The Church and Healing* (Oxford: Basil Blackwell, 1982), pp. 101–26; M. MacDonald, 'Popular Belief about Mental Disorder in Early Modern England', in W. Eckart and J. Geyer-Kordesch (eds), *Heilberufe und Kranke in 17. und 18 Jahrhundert* (Münster: Institut für Theorie und Geschichte der Medizin 1982), pp. 148–73.

16 J.M. Masson, *The Assault on Truth: Freud's Suppression of the Seduction Theory* (London: Faber and Faber, 1984). Compare E.M. Thornton, *Freud and Cocaine* (London: Blond and Briggs, 1983). An interesting feminist precursor of Masson's argument is Florence Rush, 'The Freudian Cover-up', *Chrysalis* 1 (1977): 31–45. Masson's work has been extensively criticized. See J. Malcolm, *In the Freud Archives* (London: Jonathan Cape, 1984).

17 T. Szasz, *The Manufacture of Madness* (London: Routledge & Kegan Paul, 1971). Much more generally see P. Berger and T. Luckman, *The Social Construction of Reality* (Harmondsworth: Penguin Books, 1967); and P. Wright and A. Treacher (eds), *The Problem of Medical Knowledge* (Edinburgh: Edinburgh University Press, 1982).

18 Cf. E. Midelfort, 'Madness and Civilization in Early Modern Europe' in B. Malament (ed.), *After the Reformation* (Philadelphia, Pa: University of Pennsylvania Press, 1980), pp. 247–65; Sedgwick, *Psychopolitics*; Roy Porter, 'In the Eighteenth Century, Were English Lunatic Asylums Total Institutions?', *Ego* 4 (1983): 12–34.

19 See Foucault, *Madness and Civilization*; A. Scull, 'Moral Treatment Reconsidered', in Scull, *Madhouses, Mad-doctors and Madmen* (note 1), pp. 105–20; M. Fears, 'Therapeutic Optimism and the Treatment of the Insane', in R. Dingwall (ed.), *Health Care and Health Knowledge* (London: Croom Helm, 1977), pp. 66–81; W.F. Bynum, 'Rationales for Therapy in British Psychiatry 1785–1830', *Medical History* 18 (1974): 317–34; Roy Porter, 'Was there a Moral Therapy in Eighteenth Century Psychiatry?', *Lychnos* (1981–82): 12–26.

20 Anne Digby, 'Changes in the Asylum: The Case of York, 1777–1815', *Economic History Review* 36 (1983): 218–39; and Anne Digby, *Madness, Morality and Medicine* (Cambridge: Cambridge University Press, 1985).

21 See Scull, 'The Discovery of the Asylum Revisited' (note 1) pp. 144–65.

22 M. Donnelly, *Managing the Mind* (London: Tavistock Publications, 1983); A.

Scull, *Museums of Madness* (London: Allen Lane, 1979).

23 R. Castel, F. Castel, and A. Lovell, *The Psychiatric Society* (Columbia: Columbia University Press, 1981).

24 L. Feder, *Madness in Literature* (Princeton, NJ: Princeton University Press, 1980); M. Byrd, *Visits to Bedlam* (Columbia, SC: University of South Carolina Press, 1974).

25 R. Smith, *Trial by Medicine* (Edinburgh: Edinburgh University Press, 1981).

26 Cf. Roy Porter, 'Introduction', in Roy Porter (ed.), *Patients and Practitioners* (Cambridge: Cambridge University Press, 1985).

27 For assessment and interpretation see A. Sheridan, *Michel Foucault, the Will to Truth* (London: Tavistock Publications, 1980).

28 Mainly in Foucault, *The Order of Things* (New York: Pantheon Books, 1965).

29 See Foucault, *Madness and Civilization*; (New York: Pantheon Books, 1965), and G. Rosen, *Madness in Society* (London: Routledge & Kegan Paul, 1968).

30 See Scull, *Museums of Madness*.

31 D.J. Mellett, *The Prerogative of Asylumdom* (New York: Garland Press, 1983).

32 Foucault, *Madness and Civilization* (New York: Pantheon Books, 1965).

33 S. Tomaselli, 'The First Person: Descartes, Locke and Mind-Body Dualism', *History of Science* 22 (1984): 185–205.

34 J.M. López Piñero, *Historical Origins of the Concept of Neurosis* (Cambridge: Cambridge University Press, 1983).

35 See I. Veith, *Hysteria* (Chicago: University of Chicago Press, 1965); O. Temkin, *The Falling Sickness* (Baltimore, Md: Johns Hopkins University Press, 1945). See also D.P. Walker, *Unclean Spirits* (London: Scolar Press, 1981).

36 See Alexander and Selesnick, *History of Psychiatry*; Zilboorg, *History of Medical Psychology*.

37 See also M. Screech, *Montaigne and Melancholy* (London: Duckworth, 1983); M. Screech, *Rabelais* (London: Duckworth, 1979); M. Screech, *Erasmus and the Praise of Folly* (London: Duckworth, 1980).

38 R. Klibansky, E. Panowsky and F. Saxl, *Saturn and Melancholy* (London: Nelson, 1964); M. Wittkower, *Born under Saturn* (London: Weidenfeld and Nicolson, 1963).

39 See E. Welsford, *The Fool* (London: Faber and Faber, 1935); S. Billington, *The Social History of the Fool* (Brighton: Harvester Press, 1984).

40 See, at greater length, P. Williams, 'The Making of Victorian Psychical Research' (PhD. thesis, Cambridge University, 1984).

41 W. James, *The Varieties of Religious Experience* (London: Longmans, 1902); J. Barzun, *A Stroll with William James* (London: University of Chicago Press, 1983).

42 G. Becker, *The Mad-Genius Controversy* (Beverly Hills, Calif.: Sage Publications, 1978); D.E. Stannard, *Shrinking History* (Oxford: Oxford University Press, 1980).

43 R. Baumann, *Let Your Words be Few* (Cambridge: Cambridge University Press, 1983).

44 C.A. Ryscamp, *William Cowper of the Inner Temple, Esq* (Cambridge: Cambridge University Press, 1959).

45 C. Devlin, *Poor Kit Smart* (London: Rupert Hart-Davis, 1961).

46 C. Pierce, *The Religious Life of Samuel Johnson* (London: Athlone Press, 1983).

47 M. MacDonald, *Mystical Bedlam*; M. MacDonald, 'Religion, Social Change and Psychological Healing in England 1600–1800' in W. Sheils (ed.), *The Church and*

Healing (Oxford: Basil Blackwell, 1982).

48 See also R.B. Carter, *Descartes' Medical Philosophy* (Baltimore, Md: Johns Hopkins University Press, 1983).

49 Cf. M. Berman, *The Re-enchantment of the World* (London: Cornell University Press, 1981); F. Capra, *The Turning Point* (New York: Flamingo, 1982): C. Merchant, *The Death of Nature* (San Francisco, Calif.: Harper and Row, 1980); B. Easlea, *Science and Sexual Oppression* (London: Weidenfeld and Nicolson, 1981).

50 P. Lain Entralgo, *Mind and Body* (London: Harvill Press, 1955).

51 See M. Hay, 'Understanding Madness. Some Approaches to Mental Illness, 1650–1800' (Ph.D. thesis, University of York, 1979).

52 R. Hunter and A. MacAlpine (eds), *W. Battie, A Treatise on Madness* (London: Dawsons, 1962); T. Mayo, *Remarks on Insanity* (London: Underwood, 1817); G.N. Hill, *An Essay on the Prevention and Cure of Insanity* (London: Haddock, 1789); A. Crichton, *An Inquiry into the Nature and Origin of Mental Derangement* (London: Cadell and Davies, 1798).

53 Bonnie Blustein, '"A Hollow Square of Psychological Science", American Neurologists and Psychiatrists in Conflict' (pp. 241–70); and M. Clark, 'The Rejection of Psychological Approaches to Mental Disorder in Late Nineteenth Century British Psychiatry' (pp. 271–312), in Scull, *Madhouses, Mad-doctors and Madmen* (note 1); M. Clark 'The Data of Alienism' (D.Phil. thesis, Oxford University, 1982).

54 See for example T. Trotter, *A View of the Nervous Temperament* (Newcastle: Walker, 1807).

55 W.L. Parry-Jones, *The Trade in Lunacy* (London: Routledge and Kegan Paul, 1972).

56 K. Doerner, *Madness and the Bourgeoisie* (Oxford: Basil Blackwell, 1981).

57 Cf. R. Nye, *Crime, Madness and Politics in Modern France* (Princeton, NJ: Princeton University Press, 1984).

58 S.P. Fullinwider, *Technologists of the Finite* (Westport, Conn.: Greenwood Press, 1982).

59 E. Showalter, 'Victorian Women and Insanity', in Scull, *Madhouses, Mad-doctors and Madmen*, pp. 313–38.

60 See Y. Knibiehler and C. Fouquet, *La Femme et les médecins* (Paris: Hachette, 1983).

61 See R. Sewell, *The Life of Emily Dickinson*, 2 vols (London: Faber, 1976); J. Strouse, *Alice James* (London: Jonathan Cape, 1981); S. Trombley, *'All That Summer She Was Mad': Virginia Woolf and Her Doctors* (London: Junction Books, 1981).

62 G. Bateson (ed.), *Perceval's Narrative* (Palo Alto, Calif.: Stanford University Press, 1961).

63 D. Peterson (ed.), *A Mad People's History of Madness* (Pittsburgh, Pa: University of Pittsburgh Press, 1982).

64 E. Fischer-Homberger, *Hypochondrie, Melancholie bis Neurose: Krankheiten und Zustandsbilder* (Bern: Hans Huber, 1970).

65 M. MacDonald, *Mystical Bedlam*, p. 230.

66 N. Jewson, 'Medical Knowledge and the Patronage System in Eighteenth Century England', *Sociology* 8 (1974): 369–85; cf. also Roy Porter, 'Laymen, Doctors and Medical Knowledge in the Eighteenth Century: The Evidence of the *Gentleman's Magazine*', in Porter, *Patients and Practitioners*, pp. 283–314.

67 R. Smith, *Trial by Medicine* (Edinburgh: Edinburgh University Press, 1981).

68 V. Skultans, *Madness and Morals* (London: Routledge & Kegan Paul, 1975); K. Jones, *Lunacy, Law and Conscience 1745–1845* (London: Routledge & Kegan Paul, 1955).

69 Mellett, *Prerogative of Asylumdom*, ch. 4.

70 D. Fox and C. Lawrence, *Medicine as Image* (Westport, Conn.: Greenwood Press, forthcoming).

71 G. Didi-Huberman, *Invention de l'hystérie* (Paris: Macula, 1982); S. Gilman, *Seeing the Insane* (Chichester: John Wiley, 1982).

72 R. Brandon, *The Spiritualists* (London: Weidenfeld and Nicolson, 1983); B. Inglis, *Natural and Supernatural* (London: Hodder and Stoughton, 1978); see also Williams, 'The Making of Victorian Psychical Research'.

73 H. Ellenberger, *The Discovery of the Unconscious* (London: Allen Lane, 1970).

74 See F. Sulloway, *Freud: Biologist of the Mind* (London: Fontana, 1980).

75 J. Goldstein, '"Moral Contagion": A Professional Ideology of Medicine and Psychiatry in Eighteenth and Nineteenth Century France', in G.L. Geison (ed.), *Professions and the French State 1700–1900* (Philadelphia, Pa.: University of Pennsylvania Press, 1984), pp. 181–223; and Nye,*Crime, Madness and Politics*.

76 T. Arnold, *Observations on the Nature, Kinds, Cures and Prevention of Insanity, Lunacy and Madness*, 2 vols (Leicester: G. Ireland 1782, 1786).

77 See also for England W.F. Bynum, 'Theory and Practice in British Psychiatry from J.C. Prichard (1786–1848) to Henry Maudsley (1835–1918)', in T. Ogawa (ed.), *History of Psychiatry* (Osaka: Taniguchi Foundation, 1982), pp. 196–216.

78 M. Nordau, *Degeneration* (London: Heinemann, 1913).

79 For recent discussion of these issues see S. Marcus, *Freud and the Culture of Psychoanalysis* (London: Allen and Unwin, 1984).

80 C. MacCabe (ed.), *The Talking Cure* (London: Macmillan, 1981).

81 K. Obholzer, *The Wolf-Man, Sixty Years Later* (London: Routledge & Kegan Paul, 1982). There is of course no reason to privilege this old man's reminiscences, either.

CHAPTER ONE

Good madness in Christendom

M.A. Screech

Are Christians mad?

MADNESS AND CHRISTIANITY go hand in hand. That has been true at least since the earliest surviving accounts of the central events of Christianity in the Greek New Testament. Until very recently (if that), at no time since the first century has it been possible to draw a sharp line between several kinds of Christian other-worldliness and diabolical or organic madness.

This is partly because of the way in which the four Gospel writers – especially St Mark – wrote of Jesus and his disciples; partly, also, because of the way in which the disciples themselves – especially St Paul – strove to account for the experiences which had revolutionized their lives. They had to account, too, for their startling religious certainties. What were they based upon?

The principal teachings of Christianity (the resurrection of Christ from the dead and the future resurrection of all mankind) flew in the face of mature philosophical and religious thinking in the wider world of the Roman Empire. Moreover, the resurrection of the dead of the New Testament was, from the very outset, thought of by many Greek Christians as the resurrection of the body. Yet to wish to resurrect the body once the immortal soul had got rid of it through death would be plain madness for most Greek and Roman philosophers.

That was one of the reasons why 'the Greeks' found Christianity to be 'foolish'. But it is not the only one. Other Christian beliefs, especially those concerned with ecstasies and raptures of many sorts, were held to be thoroughly compatible with Platonic notions of *mania*. They were connected with 'madness', but in another, very desirable, sense.

This is a short contribution on a very large matter. To make it manageable I shall look at this subject mainly through the eyes of Erasmus. Some of the ideas expressed here are treated in greater detail elsewhere; others will find their place in another book to appear in a few years' time.[1]

Erasmus is a good guide. He was a Christian humanist of subtlety, erudition, and complexity. He edited the first printed Greek New Testament

to be placed on sale (Basle, 1516); over the years he wrote copious annotations to show the inadequacies of the traditional Latin rendering of it; he devoted his life to exegesis, to explanation, and to humanist Christian propaganda generally; he was highly indebted to Plato and to the often Platonizing Fathers of the Church. His influence was widespread and long-lasting. And, as much as any Christian writer who ever lived, he was convinced that, at least for a chosen few, Christianity is a 'certain kind of madness'.[2]

Erasmus treats Christianity as madness, paradoxically, in the *Praise of Folly* (1511, with important subsequent expanded editions); he returned to the subject, without the paradoxes, in one of the most widely read books of the Renaissance, his ever-expanding *Adagia*; his own fundamental recension of the Latin Vulgate New Testament is marked by it; his New Testament *Annotationes* are impregnated with it in all their various editions; his other voluminous writings return to the topic again and again.[3]

Erasmus was so convinced that Christianity at its highest is a form of good madness that he put his own convictions into the very mouth of Christ, not only in paradoxical works of 'literature' but in his recension and in the accompanying *Annotationes*. When, in Matthew 11:25 and Luke 10:21, Jesus thanked the Father for hiding the 'mystery of salvation from the wise' and for having 'revealed it to *nēpiois*' ('infants'; 'babes'), Erasmus rendered *nēpioi* by *stulti* ('fools'). He defended this in his *Annotationes*. Pressure eventually made him give way, but it did not make him change his mind. He remained convinced that Jesus wanted his followers to be, in some sense, like 'fools'.[4]

Already in the first edition of the *Praise of Folly* (1511) Erasmus wrote, with a kind of bantering earnestness, that Christianity at its best is 'nothing other' than 'a kind of madness' (*insaniam quandam*). Are not enraptured Christians 'demented' – deprived of their *mens*, their mind? Do they not enjoy an experience 'very like dementedness' (*dementiae simillimum*)?

> 'As long as the soul uses its bodily organs aright a man is called sane; but, truly, when it bursts its chains and tries to be free, practising running away from its prison, then one calls it insanity. If this happens through disease or a defect of the organs, then by common consent it is, plainly, insanity. And yet men of this kind, too, we find foretelling things to come, knowing tongues and writings which they had never studied beforehand – altogether showing forth something divine. There is no doubt that this happens because the mind, a little freer from polluting contact with the body, begins to use its native powers.'[5]

The implications of all this for the history of psychiatry and madness are profound; a closer look at Erasmus within the context of his time shows that his ideas were shared by professional men in all the main disciplines.

The classical basis for Christian 'madness'

Whenever and wherever Plato's teachings are taken seriously it is quite impossible to separate inspired genius entirely from organic madness. This conviction, firmly rooted in Greek philosophy since Socrates, was adopted by the Jewish scholar Philo of Alexandria (29 B.C.–A.D. 54) in his exegesis of the Old Testament. His interpretation of the Jewish scriptures was so deeply in accord with Platonic other-worldliness that early Christians were stirred to wonder whether 'Philo had Platonized or Plato Philonized'. From Philo onwards, because of the widespread use of allegory, it was possible to interpret a surprising amount of the Old Testament in accordance with Platonic assumptions. And St Jerome, among others, welcomed Philo as a guide, despite his remaining outside the Church.

Faced with the contempt of philosophical Gentiles, Christians went on to the offensive. When they were called mad in a contemptuous sense and dismissed as fools and idiots, they revelled in the accusations: it is good to be condemned by the hostile standards of this transitory life. In I Corinthians 1, Paul is quite prepared to accept that the 'preaching of the Cross' should be 'foolishness' to them that are perishing – a stumbling-block for most of his fellow Jews, 'and unto Gentiles foolishness'.

Such reactions are humanly understandable. But long custom can weaken the force of what Paul is saying. He is not simply exulting in the fact that Christian truths seem mad to many. He is going much further: Christianity is, he insists, foolish in a very real sense. It is 'the foolishness of God' (*to mōron tou theou*).

St Paul may have meant these words to be taken quite literally; that is for New Testament scholars to try and decide. Some of the Fathers of the Church certainly believed that they meant what they bluntly said: that God, having despaired of saving the world by his wisdom, decided to save it by an act of divine 'madness'. God's 'mad' action was the crucifixion of his only Son.[6]

Christians also act in odd ways which are in conformity with this 'foolishness of God'. This may be seen in the selfless acts of charity of the Christian convert; it is to be found in the ecstasies and raptures experienced by Christian visionaries and mystics.

As Christianity spread throughout the Roman Empire, religious ecstasy (including the 'ecstasy' of selfless charity) was increasingly interpreted with the help of Platonic philosophy. This was so at least since Origen among the Greeks (A.D. 185–254) and since Tertullian among the Latins (A.D. 155–200). Because of this, these startling claims made for divine madness became, to some extent, almost commonplace; but never entirely so, since it was only too possible to follow such ideas from acceptable Platonizing within Catholic orthodoxy into Platonizing error. It was eventually seen that Plato's teachings must be modified before Christians can accept them all. Under the influence of Plato, both Origen and Tertullian fell into heresy – Tertullian resoundingly so. Nevertheless, over a thousand years later, in the

Renaissance, Plato still remained for Christian humanists, including Ficino and Erasmus, one of the most vital sources to which thinkers were compelled to turn to explain charismatic 'madness'. Theologians, poets, mystics, philosophers, lawyers, and doctors all had to come to terms with the linking of the great charismata vouchsafed to Plato's superior geniuses, and the gifts of charity, prophecy, and rapture enjoyed by the Christian elect. The link is a direct one.

The main source of Platonic teaching about charismatic madness is what Socrates taught in the *Phaedrus* (sections 244–45; 265). Socrates denied that *mania* is, in itself and in all cases, an evil. Sanity is indeed to be cherished – but only up to a point. This is because the greatest of blessings come to men through charismatic *manias* sent from the gods. These blessed manias are four in number (though sometimes reduced to three, by classifying the first and second together). They are:

(1) prophesying – the *mantic* art which, Socrates asserts, was originally called the *manic* art (without the interpolation of that 'tasteless *t*');
(2) mystical initiations and revelations;
(3) poetic inspiration; and
(4) the 'madness' of mutual lovers.

All these privileged states are characterized by frenzy. Divine spirits – or the soul of the beloved – enter the chosen vessel whose own soul is then at least partially detached from its body in ecstasy and rapture. These *manias*, being above mere earth-bound concerns, constitute man's greatest blessings and happiness. No ecstatic ever wishes to return to mundane matters, once he has experienced *ek–stasis* – what it is to be 'displaced outside himself'. Nor, it was thought, did the organically insane either; they too were 'rapturously' happy in their demented fantasies. Intense happiness was one of the many characteristics shared by both main kinds of 'maniacs', the merely mad as well as the divinely so.

Plato's theories depend on man's being a compound creature, earthbound through his body, heaven-seeking through his soul. (Intermediate between soul and body is the spirit, which forms the link between them.) When a man is a maniac from natural causes the defect is not normally thought of as being in the soul but in its organ, the body; the soul, for whatever reason, cannot use this organ aright and partially escapes from its restraints. But even at the best of times the philosophic soul also yearns to quit the 'prison' of the body and to soar aloft towards its heavenly home. Whenever the soul succeeds in freeing itself somewhat from the body's fetters – even through merely organic madness, but especially through the divine kinds – something divine may be glimpsed by it in its frenzied wanderings. The charismatic maniac is more favoured than the organic maniac, of course, but he too is 'mad' and so may share a great many signs and symptoms with the organic madman. He may even share some of his divinely privileged gifts with him. That is because, in all cases of *mania*, the basic mechanics (as it

were) are the same: the soul is striving to leave the body. Insofar as it does
so, it is exposed to extra-mundane influences.

The frenzies of both medically and charismatically insane people arise
from the soul's quest for freedom. In the case of privileged 'maniacs' this
may result from what was termed 'enthusiasm' or 'inspiration' – that is,
when good *daemons* 'possess' the favoured prophet, philosopher, or poet. It
may also result from the 'amazement' caused when the soul glimpses, even
indirectly, divine truth or beauty. In erotic mania souls are exchanged
between the two lovers, who therefore live in a state of permanent ecstasy,
permanently, that is, 'outside' themselves and 'in' the beloved. This ecstasy
is caused by divine beauty reflected in the beloved.

All the values yearned for by the divinely manic enthusiast – who is the
true philosopher – are invisible ones. They derive from realms higher than
our material world (*Phaedo*, sections 78A–80E, etc.). As far as he can, the
true philosopher spurns the body and those things which are akin to it, since
they chain him to this world. He knows that, in death, his purified soul,
having freed itself from the body, will enjoy real, eternal values, not
transient worldly ones. Meanwhile he 'practises dying' – trains himself for
the joys of the life to come – by striving, as far as it is right to do so, to
separate soul from body (*Phaedo*, sections 670; 80E–811A).

These Socratic ideas, widely known to the Greek world through Plato and
his followers, were spread to the classical Latin world through writers as
central as Cicero. In Greek the 'practising' of dying was termed *meletē*. In
Latin Cicero called it *commentatio* (*Tusculan Disputations*, I, 30). *Commentatio* means a diligent and careful preparation for something. *Commentatio
mortis* is a diligent preparation for death. Seneca, on the other hand, used the
term *meditatio* (*Epistles*, 5, 2). *Meditatio mortis* certainly represents the
Greek better. It was this more precise Latin translation which was especially
favoured by writers as diverse as St Jerome (d. A.D. 420 or, a millennium
later, by the scholarly mystic who translated Plato into Latin and adapted
him to Renaissance mysticism, Marsiglio Ficino (1433–99). The term
meditatio mortis is vital to Erasmus, and to humanists generally, for whom it
conveys a central Christian truth, not a merely pagan one. But inevitably the
Latin word *meditatio* became slackly interpreted in modern times as though
it meant 'meditation' in the current, weaker, less ancient sense of quiet
(religious) contemplation. (The confusion already existed in medieval Latin.)
Absolutely fundamental misunderstandings of Erasmus and of age-old
theories of madness have resulted from this error, right up to the present
moment. For Seneca, St Jerome, Ficino, Erasmus, and Rabelais, as well as for
a host of their contemporaries over the centuries (including doctors by the
dozen), *meditatio mortis* means – and only means – that philosophical
striving to 'practise dying' which results in one of the good manias as the
soul is loosened from its body – becoming in the process somewhat like the
ill-attached soul of the organic madman. All the Platonic *manias* are
characterized by *ekstasis*, an alienation of the mind as it is thrown out of its
normal state, whether by organic madness, by 'daemonic' possession, by

love, by awe-struck wonder (the 'ecstasy of admiration') or by the higher forms of rapture. The one fundamental change which Christians were compelled to make to these Platonic teachings – apart from replacing classical polytheism by trinitarian monotheism – was to rule out the 'possession' of a mortal by those good spirits, those good *daemons*, whom Christians termed 'angels' ('messengers'). Only evil *daemons* ('devils') can 'possess' a human being. In this way the often good classical *daemons* became the evil *demons* of Christianity.

Montanist heretics (who seduced even Tertullian) denied this. Their prophets and prophetesses claimed to be possessed by good spirits (or, indeed, by the spirit of Christ), who spoke through their frenzied mouths in such a way that, when they had 'come back to themselves' they 'did not know what they had said'. One of the Montanists' strongest points was that St Peter, enraptured at the Transfiguration, did not know what he was saying (Matthew 17; Mark 4; Luke 9). But even after Catholic orthodoxy came to make all possession diabolical, the other charismata remained.[7]

Was St Paul a madman?

For Erasmus, among others, he was certainly a 'maniac'. A great fillip was given to Platonico-Christian teachings by some late fifth-century writings of mystical theology. They became attributed, in dangerously fruitful error, to Dionysius the Areopagite – to, that is, the future patron saint of France, that 'St Denis' who, when a member of the Areopagus at Athens, was converted by St Paul in person (Acts 17:34). It was thought that he had been given rare revealed knowledge by the very apostle, Paul, whose soul had been uniquely enraptured beyond the Third Heaven, to Paradise (II Corinthians 12). Pseudo-Dionysius made Platonic ecstasy, with its attendant theories, even more at home in Christianity than it had been before and, moreover, defended it with the presumed authority of Pauline revelation. Among the major Catholic authors greatly influenced by the Platonism of Pseudo-Dionysius are Hugo of St Victor (d. 1141); Albertus Magnus (d. 1280) and, not least, Thomas Aquinas (d. 1274).

Erasmus was one of the first to doubt the authenticity of Pseudo-Dionysius; even then, he did not condemn the writings as useless, though he would not follow them in all things. Yet in some ways Erasmus went further even than Pseudo-Dionysius. Pseudo-Dionysius brought Socratic concepts into Christianity: Erasmus brought Socrates himself. For Erasmus the 'manic' Socrates could rightly be seen as a forerunner of Christ – in some ways like David. David, too, he believed to have been charismatically insane – a privileged madman – precisely when he most closely foreshadowed Christ.[8]

These Platonizing interpretations of Christian mysticism led many to classify the highest mystical rapture of Christians as the Platonic *ekstasis manikē* in its truest, purest form. A further step (taken by many, including

Pseudo-Dionysius) was to consider this *ekstasis manikē* to be also the truest, highest, most Christian form of *mania erōtikē* – that 'madness' brought on by love. In Platonic philosophy the most intense manic bliss results when mutual lovers 'die' together, as their souls leave their own bodies and live again in that of the beloved. St Paul was believed to be revealing a Christian version of this when he exclaimed (Galatians 2:20): 'I live; not I, but Christ liveth in me.' (For sound theological reasons it was found necessary to make this mean 'I live in Christ' not 'Christ lives in me').[9]

Paul knew from experience what rapture was. His own rapture (which, at least by St Ambrose among the Latins, was taken to be a two-staged one, first to the Third Heaven and then, unimaginably higher, to Paradise) is mysteriously evoked by him in II Corinthians 12. He talks of it, and of himself, in a powerfully effective impersonal way. His rapture had happened to 'a man' that he knew. And even that man (himself) did not know exactly what had happened to him.

St Paul's rapture became a corner-stone for Christian mystic doctrines. Paul's anguished cry in his letter to the Philippians (1:23) echoed down through the ages: 'I wish to be loosened asunder and to be with Christ.' It was frequently taken to mean that he yearned to die, so as to enjoy for all eternity the beatific bliss he had once enjoyed in his mystical rapture. What Paul yearned to 'loosen asunder', it was thought, was his soul from his body. When Erasmus came to paraphrase this verse he showed that he accepted this Platonic interpretation. In so doing he made Paul into a privileged Platonic 'maniac':

> 'There are reasons why I would prefer to die: others, why I should not refuse to live. Truly, consulting my own soul and balancing my own interests, I can see that it would be better for me to be freed from the tribulations of this life and to be joined more closely to Christ, returning to that ineffable happiness which I once tasted, when I was caught up into the third heaven.' (LB 7.994E, verse 23)

Erasmus does not let us see Paul's rapture merely through the eyes of the worldly-wise. It is not a case of Paul's merely appearing to the world as a maniac. He *was* a 'maniac' – charismatically enraptured by 'erotic mania' towards God.

Of course Paul was also accused of being straightforwardly insane. Erasmus brings that out too. When Paul was led as a prisoner in chains before King Agrippa and his Roman advisers, he preached the Gospel; he explained how he had obeyed heavenly visions and then told Agrippa of Christ's saving resurrection from the dead. Festus, his judge, was moved to interrupt him, 'shouting at the top of his voice: "Paul, you are raving; too much study is driving you mad."'[10] For the author of Acts, Festus was, of course, mistaken. But on another occasion Paul himself admitted – even boasted – to the Corinthians that he was indeed 'mad' – mad (in a good sense) for God. If he did remain at times 'in his right mind', it was simply to help them, his flock (II Corinthians 5:13). This was, for Erasmus, a point to stress in both commentary and translation. His Latin version brings out the contrast between Paul's sober sanity on behalf of the faithful and that ecstatic 'insanity' which he reserved for God and which is unambiguously suggested by the original Greek word used for it, *eksistēmi*. (*Eksistēmi* is cognate with *ekstasis* and means, 'to be mad', or 'deranged'.) Erasmus rendered II Corinthians 5:13 into Latin thus: 'Nam sive insanimus, Deo insanimus; sive sani sumus, vobis sani sumus'. 'For if we are insane, we are insane for God; if we are sane we are sane for you'. This is much clearer than the Vulgate which has Paul 'insane' for God but 'sober' to his flock. Erasmus was particularly pleased to be able to cite Theophylact's scriptural commentaries in support of his belief that Paul was mad with an 'erotic' madness. Theophylact was a medieval Greek Archbishop of Ochrida (Bulgaria). Through a misdating of manuscripts Erasmus had, for some time, confused him with an unknown 'Vulgarius'. Later he valued him as a follower of St Chrysostom who usefully resumed his master's teachings, some of which were already lost. In fact Erasmus first read him in the awkward fifteenth-century Latin translation of Porsena; he had misleadingly attributed these commentaries to yet a third author: to no less an authority than St Athanasius, one of the stoutest pillars of Catholic orthodoxy. The passage about to be quoted was emended to replace 'Athanasius' by Theophylact. Erasmus explained that Theophylact had found three possible ways of interpreting II Corinthians 5:13. (They are by no means mutually exclusive, since holy scripture allows multiple meanings.)

> 'Theophylact wrote a triple commentary on this: (i) [St Paul], he says, "being about to utter great things, calls it ecstasy" (*de magnis rebus loquuturus, ecstasim vocat*); (ii) again, he says, "if we seem to be insane: if we seem to be sober"; (iii) finally, he attributes madness (*insaniam*) to Paul, but a madness which is *erōtikēn*, that is amatory. For Plato taught that *furor* was of three kinds: that of seers, poets and lovers, the last of which he believed to be the most happy (*felicissimum*). Such a *furor* Theophylact attributes to St Paul, who lived not in himself but in Christ – just as the soul (*anima*) of the lover is not where it animates but where it loves (*non est ubi animat, sed ubi amat*). And Paul, for the sake of his brethren, could wish to be "anathema to Christ" [Romans 9:3]. It should be noted that unless you repeat both the verbs, the sentences seem incomplete: "If we have gone out of our mind, we have gone out to God: if we are of a sound mind (*sanae mentis*), we are *sani* (sane) for you".'[12]

Yet again Paul is not merely presented as a man who only seemed to be a maniac to the worldly-wise: he is presented in a major scriptural commentary as the supreme example of a privileged 'madman', who ecstatically loved God, happily and blessedly, with that 'erotic mania' the nature of which was revealed, by special grace, to Socrates.

Erasmus could never bring himself to think of Socrates as just one philosopher among many. So much had been revealed through him in his ecstasies.

Was Christ mad?

Paul taught that Christ, crucified and resurrected, revealed the awe-inspiring power of the 'weakness of God which is stronger than men' and, similarly, of that 'foolishness of God which is wiser than men' (I Corinthians 1:25).

Paul was claiming for Jesus a kind of folly infinitely high in the hierarchy of good manias. But, at least once, on a specific occasion, Jesus also seemed quite literally mad – mad enough to tie up. It can be seen from the third chapter of St Mark that Jesus was thought to be at least organically mad – in fact diabolically so. As many interpreted this episode, Jesus' own family, his mother included, believed him to be so mad that it was plainly their duty to restrain him. Following a tradition more completely at home in the Greek Church than in the Latin, Erasmus held that, on at least this one particular occasion, Christ's mother and brethren 'came out with chains to bind him'. (Until recent times chains were, of course, the usual means of restraining frenzied lunatics.) Erasmus' conviction arose from his reading of Mark 3 in general, and especially of verse 21.[13]

The atmosphere conveyed by St Mark at this point is one of mass excitement, with diabolical influences at work in the foreground. The crowds following Jesus as he cured the sick were so great that he planned to slip away in a boat. But 'unclean spirits' fell at his feet shouting, 'You are the Son of God.' Jesus sharply ordered them not to disclose that truth. And he commissioned the twelve disciples with authority to drive out devils. When his family learned of all this, 'they set out to take charge of him. "He is out of his mind," they said.'[14] In his New Testament *Annotationes* Erasmus explains that Christ's relatives – his *agnati* – believed they were simply doing their duty. They believed that Jesus, their kinsman, was dangerously insane. The word he used to refer to these relations – *agnati* – helps us to realize the disturbing truths which Erasmus found in this episode. Christ's mother and brethren were, he suggests, doing what the law of the occupying Romans required: 'For it is the duty of the *agnati*', he wrote, to restrain a mad relation 'if he becomes mentally deranged'.

When Erasmus came to paraphrase Mark's account of this event he was even more explicit: 'And, moreover, since they were his *agnati*, they believed it was their duty, according to the laws of men, to restrain him with chains, as one who was out of his mind (*mentis impos*) or possessed by a spirit.'[15]

In the early days of the Roman state the venerable Law of the Twelve Tables already prescribed the duty which Erasmus mentions. It ordered *agnati* to look after all frenzied lunatics (*furiosi*) belonging to their family. But Erasmus was not simply indulging in Roman legal archaism. This prescription of the Law of the Twelve Tables was very much part of Roman Law as still studied throughout Europe, for it figures in the *Institutes* of Justinian (*liber I, titulus xxii, § de curatoribus*). In addition the duties of the *agnati* are further spelled out very clearly in glosses to another law of the *Institutes*: *liber I, titulus XV, § de legitima agnatorum tutela.*

A former Roman Catholic priest, Augustine Marlorat, writing after he had become a Reformed minister, published in 1560 his *Novi Testamenti expositio ecclesiastica* in which he puzzled over Mark 3:21. He was moved to wonder that Christ should have been judged insane by his closest kinsfolk. But he did not moderate his language. These kinsfolk wanted to 'lay hands' on Christ. They wanted to confine him, by force, to the house (*domi constringere*); they wanted to treat him as a madman (*mente alienatus*).[16]

In Mark's account, Jesus, faced by such actions from his family, refused to acknowledge the kinship – 'Whoever does the will of God is my brother, my sister, my mother' (Mark 3:34–5). And he denied he was in league with devils; as Erasmus read it, the Gospel shows that Mary thought he was.

Mark's account of this violently passionate episode threw its influence over succeeding centuries. Clergymen exorcizing devils can hardly have overlooked this *locus classicus* and the warning it implies. Any patient placed under restraint was in the position that Christ's own family had wished to force upon him. If (as many thought) Christ's mother and brethren could mistake him for a madman, could not lesser mortals make the same mistake in the case of lesser people?

What was certainly recalled over the ages was the fact that the unclean spirits whom Christ rebuked were revealing the truth – acknowledging aloud what was still a secret – that Jesus was the Son of God. That devils may possess madmen and use their mouths to reveal the truth was one of the most vexatious problems that exorcists had to deal with, not least from the Renaissance onwards. Catholic exorcists might find that the devils who possessed their faithful were railing against Luther! Lutheran, Calvinist, and Anglican exorcists might well find that their faithful were in the sway of devils who railed against the Pope![17]

Erasmus faithfully expounds Mark 3 but does not, I think, advocate exorcism in any of his works. He does, however, warn his readers that, 'even today', anyone who truly tries to follow Christ's example must be prepared to be thought mad by his own family.[18]

The implications of this must again be emphasized. Any Christian doctor treating what he took to be madness had to take great care to ensure that he was not resisting the Spirit: that he was not, that is, treating as organically or diabolically mad an enraptured lover of the living God.

Prophetic powers shared by genius and madman

As we saw, Erasmus did not doubt that many kinds of maniacs, precisely because they were maniacs, had spiritual powers in common. The two spiritual gifts that he cites were the strange power to speak or read languages without having learned them and the equally disturbing power of foretelling the future, truly. Saints can do so. So can organic madmen: even in their case these signs show forth 'something divine'.

Such bland certainty needs a gloss. We are not being faced with slick irony but with medical facts as doctors saw things then.

To understand what commonly shared learning Erasmus was drawing upon we need to recall that Aristotle (or Pseudo-Aristotle) in the first section of the thirtieth book of the *Problems* had asserted that all geniuses, without exception, are of a melancholy temperament. He explained this fact with the help of the Platonic manias. In so doing he lumped together as manic 'melancholics' the insane Hercules who slew his children, Socrates, Plato, and 'other great men'. These ideas took on a new urgency throughout the Renaissance, when melancholy genius and melancholy madness were normally thought of as close and disturbing companions.[19]

Not least since the time of Ficino, it was normal to gloss Plato's account of Socrates' manias with what Aristotle wrote in *Problems* 30–1 – and *Problems* 30–1 with what Plato wrote about Socrates' manias in the *Phaedrus* and the *Phaedo*. The combined authority of Socrates, Plato, and the presumed Aristotle was all but irresistible.[20] At all events, melancholy was widely accepted as the natural cause of both organic and privileged manias. (This belief is, of course, quite consonant with God's being the first cause.) These sources and authorities explain why the two examples of special powers cited by Erasmus (speaking in tongues not learned and foretelling the future) figure in a great many medieval and Renaissance studies of melancholy. In them, both saintly 'maniacs' and organic maniacs are frequently presented as having these powers. Such phenomena were vouched for by doctors, both Arabian and Christian, over many centuries. They were still standard examples for Robert Burton in his *Anatomy of Melancholy* (I, 3; I, 3). Burton first explains what Aristotle meant when he said that 'Melancholic men are the most witty' (intelligent) by referring to 'a divine ravishment, and a kind of *enthusiasmus*, which stirreth them up to be excellent philosophers, poets, prophets, etc.'. He then goes straight on to talk of similar effects in those who suffer from 'burned' melancholy – that 'melancholy adust' which is a humour not a temperament and which often leads straight to madness. He cites Guainerius (d. 1440) on this topic: 'In their fits you shall hear them speak all manner of languages, Hebrew, Greek and Latin, that never were taught them before.' He then cites the *Conciliator* of Peter of Abano (1250–1316) for the case of a 'mad woman who spake excellent Latin' and the Arabian doctor Rhazes (865–925) for the case of a woman 'that could prophesy in her fit and foretell things truly to come'. Guainerius had a patient, 'otherwise illiterate', who wrote Latin verses 'when the moon was combust'. (Burton was loyally quoting his sources: I have checked them.)

Few doubted that these powers existed. There was disagreement whether evil spirits were involved in these cases – many insisted that they were not – but virtually everyone accepted that 'melancholy adust' might lie behind these special powers, however they are to be explained.[21]

Again, Robert Burton was certainly not twisting his sources. His own copy of the *Practica* of Dr Antony Guainerius, as edited by Dr John Falco of

Montpellier (d. 1532), is in the Bodleian (at Med. 4°. G.16). *Tractatus XV* of
it is entitled *De mania et melancolia*; chapter 4 has the title: 'Why some
illiterate melancholics are made literate and why some of them foretell the
future.' The explanation he gives, like Erasmus' own, draws upon a Platonic
interpretation of the usual passages of Aristotle's *Problems*.

The legal profession, also, was of course obliged to take note of the
problem posed by lunatics with such special powers. For example, Paul
Zacchia (1584–1659) considers them at some length in an important book
entitled *Quaestiones medico-legales, in quibus omnes eae materiae medicae,
quae ad legales facultates videntur pertinere, proponuntur, pertractantur,
resolvuntur*. He notes that:

> 'Sometimes these melancholics (that is, those labouring under a melan-
> choly defect) become frenzied (*fanatici*), foretelling the future and even
> becoming, from illiterate, literate or – what you will call wonderful – even
> shouting out in a foreign tongue without ever having learned it.'

Some say that diabolical possession, alone, can explain these phenomena.
But Zacchia disagrees, citing the usual passage from Peter of Abano, as well
as John George Schenkius (1530–98) for his *'titulus de maniacis'* and other
standard authorities such as Levinus Lemnius (1505–78) and Peter Forestus
(1522–97).[22]

These all support his contention that strange phenomena – including
illiterate madmen suddenly becoming literate, or speaking in tongues they
have never learned or else foretelling the future – 'can all proceed from a
natural cause, namely, from the simple melancholy humour'.

That charismatically blessed Christians also may have the same powers
can be shown from innumerable writers. Inspired foretelling of the future is
a saintly commonplace. But Erasmus paraphrased the account of the descent
of the Holy Ghost at Pentecost (Acts 2:13) to bring out the fact that St Peter
and his companions were accused of being diabolically possessed and that,
through *furor* ('mania') a man may speak in divers tongues. The lives of three
saints edited by Erasmus' contemporary Lefèvre d'Etaples give a very large
place to charismatic ecstasies. For example the life of St Elizabeth of Schönau
(1126–64), written by her Benedictine brother Egbert, stresses that her
ecstasies were quite exceptional. But the powers she had were, however, the
ones we have come to expect: when she was 'out of her mind' in the Spirit
she would suddenly speak in Latin – a language of which she had next to no
knowledge – or else cite highly relevant passages of Holy Writ.[23]

In a dedicatory letter to three of his friends, Lefèvre d'Etaples, too, placed
good and bad ecstasies side by side:

> 'Ecstasy is a departure of the mind from the body and a kind of calling of
> it away from it, so that some spiritual sight may be perceived. In the good
> this is done by good spirits and in the evil, the curious and the deluded,
> by evil spirits. The latter is below nature: the former, above nature. There
> is also an ecstasy which is against nature, born of illness; it is called

lipothymia, that is a defect of the soul (*animus*) and heart; doctors write learnedly about it. The first of these three ecstasies is better than *sanitas* [health or 'sanity']; the second is worse than illness; the third is merely a human illness.'[24]

Even more than his medieval counterpart, the Renaissance doctor, faced with mad-seeming behaviour or with special powers in apparently mad people, had to step with care. He might be dealing with a purely natural illness, including the madness caused by 'melancholy adust'; he might be dealing with evil spirits who require exorcizing. Or – and the signs and symptoms might not be enough to guide his judgement on this – he might be dealing, not with evil or illness at all, but with the privileged mania of a saint.

The Royal Physician André du Laurent (1558–1609), Regius Professor of Medicine in the University of Montpellier, gives a promising title to the third chapter of his authoritative treatise, *Des Maladies Melancholiques*: 'Who are the people we call melancholic; and how can we distinguish sick melancholics from healthy ones?' He signally fails to tell us. But he does remind us how even the medical pundits had to be on their guard:

'When this [melancholy] humour is heated by the vapours of the blood, it brings on a kind of holy madness (*fureur*) called 'enthusiasm', which makes men philosophise, poeticise and prophesy in such a sort that this humour seems to partake of something divine (*de sorte qu'elle semble avoir quelque chose de divin*).'

That textually agrees with what Erasmus had said years before. They both, of course, go back to Plato.

Robert Burton rehearses, for the second time, the various explanations given to explain 'whence it comes to pass that they [the maniacs] prophesy, speak several languages, talk of astronomy, and other unknown sciences to them (of which they have been ever ignorant)'. Some explain this by diabolical possession; some consider this an illness to be treated by the natural remedy of purging the melancholy humour; some evoke Plato's theory that the soul is born remembering aspects of its former glory; some accept Ficino's case for 'a divine kind of infusion'. He concludes:

'But in this I should rather hold with Avicenna and his associates, that such symptoms proceed from evil spirits, which take all opportunities of humours decayed, or otherwise, to pervert the soul of man: and beside the [melancholy] humour itself is *balneum diaboli*, the devil's bath, and as Agrippa proves, doth entice him to seize upon them.'[25]

Those special powers which Ficino saw as signs of 'a kind of divine infusion', Erasmus as *divinum quiddam* and Dr du Laurent (among a great many doctors) as *quelque chose de divin*, many others, including Peter of Abano in the early fourteenth century, Hercules Saxonia and Bodin in the sixteenth, and Robert Burton in the seventeenth, saw as symptoms proceeding from evil spirits.

Notes

1 See three of my books (all published in London by Duckworth): (1) *Rabelais* (1979), (2) *Ecstasy and the Praise of Folly* (1980), and (3) *Montaigne and Melancholy* (1983). In addition, see my contribution, 'The "Mad" Christ of Erasmus and the Legal Duties of his Brethren', in N.J. Lacy and J.C. Nash (eds), *Essays in Early French Literature Presented to Barbara M. Craig* (York, SC: French Literature Publications Company, 1982), pp. 119–27.

2 Cf. Screech, *Ecstasy and the Praise of Folly*, p. 84; and *passim*.

3 On the *Adagia*, cf. Margaret Mann Phillips, *The 'Adages' of Erasmus* (Cambridge: Cambridge University Press, 1964). Anne Reeve is bringing out now a critical facsimile edition of the *Annotationes in Novum Testamentum* (London: Duckworth, forthcoming).

4 Cf. Screech, *Ecstasy and the Praise of Folly*, pp. 30 ff., 36 ff., 39 ff., etc.

5 Screech, *Ecstasy and the Praise of Folly*, p. 84.

6 This idea is central to Erasmus' theology. There is an excellent study of Erasmus in the wider context of humanism and spiritualism from the fourteenth to the sixteenth centuries, by Professor J.-P. Massaut, in the *Dictionnaire de la spiritualité* (Paris: Beauchesne, 1969), fascicules 46–47, pp. 990–1027, under the general rubric, *Humanisme et spiritualité*. (The long entry *Extase*, in the same *Dictionnaire*, pp. 2046 ff., remains very useful.) A Renaissance work I have found helpful for its suggesting a wide acceptance of Erasmian Christian 'folly' is Bartholomew of Medina's *Expositio in primam secundae angelici doctoris divi Thomae Aquinatis* (1588): cf. pp. 302 ff.

7 Cf. Screech, *Ecstasy and the Praise of Folly*, pp. 202–12.

8 This is especially clear in Erasmus' commentary on Psalm 33 (34) *Benedicam Domino* ('A psalm of David when he changed his behaviour [or, feigned madness] before Abimelech, who drove him away, and he departed'). Cf. Screech, *Ecstasy and the Praise of Folly*, pp. 223–40.

9 Cf. Screech, *Ecstasy and the Praise of Folly*, p. 151 f.

10 This is the translation given by the *New English Bible*. It admirably conveys the sense which Erasmus attributed to the original.

11 Details in Screech, *Ecstasy and the Praise of Folly*, p. 143 f.

12 Screech, *Ecstasy and the Praise of Folly*, p. 144.

13 The Greek text of Mark 3:21 is ambiguous. It is not clear who were the *hoi par' autou* who came out to lay hands on Christ. The phrase can mean either Jesus' 'friends' or his 'relations'. Erasmus makes it refer to Christ's relations, interpreting the *hoi par' autou* as Jesus' mother and his brethren, as mentioned in verse 31. The hesitation still continues: the *Revised Version* reads 'his friends'; the *New English Bible,* 'his family'. As far as I know, Erasmus always makes the text refer to Christ's mother and brethren together. That these relations came out 'with chains' Erasmus almost certainly took from Theophylact, who says just that in his exegesis of Mark 3.

14 This is the translation given in the *New English Bible* (variant). Again, it corresponds closely to Erasmus' understanding of this verse.

15 Cf. Lacy and Nash, *Essays Presented to Barbara M. Craig*, pp. 120–21.

16 Augustine Marloratus, *Novi Testamenti Catholica expositio ecclesiastica. Id est, ex universis probatis theologis (quos Dominus diversis suis Ecclesiis dedit) excerpta* ... (Geneva: Henry Stephanus, 1561). Marlorat was, I believe, influenced by the classical adage, *Cognatio movet invidiam*, which leads one to expect envy not

from people far above or far below one but from one's nearest kinsfolk.

17 For matters such as these consult D.P. Walker, *Unclean Spirits. Possession and Exorcism in France and England in the Late Sixteenth and Early Seventeenth Centuries* (London: Scolar Press, 1981).

18 Screech, *Ecstasy and the Praise of Folly*, p. 72.

19 Cf. Screech, *Montaigne and Melancholy*, including the bibliography.

20 Cf. Screech, *Montaigne and Melancholy*, appendix B., for two Latin Renaissance versions of the text of *Problems* 30–1. The basis of modern studies of melancholy are E. Panofsky and F. Saxl, *Dürers 'Melancholia I'* (Berlin and Leipzig; Studien der Bibliothek Warburg, Hft. 2., 1923), and R. Klibansky, E. Panofsky, and F. Saxl, *Saturn and Melancholy* (London: Nelson, 1964).

21 See Robert Burton, *The Anatomy of Melancholy*, part I, section 3, member 1, subsection 3 (London, Melbourne, and Toronto: Dent; with Rowman and Littlefield, Totowa, NJ; 1978 reprint, p. 401).

22 Paul Zacchia, *Quaestiones medico-legales* (Lyons, 1688), pp. 193 ff.

23 Johannes Faber (*Stapulensis*), *Liber trium virorum et trium spiritualium virginum* (Paris: H. Estienne, 1513), p. 119 r°.

24 Faber, *Liber trium virorum*, sig. aiv°. Cf. E.F. Rice, *The Prefatory Epistles of Jacques Lefèvre d'Etaples and Related Texts* (New York and London: Columbia University Press, 1972), p. 317. (It was unusual to make this illness a defect of the soul as such. It was normally attributed to a defective organ or to a defective relationship between the soul and its bodily organ.)

25 Burton, *Anatomy of Melancholy*, p. 428 f.

CHAPTER TWO

Descartes, dualism, and psychosomatic medicine

Theodore M. Brown

Introduction

A jarring surprise greets the reader of twentieth-century American psychosomatic literature who comes to it after having been immersed in seventeenth- and eighteenth-century materials. Descartes' mind–body dualism is referred to with uncommon frequency, and, implicitly or explicitly, dualism is usually said to have exercised an overwhelmingly negative influence on the developmental course of modern medical theory. Franz Alexander, for example, condemned Descartes' extreme 'anthropocentricity' that put undue faith in the 'omnipotence of the human mind' which, at the centre of the universe, was inappropriately severed from its biological basis in the human organism.[1] Roy R. Grinker blamed Cartesian dualism for separating 'mind as subject ... from body as object ... and creating a dichotomy that even now blocks unitary concepts'.[2] George Engel claimed that Descartes' mind–body dualism 'fostered the notion of the body as a machine, of disease as the consequence of breakdown of the machine, and of the doctor's task as repair of the machine.'[3] Since the seventeenth century, according to Engel, medicine has therefore focused in a 'fractional-analytic way on biological (somatic) processes ... [while] ignoring the behavioral and psychosocial'.[4] These and similar references display many features of a shared mythology and literary convention. In place of an unfolding interpretation based on fresh readings of the primary historical documents, allusions here frequently recur and seem to be copied either from one psychosomatic theorist to another or from an influential but unnamed common source.[5] American psychosomatic theorists also show no apparent familiarity with recent Descartes scholarship.[6] Instead, like F. Capra, M. Berman, and other authors in what might be called the genre of 'liberatory eco-holism',[7] psychosomatic spokesmen are content to repeat stock phrases while offering flat and unnuanced versions of the 'Cartesian' position. Descartes is presented as a villain. His dualism is supposed to have sharply separated mind from body while leaving an earlier, more 'holistic' medicine in disarray. Modern psychosomatic medicine is an effort to restore totalistic, organismic medical theory to the position it had occupied before Descartes' devastating intrusion.

The existence in modern psychosomatic literature of what strikes a student of the seventeenth and eighteenth century as Cartesian mythology and literary convention raises two important questions. First, what was the real impact on medicine of the true historical Descartes? Second, if the actual Descartes and the putative Descartes differ substantially, then what purpose (not necessarily conscious) has the mythological reconstruction served for American psychosomaticists? Both of these questions will be considered in this essay. The impact of Descartes on the medical theory of his day has never been fully studied, especially with regard to psychosomatic issues. Consequently, the 'real Descartes' will have to be explored here first in order to establish the distance between him and the Descartes as recently perceived. This exploration will provide a foundation for attacking the second question, however briefly it can be dealt with here. The second question – of ideological fit and emotional resonance – should not be taken to imply purposeful deceit on the part of psychosomatic theorists. Rather, psychosomaticists may have been motivated by an unconscious and unrecognized desire for myth-making. Before exploring the possibility of that desire any further, however, we must turn back to the seventeenth and eighteenth century and pursue the historical Descartes.

Cartesian dualism and contemporary medical theory

To understand what the actual influence of Descartes' dualism may have been on the medicine of his day, we must examine those specific theoretical contexts in which that influence was most likely to have been felt historically, if it was felt at all. These were: the theory of the passions; the theory of the somatic influence of imagination; and the general understanding of the positive and negative effects of the patient's state of mind on the course of his illness. In these three contexts, medical theory long before Descartes had established clear precedents for a theoretical appreciation of the interaction of something very much like mind (psyche) with something very much like body (soma).[8] If Cartesian dualism truly influenced medicine in Descartes' own day or soon thereafter, it would most likely have exerted its influence in these three specific areas of medical theory, where conventional wisdom already underscored psychosomatic relationships.

The doctrine of the passions in both classical and neoclassical medical theory maintained that a definite and recurrent relationship existed between experienced affective states (anger, fear, joy, love, etc.) and transitory physical states. Hippocrates had pointed out, for example, that fear turns one pale while anger 'summons' heat to the head.[9] Galen maintained that the pulse is generally 'altered by quarrels and alarms which suddenly disturb the mind'.[10] In the early seventeenth century, Thomas Wright in his treatise *The*

Passions of the Minde (1601) claimed generally that passions are 'movements' of the soul that cause alteration of the bodily humours. Perturbations and affections of the mind cause changes in the body, as when in anger or fear men become either highly coloured or pale and their eyes heavy in sorrow but lively in joy.[11] Similarly, Robert Burton pointedly observed that 'the mind most effectually works upon the body, producing by his passions and perturbations miraculous alterations.'[12] In like manner, Hannibal Albertini maintained that sudden and great fear affects the heart, producing 'the varied, unequal and disordered beats of palpitation'.[13] In all these classical and neoclassical instances, whenever an affective state of 'passion' was experienced by an individual this 'raw feel' correlated with some physical event in his body.

The theory of the somatic influence of imagination was closely connected to that of the passions. Here the central notion held that effectively disembodied mental images could, in certain circumstances, influence somatic conditions, even the overall state of illness or health. According to one view, mental images directly affected the body. The dominant view, however, held instead that imagination only worked upon the body by the mediation of the passions. Thus, Thomas Fienus, Professor of Medicine at the University of Louvain from 1593 to 1631, wrote in his *De viribus imaginationis* (1608) as follows:

> 'The imagination is fitted by nature to move the appetite and excite the emotions, as is obvious, since by thinking happy things we rejoice, by thinking of sad things we fear and are sad, and all emotions follow previous thought. But the emotions are greatly alterative with respect to the body. Therefore, through them the imagination is able to transform the body.... Since the imagination produces change by means of the emotions and the emotions produce change by means of the natural movement of the heart and by means of the movement of the humors and the spirits, the imagination does also.'[14]

Thomas Wright echoed the same position when he stated more succinctly that passions are sensual movements of the appetitive faculty aroused by imagining some good or ill thing.[15] Both Fienus and Wright clearly believed that the interior psychological experience of imagination could lead to exterior somatic consequences.

In a third area of classical and neoclassical medical theory mental states were also presumed to cause somatic effects. This was in the consideration of the influence exerted by the patient's state of mind on the course of his illness. Hippocrates had indicated that while one patient's confidence in his physician could be important in physical recovery, another patient's emotional agitation could lead to disastrous physical deterioration: 'if the soul is burned up ... it consumes the body'.[16] Galen also called attention to these mind–body relationships, as in his recommendation of dramatic poetry and music for their emotionally enlivening effects, which had direct, positive consequences for the physical constitution.[17] Thomas Wright took it as a commonplace that the patient's positive opinion of his physician was of great importance in recovery; the emotions of hope and pleasure co-operate with nature and strengthen her in the performance of corporeal actions and vital functions.[18] By contrast, many men have lost their lives from the effects of sadness or fear.[19] Robert Burton wrote that the perturbations of the mind could produce 'cruel diseases and sometimes death itself'.[20] Obviously, it was classical and neoclassical belief that affective states could indeed cause very dramatic effects in the body.

Many of these ideas came together in classical and neoclassical writing on the hypochondriac, melancholic, and hysteric affections.[21] It is true that these conditions were understood most often in somatopsychic rather than psychosomatic terms, in the sense that relevant psychological states were typically said to derive from physiological disturbances. Nevertheless, even in these contexts disordered imagination and other psychological disorienta-tions were frequently treated as causal conditions of the disorders, which were thought of as both somatic and psychological, and direct emotional intervention was often appreciated as therapeutically efficacious. Thus, Galen listed anxiety and grief among the primary causes of melancholia and included resumption of sexual relations among the useful treatments; hysteria, he thought, was particularly a disease of widows that could also be cured by the resumption of sexual relations.[22] At the turn of the seventeenth century, André du Laurens asserted that in the melancholic condition imagination (rather than memory or reason) was primarily deranged; sudden excitement of the passions was a prime precipitating cause of deranged imagination.[23] Thomas Wright thought that a few depressing words might be sufficient to set in motion a melancholy passion terminating in death.[24] Robert Burton wrote about melancholy and related conditions at great length. He included among its causes several that specifically differed from the 'distemperature of the body':[25] apprehensive, intent, and violent im-agination; sorrow; fear; shame and disgrace; anger.[26] Among the cures for melancholy, rectification of the 'passions and perturbations of the mind' was the 'chiefest'; of specific help were 'opening up' to a trusted friend, altering one's course of life, and 'mirth, music and merry company'.[27]

It should be clear from this brief and obviously limited survey that psychosomatic relationships were given a fair amount of attention in classical and neoclassical medical theory. Before Descartes, there seemed to be no trouble conceiving various ways in which the mind influenced the body in the onset, course, and cure of physical disease. Psychological states clearly affected somatic conditions. But what was the situation after Descartes, in the later seventeenth and in the eighteenth century? Was the mind now severed from the body and did Descartes sharply mark the end of one era and the beginning of a new era, radically discontinuous with the old? One recent author has written: 'In the pre-Cartesian era, medicine was invariably holistic or psychosomatic. In the post-Cartesian, dualistic era, mechanistic physiopathology gained ascendancy, and psychophysiological events were forbidden on logical grounds.'[28] But is this an accurate historical claim? To answer this question, we must turn to medical works written in the century or so after Descartes and look carefully for a contemporary appreciation of psychosomatic interactions.

In this search it will be helpful and illuminating to carry over the classical and neoclassical categories: the passions; the role of imagination; the influence of mental states on the course of illness; and the melancholic, hypochondriac, and hysteric affections. We will again consider these areas, citing appropriate and representative late seventeenth- and eighteenth-century authors in our attempt to illustrate what continuing psychosomatic awareness can be found in the post-Cartesian medical literature. But our task here will be complicated by the fact that 'Descartes' was a presence to reckon with in various ways in that post-Cartesian period. Some medical authors, to be sure, effectively ignored Descartes, proceeding as if he had never existed or, at least, had no relevance to medicine. Other medical authors, however, tried to come to terms with Descartes in complex ways. Several used his name or alluded to his ideas but remained quite selective in what features of Cartesian philosophy they actually incorporated; others incorporated Descartes more fully.[29] Still other medical writers felt obliged to turn back to what they regarded as a more authentic statement of Cartesian dualism in order to undermine a materialist philosophical position identified, they believed inaccurately and inappropriately, with Descartes' name.[30]

Let us first consider a representative medical writer who selectively incorporated Cartesian ideas. Friedrich Hoffmann, one of the more influential medical theorists of the late seventeenth century, presented himself in *Fundamenta medicinae* (1695) as, like Descartes, a medical mechanist.[31] In all important respects, however, Hoffmann continued to adhere to basic neoclassical traditions. Thus, with regard to the passions and the transitory effect of emotional states on the body, Hoffmann noted that a disordered pulse 'always follows untimely emotional activity' and that in anger 'the heart trembles and palpitates, the face becomes now pale, now red, there is foaming at the mouth and difficulty in respiration'.[32] With regard to the imagination, Hoffmann observed: 'In those who are so disposed, terror of a particular disease may readily induce a similar disease in the body.'[33] Considering the influence of the patient's state of mind on the onset, course, and outcome of somatic disease, he noted that 'unrestrained emotion ... may act as the cause of severe diseases'[34] and that 'nothing shortens life more than continuous grief and sadness'.[35] By contrast, 'a tranquil mind is the best medicine to promote longevity' and 'moderate joy is extremely useful in prolonging life.'[36] If we (appropriately) consider Hoffmann an indicative figure, then we must conclude that psychosomatic understanding had not changed much in the wake of Descartes.

Jerome Gaub illustrates the same point. Gaub, moreover, far more fully and explicitly than Hoffmann acknowledged Cartesian dualism. He did so, in fact, some seventy years later, in 1763, to distinguish himself clearly from Julien Offray de La Mettrie and other eighteenth-century *philosophes* who had tried to legitimate their materialist views by appealing to Descartes' ideas on the 'beast-machine' and somatopsychic interactions.[37] Gaub was the widely respected Professor of Medicine at the University of Leiden who by mid-century had already established a considerable reputation for his ideas about mind–body interaction. In 1763 he published his second essay on the subject, *De regimine mentis*, which described the variety of ways by which immaterial mind influences physical human body.

Early in the essay Gaub asks the following rhetorical question:

'Are any of you unaware . . . of the extent to which a disturbed mind can affect the outward appearance of the body? Of the manner in which different affections, whatever their nature, lead to one kind of change or another in the face, eyes, forehead and the other outward parts, each one picturing itself abroad with its own peculiar characteristics, so that there is no need to wish for a little window in the breast to observe what the unquiet mind conceals beneath'?[38]

The anticipated answer, of course, was that no one in the later eighteenth century would be unaware of or surprised by these mind–body connections.

Elsewhere in the essay Gaub described the ways in which a patient's emotional state influences his physical state. He claimed, for example, that inappropriate anger exacerbates a variety of already existing diseases and 'subverts' the physician's art.[39] Undischarged sorrow is also dangerous, for if it is 'for a long time repressed and fostered, the body no less than the mind is eaten up and destroyed'.[40] Hope, on the other hand, is extremely beneficial. It 'not only arouses the mind but breathes strength into all the bodily powers as well'.[41] Patients' hope and faith in the medical art allows the physician 'to breathe new life into them with words alone' and to increase 'the power of their remedies'.[42] Finally, intense emotional experiences – of terror, for example – could function therapeutically in 'mental aberrations of all kinds whatsoever, maniacal, hysterical, hypochondriacal and febrile'.[43] Thus, Gaub, an eighteenth-century medical author explicitly loyal to Descartes and fully conversant with his formulation of mind–body dualism, continued nonetheless to adhere firmly to the neoclassical notions of psychosomatic interaction.

The same continuing loyalty was evident as well on the part of those medical authors who seemed oblivious to Descartes and his philosophy. William Heberden, one of the most brilliant clinicians and respected theorists at the end of the eighteenth century, took up the neoclassical psychosomatic themes and handled them with the astuteness typical of all of his medical work. Heberden suggested that asthma might be caused by 'grief, anger, terror, joy',[44] and that headaches could be made worse by 'anxiety and perturbation of spirits, noise, fatigue of mind or body'.[45] In the case of patients suffering for many years from chronic pain, 'In most of these patients the pain could not be traced to any certain cause; but in several they have apparently arisen from terror, grief, and anxiety, and have unquestionably been recalled and exacerbated by some disturbance of mind.'[46] As to cure, Herberden's seasoned wisdom and shrewd common sense extended to an appreciation of the patient's positive state of mind as an aid to recovery. Something so simple as replacing dirty linen with clean could 'diffuse' over patients 'a sense of ease and comfort' and thus help in the healing process.[47] And in his systematic account of hypochondriac and hysteric affections, Heberden suggested that 'terror and immoderate grief are no uncommon causes',[48] while among the most effective ways to diminish suffering was a supportive psychotherapy in which patients are encouraged to 'struggle against and resist the emotional aspects of their conditions'.[49]

In short, Heberden, like Hoffmann and Gaub before him, seemed to show all the sensitivity to psychosomatic interactions that neoclassical theorists had previously demonstrated. His medical commentaries provide additional evidence that no significant change had taken place in the understanding of mind–body relationships as a result of Descartes' formulation of dualism. Whether they acknowledged Cartesian ideas implicitly or explicitly, and even if they seemed completely oblivious to Descartes' philosophy, post-Cartesian medical writers understood psychosomatic interactions quite as well as pre-Cartesian authors had and wrote about them just as often.[50] The mythic image of a villainous Descartes, who in a stroke destroyed holistic medical theory, clearly disintegrates in the light of historical enquiry.

Dualism in Descartes

If we turn now to Descartes' writings we find still less reason to believe that he could possibly have exerted the simple, negative historical influence he was supposed to have. The principal reason for this conclusion is that Descartes' own understanding of the mind–body relationship, however original and subtle it may have been in certain ways, nonetheless includes as a central theme the notion of a functional interaction along with metaphysical or ontological dualism. As outstanding scholars have recently pointed out, Descartes' philosophical position can best be characterized as 'dualistic interactionism';[51] readings of Cartesian philosophy that fail to discover his repeated insistence on the centrality of mind–body *union* are merely 'hasty' and 'superficial glosses'.[52] Indeed, the *Discourse on Method*, which contains one of Descartes' clearest statements of metaphysical dualism, also describes the mind and body as so closely interrelated that the quality of the human mind is understood to be improvable by manipulation of the body:

> 'For the mind depends so much on the temperament and disposition of the bodily organs that, if it is possible to find a means of rendering men wiser and cleverer than they have hitherto been, I believe that it is in medicine that it must be sought'.[53]

Rather than severing mind from body, Descartes joined them closely together in an intimate interdependency. In *Meditation VI* ('Of the Existence of Material Things, and of the real distinction between the Soul and

Body of Man') he argues at length that the soul is not only 'lodged' in the body 'as a pilot in a vessel' but is 'very closely united to it, and so to speak so intermingled with it that ... [soul and body] seem to compose ... one whole'.[54] And in *The Passions of the Soul* Descartes describes at length a series of states of the mind which are the immediate consequence of preceding or simultaneous alterations of the body.

The *Passions* was, in fact, Descartes' fullest working out in his own terms of certain classically understood psychosomatic relationships. He defines the passions of the soul in contradistinction to its desires or actions. The passions are all those 'perceptions, feelings, or emotions of the soul which we relate specially to it, and which are caused, maintained, and fortified by some movement of the spirits'.[55] Examples of passions are joy, sadness, and love. In the case of each of these passions, some movement of the blood and animal spirits causes a reaction in the soul, and this reaction, is, in fact, the emotion in question. Thus in joy, 'the pulse is quicker than usual ... and that we *feel* [as] an agreeable heat which is not only in the breast, but also spreads throughout all the other exterior parts of the body with the blood'.[56] When we experience passions, our bodies also give external manifestations of our internal affective states. In joy, for example, the colour of the body becomes 'more vivid and more ruddy' and the parts of the face become moderately distended so as to take on 'a more cheerful and lively expression'.[57] In other passions, too, Descartes cites at length somatic expressions of affective states long reported by classical and neoclassical authors.

Embedded within this seemingly familiar account of the passions and their somatic manifestations is, however, a philosophically radical position *vis-à-vis* the 'passions' tradition. For Descartes asserts a sharp and rigorous distinction between the soul and the material body with which it interacts such as had not been asserted before. He states this distinction early in the treatise. The soul thinks, desires, initiates action, and experiences the passions.[58] But the body with all its solid and fluid parts is a mere machine, an automaton that performs even the most complex functions with no intervention of the immaterial soul. Thus,

> 'all the movements which we make without our will contributing thereto (as frequently happens when we breathe, walk, eat, and in fact perform all those actions which are common to us and to the brutes), only depend on the conformation of our members, and on the course which the spirits, excited by the heat of the heart, follow naturally in the brain, nerves, and muscles, just as the movements of a watch are produced simply by the strength of the springs and the form of the wheels'.[59]

Descartes' claim here clearly means that whenever 'spirits' are referred to (as in the passage above) they should be understood as fully material. Whenever we experience a feeling, that, by contrast, is an immaterial event. Every feeling of passion is the soul's immaterial reaction to some material movement in the blood or spirits. In short, the 'raw feel' of anger, joy, or even love must, of necessity, be a consequence and not a cause of material, somatic, and expressive action.

The significance of Descartes' radical move can be clarified by carefully comparing the Cartesian position on the passions to pre-Cartesian, neoclassical positions. We have already mentioned Thomas Fienus and Thomas Wright. Let us now look at certain of their ideas more closely. Consider, for example, Wright's brief comment that 'passions engender humors and humors breed passions'[60] and Fienus' more extensive statement:

> 'The imagination acts on the body through the appetitive power or by means of the emotions. This is the conclusion of the divine Thomas ... wherein he says that the soul and the imagination are unable to transform bodies *per se* but only by means of the appetite, the emotions and the motions of the humors and spirits, which indeed are moved by the appetite itself.... The imagination is fitted by nature to move the appetite and excite the emotions, as is obvious, since by thinking happy things we rejoice, by thinking of sad things we fear and are sad, and all emotions follow previous thought. But the emotions are greatly alterative with respect to the body. Therefore, through them the imagination is able to transform the body ... the appetite excites the motive power, and through the emotions the humors and spirits are borne upwards, downwards, within and without.... Since the imagination produces change by means of the emotions and the emotions produce change by means of the natural movement of the heart and by means of the movement of the humors and spirits, the imagination does also'.[61]

What is apparent in both Wright's pithy comment and Fienus' careful dialectic is the implicit neoclassical belief that passions or emotions are active causal agents of bodily change. For Fienus the complete sequence includes imagination initiating the appetite and appetite triggering the emotions, but both Fienus and Wright certainly agree that passions or emotions 'move' the heart, humours, and spirits of the body. When a person *feels* the passions, his body in one way or another is already moving concurrently. This much of the neoclassical theory is taken up by Descartes. But the other crucial feature of it – that the emotions or passions are in some sense immaterial and causally initiating – is as forcefully denied by Descartes as it is asserted by Wright and Fienus.

From another angle, the neoclassical theory of the passions seems clearly to rest on the notion, traceable ultimately to Plato, that the soul is divided into several sometimes warring parts. The higher rational part of the soul exerts some hierarchic dominance over the lower appetitive portion, but the soul is not always at peace. Passions break out from below and have to be submitted to strict rational supervision and control. Imagination can stir up the appetite and the appetite the passions. The lower parts of the soul require constant surveillance. As Fienus explains, when this sequence begins in the immaterial soul, great turbulence can soon afterwards result in the material body.

Descartes is very aware of these neoclassical theories and explicitly rejects them. He acknowledges that the rational soul may not always be able fully to control the passions, but this is only because the great mechanical 'commotion' in the spirits at such times may temporarily overwhelm efforts of the will. The 'strife' of the turbulent material spirits concentrates at the pineal gland, the locus where the conscious and wilful soul primarily interacts with the body. There,

> 'it is only in the repugnance which exists between the movements which the body by its animal spirits, and the soul by its will tend to excite in the gland at the same time, that all the strife which we are in the habit of conceiving to exist between the inferior part of the soul ... and the superior ... consists ... there is here no strife, excepting that the small gland which exists in the middle of the brain, being capable of being thrust to one side by the soul, and to the other by the animal spirits ... it often happens that these two impulses are contrary, and that the stronger prevents the other from taking effect'.[62]

Thus, the soul has no 'parts' which like persons in a power struggle strive to overcome one another. The real struggle of the unitary rational soul is to know how most effectively to beat back the tidal waves of animal spirits that sometimes come washing against the pineal gland. But just as dogs can be trained to stand still at the sound of a gun-shot, so too can men with even the feeblest of souls 'acquire a very absolute dominion over all their passions if sufficient industry is applied in training and guiding them'.[63] This is the case precisely because there is no immaterial soul so weak that it cannot in principle eventually acquire an 'absolute power' over its materially based passions.[64]

In the midst of this rejection of the internally divided and strife-torn soul of neoclassical theory, Descartes underscores the sharp separation between thinking, feeling, perceiving, and experiencing immaterial substance and brute and impassive matter. While would-be 'passions' are still in the body they are merely movements of material animal spirits; they only become the 'raw feels' of emotive experience when the soul perceives these movements. As Descartes puts it, 'all the strife which we are in the habit of conceiving to exist between the inferior part of the soul, which we call the sensuous, and the superior which is rational' reduces to the impinging of animal spirits upon the unitary soul: 'For there is within us but one soul, and this soul has not in itself any diversity of parts; the same part that is subject to sense impressions is rational, and all the soul's appetites are acts of will'.[65] For Descartes, in other words, passion and emotion are no longer earlier stages in an immaterial causal sequence that latterly causes movement in the body. Appetite is removed to the singular soul, while the experience of passion and emotion is self-consistently treated as a later reaction of the unified immaterial soul to the prior physical motions of the material animal spirits.

The full radical import of Descartes' dramatic reconstitution of the doctrine of the passions and emotions is perhaps nowhere more striking than in his account of love. For in love we experience various pleasant physical sensations, such as a gentle heat in the breast.[66] We also feel a desire to dote on the 'agreeable object'. The pleasant sensations and the desire to dote that we experience result from a particular set of bodily motions.

> '[when some object of love is present], the impression which this reflection makes in the brain leads the animal spirits ... towards the muscles which are around the intestines and stomach in the manner requisite to cause the juice of the food, which converts itself into new blood, to pass quickly towards the heart without stopping in the liver; and that being driven thither with more strength than any that is in the other parts of the body, it enters in greater abundance and excites there a stronger heat because it is coarser than that which has already been several times rarefied in passing and repassing through the heart. And this causes the spirits also to be sent to the brain, whose parts are coarser and more agitated than usual. And these spirits, fortifying the impression which the first thought of the agreeable object there makes, oblige the soul to pause over this reflection; and it is in this that the passion of love consists'.[67]

What is clear from this passage is just how passive and reactive Descartes thinks the soul is. It responds to prior material motions by feeling pleasurable warmth and the desire to dote over the object of reflection. These two emotional experiences – mild pleasure and the desire to dote – are the automatic affective consequences in the soul of physiological events which take place entirely outside it and which are prior to the soul's response.

What is still unclear in Descartes' account, however, is whether or not 'reflection' over the 'object of love' might be understood as an affective state preceding somatic behavior – that is, whether this reflection constitutes an immaterial and truly prior passion. Descartes deals with this issue in the passage below:

> 'it seems to me that the earliest passions that our soul had had when first it was joined to our body must be due to the fact that sometimes the blood or other juice which entered into the heart was a more suitable nutriment than usual for the maintenance there of heat, which is the principle of life, *and that was the cause of the soul uniting to this nutriment of its own free will, that is to say liking it,* and at the same time the animal spirits flowed from the brain to the muscles which might press or agitate the parts from which it had come to the heart, in order to cause them to send it yet more'.[68]

It seems clear that Descartes believed we first feel love as suckling infants. The soul experiences the affect of love (it 'likes' the way a 'more suitable nutriment' causes it to feel) when the particles of maternal milk first mix with ordinary blood. This physical novelty then causes an experiential novelty in the soul, and this experiential novelty is 'love'. The infant craves more milk and automatically presses for more specially suitable nutriment.

The external object of that quest – the breast, or the mother or wet nurse whose breast it is – is no doubt experienced by the ensouled infant as desirable, that is, it becomes an immediately 'agreeable object'. And just as we later recurrently experience physiological reactions first experienced as infants, so too do we later experience pleasurable associations first felt as suckling babes. This means, in turn, that Descartes' clear intent in this passage is to establish that even the fundamental passion of love is a secondary reaction in the unitary and immaterial soul to the primary motions of matter. Not even love is an appetite in the lower part of the soul but the unified soul's response to events first occurring in the body. Just as in the case of the perception of colour or of gravity, the primary reality throughout the Cartesian universe is a reality of matter and motion while the secondary experience is a feeling of emotion, a seeing of colour, or a feeling of heaviness. In all these cases, the soul has learned to 'read' the messages of the body – as love or sadness, colour or heaviness. The distinction between primary and secondary qualities and an interactionist dualism are mutually consistent parts of the new Cartesian metaphysics.

This seems, then, to have been Descartes' true philosophical position. The historical Descartes did not claim a simple severing of mind from body but a close interaction aimed at exposing the deep somatic underpinning of perceptual and affective states. Rather than denying mind–body interactions, Descartes can even be said to have facilitated them, in two senses. First, he specified a particular location – the pineal gland – where the mind and body regularly and readily interact. Second, Descartes provided a logical basis for the extensive interaction of affective states with somatic material in that he explained most aspects of all affective states as primarily somatic. Since the interior experience of 'passion' already indicates the prior action of matter, then it is of small logical consequence to expect matter to react further upon matter. For example, lovers often behave languidly because their animal spirits are so tied up representing the image of the desired object in the brain that they are relatively unavailable to flow into and move the muscles in the customary fashion.[69] Thus, in a philosophically deeper and more rigorous way than usual Descartes could still self-consistently explain how 'passions' may exert truly dramatic effects on the body.

It was very likely because of the convolutions and complexities of his views that most of Descartes' medical contemporaries and successors understood very little of his real philosophical novelty. Philosophy had already become rather separate from medicine, and writers known primarily as philosophers – like Locke, Malebranche, and Leibniz – were best able to pursue Cartesian questions with the requisite metaphysical sophistication.[70] As indicated above, *medical* spokesmen seemed largely oblivious to Descartes' philosophical exertions. Even Gaub and other post-Cartesian medical writers of the seventeenth and eighteenth century who considered themselves 'true Cartesians'[71] either missed much of what Descartes had aimed to achieve or simply ignored his more subtle philosophical efforts. For them, it seemed sufficient to identify Descartes with a reformulated dualism and then return to the medical tradition that antedated Descartes, flowed around him, and continued largely uninterrupted for many years afterwards. Reference to Descartes might simply, as for Gaub, legitimate what the medical writer had wanted to assert anyway.

The force of the largely uninterrupted medical tradition was so powerful, in fact, that there is even some evidence to suggest that Descartes himself was swept along by it at certain times. In letters to Princess Elizabeth written in the 1640s Descartes slipped into language that sounds very reminiscent of the classical and neoclassical theories he elsewhere tried to change. In one letter he explains that his mother had died of a lung disease 'caused by grief'[72] and in another he observes that the most common cause of a lingering fever is sorrow.[73] In still another letter he states with little caution or qualification that the soul 'has great power over the body, as is shown by the great changes that anger, fear and other passions excite'.[74] Descartes was here slipping into locutions common in neoclassical medical texts. And if Descartes himself could occasionally write this way, then it is no wonder that medical writers after him, who had not gone through the exquisite agonies of philosophical innovation, would largely continue in a tradition of psychosomatic etiology and interrelationship that went back to Hippocrates and Galen. The body might be thought of more as a clock-like machine and the soul might now, after Descartes, be thought of as a unity more than it had been previously, but there was little reason to change the basic causal sequence of mind–body interactions.

Real change in medical theory came in the late nineteenth and early twentieth century. For only at that late date were neoclassical conceptions abandoned and broadly replaced by views based instead on anatomical localism, cellular pathology, and microbiological etiology – each fragmenting the notion of organismic totality implicit in humoural and post-humoral physiology.[75] Specialization further fragmented the object of medicine into separate and compartmentalized organs and systems. Moreover, the advances of biomedical diagnostic technology cumulatively distanced the doctor from his patient, who was seen more and more frequently as an object to be scientifically probed rather than as a person with whom the physician could interact.[76] As the culmination of these influences, at the turn of the twentieth century mind was for the first time effectively separated from body in most of medical theory. In the majority of fields (with the notable exceptions of psychiatry and neurology),[77] somatic changes became the almost exclusive focus of biomedical attention, and affective states, if they were noticed at all, were no longer thought to exert important influences on the physical state of the organism. Scientific and technological advances and professional development achieved what metaphysical innovation had not been able to accomplish.

A few decades into the twentieth century, the new field of psychosomatic medicine arose to reassert mind–body interactions.[78] In the 1920s and 1930s most pioneers of the new field drew their intellectual inspiration from psychoanalysis and therefore often restated classic psychosomatic relationships in psychoanalytic terms.[79] As the field grew in the 1940s through the 1960s, new conceptual approaches became possible.[80] Yet as psychosomatic medicine developed, a recurrent phenomenon was evident. Leading psychosomatic theorists regularly paused to attack Descartes and the supposedly destructive effect of his mind–body dualism. They typically offered a putative history of medicine in which a villainous Descartes played a critical and destructive role. The question raised at the outset of this essay now, after our historical excursus, returns with still stronger force: why did leading psychosomatic theorists behave this way? At this juncture we are perhaps in a better position to guess why.

Cartesian dualism and the modern psychosomaticists

One of the most striking features of the attacks on Descartes in modern psychosomatic literature is that they usually occur in the midst of assertions about complex organismic wholeness. The human being is often said to be a systemic biological totality, in which 'mind' and 'body' are merely partial and imperfect expressions for different aspects of the same organic unity. Roy R. Grinker, for example, suggests that 'mind and body are two foci of an identical process'.[81] Moreover, the 'idea that a unique personality type or a specific intrapsychic conflict is essential to the development of a specific disease can no longer be entertained'.[82] Instead, one ought to bear constantly in mind that the real object of study should be 'general relationships between stress stimuli and biological processes',[83] in which biological processes *could* but do not necessarily *have to* include 'conscious emotional arousal'.[84] It is in this context of dissecting alternative approaches to psychosomatic theory and of asserting the organismic biological grounding of his own views that Grinker specifically rebukes Descartes for his artificial dualistic dichotomy that 'blocks unitary concepts'.[85]

Morton Reiser takes essentially the same stance in a generally astute essay on 'Changing Theoretical Concepts in Psychosomatic Medicine'.[86] The main thrust of Reiser's essay is an argument for a very sophisticated version of organismic psychobiological theory in which somatopsychic relationships are given as much emphasis as psychosomatic ones. His general case is most effectively made with a specific example. Reiser writes as follows:

'Mirsky identified the physiological (genetically-determined) condition necessary, but not sufficient, for the development of duodenal ulcer; that is, the hyper-secretion of pepsinogen into the blood. He postulated that this inborn trait, through its influence on the mother–infant relationship, would also play a central role in personality development and in determining the type of social-conflict situation that would later be pathogenic for the individual in adult life. This, then, is a circular rather than linear theory, i.e., it suggests somatopsychosomatic sequences rather than linear psychosomatic ones. It is supported by empirical data . . . in which independently studied psychological data were used to predict ... which, of a large number of potential ulcer patients (as determined by pepsinogen level), would actually develop the disease under the psycho-social stress of basic military training.'[87]

Reiser's point, of course, is that simple psychosomatic causal sequences will not work any longer and a more interactive organismic view is required. Yet, for all his obvious sophistication and technical command, Reiser cannot resist taking a poke at 'our bondage to Cartesian dualism'.[88] As in Grinker, this largely gratuitous sideswipe at Descartes serves primarily as an additional reminder that one should approach the field of psychosomatic relationships from a holistic biological point of view.

Reiser does more, however, than merely echo a common refrain of the modern psychosomaticists. He also provides an important clue for what may be going on at a deeper level. The clue is contained in the following illuminating passage:

'Regardless of our ultimate conviction that mind and body constitute a true functional unity, the fact remains that as observers, investigators, and theorists, we are obliged (whether we like it or not) to deal with data from two separate realms, one pertaining to mind and the other to body.... Simultaneous and parallel psychological and physiological study of a patient in an intense anxiety state produces of necessity two separate and distinct sets of descriptive data, measurements, and formulations. There is no way to unify the two by translation into a common language, or by reference to a shared conceptual framework, nor are there as yet bridging concepts that could serve, as Bertalanffy suggests, as intermediate templates, isomorphic with both realms. For all practical purposes, then, we deal with mind and body as separate realms; virtually all of our psychophysiological and psychosomatic data consist in essence of co-variance data, demonstrating coincidence of events occurring in the two realms within specified time intervals at a frequency beyond chance.'[89]

The inevitable conclusion to this shrewd observation would seem to be that because of the inherent difficulties in describing mind states and body states simultaneously and in the same language, we are left to *assert* the biological unity of the total organism yet must *behave* as if we are dealing with mind–body duality. Another way to express the same insight is to say that modern psychosomaticists *believe* in an ontological or conceptual holism but function with an operational or behavioural dualism.

Why have psychosomatic theorists found themselves in this dilemma? Why have they so regularly been caught between behaviour and assertion, action and belief? These questions are very difficult, and here I am only able to begin the search for satisfactory answers. In the future I hope to explore these questions more systematically. But for now, I will offer some preliminary speculations by way of conclusion.

Let us begin by considering the complex circumstances – intellectual and institutional – in which modern psychosomaticists have had to work. First, let us acknowledge their perplexing intellectual milieu. The most common element in the psychosomatic theoretical inheritance, as noted above, was psychoanalytic theory. Yet psychoanalytic theory was anything but clear, simple, and straightforward in its understanding of the relationship between 'mind' and 'body'. Ideas regarding psychosomatic phenomena varied considerably from one psychoanalyst to another and changed dramatically over time.[90] Freud himself regularly changed his ideas and frequently remained imprecise or unclear about certain basic concepts.[91] Freud also alleged a putative 'biological' basis for his psychoanalytic constructs but rarely presented direct empirical evidence for his theoretical speculations.[92] In general, psychoanalysts struggled – sometimes dizzyingly and inconclusively – with the mind–body relationship and often wrote in unmistakably dualistic language while simultaneously asserting biological holism.[93]

To add to these basic intellectual tangles, American psychosomatic theorists also had to contend with further confusions derived from the debates in American psychology and philosophy in the late nineteenth and early twentieth century. Leading American thinkers – like James, Santayana, and Dewey – had struggled with the implications of evolutionary biology, reductionist physiology, materialist and dialectical philosophy, and experimental and phenomenological psychology. James wrestled with these ideas in his enormously influential *Principles of Psychology* (1890). As one astute commentator has recently noted:

'A major difficulty for the reader of *Principles* is that its author so often casts *philosophical* doubt upon what seems, with considerable justification, to have been established by psychology. The reader naturally wonders where James actually stood on the issues.... James the psychologist and James the philosopher lived in unresolved conflict.'[94]

With regard specifically to dualism:

'James repeatedly ... casts doubt on dualism and yet asserts its indispensability to the scientific psychology he is presenting as persuasively as possible. Even while completing *Principles*, James was teaching his Harvard students that dualism is false, that in fact consciousness itself does not even exist!'[95]

Dewey later attempted to resolve these conflicts by being, in Morton White's words, a 'rebel against dualism'.[96] As Dewey's career evolved, he became, simultaneously, the leading voice in early twentieth century American philosophy and a strident critic of 'dualism' wherever he found it.[97] Dewey, in fact, was a principal figure in the Anglo-American movement that Arthur O. Lovejoy characterized in 1930 as 'the revolt against dualism'. Lovejoy wrote in his book of that name as follows:

'The last quarter-century, it may fairly confidently be predicted, will have for future historians of philosophy a distinctive interest and instruct-

iveness as the Age of the Great Revolt against Dualism; though it is
possible that they may prefer to describe this uprising as a phase of a wide
Revolt of the Twentieth Century against the Seventeenth. We approach
the tercentenary of the earliest writings of Galileo and Descartes; and the
occasion is being joyously celebrated in several quarters by the issuance
of declarations of independence directed against those thinkers.'[98]

By 1930, Descartes and his dualism had been sharply and unambiguously
rebuked as enemies of modern psychology and philosophy.

To complicate the picture further, we have to add the institutional
circumstances in which American psychosomatic theorists have usually
found themselves since the 1930s. For a considerable time, the majority of
identifiable psychosomaticists were trained at least partially in psychiatry
and specifically in psychoanalysis and, moreover, generally worked in
professional settings with strong linkages to psychiatry. As Wittkower
reported in 1960, 'the bulk of the research carried out in the field of
psychosomatic medicine ... is carried out by psychiatrists ... and prominent among psychiatric contributions ... are those by psychoanalysts.'[99]
Psychosomaticists have often functioned as psychiatric liaison consultants to
colleagues in internal medicine or surgery and were frequently called upon
to help manage difficult patients or to perform psychological assessments.[100]
Colleagues in internal medicine, and increasingly also those in psychiatry,
were biomedical reductionists committed to a strictly and restrictively
biological view of the organism.[101] Partly out of their own beliefs and partly
in order to accommodate themselves to their colleagues, psychosomaticists
asserted their commitment to the fundamental biological underpinning of all
organic phenomena, including the peculiar phenomena exhibited in affective
states.[102] Yet to retain their professional niche, they continued to deal
especially with affective phenomena. Lipowski described the general situation vividly:

> 'The consultant should be prepared to tolerate fluctuations in his
> colleagues' interest in his role and contribution. He may be ignored,
> especially at the beginning, or asked questions on purely medical matters.
> If he can hold his ground in these testing situations and display sound
> knowledge of general medicine, his services as a psychiatrist may then be
> sought with increasing frequency and sense of purpose.'[103]

American psychosomaticists have thus found themselves declaring belief in
ultimate biological realities but effectively operating in a special domain of
mind with a language and in a style very different from that of body.

Their complex and confusing intellectual heritage and their recurrent
professional reality have created, it seems safe to say, considerable psychological tension for American psychosomaticists. They have struggled, on the
one hand, with unresolved conflicts in their core beliefs. Their psychoanalytic and Freudian inheritance has been rife with ambiguities regarding the
meaning of the 'mind' and 'body' and 'biological holism'. At the same time,

the American philosophical and psychological tradition on which they have drawn was marked, in the early twentieth century, by its sharp repudiation of 'Descartes' and all forms of 'dualism'. Yet American psychosomaticists have been required to work in institutional settings as, in effect, dualists. They thus suffered from a dissonance between already confused beliefs and institutionally moulded behaviour. Considerable tension resulted, and one common resolution for tension of this form and magnitude is simplification of the conflict and projection of one symbolic polar representation of the simplified conflict on to an external object. American psychosomaticists seem to have done this by making that external object 'Cartesian dualism'. Descartes and his dualism were unquestionably safe targets for disdain as of the 1920s, and Descartes could be faulted because he not only *acted* dualistically (as did the psychosomaticists themselves) but because he also said that he *believed* in dualism in principle. He carefully differentiated between 'mind' and 'body' in both substance and action. The enquiry into Descartes' beliefs ended there. His actual, subtle reflections on mind–body dualism and his forceful insistence upon dualistic interactionism were expunged from what became a cartoon of his philosophical position. Descartes was also removed from his true historical context and made into a convenient symbol of villainous intrusion into medical history. It was Descartes who allegedly perpetrated nothing less than murder on previously existing holistic medical theory. Instead of having to look at themselves and their own complex, confusing, and conflict-laden circumstances, American psychosomaticists could wag their critical fingers at a mythic Descartes. Myth construction was complete as psychological and professional needs invented a historical fiction and a literary convention.

Notes

I am grateful to the following colleagues and friends who took the trouble to read and criticize this essay in an earlier draft: Jerome Bylebyl, Ian Dowbiggin, Stephen Kunitz, Ellen More, and Russell Maulitz.

1 Franz Alexander, *The Medical Value of Psychoanalysis* (New York: Norton, 1932), pp. 23–6.

2 Roy R. Grinker, *Fifty Years in Psychiatry* (Springfield, Ill.: Thomas, 1979), p. 69.

3 George Engel, 'The Need for a New Medical Model: A Challenge for Biomedicine', *Science* 96, no. 4286 (8 April, 1977): 131.

4 Engel, 'The Need for a New Medical Model'.

5 One likely candidate for an influential but unnamed common source is Dr Alan Gregg, Director of Medical Sciences at the Rockefeller Foundation from 1931 to 1951. The Rockefeller Foundation was heavily involved in funding psychosomatic research, and Gregg in 1936 wrote as follows: 'And what has medicine to say of the facile separation of "mind" from "body"? . . . [we must try] to resolve the dichotomy of mind and body left us by Descartes.' See *Harvard Medical Alumni Bulletin* 10, no. 1 (October, 1936): 2.

6 Some examples of recent, first-rate Descartes scholarship are: Margaret D. Wilson, *Descartes* (London: Routledge and Kegan Paul, 1978); Bernard Williams, *Descartes: The Project of Pure Enquiry* (Hassocks, Sussex: Harvester Press, 1978); and Edwin M. Curley, *Descartes Against the Skeptics* (Cambridge, Mass.: Harvard University Press, 1978). Richard B. Carter's *Descartes' Medical Philosophy* (Baltimore, Md.: Johns Hopkins University Press 1983) also merits a reference; unlike Wilson, Williams, and Curley, however, Carter often seems confused and chaotic in his thinking despite the many important and novel questions he raises. Additional references to modern Descartes scholarship will be cited later in this essay.

7 See, for example, Fritjof Capra's *The Turning Point* (New York: Simon and Schuster, 1982) and Morris Berman's *The Reenchantment of the World* (Ithaca NY: Cornell University Press, 1981) as representatives of what I have labelled 'liberatory eco-holism'. Although they vary considerably from one another, both Capra and Berman attack 'Cartesian dualism' as a major element in the modern western mentality that has separated instrumentalist, objectifying, and nature-destroying man from his place in a holistic and benevolent nature. Carolyn Merchant's *The Death of Nature* (New York: Harper and Row, 1980) and several of Theodore Roszak's recent books may also be considered as representative of the same genre.

8 For a review of the long-standing history of psychogenic 'psychosomatics', without that label, see Erwin H. Ackerknecht, 'The History of Psychosomatic Medicine', *Psychological Medicine* 12 (1982): 17–24.

9 Quoted in Pedro Lain Entralgo, *The Therapy of the Word in Classical Antiquity*, ed. and trans. L.J. Rather and John M. Sharp (New Haven, Conn.: Yale University Press, 1970), pp. 162–63.

10 Quoted in Stanley Jackson, 'Galen – On Mental Disorders', *Journal of the History of the Behavioral Sciences* 5 (1969): 366.

11 L.J. Rather, 'Old and New Views of the Emotions and Bodily Changes', *Clio Medica* 1(1965): 1–25, esp. pp. 2–3.

12 Robert Burton, *The Anatomy of Melancholy* (1621), ed. A.R. Shilleto (London: George Bell and Sons, 1893), vol. 1, p. 288.

13 Albertini, *De affectionibus cordis libri tres* (Venice, 1628), p. 227. Quoted in Jerome J. Bylebyl, 'The Medical Side of Harvey's Discovery', in J. Bylebyl (ed.), *William Harvey and his Age* (Baltimore, Md: Johns Hopkins Press, 1979), p. 54.

14 Quoted and translated in L.J. Rather, 'Thomas Fienus' (1567–1631) Dialectical Investigation of the Imagination as Cause and Cure of Bodily Disease', *Bulletin of the History of Medicine* 41 (1967): 349–67, esp. pp. 356 and 358.

15 Wright in Rather, 'Old and New Views', p. 2.

16 Quoted in Lain Entralgo, *The Therapy of the Word*, p. 161; see generally, pp. 158–70.

17 Jackson, 'Galen', p. 375.

18 Rather, 'Old and New Views', p. 4.

19 Rather, 'Old and New Views', p. 5.

20 Burton, *Anatomy of Melancholy*, p. 288.

21 For a discussion of these affections, their symptoms, putative etiologies, and historical interrelations over time with one another and with modern neurasthenia and neurosis, see Esther Fischer-Homberger, *Hypochondrie, Melancholie bis Neurose: Krankheiten and Zustandbilden* (Bern: Huber, 1970). See also I.E. Drabkin, 'Remarks on Ancient Psychopathology', *Isis* 46 (1955): 223–34 and

Ilza Veith, *Hysteria: The History of a Disease* (Chicago: Chicago University Press, 1965).

22 Jackson, 'Galen', pp. 375 and 379.

23 T.H. Jobe, 'Medical Theories of Melancholia in the Seventeenth and Early Eighteenth Centuries', *Clio Medica* 11 (1976): 217–31, esp. pp. 218 and 220.

24 Rather, 'Old and New Views', p. 5.

25 Burton, *Anatomy of Melancholy*, vol. 1, p. 291.

26 Burton, *Anatomy of Melancholy*, vol. 1, pp. 290–91, 298, 301, 311–12.

27 Burton, *Anatomy of Melancholy*, vol. 1, pp. 117, 124–26, 132.

28 C.E. McMahon, 'The Role of Imagination in the Disease Process: Pre-Cartesian History', *Psychological Medicine* 6 (1976): 184.

29 For an extended discussion of these issues, see Theodore M. Brown, *The Mechanical Philosophy and the 'Animal Oeconomy'* (New York: Arno, 1981).

30 For an account of the eighteenth-century reconstruction of Descartes as a materialist, see Aram Vartanian, *Diderot and Descartes: A Study of Scientific Naturalism in the Enlightenment* (Princeton NJ: Princeton University Press, 1953). See below for Jerome Gaub's attempt in his *De regimine mentis* of 1763 to distinguish himself from contemporary materialists by relying on Descartes.

31 Hoffmann, *Fundamenta medicinae*, translated and introduced by Lester S. King (London: MacDonald, 1971).

32 Hoffmann, *Fundamenta medicinae*, p. 47.

33 Hoffmann, *Fundamenta medicinae*, p. 55.

34 Hoffmann, *Fundamenta medicinae*, p. 47.

35 Hoffmann, *Fundamenta medicinae*, p. 47.

36 Hoffmann, *Fundamenta medicinae*, p. 108.

37 See L.J. Rather's *Mind and Body in Eighteenth Century Medicine* (Berkeley, Calif.: University of California Press, 1965) for an English translation of Gaub's *De regimine mentis* (1763) and an excellent commentary. See also Aram Vartanian's critical edition of La Mettrie's *L'Homme machine* (Princeton NJ: Princeton University Press, 1960), especially chapter 4, 'The Historical Background of *l'Homme Machine*'.

38 Gaub, *De regimine mentis*, p. 132.

39 Gaub, *De regimine mentis*, p. 134.

40 Gaub, *De regimine mentis*, p. 140.

41 Gaub, *De regimine mentis*, p. 173.

42 Gaub, *De regimine mentis*, p. 174.

43 Gaub, *De regimine mentis*, p. 186–87.

44 William Heberden, *Commentaries on the History and Cure of Diseases* (London: T. Payne, 1802), pp. 67–8.

45 Heberden, *Commentaries*, p. 97.

46 Heberden, *Commentaries*, p. 150.

47 Heberden, *Commentaries*, p. 5.

48 Heberden, *Commentaries*, p. 229.

49 Heberden, *Commentaries*, p. 235.

50 Ackerknecht, 'Psychosomatic Medicine', makes the same point, p. 19.

51 Margaret D. Wilson, 'Body and Mind from the Cartesian Point of View', in R.W. Rieber (ed.), *Body and Mind: Past, Present, and Future* (New York: Academic Press, 1980), p. 43.

52 Ruth Mattern, 'Descartes' Correspondence with Elizabeth: Conceiving Both the Union and Distinction of Mind and Body', in Michael Hooker (ed.),

Descartes: Critical and Interpretive Essays (Baltimore, Md: Johns Hopkins University Press, 1978), p. 221.

53 Descartes, *The Philosophical Works*, trans. Elizabeth S. Haldane and G.R.T. Ross (New York: Dover, 1955), vol. 1, p. 120.

54 Descartes, *The Philosophical Works*, p. 192.

55 Descartes, *The Philosophical Works*, p. 344.

56 Descartes, *The Philosophical Works*, p. 375; italics added.

57 Descartes, *The Philosophical Works*, p. 382.

58 Descartes, *The Philosophical Works*, p. 340.

59 Descartes, *The Philosophical Works*, pp. 339–40.

60 Quoted in Rather, 'Old and New Views', p. 5.

61 Quoted and translated in Rather, 'Thomas Fienus', pp. 356–58 *passim*.

62 Rather, 'Thomas Fienus', pp. 352–53.

63 Rather, 'Thomas Fienus', p. 356.

64 Rather, 'Thomas Fienus', p. 355. Cf. Carter, *op. cit.*, pp. 110–42 and 233–49 for an account of the *Passions* that stresses Descartes' 'ethical' intent.

65 Rather, 'Thomas Fienus', p. 353.

66 Rather, 'Thomas Fienus', p. 375.

67 Rather, 'Thomas Fienus', p. 376.

68 Rather, 'Thomas Fienus', p. 378; italics added.

69 Rather, 'Thomas Fienus', pp. 383–84.

70 For a recent account of post-Cartesian philosophy concentrating on issues closely related to dualism, see John W. Yolton, *Thinking Matter: Materialism in Eighteenth-Century Britain* (Minneapolis, Minn.: University of Minnesota Press, 1983).

71 Gaub called Descartes 'the most ingenious philosopher of his age'; see Rather, 'Mind and Body', p. 74.

72 Quoted by Walther Riese, 'Descartes as a Psychotherapist', *Medical History* 10 (1966): 243.

73 Quoted by Rather, 'Old and New Views', p. 16.

74 Quoted by Riese, 'Descartes as a Psychotherapist', p. 244.

75 For a clear statement of the broad historical sweep, see Rather, 'Mind and Body', pp. 10–17.

76 Joel Stanley Reiser, *Medicine and the Reign of Technology* (New York: Cambridge University Press, 1978), quite effectively argues the case for the negative impact of biomedical technology.

77 For a sophisticated account of the 'covert psychology' and psychosomatic presumption widespread in the putatively somatic disciplines of psychiatry and especially neurology, see Nathan G. Hale, *Freud and the Americans: The Beginnings of Psychoanalysis in the United States, 1876–1917* (New York: Oxford University Press, 1971), ch. 3.

78 See Ackerknecht, 'Psychosomatic Medicine' (note 8), pp. 22–3.

79 Ackerknecht, 'Psychosomatic Medicine'. Cf. Robert C. Powell, 'Helen Flanders Dunbar (1902–1959) and a Holistic Approach to Psychosomatic Problems. I. The Rise and Fall of a Medical Philosophy', *Psychiatric Quarterly* 49 (1977): 133–52, for an account that, without discounting the contribution of psychoanalysis to psychosomatic medicine, stresses the role of American psychobiology.

80 For helpful overviews, see Chase P. Kimball, 'Conceptual Developments in Psychosomatic Medicine: 1939–1969', *Annals of Internal Medicine* 73 (1970):

307–16; Eric D. Wittkower, 'Historical Perspective of Contemporary Psycho-somatic Medicine', *International Journal of Psychiatry in Medicine* 5 (1974): 309–19; and Margaret Thaler Singer, 'Psychological Dimensions in Psycho-somatic Patients', *Psychotherapy and Psychosomatics* 27 (1977): 13–27.

81 Grinker, *Fifty Years in Psychiatry* (note 2), p. 69.

82 Grinker, *Fifty Years in Psychiatry*, p. 71.

83 Grinker, *Fifty Years in Psychiatry*, p. 71.

84 Grinker, *Fifty Years in Psychiatry*, p. 74.

85 Grinker, *Fifty Years in Psychiatry*, p. 69.

86 In Silvano Arieti (ed.), *American Handbook of Psychiatry* (New York: Basic Books, 1975), vol. 4, pp. 477–500.

87 Arieti, *American Handbook*, p. 487.

88 Arieti, *American Handbook*, p. 487.

89 Arieti, *American Handbook*, p. 479.

90 Powell, 'Helen Flanders Dunbar', esp. pp. 141–47.

91 For a sophisticated recent critique, see John Forrester, *Language and the Origins of Psychoanalysis* (New York: Columbia University Press, 1980).

92 See particularly, Frank J. Sulloway, *Freud, Biologist of the Mind: Beyond the Psychoanalytic Legend* (New York: Basic Books, 1979).

93 See Forrester, *Language and the Origins of Psychoanalysis*, pp. 24–5, 215 n.2 and Sulloway, *Freud*, pp. 48, 50–1, 67–8, 105–06, 130, 333 n.14, 511 on Freud's unmistakable 'dualism'.

94 Gerald E. Myers, 'Introduction: The Intellectual Context', William James, *The Principles of Psychology* (Cambridge, Mass.: Harvard University Press, 1981), vol. 2, p. xiii.

95 Myers, 'Introduction', p. xiv.

96 Morton White, *Science and Sentiment in America* (New York: Oxford University Press, 1972), ch. II. Cf. Elizabeth Flower and Murray G. Murphey, *A History of Philosophy in America* (New York: Capricorn Books, 1977), vol. 2, where the chapter on Dewey is entitled 'Dewey: Battling against Dualisms'.

97 One of Dewey's most forceful and popular books was *The Quest for Certainty* (New York: Minton, Balch, 1929). Here he wrote, p. 76: 'the survey that has been made of the classic philosophic statement of the dualism between theory and practice, between mind and body, between reason and experience ... is much more than a piece of historic information. For in spite of enormous extension of secular interests, of expansion of practical arts and occupations, of the almost frantic domination of present life by concern for definite material interests and the organization of society by forces fundamentally economic, there is no widely held philosophy of life which replaces the traditional classic one as that was absorbed and modified by the Christian faith.'

98 Arthur O. Lovejoy, *The Revolt against Dualism* (New York: Open Court, 1930), p. 1.

99 E.D. Wittkower, 'Twenty Years of North American Psychosomatic Medicine', *Psychosomatic Medicine* 22 (1960): 311.

100 See Z.J. Lipowski, 'Consultation-Liaison Psychiatry: Past, Present, and Future', in Robert O. Pasnau (ed.), *Consultation-Liaison Psychiatry* (New York: Grune and Stratton, 1975), pp. 1–28; and Maurice H. Greenhill, 'The Development of Liaison Programs', in Gene Usdin (ed.), *Psychiatric Medicine* (New York: Brunner/Mazel, 1977), pp. 115–91.

101 See Engel, 'New Medical Model', pp. 129–30.

102 For striking testimony to the accommodationist tactic, see Greenhill, 'Liaison Programs', p. 152.

'resistance against psychological medicine is complicated, puzzling, and stubborn. It has been discussed thoroughly through the years and many methods have been attempted to combat it. Conciliation, concession, internist identification, use of somatic language, joint rank, emphasis on physiology and biochemistry, and attitudes denoting validity of psychiatric approach are among the methods which have been used by liaison psychiatrists.'

103 Z.J. Lipowski, 'Review of Psychiatry and Psychosomatic Medicine: I. General Principles', *Psychosomatic Medicine* 29 (1967): 156.

CHAPTER THREE

'The Hunger of Imagination': approaching Samuel Johnson's melancholy

Roy Porter

IN RECENT YEARS our understanding of the history of the mad in Britain has advanced greatly on a broad front. Thanks to Kathleen Jones, Nigel Walker, and Roger Smith, we now have overviews of the making of law, public policy, and administration concerning the insane.[1] The rise of the asylum, its therapeutic order, and of the profession of psychiatrist has been researched and distinctively interpreted by Scull, Mellett, Walton, and others.[2] Bynum and Donnelly have offered important readings of the cognitive foundations and medical standing of psychiatry as it crystallized in the nineteenth century.[3] And, not least, the basic question of the *meaning* of the rise to public prominence of insanity, the asylum, and psychiatry has been opened up and addressed. Thanks to the critiques of Foucault, Doerner, Sedgwick, and others, we no longer see the growth of psychiatric care and institutions as historically unproblematic.[4] In all this, however, there remains a key absence, a silence at the centre.

For we continue to know very little about mad people themselves. From one point of view, it could be argued that this is as it should be; for it underlines – as is only proper – to what a great degree the 'madman' is a construct, analogous to Frankenstein's monster, almost an assumed identity, the product of a whole cluster of representations assembled by psychiatry and culture.[5] Every age, one might say, invents the mad people it deserves, their image refracted through rules of normality and systems of psychiatry. Yet this way of thinking is ultimately glib and cruel, a modish idealism. It is not, after all, mad people who are the invention of psychiatrists, but only the ways of classifying them. The mad are not merely the unlucky victims of stigma, but another group scapegoated by society, penalized alongside blacks, Jews, women, midgets, and other outcasts and aliens.[6] For all cultures have recognized that there are individuals who are indisputably disturbed, pained, incapacitated, a danger to themselves and others. It is to do the mad a disservice, and to dissolve away the suffering of history by sleight of hand and a trick of words, to suggest that 'madness' is wholly invented through just another kind of societal conspiracy.

Of course, it is difficult to know the minds of the mad. For mostly we know *about* them, as refracted through the doctors, the institutions, the legal and administrative frameworks which have labelled, treated, and recorded them. We encounter the insane through medical casebooks and admission registers, but we encounter them there not raw but predigested. Yet intelligent interrogation and decoding of these records can be accomplished, as for example, in Michael MacDonald's illuminating resurrection of the mad and sad of early Stuart England, out of the casebooks of the parson-physician, Richard Napier.[7]

But to some degree we can also bring the troubled to life through the agency of their own writings. Numerous of the insane have left their testaments and *apologiae* (excerpts from some of these have been recently conveniently collected in Dale Peterson's *A Mad People's History of Madness*).[8] Yet these cannot be taken at face falue: their reading is deeply problematic. For autobiographical accounts of being mad were mostly penned long after the event – the event of incarceration, the event of treatment. They are almost all agonized howls of protest – self-vindications, 'proving' the sufferer was never mad at all, protesting against cruel treatment, illegal detention, alleging that the really mad are their captors or society at large (they do protest too much). Alternatively, they are religious or spiritual autobiographies, or moral tracts couched in the language of dire warning. All such memoirs of madness are nevertheless valuable; and reading between the lines can give us insights – albeit necessarily retrospective ones – into the terrors and ecstasies of being different, being treated as crazy, or what it felt like to be a scarred survivor, or a mind that found itself.

But what we know least of all about is the first-hand experience, from day to day, of *becoming* disturbed, of teetering towards the precipice. Yet it shouldn't prove impossible for historians to recreate what it felt like to dread breakdown, to descend towards the brink of insanity, for no small number of prolific recorders of their own lives – self-absorbed diarists, and men of letters like Coleridge and De Quincey – have actually lived and written on the margins of sanity. Now studies have been made of course of the 'abnormality' of such distinguished writers and 'geniuses'. But generally these have been the work either of literary biographers or of psychiatric doctors, whose interests and questions are not necessarily identical to the historian's. In particular such studies are often conducted within the ghoulish 'madness of genius' genre, or alternatively are prey to the lure of exact retrospective diagnosis (did Darwin have Chagas' disease, or was his a bad case of Oedipal complex? Can Freud's writings be explained by cocaine addiction?).[9]

There are grave dangers of dogmatism in all this, particularly in the expectation of wrapping up and pigeon-holing generations of the mad through the convenience of a diagnostic label. Something more tentative and exploratory, rather, is required, an attempt to reconstruct the experienced world and the crises of the disturbed through getting under their skins. This has traditionally been neglected and will not be easy; but fortunately, reinforcing our attempts to see madness from the viewpoint of the mad, a parallel movement is getting up steam within the history of medicine in general, the desire to reconstruct the history of health and sickness not just through the doctor's, but also through the sick person's, eyes. In general medicine, as Nicholas Jewson has stressed, the crucial period lies before the threshold of the nineteenth century. In these early times, characterized by the absence of specialist medical expertise, it was routine for the patient – the well-off patient, that is – to be actively involved in specifying his own 'complaint' and negotiating his own therapy.[10]

My aim in the body of this present paper is to explore a particular instance of mental disturbance and threatened collapse into madness from this period. It is the case of a man who suffered the torments of melancholy on and off all his life, who feared that his melancholy would career downhill into madness proper; a man who recorded symptoms, speculated on causes, and reported his experience of that affliction and attempted remedies in some detail. Through such an exploration we can get beneath the skull of madness, and thereby sketch in a better rounded picture of the complex interplay between sufferer, society, and the doctors.

The sufferer is Samuel Johnson. The fact that he was a celebrity is no hindrance to the study. For Johnson certainly did not use his melancholy as a public act towards his own career advancement, nor was it a useful, creative malady,[11] in the way non-specific functional disorders could be for Florence Nightingale or Charles Darwin. We are not merely examining a persona, an artificial construct. Rather, in this case Johnson's celebrity is helpful since it permits us to draw on the records of a wide range of friends and contemporary biographers, filling out the picture. And, not least, Johnson was scrupulously honest, a man who when writing autobiographically was always on oath with himself. In the main body of this paper I shall explore the course, nature, and possible explanations of Johnson's melancholy, and I will then conclude by briefly indicating what wider conclusions Johnson's sufferings might help us to draw about mental disturbance in Georgian England.

In June 1766 the Thrales dropped in unexpectedly on their new friend Samuel Johnson. They were horrified to find him grovelling in front of a clergyman, Dr Delap, 'beseeching God to continue to him the use of his understanding'. The embarrassed Delap fled, whereupon Johnson cried out 'so wildly' in self-condemnation that Henry Thrale 'involuntarily lifted up one hand to shut his mouth'.[12]

Johnson was undergoing prolonged mental collapse. Indeed, for all his 'John Bull' qualities, he was no stranger to depression, that 'general disease of my life'. 'My health has been, from my twentieth year, such as has seldom afforded me a single day of ease,' he reflected in old age;[13] and though he was plagued by *physical* ailments – chronic bronchitis, and eventually gout

and dropsy[14] – it was clearly his melancholy which he had in mind, since it
had been at the age of twenty, in 1729, that his spirits first failed him.
Kicking his heels at his parental home (that 'house of discord')[15] after being
forced by chill penury to quit Oxford, degreeless and careerless, Johnson
sank into suicidal lethargy, 'overwhelmed [Boswell put it] with an horrible
hypochondria, with perpetual irritation, fretfulness and impatience; and
with a dejection, gloom and despair, which made existence misery. From
this dismal malady he never afterwards was perfectly relieved.'[16]

What intensified melancholy's terrors at this stage was the inept interference of his godfather, the physician Dr Swynfen. Encouraged by him to
record his symptoms, Johnson was aghast to hear the doctor's prognosis of
probable future madness.

Profound melancholy crushed Johnson again after the death of his wife
Tetty in 1753 (he was 'distracted' and 'hardly supportable'), and then during
the 1760s. In 1764, for example, 'Dr Adams ... found him [Boswell wrote]
in a deplorable state, sighing, groaning, talking to himself, and restlessly
walking from room to room.'[17]

Welcomed into the Thrales' household, and exhilarated by Boswell,
Johnson enjoyed something of an Indian summer during his sixties; but even
then the spectre of incapacitation continued to haunt him. In 1768 he
entrusted a padlock to Hester Thrale's care,[18] and three years later jotted in
his diary: '*De pedicis et manicis insana cogitatio*' ('an insane thought about
fetters and manacles').[19] 'Mind-forg'd manacles' were evidently paralysing
Johnson with fears of collapse and future confinement, culminating in 1773
in a terrible letter written in French to Hester Thrale, begging her to exercise
discipline and governance over his 'fancied insanity'.[20]

Johnson saw himself as the victim of a 'vile melancholy, inherited from
my father'.[21] 'When I survey my past life', he confided to his diary on Easter
Day 1777, 'I discover nothing but a barren waste of time with some
disorders of body and disturbance of the mind, very near to madness.'[22]
Such reflections are not incidental flourishes but a minor key running
through his writings. Following his exposure of *The vanity of human
wishes*, *Rasselas* (1759) is a sustained anatomy of self-delusion, lacking even
Candide's optimism about cultivating gardens; and the *Rambler* and *Idler*
papers can be read as lay sermons exposing both the 'vacuity of existence'
and the pathology of escapism.[23]

For certain of Johnson's contemporaries, self-absorbed dejection was in
vogue as a badge of identity. The Augustan generation of Swift and Pope had
satirized lunatics, but by Johnson's day sentimental and sympathetic
attitudes were gaining ground, making melancholy fashionable as the poet's
affliction or the mark of refinement in the man of feeling.[24] Boswell himself
freely indulged his sensibilities in this direction, awarding himself the
pseudonym of 'HYPOCHONDRIACK' for his persona as periodical journalist,
and asserting that '*we Hypochondriacks* ... console ourselves in the hour of
gloomy distress, by thinking that our sufferings mark our superiority'.[25]
Johnson, however, had no patience with this 'foolish notion that melancholy

is a proof of acuteness';[26] he detested all that trivialized real suffering, and in any case thought it was playing with fire. Boswell might believe he could safely cultivate his 'turn for melancholy', because (so Professor Gaubius himself told him) melancholy was a distemper allegedly quite distinct from dementia proper. But Johnson had no such confidence. He dreaded that melancholy was the jaws of hell, leading inevitably down into the very pit of insanity. The distinction between them was paper-thin – in fact, merely in the mind. Why else had his friend Kit Smart been locked up as a lunatic? Though obsessive, dirty, and a pentecostal enthusiast, Smart was harmless. Smart had prayed in public, but 'I'd as lief pray with Kit Smart as anyone else; another charge was that he did not love clean linen, and I have no passion for it.'[27] The nervous jocularity betrays Johnson's lurking dread that, a misfit himself, one day it would be his turn to be taken for mad. And such fears, of course, only fanned his anxieties, as Hester Thrale pointed out: 'Mr Johnson's health had been always bad since I first knew him, and his over-anxious care to retain without blemish the perfect sanity of his mind, contributed much to disturb it.'[28]

Thus Johnson's melancholy wasn't an occasional whim or a *litterateur*'s affectation. It suffused the authentic Johnson known to Boswell, Mrs Thrale, Joshua and Frances Reynolds; and was even notorious to the wider circles of obituarists and early biographers, inseparable from Johnson in the round, that colossus of extremes and contradictions. Everyone found him bizarre: abnormal in bulk, demeanour, gait, opinions. In caricaturing him as 'a respectable Hottentot', Lord Chesterfield aptly evoked the wild man within, a caged animal full of pent-up energy: *ursa major*. Overbearing, dictatorial, truculent, the man who talked for victory, tossing and goring his opponents, Johnson yoked pride with abjection, lethargy (lying abed till two) with bouts of physical frenzy (he was a habitual midnight rambler, and was still climbing trees in his fifties). Always, as he told Mrs Thrale, 'in extremes' he could be piggishly indulgent in food and drink ('madmen are all sensual in the lower stages of the distemper'),[29] or mortifyingly abstinent: only moderation escaped him.[30]

The trials of living in extremes etched themselves on to his very countenance, there for all to see. Running into Johnson for the first time at Samuel Richardson's, Hogarth 'perceived a person standing at a window in the room, shaking his head and rolling himself about in a strange ridiculous manner, and concluded that he was an ideot [sic], whom his relations had put under the care of Mr Richardson.'[31] Fanny Burney was no less staggered at her first meeting:

> 'He is, indeed, very ill-favoured, tall and stout but stoops terribly. He is almost bent double. His mouth is almost constantly opening and shutting as if he were chewing. He has a strange method of frequently twirling his fingers and twisting his hands. His body is in constant agitation, see-sawing up and down.'[32]

For by middle age, Johnson had developed an elaborate repertoire of tics, spasms, and mannerisms[33] ('a convulsionary' was his obituarist Thomas Tyers' verdict).[34] 'He often had', wrote his step-daughter Lucy Porter, 'convulsive starts and odd gesticulations, which tended to excite at once surprise and ridicule'[35] – muttering under his breath, rubbing bits of orange peel together, making clucking noises, obsessively fingering posts as he lurched along the street, retracing his steps if he omitted one. 'He had another particularity,' added Boswell,

> 'some superstitious habit, which he had contracted early, and from which he had never called upon his reason to disentangle him. This was his anxious care to go out or in at a door or passage, by a certain number of steps from a certain point, or at least so as that either his right or left foot (I am not certain which), should constantly make the first actual movement when he came close to the door or passage. Thus I conjecture: for I have, upon innumerable occasions, observed him suddenly stop, and then seem to count his steps with a deep earnestness; and when he had neglected or gone wrong in this sort of magical movement, I have seen him go back again, put himself in a proper posture to begin the ceremony, and, having gone through it, break from his abstraction, walk briskly on, and join his companion.'[36]

Johnson was thus riddled with private phobias and grotesque compulsions. He even developed petty superstitions, like fretting over adding milk to his tea on Good Friday,[37] and Mrs Thrale sometimes discovered him buried deep in fantastical arithmetic:

> 'When Mr Johnson felt his fancy, or fancied he felt it, disordered his constant recurrence was to the study of arithmetic; and one day that he was totally confined to his chamber, and I enquired what he had been doing to divert himself, he showed me a calculation which I could scarce be made to understand, so vast was the plan of it, and so very intricate were the figures: no other indeed than that the national debt, computing it at one hundred and eighty millions sterling, would, if converted into silver, serve to make a meridian of that material, I forget how broad, for the globe of the whole earth, the real globe.'[38]

Here is a man, *sui generis*, deaf to the *mores* of polite society, possessed by obsessions and oppressed by bugbears: 'The great business of his life', judged Reynolds, 'was to escape from himself; this disposition he considered as the disease of his mind.' For Johnson thought himself mad: 'I have been mad all my life, at least not sober.'[39] What exactly then was his affliction? And how are we to explain his melancholy disorder?

Common sense's scythe through the thicket of explanations would be simple: no wonder Johnson was odd and melancholy; he had good reason for it; he was a man apart. Scarred from birth by physical stigmata, exceptionally big-boned and clumsy, blighted by scrofula, he was half-blind in his left eye and half-deaf in his left ear. Yet he also towered above his fellow schoolboys in acuteness, memory, argument, and powers of speech. Always different, he couldn't shake off the dread of isolation or the torment of talent thwarted, and never relaxed his instinct to struggle. Starting life (as he told Fanny Burney) as 'nothing and nobody', hating his Oxford poverty (where he was 'rude and violent', his fellows mistaking his 'bitterness' for 'frolick'), but then humiliated by being forced to quit, he spent the bloom of youth careerless and then failed as a schoolmaster, partly because of his shambling, convulsive mien. And when finally he found his feet it was by undertaking soul-destroying Grub-Street literary hack-work.[40] In a poignant aside in his *Lives of the Poets*, he wrote of Pope that he 'was one of those few whose labour is their pleasure'.[41] For Johnson, by contrast, hounded by publishers and by chill penury, labour was a curse; and unlike his erstwhile pupil David Garrick, who had trudged with him to London to seek his fortune, recognition came late to Johnson, not least because his early publications had to remain anonymous. 'Slow rises worth, by poverty depress'd,' runs the *leitmotif* of *London*. Till his fifties he was struggling for life in the water, and at least once was arrested for debt, and want dogged him till the grant of his pension in 1762. Moreover, after the death of his wife, Tetty, grief and loneliness were his boon companions. Proud and combative, Johnson sometimes could triumph, as in his rasping letter to Lord Chesterfield; but life always threatened to become weary, stale, flat, and unprofitable; merely exhausting.

Johnson believed his own experience epitomized the human condition: 'Every man will readily confess that his own condition discontents him.'[42] He never tired of ringing the changes on that theme. 'The general lot of mankind is misery,' explains his *Life of Savage*;[43] it is 'the condition of our present state, that pain should be more fixed and permanent than pleasure';[44] 'life is progress from want to want, not from enjoyment to enjoyment', he assured Boswell.[45]

Life rained down so many disappointments as to be bearable only when gilded by pretence:

> 'The world, in its best state, is nothing more than a larger assembly of beings, combining to counterfeit happiness which they do not feel, employing every art and contrivance to embellish life, and to hide their real condition from the eyes of one another.'[46]

Did he here betray a pathological streak, the fear that someone, somewhere, genuinely was happy? But if, like Jaques, he was suspiciously swift to prick others' illusions, his scorn was savage for the glib 'all is for the best' optimism of coxcombs such as Soame Jenyns.[47] What were their fatuous rationalizations, proving it was a happy world after all, but insults to real affliction?

Why, as he told *Rambler* readers, was the world so 'full of calamity'?[48] Stupidity and ignorance, greed and tyranny must all shoulder some blame – affording in turn some prospect of remedy ('Here's to the next insurrection of the negroes in the West Indies').[49] But most evil was threaded into the very fabric of the lapsarian world: disease, disaster, and death, phantom day-dreams, and all the vanities which *Ecclesiastes* lamented. For Johnson subscribed to original sin – 'the natural depravity of mankind'[50] – and grudgingly respected Mandeville's cynical realism. Asked by Lady Macleod whether man was naturally good, he responded, 'No Madam, no more than a wolf,' which she found 'worse than Swift' – no doubt a sore point with Johnson, if he heard her, since he reviled Swift's misanthropy ('life wasted in discontent'), perhaps seeing too much of himself in that fellow Christian pessimist consumed by spleen.[51]

> 'When an offer was made to Themistocles [Johnson told *Idler* readers] of teaching him the art of memory, he answered, that he would rather wish for the art of forgetfulness. In this we all resemble one another; the hero and the sage are, like vulgar mortals, over-burthened by the weight of life, all shrink from recollection, and all wish for an art of forgetfulness.'[52]

Johnson sympathized. Consciousness – of how reality was more to be endured than enjoyed – was a millstone round the neck of hope. As Peter Pinero Chase suggested, Johnson was melancholy because he had every reason to be.[53]

Yet we need to be more specific than that. Not all who trod life's treadmill sank into Johnson's occasional paralysis of the will. And Johnson himself recognized his despondency was inordinate; he saw himself as sick, alluding frequently to his 'diseased mind'.[54] So if Johnson's mind was diseased, what disease did he have? Various physicians have diagnosed that his disturbances had an organic seat (not a foolish view: after all, in his *Dictionary* Johnson himself opted for a physical basis, defining melancholy as 'a disease, supposed to proceed from a redundance of black bile; but it is better known to arise from too heavy and too viscid blood.')[55]

Playing 'hunt the lesion', doctors have looked back to Johnson's birth. First child of a forty-year-old, Sam was 'born almost dead, and could not cry for some time'. It is reasonable to infer he was deprived of oxygen, which possibly caused anoxia and some form of cerebral damage. Scrutinizing later symptoms, others have suggested Johnson's disturbances stemmed from cerebral palsy, epilepsy, De La Tourette's syndrome, or – the favourite view, echoing Johnson's contemporaries – St Vitus' Dance.[56] Dr Verbeek has alleged serious brain lesion at birth, giving rise to non-hereditary epilepsy which combined with a hereditary degenerative tendency to produce a borderline psychosis.[57] But this reading is extravagant, and it is hard to evaluate the case for organic brain disease for want of firm evidence. And it is important not to lose sight of the fact that Johnson himself denied his tics and mannerisms were physical in origin. Asked by Elizabeth Smart why he made such gestures he answered: 'from bad habit'[58] – a judgement borne out by Reynolds who thought, 'Dr Johnson's extraordinary gestures were only habits in which he indulged himself at certain times. When in company, where he was not free, or when engaged earnestly in conversation, he never gave way to such habits, which proves that they were not involuntary.'[59]

In view of this, most commentators argue that Johnson's disturbance was basically psychological.[60] But the idea of Johnson the obsessional neurotic has met a mixed reception, since it may seem to impugn his greatness.[61] Boswell allowed instability; but only to a limited degree (rightly denying his judgement and reason were ever vitiated), and then put a heroic gloss on it, imagining Johnson as an intellectual gladiator constantly combating 'apprehensions that, like the wild beasts of the Arena, were . . . ready to be let out upon him. After a conflict he drove them back into their dens; but not killing them, they were still assailing him,'[62] and concluding: 'we cannot but admire his spirit when we know, that amidst a complication of bodily and mental distress, he was still animated with the desire of intellectual improvement.'[63]

Scholars such as George Birkbeck Hill have likewise been unwilling to admit mental illness, thereby, as they saw it, supplying ammunition to Johnson's detractors. Yet inevitably Freud's century has produced its prize crop of psychoanalytical diagnoses, superseding the discredited theories of 'degenerate genius' which held sway late in the last century. In the 1940s, Lord Brain pondered Freudian, Jungian, and Adlerian analyses, but inconclusively.[64] Arguing that the portrait of the mad astronomer in *Rasselas* – guilt-ridden, self-absorbed, monomaniacal – was a projection, Kathleen Grange[65] seems to imply that Johnson suffered from 'schizophrenia', a view at least congruent with Mrs Thrale's opinion that Johnson's madness was 'delusive' not 'impulsive'. By contrast, Katherine Balderston has seized the Freudian heartland, explaining Johnson's 'psychic maladjustment' in sexual terms.[66] Focusing on Johnson's letter to Mrs Thrale, pleading for domination, Balderston finds a pathologically sick personality betraying 'erotic maladjustment'. Johnson's problem, she suggests, lay in a masochistic disposition, the letter showing 'all the stigmata of the masochist's state', familiar 'in the records of sex pathology'. Johnson's true sexual desires, long repressed, found vent in perverted form with Hester Thrale, accompanied by the shame and guilt which triggered psychic collapse.

Yet this is improbable. Johnson's calls for domination are symptoms not causes; they are a pitiable cry for help not an invitation for the gratification of shackled libido. They are not sexual but the SOS signals of a shipwrecked soul.[67]

All such reconstructions of Johnson's unconscious are more precise than the data warrant. Yet this is not to pooh-pooh a broadly psychoanalytical approach. 'Johnson's own sense of the working of the human imagination', writes Walter Jackson Bate, 'probably provides us with the closest anticipation of Freud to be found in psychology or moral writing before the twentieth century';[68] and though such ancestor-hunting is dubious, as an anatomist of the psyche Johnson certainly has affinities with Freud. No one paid greater tribute to desire, or saw more clearly that, deprived and frustrated, mankind easily becomes reduced to wishing, and wishes themselves fester. How alarmingly did imagination build houses of reality out of its own fictions![69] How the rationalizing mind masked its true intentions ('we are seldom sure that we sincerely meant what we omitted to do')![70] No wonder he dreaded the tyranny of dreams, warning Mrs Thrale, 'Make your boy tell you his dreams: the first corruption that entered into my heart was communicated in a dream.' And when she tried to draw out of him what it was, he replied 'Do not ask me,' and walked away in agitation.[71]

Attuned thus to the psyche's undercurrents, it is not surprising that Johnson himself had some inkling of how he was his parents' child: 'I have often heard him lament [wrote Frances Reynolds] that he inherited from his Father a morbid disposition both of Body and Mind. A terrifying melancholy, which he was sometimes apprehensive bordered on insanity.'[72] Yet, regardless of whether melancholy is heritable, problems lurk here. How far is Johnson blaming his father, identifying with him, or excusing himself? Moreover, it is not certain that – however bumbling, henpecked, and distant – Michael Johnson was particularly melancholy. But Johnson emphatically despised his parents for failing to give him the right start in life, compounding his physical handicaps with social inferiority ('when I was beginning in the world', he assured Fanny Burney, 'I was nothing and nobody').[73]

It cannot have been a serene childhood. His parents, recollected Johnson, had little pleasure of each other. They were old – his father fifty-four, his mother forty when he was born – and remote, and within three years a younger brother, Nathaniel, came along. Johnson's silence about Natty speaks volumes of his jealousy.

Like Gibbon, Johnson probably resented his father's slide from affluence, and he certainly loathed being paraded for his precocious talents like a performing seal. And he found his mother petty, impossible to satisfy, and punitive. It was she who warned him of hell before his third birthday, and, as he told Boswell, 'Sunday was a heavy day to him when he was young. His mother made him read The Whole Duty of Man on that day.'[74]

Johnson grew up seething with inner revolt. Maybe the main debt he felt to his parents was to Michael Johnson, Bookseller, though even here the gratitude had a sting in the tail, for he was later to urge on Mrs Thrale the stark advice: 'Get your children into habits of loving a Book by every possible means; You do not know but that it may one Day save them from suicide.'[75]

Later in life, guilt towards his father overtook him. In his seventies he performed an extraordinary act of atonement, as he explained to Boswell:

> 'I was disobedient; I refused to attend my father to Uttoxeter market. Pride was the source of that refusal, and the remembrance of it was painful. A few years ago, I desired to atone for this fault; I went to Uttoxeter in very bad weather, and stood for a considerable time bareheaded in the rain, on the spot where my father's stall used to stand. In contrition I stood, and I hope the penance was expiatory.'[76]

Longer-lived, more demanding, and less easily exorcized, his mother had to be held at bay. Installed in London, Johnson did not once make the two-day journey back to Lichfield in the nineteen years that remained of her life. Hearing she was dying, he didn't speed north but plunged into writing *Rasselas*, exculpating himself by earmarking the proceeds for her funeral. If he felt love, it was clearly a love overlaid and warped by other emotions; not once in his private diaries and prayers did he call his mother 'dearest', though commonly using the term for his female friends. But his unresolved relations with her may have shaped his choice of a wife twenty-one years his senior, and led later to filling his house with dependents such as the blind and grumpy Anna Williams, surrogate parents to care for by way of penance. Perhaps his paralysing grief on Tetty's death – neglected during her life – and his retrospective sentimentalization of his marriage, were ways of mourning a mother for whom there was no love lost.

But what Johnson repressed will probably yield few further clues to his melancholy. The evidence is lacking, for we have scant detail of his childhood: tantalizingly, he burnt the relevant leaves of his journals just before his death. What he had to hide we can't know. But we probably don't need to, for his adult and conscious life provides abundant leads.

Like a moth to a candle, Johnson was drawn to idleness. Idleness had of course been yoked with melancholy in religion and medicine ever since antiquity, and the Church had condemned sloth (*acedia*) as one of the deadly sins.[77] Johnson's own inner experience of idleness must have been coloured by such traditional associations; but it also veered from the mainstream in important ways. For in Enlightenment England, psychiatric opinion, headed by physicians such as George Cheyne, Sir Richard Blackmore, Richard Mead, and Bernard Mandeville, argued that it was the leisured elite (Johnson's 'votaries of idleness') who were most prone to melancholy, or, in vogue parlance, nervous complaints. With time upon their hands, the demands of fashion and politeness, coupled with the need to shine in arts and letters, senate and salon, took a heavy toll of the refined souls who made up England's elite. These pressures were often accentuated by finely tuned sensibility or compounded by the excesses of the *dolce vita* – gourmandizing, toping, sedentary habits, irregular hours, gambling, and so forth.[78] Johnson's own *Rambler* and *Idler* vignettes follow Addison and Steele in painting a sick parade of the idle rich.

But idleness threatened Johnson's mental health in a completely different register. For him it was not primary but secondary, not cause but effect. Idleness was not having nothing to do, but being unable to face having to do too much of it, under the silent rebuke of the text Johnson had engraved on his watch and doubtless also on his mind: 'that night cometh, when no man can work'.[79] For Johnson of course was no man of leisure, time on his side, measuring out a balanced Chesterfieldian diet of recreation. Quite the reverse; in the prime of life, pride and poverty had forced him into gargantuan projects, single-handedly writing the parliamentary reports and reams of other journalism for the *Gentleman's Magazine*, compiling his

Dictionary, and producing the *Rambler* and the *Idler*. His daily bread was endless toil, menial, grinding, against the clock; the lexicographer was indeed a drudge. Johnson's psyche rebelled against the humdrum and tedious; he fled into idleness.

Of course, it was not only Johnson amongst Georgian writers who found the lonely vigils of composition, constantly self-scrutinizing, squeezing inspiration dry, excruciatingly painful. His contemporary, David Hume, was undergoing a similar crisis, finding that his introspections into the filigree structures of the self left him prostrate and disorientated.[80] Hume eventually forged his own *modus vivendi*, uniting deep study with *eclat* as a man of the world, basking in the dignified recognition of the polite. Others of course went under – in madness, like Cowper and Collins;[81] or suicide, like Chatterton; or, like Savage, found oblivion in strong liquor – as Johnson himself did for a time, in line with his dictum: Claret for boys, port for men, brandy for heroes, preferring the latter as it did its work (of intoxication) most rapidly, and so, as he said, enabled him "to get rid of myself; to send myself away".[82]

But with Johnson, struggle ended neither in flight nor resolution. 'To have the management of the mind [he told Boswell] is a great art, and it may be attained in a considerable degree by experience and habitual exercise.'[83] But did he attain it himself? He dramatized the dilemma through the character of 'Sober' in the *Idler*. A man of 'strong desires and quick imagination', 'Sober' finds solace in 'love of ease', particularly in 'conversation; there is no end of his talk or his attention; . . . for he still fancies that he is teaching or learning something, and is free for the time from his own reproaches.' But the cameo acknowledged that no Horatian happy mean lay to hand. 'Sober's' drives and imagination 'will not suffer him to lie quite at rest,' but rather leave him 'weary of himself'. Above all, he cannot bear to be alone with his thoughts. For 'there is one time at night when he must go home, that his friends may sleep; and another time in the morning, when all the world agrees to shut out interruption. These are the moments which poor Sober trembles at the thought.'[84]

So precarious was Johnson's dilemma. Fleeing from toil, left on his own, his conscience would begin corrosive self-accusations, arraigning himself of idling, wasting his life, and sinking into vacuity, mere oblivion. Thus the alluring escape from the melancholy of the daily grind ended in paralysing him yet further. As he confessed to his diary on 21 April, 1764:

'My indolence, since my last reception of the Sacrament, has sunk into grosser sluggishness, and my dissipation spread into wilder negligence. My thoughts have been clouded with sensuality, and, except that from the beginning of this year I have in some measure forborn excess of Strong Drink, my appetites have predominated over my reason. A kind of strange oblivion has overspread me, so that I know not what has become of the last year.'[85]

This strain became the signature of his life. His diary for 7 April, 1776 reads:

'My reigning sin, to which perhaps many others are appendent, is waste of time, and general sluggishness, to which I was always inclined and in part of my life have been almost compelled by morbid melancholy and disturbance of mind. Melancholy has had in me its paroxism and remissions, but I have not improved the intervals nor sufficiently resisted my natural inclination, or sickly habits.'[86]

And resolutions to reform lie scattered along his pilgrim's way like futile signposts; as far back as 1729 he had been chivying himself with memoranda: 'I bid farewell to Sloth, being resolved henceforth not to listen to her siren strains.'[87]

Why precisely such terror of idleness? Because it handed a blank cheque to the demons of imagination. Idleness created vacuities or 'vacancies of life'. These permitted the old peripatetic principle that 'Nature abhors a vacuum' to come into play, crowding the vacant mind with 'vain imaginations'.[88]

Obviously Johnson was perturbed by the content of the phantasms that flooded into his head. Soon after Tetty's death he refers to being 'depraved with vain imaginations' and calls upon himself to 'reclaim imagination'; he was clearly beset by sexual fantasies.[89] Beseeching God to 'purify my thoughts from pollutions', he was relieved to find at Easter 1753 that at church he was not 'once distracted by the thoughts of any other woman'.[90] Over the years he was to brood wistfully, guiltily on the past, and wishfully about the future ('no mind is much employed upon the present', he writes in *Rasselas*, 'recollection and anticipation fill up almost all our moments').[91]

But Johnson's terror did not lie simply in *what* he imagined, but in the very surrender of being invaded by fictions and fantasies. Impelled by the 'hunger of imagination',[92] he dreaded succumbing to a never-never land of wishes. Open the sluicegates to dreaming and you would end up drowning in unreality. At times he feared that fate was indeed overtaking him, as his self-control over the urge to make-believe began to cave in:

'I had formerly great command of my attention [he wrote in 1772] and what I did not like could forbear to think. But of this power which is of the highest importance to the tranquillity of life, I have for some time past been so much exhausted.'[93]

The mad astronomer episode in *Rasselas* is Johnson's imaginative exploration of this doom. The sage's solitary fantasizings about the heavens have turned monstrous, unchecked by the judgements of his peers. His yearnings for knowledge have swollen into the *idée fixe* that command of the elements lies at his nod:

'all other intellectual gratifications are rejected, [explains Imlac] the mind, in weariness of leisure, recurs constantly to the favourite conception, and feasts on the luscious falsehood whenever she is offended with the bitterness of truth. By degrees the reign of fancy is confirmed; she grows first imperious, and in time despotic. Then fictions begin to operate as realities, false opinions fasten upon the mind, and life passes in dreams of rapture or of anguish.'[94]

Johnson was thus haunted by dread that his 'mind corrupted with an inveterate disease of wishing', would eventually succumb to monomania.

The diagnosis was not, of course, uniquely Johnsonian – far from it. For Johnson was introspecting within a paradigm of insanity sharp-focused by Locke's *Essay on Human Understanding*, a work which achieved great popularity through its psychology of the normal mind.[95] Traditionally, madness had been regarded as stemming either from constitutional imbalance of the humours, particularly black bile, from ruling passions, or from diabolical possession. Locke, by contrast, contended that madness was typically intellectual *delusion*, the overrunning of the mind by false ideas pieced together into a logical system of unreality.[96] Because knowledge sprang from sensations, ideas accurately reflecting reality had to be gradually pieced together out of fragmentary sensations, and were hence at best probable and provisional. What scope there was for mistaken sensations or false associations, impelled by fear, hope, or other passions, to fill the mind with error, creating a *summa* of delusion! Johnson did not use precisely Locke's terminology, but endorsed his view that madness was essentially 'in the mind', consequential upon 'voluntary delusion'. The sleep of reason allowed imagination to spawn monsters. The prospect tallied with his traditional Christian sense of human frailty and distrust of egoism, pride, and presumption:

> 'There is no man whose imagination does not sometimes predominate over his reason, who can regulate this attention wholly by his will, and whose ideas will come and go at his command. No man will be found in whose mind airy notions do not sometimes tyrannise, and force him to hope or fear beyond the limits of sober probability. All power of fancy over reason is a degree of insanity; but while this power is such as we can control and repress, it is not visible to others, nor considered as a depravation of the mental faculties: it is not pronounced madness but when it comes ungovernable, and apparently influences speech or action.'[97]

It was precisely this prognostication of the despotism of imagination which preyed upon Johnson. Fleeing to idleness to escape the melancholy round would prove but a leap out of the frying pan into the fire. Impressed early in life by the *Anatomy of Melancholy*, he knew the wisdom of Burton's adage, 'Be not solitary, be not idle',[98] often advising *Rambler* readers: 'That mind will never be vacant, which is frequently recalled by stated duties to meditations on eternal interests; nor can any hour be long, which is spent in obtaining some new qualification for celestial happiness.'[99] For otherwise there was the descending spiral: 'Idleness produces necessity, necessity incites to wickedness, and wickedness again supplies the means of living in idleness.'[100]

Johnson was thus trapped. Unable, through poverty, situation, and temperament, to assimilate himself to the *bourgeois gentilhomme*'s ease, unable to fuse learning and sociability in Addisonian moderation, he lurched from melancholy toil to melancholy indolence, fearing all the time that way madness lay.

But why – unlike, say, Hume – couldn't Johnson haul himself out of this slough of despond? I believe the answer lies in his religion.[101] To use Burton's terms, Johnson's melancholy was ultimately religious melancholy. Religion, after all, was in Johnson's blood. His mother had dinned *The Whole Duty of Man* into him in early childhood, with its vision of sinful man humbled by a God of Justice, omnipotent and vengeful, dictating duties for man to obey, without respite, to redeem his sin. That message – which young Sam resisted, perhaps guiltily, leading to scoffing in his teens – seized Johnson's heart when he read and was 'overmatched' by William Law's *A Serious Call to a Devout and Holy Life* around 1729.[102] Under the rule of Law, Johnson remained awed by the terrifying mysteries of sin and damnation to the end of his days. Christianity's attraction was that it promised Johnson a solution to the enormity of death.[103]

Johnson could not get death off his mind. 'Is not the fear of death natural to man?' queried Boswell, equally death-obsessed. 'So much so, Sir,' replied Johnson, 'that the whole of life is but to keep away the thoughts of it.' Johnson strove mightily enough to fend it off. Sometimes when Boswell raised the issue, Johnson bellowed him down. Little things triggered great fears. When Bennet Langton drew up his will, Johnson made hysterical sport of him all day. Being 'of dreadful things the most dreadful' (as he put it in the *Rambler*), 'the fear of death' was naturally 'the great disturber of human quiet'.[104] Johnson's dread of extinction, of annihilation, became obsessive, and, as he well knew, fear ate the soul: 'Fear, whether natural or acquired, when once it has full possession of the fancy, never fails to employ it upon visions of calamity, such as, if they are not dissipated by useful employment, will soon overcast it with horrors, and embitter life.'[105]

Christianity gave Johnson a prospect of managing mortality, a vision of triumph over the Grim Reaper, an earnest of life eternal. But only at a terrible price, that of obeying Law's injunction to keep your mind so 'possessed with such a sense of [death's] nearness that you may have it always in your thoughts'. For Johnson's God was wrathful and arbitrary: 'The quiver of Omnipotence is stored with arrows, against which the shield of human virtue, however adamantine it has been boasted, is held up in vain.'[106] God stretched mankind upon a rack of superhuman duties, and punished the sinful by damning them (which meant, Johnson explained, being 'sent to hell and punished everlastingly').[107] Johnson buckled under the onerousness of God's 'call', a *via crucis* of religious duties – prayers, fasting, church attendance, bible reading, soul-searching – which he equally continually shied away from, because they all brought him inescapably face-to-face with his own worthlessness. Not least he felt drilled to intellectual and literary hard labour. Under this regime Johnson condemned himself as idle. Yet what *homme de lettres* could possibly have deemed himself idle, whose output included the *Dictionary*, the *Rambler*, *Idler*, and *Adventurer*, the edition of Shakespeare, the *Lives of the Poets*, and mountains of hack journalism? Johnson's morbid anxiety about wasting time makes sense only under the ultimatums of religious terrorism, under the lash of a divine taskmaster. He abased himself with prayer upon prayer: 'O Lord, enable me by thy Grace to use all diligence in redeeming the time which I have spent in Sloth, Vanity, and wickedness.'[108] But successive promises of reformation only exposed his inability to reform (the demands were superhuman: how could he rise at six, as he continually pledged, when dread insomnia kept him awake till deep into the early hours?[109] How could he be dutiful in soul-searching when it brought to light only fresh proofs of wickedness?). In turn this produced more guilt, more confessions of 'manifold sins and negligences', spawning yet more 'oppressive terrors'.[110]

Johnson's religion proved a torment. He never found religious peace. Even as he neared his deathbed, he confessed to William Hoole, 'he had himself lived in great negligence of Religion and Worship for forty years, that he had neglected greatly to read his Bible and that he had since often reflected what he could hereafter say when he should be asked why he had not read it.'[111] Mrs Thrale knew it only too well. As she perceived, it was precisely Johnson's religion which animated his fears of madness, 'daily terror lest he had not done enough originated in piety, but ended in little less than disease. . . . He . . . filled his imagination with fears that he should ever obtain forgiveness for omission of duty and criminal waste of time.'[112] And Johnson himself was helplessly aware how he made rods for his own back, for example by his 'scruples'.[113] To assuage guilt, strengthen his resolve, and placate the deity, Johnson habitually bound himself by vows and resolutions (which he called 'scruples'). As with his nervous tics and mannerisms, these 'scruples' relieved tension, acting as charms against further backslidings. But they too had their revenges. For making them created guilt, aware as he was of their superstitious, quasi-magical nature ('a vow is a horrible thing, . . . a snare for sin'); and he was still guiltier about not keeping them: 'I have resolved till I am afraid to resolve again,' he confessed, in despair, in 1761.[114]

At almost the same time, another Christian and budding London man of letters was sinking in a similar slough of despond, yet with crucial differences. William Cowper – then in his early thirties – likewise felt that the burdens God had piled on his back were more than he could bear.[115] Rather differently from Johnson, Cowper had a Calvinist conviction of being preordained for perdition. And more in tune with the age of feeling, Cowper wallowed in his own weakness. At crisis point he actually sought release in 'the chastisement of madness'. When madness didn't materialize, he tried suicide, failed, and was ultimately rescued by being taken for mad by his clergyman brother, and despatched to an asylum. There was no such way out for Johnson, whose self-control was iron.

For Johnson was utterly tenacious of his reason; nothing meant more to him. Others like Cowper could ache for its eclipse, but Johnson's religion forbade such euthanasia of the spirit, since he believed it was his cardinal responsibility to 'render up my soul to God unclouded'. Johnson consistently prized the mind infinitely above the body. Physical pain was as nothing; undergoing lancing for dropsy, he demanded deeper incisions, chiding the apothecary, 'I want length of life and you are afraid of giving me pain';[116] characteristically, he had confided to Dr Adams, 'I would consent to have a limb amputated to recover my low spirits.'[117] When he suffered a stroke, his real fear was for his mental powers. These he tested by composing a thematic Latin prayer:

'Summe Pater, quodcunque tuum de corpore
Numen Hoc statuat, precibus Christus adesse velit;
Ingenio parcas, nec sit mihi culpa rogasse,
Qua solum potero parte, placere tibi.'
('Almighty Father, whatever the Divine Will ordains concerning this body of mine, may Christ be willing to aid me with his prayers. And let it not be blameworthy on my part to implore that thou spare my reason, by which faculty alone I shall be able to do thy pleasure.')[118]

Characteristically Johnson gave up the medically prescribed opiates on his deathbed, to pass over with his mind clear.

Religion thus made the mind a jewel of infinite price, confirming Johnson's intuition that whatever he was, he was through his mind. But he also knew only too well that 'of the uncertainties of our present state, the most dreadful is the uncertain continuance of reason'.[119] And it was religious terrors precisely which raised those storms in Johnson's mind that jeopardized his reason. With what enormous pathos of other possible lives unlived we find him writing: 'If I had no duties, and no reference to futurity, I would spend my life in driving briskly in a post-chaise with a pretty woman, but she should be one who could understand me, and would add something to the conversation.'[120]

Rasselas ends with a 'conclusion in which nothing is concluded', and the final *Idler* essay sombrely analyses the 'secret horrour of the last'. Rounding off this paper is thus not easy. But I should like to suggest ways in which the study of how Johnson experienced and coped with melancholy could illuminate the wider history of mental disturbance. We do not altogether lack sufferers' accounts of personality breakdown. But much autobiography of melancholy, particularly that written by men of letters, reeks of literary convention, the stilted clichés of role-players.[121] Furthermore most writings by the mad about their derangement – such as those of Cowper – were penned after the event, as retrospective vindications, proving their sanity, indicting persecutors, demonstrating their role as God's instruments. Moralistic, homiletic, dramaturgic, few have the ring of minute-by-minute authenticity. With Johnson, by contrast, the daily range of letters, prayers, and reflective writings penned by a man of peculiar honesty and self-awareness affords a private view of a soul in turmoil – a portrait almost uniquely enhanced by a wealth of contemporary biography. This richness of materials – I have tried to present a generous slice in this paper – affords an opportunity to attempt a history of mental illness from the sufferer's point of view, rather than merely from the customary standpoints of medicine and psychiatry. We may not be able to make satisfactory diagnoses of Johnson's organic syndromes, but we can reconstruct in some detail how he experienced and vocalized his disturbance, and negotiated it with friends and doctors.

The case study confirms the shaping, constitutive, role of culture in sickness.[122] For Johnson suffered his afflictions – one almost says, enacted his passion – in the idiom of his day, above all perceiving derangement through the Lockean lens that located madness in the mind, the deluge of delusion invading the realm of reason. Johnson had no premonition of the way people were to 'act crazy' a century later (the dissociation of personality, *dementia praecox*).[123] Neither was he melancholy as his forebears had been. For though Johnson certainly laboured under 'religious melancholy', the form that took was not at all as described by his hero and mentor, Robert Burton, for Johnson had no experience of demonic possession in his own case.[124]

Does analysis of Johnson help us to evaluate recent historiography dealing with eighteenth-century nervous afflictions and the therapies of medicine and psychiatry? Consider his experiences in the light of the interpretations developed by Klaus Doerner, Michel Foucault, and Michael MacDonald.[125] In their distinctive but generally convergent ways, they have suggested that madness came to be conceptualized in the Enlightenment essentially in polar opposition to reason. In fact, argues Foucault, it was seen as the negation of reason (unreason). The age of reason thus penalized madness, in company with such other faces of unreason as crime, vice, and idleness. Shorn of its earlier prestigious associations with freedom, prophecy, ecstasy, and poetic genius, madness became suppressed, increasingly through the pseudo-medical means of mechanical therapeutic intervention and incarceration. 'The eighteenth century', concludes MacDonald, 'was a disaster for the insane.'[126]

Johnson's experience corroborates some of these points, at least to some degree. For example, his condemnation of the institutionalization of Kit Smart, and his pleas to be disciplined by Mrs Thrale, show how the threat of public confinement was looming large. Yet the resemblances between the historians' reading and Johnson's experiences are often merely superficial and possibly misleading. Thus no one would deny that Johnson saw madness as the eclipse of reason. But Johnson's conception of reason was far richer than the image of Enlightenment scientific secularism presented by Foucault and MacDonald; he viewed it rather as the embodiment of the soul, in the mainstream of Christian humanism.[127] And in arguing that it was the tyranny of secularizing rationalism that drove the Georgians mad, our modern revisionist historiography underestimates just how many of the mentally afflicted then experienced their tribulations as arising from specifically Christian hopes and fears and agonies (a fact which was no surprise to contemporary physicians, many of whom deplored how commonly religion was the source of depression and derangement).

MacDonald has of course made the important observation at this juncture that the ancient traditions of spiritual healing and exorcism shrivelled up in the eighteenth century, under the hostile glare of Anglicanism and medicine. And it is noteworthy that – despite the episode with the Rev. Dr Delap – Johnson did not regularly seek the ministrations of the clergy for comfort and consolation. Yet MacDonald's corollary – that madness was becoming medicalized – surely does not apply here. Johnson's sufferings show no sign whatever of falling under a strict medical regime. A 'great dabbler in physick' himself,[128] Johnson enjoyed the warmest relations with doctors,[129] eagerly swallowed their remedies for his bodily ills, and absorbed himself in close study of texts such as George Cheyne's *The English Malady*, recommending them to his friends.[130] But he had no notion that medicine would do the slightest good for his own melancholy; nor is there any sign that his physicians tried to urge any on him. Quite the reverse. When Johnson asked of his friend Dr Brocklesby:

'Canst thou not minister to a mind diseased;
Pluck from the memory a rooted sorrow;
And with some sweet oblivious antidote
Cleanse the stuffed bosom of that perilous stuff
Which weighs upon the breast?'

Brocklesby also knew his Shakespeare, replying:

'Therein the patient must minister to himself.'[131]

It is, I think, a fitting comment on lay participation and power in managing sickness in that era, that the person to whom Johnson turned – and turned successfully – for a form of therapy was indeed Hester Thrale.[132] The moral is that if we are to achieve a balanced and sensitive history of psychic affliction and its therapies we must change focus, even transpose subject and object, and start from the sufferers themselves.

Notes

1 K. Jones, *A History of the Mental Health Services* (London: Routledge and Kegan Paul, 1972); K. Jones, *Mental Health and Social Policy 1845–1959* (London: Routledge and Kegan Paul, 1960); N. Walker, *Crime and Insanity in England*, vol. 1, *The Historical Perspective* (Edinburgh: Edinburgh University Press, 1968); N. Walker and S. McCabe, *Crime and Insanity in England*, vol. 2, *New Solutions and New Problems* (Edinburgh: Edinburgh University Press, 1981); Roger Smith, *Trial by Medicine* (Edinburgh: University Press, 1981) For broad discussion of trends in the history of the mad and of psychiatry in Britain see the 'Introductions' to this and the companion volume.
2 A. Scull, *Museums of Madness* (London: Allen Lane, 1979); A. Scull (ed.), *Mad-*

Houses, Mad-Doctors and Madmen (London: Athlone Press, 1981); A. Scull, *Decarceration* (Englewood Cliffs, NJ: Prentice Hall, 1977); D.J. Mellett, *The Prerogative of Asylumdom* (New York: Garland, 1983); John Walton, 'The Treatment of Pauper Lunatics in Victorian England' in Scull (ed.), cited above in this footnote, and his essay in volume 2 of the present work.

3 W.F. Bynum, 'Rationales for Therapy in British Psychiatry 1785–1830', *Medical History* 18 (1974): 317–34; W.F. Bynum, 'Theory and Practice in British Psychiatry from J.C. Prichard (1786–1848) to Henry Maudsley (1835–1918)', in T. Ogawa (ed.), *History of Psychiatry* (Osaka: Taniguchi Foundation, 1982), pp. 196–216; M. Donnelly, *Managing the Mind* (London: Tavistock Publications, 1983).

4 M. Foucault, *Madness and Civilization*, abridged English edition, trans. Richard Howard (London: Tavistock Publications, 1967); K. Doerner, *Madmen and the Bourgeoisie* (Oxford: Basil Blackwell, 1981); P. Sedgwick, *Psychopolitics* (London: Pluto Press, 1981); and for a broad theoretical perspective, D. Ingleby, 'The Social Construction of Mental Illness', in P. Wright and A. Treacher (eds), *The Problem of Medical Knowledge* (Edinburgh: Edinburgh University Press, 1982), pp. 123–43.

5 On the making of images of patients see D. Armstrong, 'The Doctor–Patient Relationship, 1930–80', in Wright and Treacher, *The Problem of Medical Knowledge*, pp. 109–22; and generally, for 'mental illness', see T. Szasz, *The Manufacture of Madness* (London: Routledge and Kegan Paul, 1971).

6 For the mad as scapegoats see Szasz, *The Manufacture of Madness*, and S. Gilman, *Seeing the Insane* (New York: John Wiley, 1982).

7 M. MacDonald, *Mystical Bedlam* (Cambridge: Cambridge University Press, 1981).

8 D. Peterson (ed.), *A Mad People's History of Madness* (Pittsburgh, Pa.: University of Pittsburgh Press, 1982). Compare G. Bateson (ed.), *Perceval's Narrative* (New York: William Morrow, 1974).

9 See R. Colp, *To Be an Invalid* (Chicago: University of Chicago Press, 1977); E.M. Thornton, *Freud and Cocaine* (London: Blond and Briggs, 1983). See the discussion by W.F. Bynum and M.R. Neve, 'Hamlet on the Couch', in this volume.

10 N. Jewson, 'The Disappearance of the Sick Man from Medical Cosmology 1770–1870', *Sociology* 10 (1976): 225–44; N. Jewson, 'Medical Knowledge and the Patronage System in Eighteenth Century England', *Sociology* 8 (1974): 369–85; and Roy Porter (ed.), *Health, Healing and the People* (Cambridge: University Press, 1985).

11 G. Pickering, *Creative Malady* (London: Allen and Unwin, 1974).

12 W.J. Bate, *Samuel Johnson* (New York: Harcourt, Brace, Jovanovich, 1977), p. 117. For Johnson's life the major early biographies are Hester Lynch Piozzi (Mrs Thrale), *Anecdotes of the Late Samuel Johnson, LL.D.*, ed. A. Sherbo (Oxford: Oxford University Press 1974); Sir J. Hawkins, *The Life of Samuel Johnson LL.D.*, 2nd edn (London, 1787); J. Boswell, *Life of Johnson*, ed. G.B. Hill, revised and enlarged by L.F. Powell, 6 vols (Oxford: Clarendon Press, 1934); J.T. Callender, *The Deformities of Johnson* (Edinburgh: W. Creech, 1782); O.M. Brack, Jr and R.E. Kelly (eds), *The Early Biographies of Samuel Johnson* (Ames, Ia: University of Iowa Press, 1971). For modern biographies see J.L. Clifford, *Young Sam Johnson* (New York: McGraw-Hill, 1955): J.L. Clifford, *Dictionary Johnson. The Middle Years of Samuel Johnson* (London:

Heinemann, 1980); W.J. Bate, *Samuel Johnson* (New York: Harcourt-Brace Jovanovich, 1977); J. Wood Krutch, *Samuel Johnson* (New York: H. Holt, 1944); B.H. Bronson, *Johnson Agonistes* (Berkeley, Calif.: University of California Press, 1944); C. Hibbert, *The Personal History of Samuel Johnson* (London: Longman, 1971); J. Wain, *Samuel Johnson* (London: Macmillan, 1974).

13 R.W. Chapman (ed.), *The Letters of Samuel Johnson*, 3 vols (Oxford: Clarendon Press, 1952), vol. 2, no. 772 (28 Aug.), p. 474.

14 For Johnson's physical afflictions see L.C. McHenry, 'Dr Samuel Johnson's Emphysema', *Archives of internal medicine*, 119 (1967): 98–105; L.C. McHenry, 'Medical Case Notes on Samuel Johnson in the Heberden Manuscripts', *Journal of the American Medical Association*, 195 (1966): 89–90; B.S. Abeshouse, *A Medical History of Dr Samuel Johnson* (Norwich, NY: Eaton Laboratories, 1965); Anon., 'Dr Johnson as a "Dabbler in Physick"', *Guy's Hospital Gazette* 76 (1962): 321–24; R.W. Sagebiel, 'Medicine in the Life and Letters of Samuel Johnson', *Ohio State Medical Journal* 53 (1961): 382–84; Sir H. Rolleston, 'Samuel Johnson's Medical Experiences', *Annals of Medical History* n.s. 1 (1929): 540–52.

15 W.J. Bate and A.B. Straus (eds), *Samuel Johnson: The Rambler*, 3 vols (New Haven, Conn.: Yale University Press, 1969), vol. 2, no. 95, p. 143.

16 Boswell, *Life of Johnson*, vol. 1, pp. 63–4. Similar sentiments appear in the 'Introduction' to the *Dictionary*. The phrase 'general disease of my life' recalls Pope: see M.H. Nicolson and G.S. Rousseau, *This Long Disease My Life* (Princeton, NJ: Princeton University Press, 1968).

17 Boswell, *Life of Johnson*, vol. 1, p. 483.

18 J.L. Clifford, *Hester Lynch Piozzi – Mrs Thrale*, 2nd edn, (Oxford: Clarendon Press, 1952).

19 E.L. McAdam, Jr (ed.), *Samuel Johnson, Diaries, Prayers and Annals* (New Haven, Conn.: Yale University Press, 1958), p. 140.

20 The fullest discussion is in Bate, *Samuel Johnson*, pp. 382 ff.

21 Boswell, *Life of Johnson*, vol. 2, p. 35.

22 McAdam, *Diaries, Prayers and Annals*, p. 264.

23 Boswell, *Life of Johnson*, vol. 1, p. 35.

24 See L. Feder, *Madness in Literature* (Princeton, NJ: Princeton University Press, 1980); M.V. De Porte, *Nightmares and Hobbyhorses* (San Marino, Calif.: Huntington Library, 1974); M. Byrd, *Visits to Bedlam* (Columbia, SC, 1974); C. Moore, *Backgrounds to English Literature, 1700–1760* (Minneapolis, Minn.: University of Minnesota Press, 1953); G.S. Rousseau, 'Psychology', in G.S. Rousseau and Roy Porter (eds), *The Ferment of Knowledge* (Cambridge: Cambridge University Press, 1980), pp. 143–210.

25 A.M. Ingram, *Boswell's Creative Gloom* (London: Macmillan, 1982); M. Bailey (ed.), *Boswell's Column* (London: William Kimber,1951). The quotation is on pp. 42–3.

26 Boswell, *Life of Johnson*, vol. 3, pp. 175–76.

27 Boswell, *Life of Johnson*, vol. 1, p. 397.

28 Mrs Thrale (Piozzi, *Anecdotes*), in G.B. Hill (ed.) *Johnsonian Miscellanies*, 2 vols (Oxford: Clarendon Press, 1897), vol. 1, pp. 199–200.

29 Boswell, *Life of Johnson*, vol. 2, p. 176.

30 J.S. Madden, 'Samuel Johnson's Alcohol Problem', *Medical History* 11 (1967): 141–49. Johnson had a contemporary public reputation as coarse and ill-

mannered. See the comment for 1756 by a parson, the Rev. George Woodward, a man personally unacquainted with him: 'When I came home, I found the Critical Review of last month. I am told the chief person concerned in this work is Johnson the Dictionary man, a person noted for great invectives in all his writings, and much ill nature in his private character' (quoted in D. Gibson (ed.), *A Parson in the Vale of White Horse* (Gloucester: Allan Sutton, 1982), p. 92).

31 Boswell, *Life of Johnson*, vol. 1, pp. 145–47.

32 Quoted in L.C. McHenry, 'Samuel Johnson's Tics and Gesticulations', *Journal of the History of Medicine* 22 (1967): 152–70 (p. 157), from *Memoirs of Dr Burney* (London: Edward Moxon, 1832), vol. 1, p. 241.

33 Quoted in McHenry, 'Tics and Gesticulations', p. 157.

34 From Thomas Tyers's biography reprinted in Brack and Kelly, *The Early Biographies of Samuel Johnson*, p. 63. For the religious overtones of 'convulsions' see B.R. Kreiser, *Miracles, Convulsions and Ecclesiastical Politics in Early Eighteenth Century Paris* (Princeton, NJ: Princeton University Press, 1978).

35 Quoted in McHenry, 'Tics and Gesticulations', p. 155.

36 Boswell, *Life of Johnson*, vol. 1, pp. 95, 98, 144, 485; vol. 3, p. 140.

37 Boswell, *Life of Johnson*, vol. 4, p. 397.

38 Mrs Thrale, in Hill, *Johnsonian Miscellanies*, vol. 1, p. 200.

39 Boswell, *Life of Johnson*, vol. 1, p. 35.

40 E.A. Bloom, *Samuel Johnson in Grub Street* (Providence, RI: Brown University Press, 1957).

41 Samuel Johnson, *Lives of the Poets*, extracted in B.H. Bronson, *Samuel Johnson, Rasselas, Poems and Selected Prose* (San Francisco, Calif.: Rinehard Press, 1971), p. 446.

42 J.H. Hagstrum and J. Gray (eds), *Samuel Johnson: Sermons* (New Haven, Conn.: Yale University Press, 1978), no. 12, pp. 127 ff.

43 Samuel Johnson, *The Life of Mr Richard Savage* (London, 1747), p. 9.

44 Bate and Straus, *The Rambler*, vol. 2, no. 78, p. 45.

45 Boswell, *Life of Johnson*, vol. 3, p. 53; cf. 'Life is a pill which none of us can bear to swallow without gilding; yet for the poor we delight in stripping it still barer, and are not ashamed to shew even visible displeasure, if ever the bitter taste is taken from their mouths' (in Piozzi, *Anecdotes*, p. 89).

46 Quoted in Hill, *Johnsonian Miscellanies*, vol. 1, pp. 334–35.

47 See Samuel Johnson, 'A Review of Soame Jenyns' *A Free Enquiry into the Nature and Origin of Evil*', in B. Bronson (ed.). *Samuel Johnson, Rasselas, Poems and Selected Prose* (San Francisco, Calif.: Rinehart Press, 1971), p. 219.

48 Bate and Straus, *The Rambler* vol. 3, no. 203, p. 291.

49 Boswell, *Life of Johnson*, vol. 2, p. 476; vol. 3, p. 200.

50 Piozzi, *Anecdotes* in Hill, *Johnsonian Miscellanies*, vol. 1, p. 268.

51 Bate, *Samuel Johnson*, pp. 196, 375.

52 Samuel Johnson, *The Idler and Adventurer*, ed. W.J. Bate, J.M. Bullitt, and L.F. Powell (New Haven, Conn.: Yale University Press, 1963), p. 139.

53 P.P. Chase, 'The Ailments and Physicians of Dr Johnson', *Yale Journal of Biology and Medicine* 23 (1951): 370–79.

54 A.L. Reade, *Johnsonian Gleanings*, 11 vols (London: privately printed, 1909–52), vol. 10, p. 22.

55 Samuel Johnson, *A Dictionary of the English Language* (London, 1755).

56 McHenry, 'Tics and Gesticulations'; M. Critchley, 'Dr Samuel Johnson's Aphasia', *Medical History* 6 (1962): 27–44. The case for De La Tourette's

Syndrome has recently been argued in T.J. Murray, 'Doctor Samuel Johnson's Abnormal Movements', in A.J. Friedhoff and T.N. Chase (eds), *Gilles de la Tourette Syndrome* (New York: Raven Press, 1982), pp. 25–30.

57 E. Verbeek, *The Measure and the Choice. A Pathographic Essay on Samuel Johnson* (Ghent: Leuven E. Story Scienta, 1971). Cf. M.L. Astaldi, *Tre Inglesi Pazzi* (Milano: Rizzoli, 1974).

58 Quoted in McHenry, 'Tics and Gesticulations', p. 164.

59 Quoted in McHenry, 'Tics and Gesticulations', p. 165.

60 R. Macdonald Ladell, 'The Neurosis of Dr Samuel Johnson', *The British Journal of Medical Psychology* 9 (1929): pp. 314–23.

61 See the discussion in Bate, *Samuel Johnson*, pp. 117 f.

62 Boswell, *Life of Johnson*, vol. 2, p. 106.

63 Boswell, *Life of Johnson*, vol. 2, p. 549.

64 W.R. Brain, 'The Great Convulsionary', and 'A Post-Mortem on Dr Johnson', in *Some Reflections on Genius and Other Essays* (London: Pitman Medical, 1960), pp. 69–91, 92–100.

65 K. Grange, 'Dr Samuel Johnson's Account of a Schizophrenic Illness in *Rasselas* (1759)', *Medical History* 6 (1962): 162–68; R.B. Hovey, 'Dr Samuel Johnson, Psychiatrist', *Modern Language Quarterly* 15 (1954): 321–55; K.T. Reed, 'This Tasteless Tranquillity: A Freudian Note on Johnson's *Rasselas*', *Literature and Psychology* 19 (1969): 61–2. For Mrs Thrale, see K. Balderston, *Thraliana*, 2 vols (Oxford: Clarendon Press, 1942), vol. 1, p. 728.

66 K. Balderston, 'Johnson's Vile Melancholy', in *The Age of Johnson*, ed. F.W. Hilles and W.S. Lewis (New Haven, Conn.: Yale University Press, 1964), pp. 3–14. Ladell, 'Neurosis', also suggests at root a sexual problem.

67 Bate, *Samuel Johnson*, pp. 382 f.

68 W.J. Bate, *The Achievement of Samuel Johnson* (New York: Oxford University Press, 1955), p. 93.

69 Bate and Straus *The Rambler*, vol. 2, no. 73, p. 22.

70 Johnson, *Letters*, vol. 2, p. 70, no. 422 (1774) (to Mrs Thrale).

71 Piozzi, *Anecdotes*, in Hill, *Johnsonian Miscellanies*, vol. 2, p. 159.

72 Quoted in Hill, *Johnsonian Miscellanies*, vol. 2, p. 257. See also p. 280.

73 F. Burney, quoted in R. Napier (ed.), *Johnsoniana* (London: Bell, 1892), 309.

74 Boswell, *Life of Johnson*, vol. 1, p. 67.

75 Cited in G. Irwin, *Samuel Johnson, A Personality in Conflict* (Auckland: Auckland University Press, 1971), p. 60.

76 Boswell, *Life of Johnson*, vol. 1, p. 373.

77 Gilman, *Seeing the Insane*; P.B.R. Doob, *Nebuchadnessar's Children* (New Haven, Conn.: Yale University Press, 1974); B. Clarke, *Mental Disorders in Earlier Britain* (Cardiff: University of Wales Press, 1975); R. and M. Wittkower, *Born under Saturn* (London: Weidenfeld and Nicolson, 1963); R. Klibansky, E. Panofsky, and F. Saxl, *Saturn and Melancholy* (London: Nelson, 1964).

78 Roy Porter, 'The Rage of Party: a Glorious Revolution in English Psychiatry?', *Medical History* 27 (1983): 35–50.

79 See M. Golden, *The Self Observed* (Baltimore Md: Johns Hopkins Press, 1972), pp. 68 f.

80 For Hume see E.C. Mossner, *The Life of David Hume* (London: Nelson, 1954), pp. 67 ff.; S.D. Cox, *'The Stranger Within Thee': The Concept of the Self in Late Eighteenth Century Literature* (Pittsburgh, Pa.: University of Pittsburgh

Press, 1980); J.O. Lyons, *The Invention of the Self* (Carbondale, Ill.: Southern Illinois University Press, 1978).

81 Samuel Johnson, *The Poems of Mr Collins* (London, 1779).

82 Boswell, *Life of Johnson*, vol. 3, p. 381; vol. 4, p. 79. Remember, however, Johnson's ambiguous feelings about heroes.

83 Boswell, *Life of Johnson*, vol. 2, p. 440.

'Disorders of intellect, answered Imlac, happen much more often than superficial observers will easily believe. Perhaps, if we speak with rigorous exactness, no human mind is in its right state. There is no man whose imagination does not sometimes predominate over his reason, who can regulate his attention wholly by his will, and whose ideas will come and go at his command. No man will be found in whose mind airy notions do not sometimes tyrannise, and force him to hope or fear beyond the limits of sober probability. All power of fancy over reason is a degree of insanity; but while this power is such as we can controul and repress, it is not visible to others, nor considered as any deprivation of the mental faculties; it is not pronounced madness but when it comes ungovernable, and apparently influences speech or action.'

(S. Johnson, *Rasselas*, quoted in Bronson,
Samuel Johnson, Rasselas, Poems and Selected Prose, pp. 693–94)

84 Johnson, *The Idler*, ed. W.J. Bate, J.M. Bullitt, and L.F. Powell (New Haven, Conn.: Yale University Press, 1963), no. 31, p. 95 f.

85 McAdam, *Diaries, Prayers and Annals*, p. 77. Cf. Golden, *The Self Observed*, pp. 69 f.

86 McAdam, *Diaries, Prayers and Annals*, p. 257.

87 McAdam, *Diaries, Prayers and Annals*, p. 26.

88 Bate and Straus, *The Rambler* vol. 2, no. 85, p. 86.

89 McAdam, *Diaries, Prayers and Annals*, p. 47 (May 6, 1752).

90 McAdam, *Diaries, Prayers and Annals*, 25 April, 1752; 6 May, 1752; 6 May, 1752; Easter 1757; Easter 1753.

91 Johnson, *Rasselas*, quoted from Bronson, *Samuel Johnson, Rasselas, Poems and Selected Prose*.

92 For the wider context of Johnson's view of the interconnectedness of idleness, imagination, and madness see R. Voitle, *Samuel Johnson the Moralist* (Cambridge, Mass.: Harvard University Press, 1961); W.B.C. Watkins, *Perilous Balance* (Princeton, NJ: Princeton University Press, 1939); Irwin, *Samuel Johnson: A Personality in Conflict*; A. Sachs, *Passionate Intelligence* (Baltimore, Md: Johns Hopkins Press, 1967); P.K. Alkon, *Samuel Johnson and Moral Discipline* (Evanston, Ill.: 1967).

93 McAdam, *Diaries, Prayers and Annals*, p. 65.

94 Johnson, *Rasselas*, quoted from Bronson, *Samuel Johnson, Rasselas, Poems and Selected Prose*, p. 694.

95 For Locke and the imagination in the eighteenth century see J. Engell, *The Creative Imagination* (Cambridge, Mass.: Harvard University Press, 1981); J. Wright, 'Hysteria and Mechanical Man', *Journal of the History of Ideas* 41 (1980): 223–47; E.L. Tuveson, *Imagination as a Means of Grace* (Berkeley Calif.: University of California Press, 1960); M.H. Abrams, *The Mirror and the Lamp* (New York: Oxford University Press, 1953).

96 D.F. Bond, '"Distrust" of Imagination in English Neo-Classicism', *Philological Quarterly* 14 (1935): 54–69; D.F. Bond, 'The Neoclassical Psychology of the

Imagination', *English Literary History* 4 (1937): 245–64; P. Fussell, *The Rhetorical World of Augustan Humanism* (Oxford: Clarendon Press, 1965).

97 Johnson, *Rasselas*, quoted from Bronson, *Samuel Johnson, Rasselas, Poems and Selected Prose*, pp. 693–94.

98 R. Burton, *Anatomy of Melancholy* (Oxford: John Lichfield and James Short for Henry Cripps, 1621).

99 Bate and Straus, *The Rambler*, ii, 142.

100 Bate and Straus, *The Rambler*, ii, 146.

101 For Johnson's religion see C. Pierce, *The Religious Life of Samuel Johnson* (London: Athlone, 1983); M. Quinlan, *Samuel Johnson, a Layman's Religion* (Madison, Wis.: University of Wisconsin Press, 1964); C. Chapin, *The Religious Thought of Samuel Johnson* (Ann Arbor, Mich.: University of Michigan Press, 1968); R.B. Schwarz, *Samuel Johnson and the Problem of Evil* (Madison, Wis.: University of Wisconsin Press, 1975); S.G. Brown, 'Dr Johnson and the Religious Problem', *English Studies* 20 (1938): 1–17.

102 K. Balderston, 'Doctor Johnson and William Law', *Proceedings of the Modern Language Association* (1960), pp. 382–94.

103 For Johnson and death see J.H. Hagstrum, 'On Dr Johnson's Fear of Death', *ELH* 14 (1947); 308–19.

104 Bate and Straus, *The Rambler*, vol. 2, no. 114, p. 244.

105 Bate and Straus, *The Rambler*, vol. 2, no. 134, p. 347.

106 W.J. Bate, J.M. Bullitt, and L.F. Powell (eds), *Samuel Johnson: The Idler and Adventurer* (New Haven, Conn.: Yale University Press, 1963), p. 468.

107 Boswell, *Life of Johnson*, vol. 4, p. 299; vol. 2, p. 360; vol. 3, p. 293.

108 McAdam, *Diaries, Prayers and Annals*, p. 40.

109 See the discussion in Bate, *Samuel Johnson*, p. 119.

110 McAdam, *Diaries, Prayers and Annals*, p. 38. Cf. also pp. 48, 55, 63, 69, 143, 257, 278, 300, 303, 305, 393.

111 O.M. Brack, Jr., *Journal Narrative Relative to Doctor Johnson's Last Illness* (Iowa City, Windhover Press, 1972), unpaginated.

112 Piozzi, *Anecdotes*, in Hill, *Johnsonian Miscellanies*, vol. 2, 157.

113 McAdam, *Diaries, Prayers and Annals*, p. 71. See also pp. 64, 82, 99, 105–08, 110, 161, 266, 276, 363, 368.

114 On scruples see McAdam, *Diaries, Prayers and Annals*, p. 73.

115 For Cowper see M. Quinlan, *William Cowper* (Minneapolis, Minn.: University of Minnesota Press, 1953); C.A. Ryskamp, *William Cowper of the Inner Temple Esq.* (Cambridge: Cambridge University Press, 1959); C.A. Ryskamp, *Johnson and Cowper* (London, 1965).

116 See the discussion in Bate, *Samuel Johnson*, p. 598.

117 Boswell, *Life of Johnson*, vol. 1, p. 483.

118 Boswell, *Life of Johnson*, vol. 4, p. 230.

119 Johnson, *Rasselas*, quoted in Bronson, *Samuel Johnson, Rasselas, Poems and Selected Prose*, p. 693.

120 Boswell, *Life of Johnson*, vol. 2, p. 453; cf. vol. 3, pp. 162, 458; vol. 5, p. 16.

121 D. Peterson, *A Mad People's History of Madness* (Pittsburgh, Pa.: University of Pittsburgh Press, 1982); Roy Porter, 'Being Mad in Georgian England', *History Today*, vol. 31 (1981): 42–8.

122 See Wright and Treacher, *The Problem of Medical Knowledge*.

123 See S.P. Fullinwider, *Technicians of the Finite* (Westpoint, Conn.: Greenwood Press, 1982); Donnelly, *Managing the Mind*; W.F. Bynum, 'The Nervous

Patient' (this volume).

124 See MacDonald, *Mystical Bedlam*; D.P. Walker, *Unclean Spirits* (London: Scolar, 1981); L. Babb, *Sanity in Bedlam* (East Lansing, Mich.: Michigan State University Press, 1959); B.G. Lyons, *Voices of Melancholy* (London: Routledge and Kegan Paul, 1971); B. Evans, *The Psychiatry of Robert Burton* (New York: Columbia University Press, 1944).

125 Doerner, *Madmen and the Bourgeoisie*; M. Foucault, *Madness and Civilization* (New York: Pantheon Press, 1965); MacDonald, *Mystical Bedlam*. For discussion see Sedgwick, *Psychopolitics*; Roy Porter, 'In the Eighteenth Century, Were English Lunatic Asylums Total Institutions?', *Ego* 4 (1983): 12–34.

126 MacDonald, *Mystical Bedlam*, p. 230.

127 For example N. Robinson, *A New System of the Spleen* (London: A. Bettesworth, 1729). See H. Schwarz, *Knaves, Fools, Madmen and that Subtle Effluvium* (Gainesville: University of Florida Press, 1978); R. Knox, *Enthusiasm* (London, 1950); Porter, 'The Rage of Party' (note 78).

128 Boswell, *Life of Johnson*, vol. 3, p. 152. J. Mulhallen and D.J.M. Wright, 'Samuel Johnson: Amateur Physician', *Journal of the Royal Society of Medicine* 76 (1983): 217–22.

129 H.E. Bloxome, 'Dr Johnson and the Medical Profession', *Cornhill Magazine* n.s. 63 (1925): 455–71; J.P. Warbasse, 'Doctors of Samuel Johnson and His Court', *Medical Library and Historical Journal* 5 (1907): 65–87; R. Hutchinson, 'Dr Samuel Johnson and Medicine', *Edinburgh Medical Journal* 97 (1925): 389–406; A.F. Hazen, 'Samuel Johnson and Dr Robert James', *Bulletin of the History of Medicine* 4 (1936): 455–65; L.C. McHenry, Jr. 'Dr Johnson and Dr Heberden', *Clio Medica* (1976): 117–23; F. Doubleday, 'Some Medical Associations of Dr Johnson', *Guy's Hospital Reports* 101 (1952): 45–51.

130 See G.S. Rousseau, 'Medicine and Millenarianism: Immortal Dr Cheyne', in R. Popkin (ed.), *Millenarianism and Messianism in the Enlightenment* (Berkeley, Calif.: University of California Press, forthcoming). Mrs Thrale wrote that Johnson had 'studied medicine diligently in all its branches but had given particular attention to the diseases of the imagination' Piozzi, *Anecdotes*, in Hill, *Johnsonian Miscellanies*, vol. 1, p. 199.

131 Boswell, *Life of Johnson*, vol. 4, p. 400.

132 Hester Thrale was herself medically quite expert. She later contrasted Johnson's and George III's conditions, using Thomas Arnold's classification of madness.

CHAPTER FOUR

The nervous patient in eighteenth- and nineteenth-century Britain: the psychiatric origins of British neurology

W.F. Bynum

'The more marked the mental disturbance the fewer the neurological signs, and vice versa. Psychiatrically noisy, neurologically silent, is no bad adage.'[1]

My epigram comes from the late Richard Hunter. It was one of Hunter's firm professional and historical convictions that psychiatric disorders are at bottom physical, and that psychiatry and neurology developed as separate specialities because of the curious fact that patients can suffer substantial impairments of their nervous systems without signs of mental derangement, and that individuals with bizarre affects, mental states, or behavioural characteristics can die with brains which stubbornly refuse to yield evidence of abnormality to the dissecting scalpel or chemical analyst. However, a more astute diagnostician than many psychiatrists, Hunter could often find evidence of neurological deficit where more casual observers had found only psychiatric disorder. For instance, he suggested that the earliest picture of a patient in Bethlem – or Bedlam – taken from the title page of Robert Burton's *Anatomy of Melancholy*, showing a patient with 'mania', actually depicts an abnormal arm and hand posture associated with choreo-athetosis.[2]

The historical relationships between psychiatry and neurology have been markedly different in different national contexts. In the German-speaking lands, they merged in the middle of the nineteenth century to form the rich neuropsychiatric tradition of Griesinger, Wernicke, Krafft-Ebing, Meynert, and Korsakoff. These German and Austrian neuropsychiatrists made no real distinction between diseases of the brain and diseases of the mind, for they held that mental processes were always the unvarying result of underlying brain functions; Meynert subtitled his psychiatric textbook 'A Treatise on Diseases of the Forebrain'.[3] Not surprisingly, they were more interested in scientific research than in practice, and although psychopharmacology came within their ken, they were little concerned with psychotherapy, and the tradition made little concession to psychoanalysis, even if, ironically, the tradition actually nourished the young Sigmund Freud. The German neuropsychiatric approach was taken up in many parts of Europe – Italy, Greece, and Spain, for instance – and is still alive and well in places like Japan.[4]

In the English-speaking world, however, the pattern was different. In both the United States and Britain, a formal psychiatric profession developed in the first half of the nineteenth century, decades before medical specialities such as cardiology, gastroenterology, or neurology. In both countries, the psychiatric profession coalesced around specialized hospitals – the insane asylum – whose medical superintendents became, for the most part, administrators and overlords of vast establishments filled with chronically incapacitated patients. Richard Hunter and Ida Macalpine's history of one such establishment – at Colney Hatch in North London – has reminded us that these institutions were not simply museums of madness: they were also museums of neuropathology where unwanted patients with neurosyphilis, epilepsy, ataxias, and many other organic diseases of the nervous system spent their monotonous lives.[5] But neuropsychiatry never really flourished in Britain or America, despite continued lip-service paid to the notion of the organic nature of insanity.[6] In America, neurology as a clinical speciality developed largely in the private sector associated, above all, with men such as William Hammond, Silas Weir Mitchell, and George Beard.[7] Early on American neurology was identified with neurasthenia and the rest cure. The tensions between American psychiatrists and neurologists have recently been explored by Bonnie Blustein, and Russell Dejong has looked at more traditional features of American neurology.[8]

But what of the nervous British patient? I should like here to consider briefly some of the traits of patients suffering from nervous diseases from the early eighteenth to the early twentieth century. These nervous diseases were a class in which physical symptoms predominated but for which the evidence for structural derangement was lacking. Historians have been particularly intrigued by these 'functional' diseases, as they have come to be called, for they seem to show most clearly the cultural, social, and ideological factors which influence definitions and perceptions of disease and constrain the behaviour of both patients and their doctors.[9] Hysteria is perhaps the best known of these disorders, all the more famous since hysteria played such a crucial role in Freud's elaboration of the principles of psychoanalysis. But of course hysteria was only one of a cluster of these functional disorders. As Thomas Trotter wrote in 1807, in his *View of the Nervous Temperament*: 'They have been designated in common language, by the terms NERVOUS; SPASMODIC; BILIOUS; INDIGESTION; STOMACH COMPLAINTS; LOW SPIRITS; VAPOURS etc.'[10] Earlier, George Cheyne, in his treatise on the *English Malady* (1733) had identified the spleen, vapours, lowness of spirits, hypochondriacal and hysterical distempers as constituting the cluster of nervous diseases to which he believed the English were especially prone.[11]

It was, in fact, only in the eighteenth century that it became possible to suffer from the 'nerves'. If a patient had gone to his doctor in Hippocratic times and complained of being 'nervous' his doctor would have expected to see a sinewy fellow, strong and vigorous.[12] Shakespeare never used the word 'nervous', but he used the cognate adjective, 'nervy', to describe the arm of a strong warrior in *Coriolanus*:

'Death, that dark spirit, in's nervy arm doth lie,
Which, being advanc'd, declines, and then men die.' (II. i, 177–78)

Thomas Willis, whose English translator Samuel Pordage gave us the word 'neurologie', as the 'doctrine of the nerves', occasionally described patients without, as he said, 'any notable sickness', but his vocabulary for these functional disorders was traditional, even if he helped dismantle the old notion that hysteria is a disease of the uterus.[13]

Half a century after Willis's death, however, George Cheyne put the nerves on the map. His popular treatise, which went through five quick editions, described a personality type found in those with 'weak, loose, and feeble or relax'd nerves', the result of which was extreme sensitivity to hot and cold, weak digestion, a tendency to alternative diarrhoea and costiveness, and other signs of valetudinarianism. This English disease, affecting, he insisted, as many as one-third of all people of quality in England, was the result of the high living, prosperity, and progress unique on such a wide scale in early eighteenth-century England. Cheyne flattered his patients: only those of quick and lively dispositions and good breeding suffered from the nerves. 'We *Hypochondriacks*,' James Boswell mused to himself, 'may console ourselves in the hour of gloomy distress, by thinking that our sufferings make our superiority.'[14] With Cheyne, 'nervous' acquired some of its modern connotations, although Dr Johnson, with his firm sense of historical etymology, lamented its new and trendier meaning. He described in a letter to Mrs Thrale a person with 'a tender, irritable, and as it is not very properly called, a nervous constitution'. In his *Dictionary*, Johnson gave as the first meaning of 'nervous' the older one: 'well strung; strong; vigorous'. Its second meaning was also acceptable to him: 'Relating to the nerves; having the seat in the nerves.' Finally, with Cheyne as his authority, Johnson recorded a third meaning of 'nervous': 'Having weak or diseased nerves', indicating his disapproval by the stern caveat that this usage was '*medical cant*'.[15]

In the meantime, Cheyne's Scottish colleagues, Robert Whytt and William Cullen, elevated the nervous system to a prime position within physiology, pathology, and nosology. 'In my opinion', wrote Whytt, 'the generality of morbid affections so depend on the nervous system, that almost every disease might be called nervous.'[16] To Cullen, we owe the invention of the term, and the original elaboration of the concept, of neurosis.[17] Cullen's lectures on physiology were about two-thirds devoted to the nervous system; his *First Lines of the Practice of Physic*, which became a textbook for a whole generation of British and American medical students, included as one of his major classes of diseases the neuroses, defined by him as affections of sense and motion, without fever or evidence of local disease. Cullen further divided the neuroses into four orders, the *comata* (apoplexy, paralysis); *adynamiae* (syncope, hypochondriasis, chlorosis), *spasmi* (convulsions, chorea, hysteria, hydrophobia), and *vesaniae* (melancholia, mania, and other diseases of impaired judgement).[18] It was, of course, a classification which did not stand the test of time, but its *functional* orientation, its division of diseases of the nervous system essentially into those of sensation and those of motion, continued to dictate neurological nosology throughout the nineteenth century, particularly through the *locus classicus* of modern neurology, Moritz Romberg's *Manual of the Nervous Diseases of Man*, published in parts between 1840 and 1846, and translated, from its second edition, into English in 1853. The title was significant: Romberg wrote about nervous diseases, rather than diseases of the nervous system: a functional rather than structural outlook.[19] Earlier, John Cooke's *Treatise of Nervous Diseases* had quietly adopted the same approach.[20]

This functional orientation is one of the common strands of nineteenth-century neurology and psychiatry and continues to be a soft spot in modern psychiatric diagnoses. Initially, for neither speciality did the anatomico-pathological thrust so successfully cultivated by the French school seem to be of much systematic use. John Cooke devoted 150 pages to general considerations of the functions of the nervous system, and only about 10 per cent of that amount to post-mortem dissections. He knew that apoplexies could be correlated with contralateral lesions in the brain, but the range of post-mortem appearances, and the absence of precise correlations with clinical symptoms, led him to devalue this avenue to medical knowledge. Likewise, his contemporaries who were primarily intrigued with psychiatric disorders such as melancholia and mania, sometimes puzzled over their inability to discover those footsteps of disease which Francis Bacon long before had suggested were the tangible legacies of suffering and sickness, and whose precise elaboration offered the surest hope of an efficacious medical science. James Cowles Prichard, for instance, used an appendix to his *Treatise on Insanity* (1835) to consider the French alienists' attempts to apply the methods of clinico-pathological correlation to the mad. The result, Prichard insisted, was a failure: there were simply too many instances where overt insanity could not be correlated with structural abnormalities of the brain and nervous system.[21]

One consequence of this common functional mould was the mixture of moral and medical language so emphasized by recent historians. Many of the characteristics of the nervous patient as he – or, increasingly in the nineteenth century, she – was described by Enlightenment doctors and moralists were pulled together in the view of the nervous temperament, elaborated by one of Cullen's pupils, Thomas Trotter. Trotter's nervous patient has such persistence throughout the nineteenth century that he deserves a closer look. For this nervous patient, in Trotter's opinion, was extremely easy to find. As he wrote:

'Sydenham at the conclusion of the seventeenth century, computed fevers to constitute two thirds of the diseases of mankind. But, at the beginning of the nineteenth century, we do not hesitate to affirm, that *nervous disorders* have now taken the place of fevers, and may be justly reckoned two thirds of the whole, with which civilized society is afflicted.'[22]

A bold claim, that, but one which Trotter sought to substantiate by extending the typical eighteenth-century assumption that nervous complaints are diseases of the leisured classes – diseases of luxury – to encompass virtually all of the urban population of Britain. A simple, energetic country life engenders health and vigour; anything which deviates from it is debilitating: want of fresh air, highly refined foods, tea, excessive alcohol consumption, fashionable dress, competitiveness, lack of sleep, novel reading, adultery, excessive passion, abuse of medicine, excessive study: these and a thousand other pitfalls await the unwary business man, labourer, or woman of leisure. Trotter could see no real and lasting solution save that which Charles Dickens was later to propose for all the social ills of his own day: the individual change of heart. Civilization bred its own discontents and provided no easy solutions. To obtain health, men and women must return to the simple life which Tacitus had described for the ancient Germans: the life of fresh air, vigorous outdoor pursuits, simple food, uncomplicated relations between the sexes. What Trotter mourned was the passing of an England which he located in a romantic, organic past:

'The rise and fall of a large commercial town, may be taken as an example of a nation. From a few fishermen's huts, on some river, or arm of the sea, it gradually extends and improves, till the exchange for business, and the theatre for amusement, become its ornaments. A narrow port is by degrees, widened into a capacious harbour: and the warehouse, manufactory and shop, increase in proportion, till wealth and elegance dazzle in every lane and alley. The coffee-house, the inn, and the tavern, grow necessary appendages to business and pleasure: the morning begins with a bargain, and the evening closes with a banquet. Then the rout commences, to teach the young the arts of gaming: and the midnight masquerade initiates them into the wiles of intrigue. The riot disturbs sleep; the drunkard is seen staggering home, in danger of robbery and death; and the woman of the town, deserted by her destroyer, is seeking reprisals, and looking for prey in the streets. Now the hospital and bedlam appear in the suburbs; the first to receive the poor, sick and lame; and the other to confine the more wretched in mind. The physician and apothecary are seen gliding in their chariots, with retinues sometimes not much like men who are conversant with human affliction, and enriched by the luxuries and vices of their fellow mortals. Morals and health are alike committed in this vortex of wealth and dissipation.'[23]

Trotter's nervous patient might suffer from almost any organ of the body, because the nerves go everywhere. Thus, gout, liver disease, dyspepsia, and kidney stone were diseases of the nervous temperament as much as hysteria, hypochondria, and frank disorders of the mind.

During the half-century following Trotter's work, however, the new concern for spinal physiology directed medical attention towards the spinal cord and reflexes, provided a much more scientific-sounding vocabulary to describe nervous symptoms, and brought other disorders – particularly epilepsy – within the nervous pale.[24] Of especial importance for the British scene were Marshall Hall and Thomas Laycock.

Hall was a controversial figure in his own lifetime and has continued to attract a divided historical commentary. That he was a thoroughly disagreeable man few would deny. He was vain, ambitious, opionated, self-serving, arrogant, and gratingly pious. He was also exceptionally intelligent and hard-working, an inveterate experimentalist at a time when vivisectional experimentation in Britain was rather frowned upon. He ran afoul of the Royal Society, whose physiological committee turned down his papers as essentially derivative from Whytt, Prochaska, and earlier pioneers of reflex physiology.[25] He never held a proper hospital appointment in a period when such consultancies were virtually essential for a place within the elite of medical London. Denied a hospital-based practice, he set himself up in a practice which cultivated nervous disorders, trying to develop a speciality of neurology a generation before the British were ready to accept medical specialisms.[26] He lived and died an aggrieved man; he wanted desperately, like Charles Bell before him, to be the William Harvey of the nervous system.

Yet, like Bell, Hall's achievements were considerable, for, after him, it was impossible to think about neurological disorders without considering the reflex concept, even though Hall was not so successful at applying clinically his reflexology as he was at working out its experimental basis. Previous divisions of the nervous system had been into two: cerebro-spinal and the ganglionic or sympathetic, or as it was sometimes conceived, the voluntary and the automatic. Hall proposed to divide the cerebro-spinal system further, into separate cerebral and spinal systems, or as he came to call the latter, the diastaltic nervous system. Diastaltic was congeneric with peristaltic, the chief characteristic of the sympathetic system; and this diastaltic system was the source of much physiological activity and the seat of many of the diseases called nervous: epilepsy, hysteria, tetanus, and other disorders characterized above all by their spasmatic qualities.[27]

Hall's division of the central nervous system into two was not without its difficulties, for in emphasizing the importance of his diastaltic system he made ambiguous the nature of the links between the higher, voluntary system, and the lower reflex one. He had difficulty integrating moral and psychological factors, associated by him with the voluntary system, into the overall clinical picture of those spasmatic diseases of the diastaltic system which were his especial province. But the reflex model was promptly applied to the higher centres by William Carpenter, Thomas Laycock, and others, and served as the basis of John Hughlings Jackson's mature work.[28] Jackson, and the work of Fritsch and Hitzig and, above all, David Ferrier on cerebral localization, provided the basic neurological paradigms from which, from the 1880s, developed a structurally orientated neurology that gradually left the care of the nervous patient to the obstetricians and gynaecologists, the general physicians, and the office-based psychiatrists. Before looking briefly at this heroic, formative period in British neurology, let us glance at a work which pulls together many of the older strands, Charles Handfield-Jones's *Studies on Functional Nervous Disorders*, published in an enlarged second edition in 1870.

Handfield-Jones was a physician to St Mary's Hospital who had earned his fellowship in the Royal Society early in his career through his pathological and microscopical researches, particularly on the liver. In his later work, he sought to systematize current thinking on functional nervous disorders from the standpoint of general medicine. Three characteristics of his 800-page treatise on functional nervous disorders are worth noting. First, he refused to admit that the functional diagnosis was simply one of exclusion: a second-class disease to be invoked only when organic disease was eliminated. Rather, they were real diseases, possibly caused by molecular changes as yet undetected, but more significantly diseases in which the nervous system's vital powers were affected. Second, however, functional diseases were individual, occasionally, as in the case of hysteria, caused by a mixture of moral and physical factors; but always affecting individual patients in idiosyncratic ways. Handfield-Jones doubted if clinical medicine could ever achieve the simple cause and effect status of the physical sciences. Rather, the same morbid phenomena could be dependent on a variety of causes, the same causes produce a variety of effects in different individuals. For all diseases, especially functional ones, diagnosis and treatment must be individualized: 'I hold that a diagnosis which goes no further than distinguishing a disease as gout, ... erysipelas, chorea, etc., and does not attempt to appreciate the peculiar circumstances of the individual sick man, falls very far short of what is needed for a rational therapy.'[29] Finally, it is worth noting the wide spectrum of conditions that Handfield-Jones included within the functional category: hysteria, headache, chorea, tetanus, and epilepsy had established places within the nervous camp, but malaria, Graves' disease, asthma, angina pectoris, and whooping cough are more surprising inclusions. Their presence in his book testifies to the continuing importance of periodicity and spasm in the definition of the functional disorder. That Handfield-Jones used the phrase 'cardiac neurosis' to refer to cases of angina (which he recognized frequently terminated in sudden death) reminds us that, in 1870, neurosis was still primarily a neurological, rather than a psychiatric, category.[30]

Despite the impressive increase in neurophysiological and neuropathological knowledge between John Cooke in 1823 and Handfield-Jones in 1870, Handfield-Jones belongs more to that earlier world than he does to the neurological milieu which came just after. The years between 1870 and 1890 saw the emergence of a critical and mature neurological profession in Britain. It was located largely in the London hospitals – general hospitals like University College Hospital, King's College Hospital, and the London Hospital, but also in the specialized neurological hospitals – the National Hospital at Queen Square and the Hospital for Epilepsy and Paralysis, now the Maida Vale Hospital, both founded in the 1860s.[31] This new hospital orientation created the institutional basis for the systematic investigation of the neurological lesion.

If the flowering was in London, the roots are usually placed in the West Riding of Yorkshire, in the fruitful interchange between neurologists, psychiatrists, scientifically orientated general physicians, and pathologists in the newly created pathology laboratory of the West Riding Lunatic Asylum, presided over by the genial and long-lived psychiatrist, James Crichton-Browne. Crichton-Browne, who died when he was ninety-seven, and had strong views against teetotalism, maintaining that no writer had achieved much without alcohol.[32] As medical director of the asylum, he encouraged neuropathological and physiological experimentation in the asylum's laboratories; he held periodic scientific *conversazioni* – with music by the asylum band – which brought together a number of young like-minded doctors from Leeds and further afield, including London. The group included Thomas Clifford Allbutt, who helped introduce the ophthalmoscope into British medicine (and ended his long career as Regius Professor of Medicine at Cambridge); W.B. Carpenter the physiologist and Thomas Lauder Brunton the pharmacologist; John Hughlings Jackson and David Ferrier, both at the beginnings of their careers.[33] The fruits of the new ethos were recorded in the *Reports of the West Riding Asylum*, edited by Crichton-Browne in six volumes between 1871 and 1876. The seventy-nine papers published in the *Reports* detail a variety of approaches to both psychiatric and neurological disease: the use of modern diagnostic equipment such as the ophthalmoscope, sphygmograph, and laryngoscope; histological analyses of neuropsychiatric diseases; the investigation of pharmacological preparations such a hyoscyamine, amyl nitrite, and chloral hydrate; and the application of experimental physiology to the understanding of diseases of the human brain and spinal cord.[34] Two diseases predominated: epilepsy and general paralysis, both commonly seen in patients in Victorian asylums and both amenable to the neuropsychiatric approach characteristic of many of the contributors to the *Reports*. Although short-lived, the *Reports* were the natural predecessor to *Brain*, founded in 1878 by Crichton-Browne, Jackson, Ferrier, and J.C. Bucknill, long-time editor of the *Journal of Mental Science*. *Brain* was thus founded and initially edited by two psychiatrists and two neurologists.[35] In 1866, *Brain* passed over to the control of the Neurological Society of London, founded that year under the presidency of Hughlings Jackson. The Neurological Society and its journal continued to a certain extent to represent the continued interest of psychiatrists and neurologists, but the successive meetings of the Society, and the successive volumes of *Brain*, reflect a growing alliance between neurologists and experimental physiologists such as Charles Sherrington, Edward Sharpey Schaefer, John Scott Burdon-Sanderson, Ernest Starling, and Michael Foster, all of whom were active members of what might at first blush be thought of as a purely clinical society.[36]

Two events symbolized this increasing emphasis on diagnostic precision based whenever possible on localized, structural identification, which characterizes this period of British neurology. The first was the operation, at the Hospital for Epilepsy and Paralysis, by Rickman Godlee, on a Scottish labourer named Henderson, for a brain tumour. His symptoms had been a succession of motor fits, which would now be called Jacksonian epilepsy, and the diagnosis of his tumour and its localization had been confirmed by Jackson and Ferrier. It was performed in 1884, at which point Ferrier was under attack from antivivisectionists because of his experimental work (involving monkeys) on cerebral localization. The operation provoked Crichton-Browne, as he revealed fifty years later, to defend Ferrier in *The Times*, under the nom-de-plume F.R.S. Two leading articles and sixty-four letters were published in *The Times*, debating the pros and cons of medical research which involved the sacrifice of animals. *The Times* was firm in its support of the doctors.[37]

The second event, two years later, was the publication of the first edition of William Gowers's *Manual of Diseases of the Nervous System*. Gowers systematized the newer knowledge of neurological localization, neurophysiology, and pathology. His section on functional disorders, while extensive, reduced considerably from Handfield-Jones the range of diagnostic categories. Although hysteria and one of its varieties, anorexia, were fully described, he believed that the most important feature of the Weir-Mitchell treatment was the 'opportunity for influencing the mind and to this the unquestionable success of the treatment is largely due'.[38] As he pointed out, the main British exponent of the Weir-Mitchell rest cure was W.L. Playfair, an obstetrician, not a neurologist. Gowers relegated Beard's concept of neurasthenia to the neurological dustbin: it was, he insisted, a descriptive term but not a proper diagnostic category. 'It is often better not to gratify the craving for nomenclature that is manifested by many patients, but rather to explain to them that to give their ailments a definite name would involve more error than truth.'[39]

The nervous patient of course had not disappeared by 1890 and neurologists did not entirely abandon him to the care of psychiatrists and others. In fact, recent works about two Victorian patients record the extent to which nervousness and the 'nerves' continued to play a significant role in both patient and medical perceptions of illness and major life events. The recent biography of Alice James (1848–92), the sister of William and Henry James, shows how she lived her claustrophobic life in the shadow of the two brothers, who shared much of her valetudinarianism and much of the same vocabulary concerning nervous energy and neurasthenia.[40] Alice's life, always plagued by ill-health, became, in its last decade, almost a quest for what she described as 'divine cessation'. She had been seen by many doctors in the United States and Britain, who had given her various functional diagnoses: hysteria, spinal neurosis, suppressed gout, neurasthenia, among others. Then, in May 1891, Sir Andrew Clark diagnosed a breast tumour. She felt 'enormous relief' at his 'uncompromising verdict'. As she confided to her Diary,

> 'To him who waits, all things come! My aspirations may have been eccentric, but I cannot complain now, that they have not been brilliantly fulfilled. Ever since I have been ill, I have longed and longed for some *palpable disease*, no matter how conventionally dreadful a label it might have, but I was always driven back to stagger alone under the monstrous mass of subjective sensations, which that sympathetic being "the medical man" had no higher inspiration than to assure me I was personally responsible for, washing his hands of me with a graceful complacency under my very nose.'[41]

In a 'beautiful and fraternal letter', William responded to the news that Alice had been given a 'real' diagnosis:

> 'So far from being shocked I am, although made more compassionate, yet (strange to say) rather relieved than shaken by the more tangible and immediate menacing source of woe. Katherine [Alice's friend and nurse] describes you as being so too; and I don't wonder. *Vague nervousness has a character of ill about it that is all its own*, and in comparison with which any organic disease has a good side.'[42]

Even at cost of an ominous diagnosis, Alice embraced this reality of a palpable lesion.

The second 'patient' was Virginia Woolf, whose treatment by four doctors a decade or two after Alice James's death has recently been examined by Stephen Trombley.[43] The cases cannot be easily compared: for one thing, Virginia Woolf never developed that 'palpable disease' which characterized the end of Alice James's medical history. For another, her breakdowns occurred after 'dynamic psychiatry' had begun to make a little impact on British medicine.[44] Of the four primary physicians who treated her, three are recognizable as psychiatrists: Maurice Craig (1866–1935), T.B. Hyslop (1864–1933) and George Savage (1842–1921). One – Henry Head (1861–1940) – was a neurologist. That Head seems to have adopted the most sensible attitude to Virginia Woolf's difficulties may or may not have been a direct consequence of his neurological orientation, but he believed that many 'nervous' diagnoses were but 'camouflaged ignorance'. 'Diagnosis of the psycho-neuroses is an individual investigation; they are not diseases, but morbid activities of a personality which demand to be understood,'[45] he wrote in 1920. More than his psychiatric colleagues, Head treated Virginia Woolf as a disturbed person rather than a patient. He distinguished between mental and physical diseases, and spent most of his professional time with the latter.

By the First World War, most leading neurologists in Britain had followed Gowers's lead and had left the treatment of functional disorders to their psychiatric colleagues. Neurologists' professional identities were much more closely bound up with the new precision in structural localization which the work of Jackson, Ferrier, and Gowers offered them. The reflex hammer rather than the couch, the rest cure, or the talking cure had become their symbol. In fact, what had happened during the course of the nineteenth century was a quiet reversal: in 1800 the 'nervous doctor had treated functional diseases of the nervous system, whereas psychiatrists had confidence in the underlying organic nature of the diseases which concerned them. By the century's end, the roles were reversed: nerve doctors – neurologists – were concerned primarily with organic diseases, whereas the psychiatrists had accepted the reality of primary mental disease and were the principal doctors for nervous patients.

Notes

Earlier versions of this paper have been given as lectures, particularly as a Hannah Visiting Professor at the medical schools in Ontario in March 1982, and as the Squibb Lecture at the Institute of Psychiatry, London, in June 1983. I have benefited from discussions following those lectures, and from the useful comments of Edwin Clarke, Chris Lawrence, Michael Neve, and Roy Porter. Research expenses were generously met by the Wellcome Trustees.

1 Richard Hunter, 'Psychiatry and Neurology: Psychosyndrome or Brain Disease', *Proceedings of the Royal Society of Medicine*, 116 (1973): 359–64.
2 The patient depicting 'Maniacus' was engraved on the title page of the fourth edition of Burton's *Anatomy of Melancholy* (Oxford: Cripps, 1632), and has been reproduced in Hunter, 'Psychiatry and Neurology', and on the dust wrapper of Michael MacDonald, *Mystical Bedlam* (Cambridge: Cambridge University Press, 1981). The borderlands between neurology and psychiatry have been recently explored by Oliver Sacks, especially in *Awakenings* (Harmondsworth: Penguin, 1976) and *A Leg to Stand On* (London: Duckworth, 1984).
3 Theodor Meynert, *Psychiatrie. Klinik der Erkrankungen des Vorherhirns* (Vienna: Braumüller, 1884).
4 Cf. J.G. Howells (ed.), *World History of Psychiatry* (New York: Brunner/Mazel, 1975); Yasuo Okada, '110 Years of Psychiatric Care in Japan', in T. Ogawa (ed.), *History of Psychiatry* (Tokyo: Saikon Publishing, 1982), pp. 108–28. A good survey of the German tradition is in E.H. Ackerknecht, *A Short History of Psychiatry*, trans. S. Wolff (New York: Hafner, 1968).
5 R.A. Hunter and I. MacAlpine, *Psychiatry for the Poor. 1851 Colney Hatch Asylum, Friern Hospital 1973: A Medical and Social History* (London: Dawsons, 1974).
6 Michael J. Clark, 'The Rejection of Psychological Approaches to Mental Disorder in late Nineteenth-Century British Psychiatry', in Andrew Scull (ed.), *Madhouses, Mad-doctors and Madmen* (Philadelphia, Pa. and London: University of Pennsylvania Press and Athlone Press, 1981), pp. 271–312; and M.J. Clark, 'The Data of Alienism: Evolutionary Neurology, Physiological Psychiatry, and

the Reconstruction of British Psychiatric Theory, c. 1850–c. 1900' (unpublished D.Phil. thesis, Oxford University, 1982).

7 Bonnie E. Blustein, 'A New York Medical Man: William Alexander Hammond, M.D. (1829–1900), Neurologist' (unpublished Ph.D. thesis, University of Pennsylvania, 1979); Charles Rosenberg, 'The Place of George M. Beard in Nineteenth-century Psychiatry', *Bulletin of History of Medicine 36* (1962): 245–59.

8 Bonnie E. Blustein, '"A Hollow Square of Psychological Science": American Neurologists and Psychiatrists in Conflict', in Scull, *Madhouses, Mad-doctors and Madmen*, pp. 241–70; Russell Dejong, *A History of American Neurology* (New York: Raven Press, 1982).

9 M.R. Trimble, *Post-Traumatic Neurosis: From Railway Spine to the Whiplash* (Chichester: John Wiley, 1981); Esther Fischer-Homberger, *Hypochondrie* (Bern: Huber, 1970); Alan Krohn, *Hysteria: the Elusive Neurosis* (New York: International Universities Press, 1978).

10 Thomas Trotter, *A View of the Nervous Temperament* (London: Longman, 1807), p. xv.

11 Roy Porter, '"The Rage of Party": a Glorious Revolution in English Psychiatry?', *Medical History* 27 (1983): 35–50; and G.S. Rousseau, 'Psychology', in G.S. Rousseau and Roy Porter (eds), *The Ferment of Knowledge* (Cambridge: Cambridge University Press, 1980), pp. 143–210, are two useful introductions to the literature of 'nerves' during the period.

12 The *Oxford English Dictionary*, while noting that by the late nineteenth century the usage was 'rare', gives the original definition of 'nervous' as 'Sinewy, muscular; vigorous, strong'.

13 Good expositions of Willis's work may be found in John D. Spillane, *The Doctrine of the Nerves: Chapters in the History of Neurology* (Oxford: Oxford University Press, 1981); and Kenneth Dewhurst, 'Thomas Willis and the Foundations of British Neurology', in F.C. Rose and W.F. Bynum (eds), *Historical Aspects of the Neurosciences: A Festschrift for Macdonald Critchley* (New York: Raven Press, 1982), pp. 327–46.

14 For Boswell, cf. Roy Porter, 'The Hunger of Imagination: Approaching Samuel Johnson's Melancholy', in this volume.

15 I have considered some of Johnson's attitudes to the 'new' neurophysiology and neuropathology in a talk (which I hope to publish) given at the Wellcome Institute, entitled 'Doctor and Dictionary'. The definitions are taken from the first edition of his *A Dictionary of the English Language*, facsimile reprint (London: Times Books, 1983).

16 Robert Whytt, *Works* (Edinburgh: J. Balfour 1768), p. 487; cf. C.J. Lawrence, 'Medicine as Culture: Edinburgh and the Scottish Enlightenment' (unpublished PhD thesis, University of London, 1984).

17 José M. López Pinero, *Historical Origins of the Concept of Neurosis*, trans. D. Berrios (Cambridge: Cambridge University Press, 1983); and J.M. López Piñero and J.M. Morales Meseguer, *Neurosis y psicoterapia; un estudio histórico* (Madrid: Espasa Calpe, 1970).

18 The standard work on Cullen is John Thomson, *Account of the Life, Lectures and Writings of William Cullen, M.D.*, 2 vols (Edinburgh: William Blackwood, 1859), and the standard edition of his works is that edited by John Thomson, *The Works of William Cullen, M.D.*, 2 vols (Edinburgh: William Blackwood, 1827). An illuminating discussion of Cullen's attitudes towards progress and luxury may

be found in Lawrence, 'Medicine as Culture'. He points out that Cullen's colleague James Gregory was more ardent in relating the increase of nervous disorders to 'modern' civilization.

19 Moritz Romberg, *A Manual of the Nervous Diseases of Man*, trans. E.H. Sieveking, 2 vols (London: Sydenham Society, 1853).

20 John Cooke, *A Treatise on Nervous Diseases*, 2 vols (London: Longman, 1820–23); for an assessment, cf. Spillane, *Doctrine of the Nerves*.

21 J.C. Prichard, *A Treatise on Insanity and other Disorders affecting the Mind* (London: Sherwood, Gilbert, and Piper, 1835).

22 Trotter, *A View of the Nervous Temperament*, p. xvii.

23 Trotter, *A View of the Nervous Temperament*, pp. 144–45; John Sekora, *Luxury: The Concept in Western Thought, Eden to Smollett* (Baltimore, Md and London: Johns Hopkins University Press, 1977); and, in a more contemporary vein, Brian Inglis, *The Diseases of Civilization* (London: Hodder and Stoughton, 1981).

24 On epilepsy, cf. the magisterial work of Owsei Temkin, *The Falling Sickness*, 2nd edn (Baltimore and London, Johns Hopkins University Press, 1971); an intriguing, but ultimately unconvincing account of its role in nineteenth-century medical thinking is E.M. Thornton, *Hypnotism, Hysteria and Epilepsy: an Historical Synthesis* (London: Heinemann, 1976).

25 Charlotte Hall, *Memoirs of Marshall Hall* (London: Bentley, 1861); Diana E. Manuel, 'Marshall Hall, F.R.S. (1790–1857): A Conspectus of His Life and Work', *Notes and Records of the Royal Society of London* 35 (1980): 135–66.

26 On the importance of hospital appointments, cf. M. Jeanne Peterson, *The Medical Profession in Mid-Victorian London* (Berkeley, Calif.: University of California Press, 1978); a good contemporary account of reasons against specialisms may be found in Sir J. Russell Reynolds, 'Specialism in Medicine', in his *Essays and Addresses* (London: Macmillan, 1896), pp. 194–207: Reynolds admits the value of psychiatry as a speciality, but 'only when the physician is at the same time competent to treat the other bodily ailments that may range themselves around the brain disease with which he has primarily to deal' (p. 203).

27 Marshall Hall, *Synopsis of the Diastalic Nervous System* (London: Joseph Mallett, 1850); a clear exposition of traditional ideas of nervous action in mid-century is Robert Brudenell Carter, *On the Influence of Education and Training in Preventing Diseases of the Nervous System* (London: John Churchill, 1855).

28 R.M. Young, *Mind, Brain and Adaptation in the Nineteenth Century. Cerebral Localization and Its Biological Context from Gall to Ferrier* (Oxford: Clarendon Press, 1970); Roger Smith, 'The Background of Physiological Psychology in Natural Philosophy', *History of Science* 11 (1973): 75–123; Kenneth Dewhurst, *Hughlings Jackson on Psychiatry* (Oxford: Sandford Publications, 1982).

29 Charles Handfield-Jones, *Studies on Functional Nervous Disorders*, 2nd edn (London: John Churchill, 1870).

30 Handfield Jones, *Studies on Functional Nervous Disorders*, ch. 38.

31 Gordon Holmes, *The National Hospital Queen Square 1860–1948* (Edinburgh: Livingstone, 1954); Anthony Feiling, *A History of The Maida Vale Hospital for Nervous Diseases* (London: Butterworth, 1958).

32 There is no systematic study of Crichton-Browne, although his volumes of semi-autobiographical essays, published in his old age, are useful. They include *Stray Leaves from a Physician's Portfolio* (London: Hodder and Stoughton, 1927); and *What the Doctor Thought* (London: Benn, 1930).

33 Henry R. Viets, 'West Riding, 1871–1876', *Bulletin of the History of Medicine* 6

(1938): 477–87.

34 C.A. Gatehouse, 'The West Riding Lunatic Asylum: the History of a Medical Research Laboratory, 1871–1876' (unpublished M.Sc. thesis, University of Manchester, 1981).

35 R.A. Henson, 'The Editors of *Brain*', *Practitioner* 221 (1978): 639–44.

36 Membership lists were published in *Brain*. There appears to have been little written about the Society.

37 The operation has been written about several times, recently by J.M.S Pearce, 'The First Attempts at Removal of Brain Tumors', in Rose and Bynum, *Historical Aspects of the Neurosciences*, pp. 234–43. The antivivisection movement is well covered in R.D. French, *Antivivisection and Medical Science in Victorian Society* (Princeton, NJ: Princeton University Press, 1975).

38 W.R. Gowers, *A Manual of Diseases of the Nervous System*, 2 vols (London: Churchill, 1886–88), vol. 2, p. 938.

39 Gowers, *Manual of Diseases*, p. 960.

40 Jean Strouse, *Alice James. A Biography* (London: Jonathan Cape, 1980); Ruth Bernard Yeazell, *The Death and Letters of Alice James* (Berkeley, Calif.: University of California Press, 1981); Leon Edel (ed.), *The Diary of Alice James* (New York: Dodd, Mead, 1964).

41 Edel, *Diary of Alice James*, pp. 206–07, entry for 31 May, 1891; my emphasis.

42 William James to Alice James, 6 July, 1891, in Strouse, *Alice James*, p. 303; my emphasis.

43 Stephen Trombley, '*All That Summer She Was Mad*': *Virginia Woolf and Her Doctors* (London: Junction Books, 1981).

44 Cf. the essay by Martin Stone, 'Shellshock and the Psychologists', in the companion volume.

45 Quoted in Trombley, '*All That Summer She Was Mad*', pp. 170–71.

CHAPTER FIVE

A Victorian alienist: John Conolly, FRCP, DCL (1794–1866)

Andrew Scull

'We have in this asylum, Sir
Some doctors of renown,
With a plan of non-restraint
Which they seem to think their own
All well meaning men, Sir,
But troubled with a complaint
Called the monomania
Of total non restraint'.
(Epistle to Mr Ewart, MP,
by a Reverend Gentleman lately a patient
in the Middlesex Asylum, 1841)

John Conolly's place in the pantheon of heroes of English psychiatric history seems secure. Contemporaries likened his achievement in introducing non-restraint in the treatment of the insane paupers at Hanwell Lunatic Asylum to Howard's labours in the cause of penal reform and Clarkson's role in the abolition of slavery.[1] Lord Shaftesbury, for forty years the chairman of the English Lunacy Commissioners and chief spokesman for the lunacy reform movement, referred to Conolly's work as 'the greatest triumph of skill and humanity that the world ever knew'.[2] And the doyens of late nineteenth-century medicine were only marginally less hyperbolic: for Sir James Crichton-Browne, 'no member of his profession – except Jenner and Lister – has done a tithe as much as he to ward off and alleviate human suffering'.[3] 'It is to Conolly', said Sir Benjamin Ward Richardson, 'that we really owe the modern humane treatment of the insane as it exists today in all its beneficent ramifications ... the abolition of restraint ... has placed us first among all the nations as physicians of mental disease'.[4] These are judgements which historians have for the most part been content to echo,[5] crediting Conolly with completing the work begun by Pinel and Tuke, by introducing 'reforms which simultaneously gave freedom to the mentally ill and psychiatry to medicine'.[6]

But Conolly's medical career is too long and varied to be reduced to a simple tale of his triumph as the author of 'non-restraint'. Quite apart from any other considerations, the system which he is popularly assumed to have initiated[7] was, as he periodically acknowledged, not his invention at all. Moreover, he was well into middle age before he became the resident physician at Hanwell, and he occupied that post for less than four years. A more extended look at his professional life provides valuable insight into some of the vicissitudes attending the choice of a medical career in Victorian England; and the sharp transformations that mark his thinking on psychiatric matters, closely paralleling the twists and turns of his own career, point up the intimate relationship that often exists between developments in disinterested medical 'knowledge' and the varying social interests of those propounding it.

John Conolly was born at his grandmother's house in the small town of Market Rasen in Lincolnshire, in 1794. His father, 'a younger son of a good Irish family ... had been brought up to no profession; had no pursuits; died young'; leaving his wife with three young children to raise. The three boys were soon separated, and John, at the age of five, found himself boarded out, like 'an inconvenient superfluity', with an elderly widow, a distant relative of the family, in the decaying borough of Hedon. Here he spent a 'barren' and 'wretched' boyhood, receiving a 'dull, mechanical' and, as he later confessed, grossly inadequate education at the local grammar school. 'In all these years my school master, the vicar, never that I remember, gave me any assistance except by blows on the head ... I read [Latin] with difficulty and understood nothing'. The descent from even a shabby gentility 'to the commoner arrangements inseparable from school, and to a society of the lower kind, where nothing was tasteful, and nothing was beautiful, and nothing was cheerful' made a profound impression on Conolly. 'Antiquated residences, rooms of which chairs and tables constituted all the furniture, shabby neglected gardens, coarse or common companions, and general neglect of all that could promote happy feelings, were productive of a kind of desolation neither expressed nor quite understood'.[8] Such feelings may have contributed to the insistent concern he displayed in his later years that others acknowledge his gentlemanly status; and they certainly must have intensified the pressures engendered by the uncertain course that marked his professional and financial life until the age of forty-five.

Conolly's mother had moved to Hull in 1803 and supported herself by opening a boarding school for 'young ladies'. Within a few years she remarried a Mr Stirling, an emigré Scot from Paris who taught languages, and in 1807, she brought her son John home to live with them. Despite the further decline in social status that these domestic arrangements implied, Conolly seems to have enjoyed the next five years. With his step-father's encouragement, he became fluent in French, dabbled in Enlightenment philosophy and obtained a rudimentary general and literary education. In 1812, at the age of eighteen, he procured a commission as an ensign in the Cambridgeshire militia and spent the closing years of the Napoleonic Wars in Scotland and Ireland. Apparently he found military life to his taste, for Henry Maudsley reports enduring many conversations filled with 'lively and pleasant recollections' of his service.[9] Napoleon's defeat and exile, however, foreclosed the possibility of a military career, and by 1816, Conolly had resigned his commission and returned to Hull.[10] With the death of his mother and stepfather he received a small inheritance, and in March of 1817, married Eliza Collins, daughter of the recently deceased Sir John Collins (himself the illegitimate son of the second Earl of Albemarle). Such as early marriage, with very little capital and no real prospects, would by itself have struck most Victorians as foolhardy, and the couple quickly compounded their difficulties by the sort of financial ineptitude that Conolly was to exhibit throughout his life. After the marriage, they left immediately for France and spent an idyllic year in a cottage near Tours, on the banks of the Loire. At the end of this period, with the arrival of his first child and the rapid shrinking of his capital, it seems finally to have dawned on Conolly that he had to develop some stable source of income.

For those in early nineteenth-century England who were without independent means but aspired to gentlemanly status, the choice of careers was meagre indeed.[11] Anything connected with 'trade' was out of the question, leaving only law, the Church, the army, and perhaps medicine as ways of gaining a livelihood without irrevocable loss of caste. Medicine, in fact, was not an unambiguously acceptable choice: as Trollope observed (in the person of Miss Marable), 'She would not absolutely say that a physician was not a gentleman, or even a surgeon; but she would not allow to physic the absolute privilege which, in her eyes, belonged to the law and the church'.[12] Still, it was on medicine that Conolly settled (based in part on the advice of his older brother William, who was already medically qualified); and like many an ill-connected and impecunious provincial, he elected to obtain his training in Scotland, first at Glasgow and then, for two years, at Edinburgh.

Possessed of a talent for making friends and for moving easily in society,[13] Conolly enjoyed a moderately successful student career, becoming one of the four annual presidents of the Royal Medical Society in his second year. He was strongly influenced by Dugald Stewart, the Professor of Moral Philosophy,[14] and like a number of Edinburgh students of this period[15] he developed a special interest in the problem of insanity. Reflecting this, his MD dissertation of 1821 was devoted to a brief discussion of *De statu mentis in insania et melancholia*.[16]

He now had to earn his living, and faced immediately the dilemma of where to set up his practice. Lacking the means to buy into an established practice, and without any family ties he could call on to help obtain a clientele, Conolly faced an uphill battle.[17] His difficulties were further compounded by the fact that he already had a wife and child to support. And since his Scottish training left him without any institutional or personal linkages to the London hospitals and medical elites, he had perforce to begin his career in a provincial setting. Inevitably, this meant engaging in general practice in an isolated and highly competitive environment, in which it generally took several years before one began to earn even a modest competence and where one was highly dependent on somehow securing the approval and patronage of the well-to-do.[18] To make matters worse, medical men working in such settings were regarded with ill-concealed contempt by the professional elites of Edinburgh and London, reflecting their marginal status in the larger social world. They were, sniffed the *Edinburgh Medical and Surgical Journal*, 'engaged in the trading, money making parts of the profession, and not one in a hundred of them distinguished by anything like science or liberality of mind'.[19]

Conolly's first efforts to make his way in this difficult environment met with abject failure. After a three-month stay in Lewes, he abandoned the attempt to build a practice there, and removed his family to Chichester to try again. Here, however, he had to compete with another young practitioner, John Forbes.[20] Though the two were to become lifelong friends, there was insufficient work to support them both, and within a year it had become apparent that it was Conolly who would have to leave. Of the two, he was undoubtedly 'the greater favourite in society, his courteous manner, his vivacity of character, and his general accomplishments, rendered him an agreeable companion'.[21] But however enjoyable the local notables found his company, when they required professional medical services, they turned instead to Forbes. Conolly, as his son-in-law Henry Maudsley later remarked, was a poor 'practical physician', with little talent or ability to inspire confidence in 'the exact investigation of disease, or in its treatment; he had little faith in medicines, and hardly more faith in pathology, while the actual practice of his profession was not agreeable to him'.[22]

Now blessed (or burdened) with a second child, his son Edward Tennyson, Conolly once more uprooted his family and moved, this time to Stratford-upon-Avon, then a small town of some 4000 inhabitants. Here he at last began to prosper, albeit in a very modest way. He was elected to the town council and twice served as mayor, the £80 salary serving as a useful supplement to his still slender professional income. He took a leading role in establishing a dispensary for the treatment of the sick poor and was active in civic affairs more generally, the well-worn path for a young practitioner trying to make his way.[23] Perhaps because of the interest he had developed in the subject while in Edinburgh, and no doubt because the honorarium attached supplemented his inadequate income, he also secured an appointment as 'Inspecting Physician to the Lunatic Houses for the County of Warwick', a position which required only that he accompany two local justices of the peace on their annual inspection of the country's half-dozen mad houses.

In his best year at Stratford, though, Conolly's income is reported 'not to have exceeded 400 pounds', an amount barely sufficient to maintain a suitable lifestyle for a professional man with a growing family.[24] Quite suddenly, however, the prospect arose of substituting the rewards of a London teaching and consulting practice for the dull routines of general practice in a provincial backwater. The founders of the new University of

London had decided to include a medical school in the new foundation. Somewhat to his surprise, Conolly managed to obtain an appointment as Professor of the Nature and Treatment of Diseases, helped in part by being previously known to Dr George Birkbeck[25] and Lord Brougham,[26] two of the prime movers in the project. While the university had 'sought to engage men of high standing ... it could offer but small emoluments and a precarious future' in its early years.[27] And accordingly, a number of the early appointments were of young or relatively unknown men.[28]

In general, however, 'assured income and national visibility ... went with status as full physician or surgeon at a hospital and as teacher at a medical school' in London,[29] and Conolly undoubtedly thought that he was about to cross successfully the great divide that marked off the social and financial world of elite London physicians from the humble surroundings of the rest of the profession. He instantly wrote back accepting: 'Gratified, as I cannot but be, by the confidence which has been placed in me, an untried person, I know that it only remains for me to justify it by my services'.[30] Though the first scheduled teaching session was not to begin until October 1828, some fourteen months hence, he at once refused offers to write and edit for London publishers on the grounds that 'the attention and care required by the lectures of so inexperienced a teacher as I am ... occupy almost every hour of my time',[31] And towards the end of 1827, he announced plans to travel to Paris for three months to obtain materials that would assist him in preparing his lectures.[32]

On 2 October 1828, Conolly gave his inaugural lecture, the second at the new medical school.[33] It was apparently quite successful,[34] although largely given over to some rather platitudinous advice to his students. He told them:

> 'I have watched with some interest, the fate and conduct of many of those who were pursuing their studies at the same time as myself. Of these, some were of course idle, and despised the secluded pursuits of the studious: I do not know *one* whose progress has been satisfactory: many of them after trying various methods of dazzling the public, have sunk, already, into merited degradation. But I do not know one among the industrious, who has not attained a fair prospect of success; many of them have already acquired it; and some of them will doubtless be the improvers of their science in our own day, and remembered with honour when they are dead'.[35]

Naturally enough, Conolly aspired to belong to the latter group. Nevertheless, his lecture's one departure from the expected was an announcement that 'It is my intention to dwell somewhat more fully on Mental Disorders, or to speak more correctly, of disorders affecting the manifestations of the mind than has, I believe, been usual in lectures on the practice of medicine'.[36]

Conolly's attempts, over the next two years, to get permission to give students clinical instruction in mental disorders at a London asylum proved unavailing. After initially encouraging him, the university council rejected the idea.[37] Thwarted in this direction, he decided instead to publish a book on the subject, not least because 'I disapprove entirely of some part of the usual management of lunatics'.[38]

An Inquiry Concerning the Indications of Insanity, published in 1830, is, in many respects, a rather conventional treatise, 'investigating the mind's history, from its most perfect state, through all its modifications of strength and through all its varieties of disease, until it becomes affected with confirmed madness'.[39] But Conolly broke sharply with contemporary orthodoxy over the key issue of how and where the lunatic ought to be treated. His book appeared in the midst of the early nineteenth-century campaign for 'reform' in the treatment of lunatics – a movement that took some thirty years to achieve its goals, and one whose proponents were absolutely convinced that asylum care was the only appropriate form of treatment for the insane. The heightened public attention to the problems posed by the mentally disturbed stimulated a large number of medical men to produce books and pamphlets on insanity, and running through this literature, and repeated with growing emphasis and conviction, was the assertion that all forms of madness required institutional care and treatment, and that the sooner those displaying signs of mental imbalance were removed from domestic to asylum care, the greater their chances of ultimate recovery.[40]

From this almost universal consensus about 'the improbability (I had almost said moral impossibility) of an insane person's regaining the use of his reason, except by removing him early to some Institution for that purpose',[41] Conolly issued a lengthy and closely argued dissent. Seeking to offer 'no opinions which have not received some confirmation from observation and experience',[42] he asserted that the emphasis on the centrality of the asylum 'originated in erroneous views of mental disorders, and has been perpetuated with such views'.[43] Existing authorities argued that any and all forms of mental unsoundness warranted – indeed required – confinement. If this doctrine of 'indiscriminate treatment, including deprivation of property and personal liberty' were to prevail, then, said Conolly,

> 'no man can be sure that he may not, with a full consciousness of his sufferings and wrongs, be one day treated as if all sense and feeling were in him destroyed and lost; torn from his family, from his home, from his innocent and eccentric pursuits, and condemned, for an indefinite period, to pass his melancholy days among the idiotic and the mad'.[44]

'Restraint', as he saw it, was 'seldom apportioned to the individual case, but is indiscriminate and excessive and uncertain in its termination'.[45] (Later in Conolly's career, restraint was to acquire a narrower meaning, referring to the use of chains, strait-jackets, and the like to impose physical controls on the insane, but here, significantly, it is used in the broad sense of removal from ordinary social life and confinement in an institution.) It was precisely the expert's task, not just to distinguish the mad from the sane, but 'to point out those circumstances which, even in persons decidedly insane, can alone justify various degrees of restraint'.[46] And the latter was clearly the more

difficult accomplishment. At present, 'certificates of insanity' were heed-
lessly and ignorantly ... signed',[47] with the result that 'the crowd of most
of our asylums is made up of odd out harmless individuals, not much more
absurd than numbers who are at large'.[48] Moreover,

> 'once confined, the very confinement is admitted as the strongest of all
> proofs that a man must be mad ... it matters not that the certificate is
> probably signed by those who know very little of madness or of the
> necessity of confinement; or by those who have not carefully examined
> the patient; a visitor hesitates to avow, in the face of such a document,
> what may be set down as a mere want of penetration in a matter wherein
> nobody seems in doubt but himself; or he may be tempted to affect to
> perceive those signs of madness that do not exist'.[49]

Hence the central importance of clinical instruction of medical students in
the recognition and treatment of insanity. As the medical curriculum was
presently constructed,

> 'during the term allotted to medical study, the student never sees a case of
> insanity, except by some rare accident ... the first occurrence, conse-
> quently, of a case of insanity, in his own practice, alarms him: he ... has
> recourse to indiscriminate and, generally, to violent or unnecessary
> means; or gets rid of his anxiety and his patient together, by signing a
> certificate, which commits the unfortunate person to a mad house'.[50]

Such an outcome might be avoided by teaching students not only how to
solve the relatively simple problem of distinguishing those of unsound mind,
but also how to decide *'whether or not the departure from sound mind be of
such a nature to justify the confinement of the individual, and the imposition
of restraint upon him, as regards the use or disposal of his property'*.[51]

The task was rendered the more urgent by the fact that asylum treatment
was, as he saw it, more pernicious than beneficial. Perhaps a trifle dis-
ingenuously, Conolly announced that he had 'no wish to exaggerate the
disadvantages of lunatic asylums'.[52] There were, after all, certain classes of
patients for whom public asylums were 'unavoidable evils'.[53] 'For a hopeless
lunatic, a raving madman, for a melancholy wretch who seems neither to see
nor to hear, or for an utter idiot, a lunatic asylum is a place which affords all
the comforts of which unfortunate persons are capable'.[54] But their regrettable necessity as places of last resort must not be allowed to obscure the fact
that

> 'it is a far different place for two-thirds of those who are confined there
> ... to all these patients confinement is the very reverse of beneficial. It
> fixes and renders permanent what might have passed away and ripens
> eccentricity or temporary excitement or depression, into actual insanity'.[55]

The first principle of asylum treatment was the isolation of the mad from
the sane. This sequestration from the world was alleged to be therapeutic, a
notion Conolly scathingly attacked:

'whatever may be said, no one in his senses will believe, that a man whose mind is disordered is likely in any stage of his disorder to derive benefit from being surrounded by men whose mental faculties are obscured, whose passions and affections are perverted, and who present to him, in place of models of sound mind, in place of rational and kind associates, in place of reasonable and judicious conversation, every specimen of folly, of melancholy, and of extravagant madness.'[56]

People's mental and moral capacities varied markedly according to the circumstances in which they were placed, and their thoughts and actions were, in large degree, the product of an interaction between habits, situational pressures, and the influence and reactions of their associates. The capacity to control one's wayward passions and imagination and to avoid the perils of morbid introspection[57] was thus essentially dependent upon social reinforcement and support. Granting these realities of our mental life,

'who can fail to perceive that in such an unhappy situation [as asylum life provided] the most constant and vigorous assertion of his self-command would be required to resist the horrible influences of the place; – a place in which a thousand fantasies, that are swept away almost as soon as formed in the healthy atmosphere of our diversified society, would assume shapes more distinct; a place in which the intellectual operations could not but become, from mere want of exercise, more and more inert; and the domination of wayward feelings more and more powerful.'[58]

Taking even 'the most favourable case for the asylum', its effects were likely to be harmful.[59]

Of course, the men running such places sought to reject these charges. They claimed that the inmates of the asylums were not abandoned and subjected to a pernicious atmosphere of uncontrolled ravings and delusions. Instead their environment was carefully monitored and controlled by a sane superintendent and they were judiciously coaxed and encouraged to resume an independent, self-governing existence. Conolly remained unconvinced:

'To say that persons in this state are not left, are not abandoned, is by no means satisfactory to those who have opportunities of knowing how little of the time of the superintendent is, or can be, commonly devoted to the professed objects of his care, and yet who, like children, demand constant watching and attention.[60]

Hence the 'numerous examples' to be found 'in which ... a continued residence in the asylum was gradually ruining the body and the mind'.[61]

To some extent, the antitherapeutic effects of the asylum derived from 'the monotonous wretchedness of the unhappy patient's existence; debarred from home, from the sight of friends, from the society of their families; ... shut out from even a hope of any change that *might* prove beneficial to them'.[62] But criticisms of this sort suggested that a more enlightened and flexible administration, and the provision of more varied amusements and diversions could obviate the difficulty. They could not. Superintendents, some of whom

> 'are men of great intelligence and humanity ... may point to the spaciousness of their grounds, to the variety of occupations and amusements prepared for their patients, to the excellence of their food and the convenience of their lodging; and urge that as little restraint is employed as is compatible with their safety: but the fault of the association of lunatics with each other, and the infrequency of any communication between the patient and persons of sound mind, mars the whole of the design'.[63]

The defect was thus, as Conolly saw it, a structural one, and hence not removable by any conceivable reform. Confinement in an institution acted like a self-fulfilling prophecy, intensifying and even creating the very behaviours that were its alleged justification:

> 'the effect of living constantly among mad men and women is a loss of all sensibility and self-respect or care; or not infrequently, a perverse pleasure in adding to the confusion and diversifying the eccentricity of those about them ... in both cases the disease grows inveterate. Paroxysms of violence alternate with fits of sullenness; both are considered further proofs of the hopelessness of the case.'[64]

For whole classes of lunatics, therefore, asylum treatment was grossly inappropriate. Given that 'so long as one lunatic associates with another, supposing the case to be curable, so long must the chances of restoration to sanity be very materially diminished',[65] recent and curable cases did not belong in an institution. This was particularly the case 'during the mental weakness of their convalescence', when confinement exposed them to 'the presence of a company of lunatics, their incoherent talk, their cries, their moans, their indescribable utterances of all imaginable fancies or their ungovernable frolics and tumult' – these, said Conolly, 'can have no salutary effect on a mind just reviving from long depression'.[66] On the contrary, they were 'the very circumstances most likely to confuse or destroy [even] the most rational and healthy mind'.[67]

> 'Another class of patients for whom a lunatic asylum is a most improper place consists of those who, in various periods of life become afflicted with various degrees of weakness of intellect ... but there is little or no extravagance of action, still less is there anything in the patient which would make his liberty dangerous, or, if he were properly attended to and watched, even inconvenient to others or himself.'[68]

Such patients, along with the chronically insane, where subject to a more insidious but equally debilitating and damaging effect of confinement in an institution, the gradual atrophy of their social capacities: 'after many hopeless years, such patients become so accustomed to the routine of the house, as to be mere children; and are content to remain there, as they commonly do, until they die.'[69]

If social practices could be brought to reflect these realities, 'the patients *out* of the asylum being the majority, and consisting of all whose circumstances would insure them proper attendance – better arrangements might be made for the smaller number of public asylums, or central houses of reception'.[70] Such asylums must, first of all, be public, that is, state supported, for only by removing the distorting effects of the profit motive, could one avoid the problems created by a system in which 'the patients are transmitted, like stock-in-trade, from one member of a family to another, and from one generation to another': a free trade in lunacy which attracts, besides a handful of 'respectable, well-educated, and humane individuals', the 'ignorant and ill-educated' and those 'capable of no feeling but a desire for wealth'.[71] Second, each asylum should become a centre in which aspiring medical men could be taught to recognize and treat mental disorder. 'If each establishment of that kind became a clinical school' it would allow 'the acquisition of principles of practice which can alone prepare them for . . . this department of medicine'.[72] And the possession of such clinically derived skills and knowledge – the fruit of the sort of arrangement he had unsuccessfully urged on the university – would give the average medical practitioner both the competence and the confidence to treat most cases of insanity on a domiciliary basis.

If Conolly hoped that the publication of *An Inquiry Concerning the Indications of Insanity* would serve to advance his reputation and enlarge his private practice, he was soon disabused. One reviewer, in the *Medico-Chirurgical Review*, did praise him for performing 'a very important service to the profession, in calling their attention to the construction and properties of the mind', and for the superior 'language and style' in which he expressed himself.[73] But for the most part, Conolly's suggestions were not even debated,[74] but simply ignored. For by now the overwhelming weight of opinion among both the profession itself and those laymen interested in lunacy reform was that in cases of insanity, asylum treatment was indispensable and could not be embarked upon too quickly for the patient's own good – a position Conolly himself was to embrace less than a decade later.

In the meantime, he was involved in a series of controversies at the medical school, which, within six months, were to prompt his resignation. The early years of the university were stormy ones. The council, chosen from among the university's proprietors, exhibited a constant disposition to interfere with the conduct of the institution, threatening to send inspectors to check on the quality of lectures given, to exercise the power to censor the books used in teaching, and 'to regulate minutely not only the number, length, and hours, but also the scope and content of the various courses'.[75] In general, 'it regarded the professors in the same light as any other of its employees, and all its employees with suspicion'.[76] The friction such conduct was sure to arouse was exacerbated by the activities of the warden, Leonard Horner, the salaried officer to whom the council had delegated day-to-day supervision of university affairs. For Horner, too, had an exalted view of his position, and his arrogant and autocratic manner, his constant petty interference and intrigue, aroused widespread discontent among the professoriate – an antipathy strengthened by the fact that the warden, though paid four or five times as much as those he supervised, was an erstwhile linen manufacturer possessed of limited education and no scholarly qualifications.[77]

The medical faculty considered that 'a Hospital is absolutely necessary for the prosperity of the Medical School',[78] since only by providing clinical instruction could they hope to compete effectively with rival London institutions for students. For a time it appeared that a suitable arrangement could be reached with the nearby London Fever Hospital, but when the council insisted on being given complete control, its intransigence led to the collapse of the negotiations. As a temporary, if inadequate, substitute, Conolly and his colleagues proposed the establishment of a university dispensary, which they would attend 'without compensation . . . as a help to a rising school'[79] – a plan to which the parsimonious council quickly agreed.[80] But the dispensary soon became a new source of friction. It was to have a resident apothecary, and Conolly and his colleague Anthony Todd Thomson immediately expressed concern that the appointee be someone who aspired 'solely to being efficient in that useful but still subordinate capacity'.[81] Their concern to protect their status soon proved prescient, for Horner began to use John Hogg, who had secured the position, to check on the professors' performance of their duties. Conolly viewed such 'very offensive' machinations as an intolerable affront to his dignity:

> 'you have constituted the Apothecary, who ought to be under the orders of the physicians and surgeons, a kind of spy over those physicians and surgeons, and have thereby completely subverted the discipline of the establishment. Among respectable men of my own rank in the medical profession, I find but one opinion concerning this matter; and that opinion makes it impossible for me to continue my attendance at the Dispensary . . . the Council have no right to impose a degradation on me, and I cannot submit to it.'[82]

Two months later, Horner informed him that 'the Council considered it a part of the duty of the Professor of the Practice of Medicine to attend as Physician at the Dispensary'.[83] But Conolly stood his ground: 'No opinion of the Council, or of any body of men, can, or ever shall, induce me to act inconsistently to my character as a physician and a gentleman.' Only a change in the lines of authority at the dispensary would induce him to return.[84] Eventually a meeting with the council itself led to the quarrel being patched up, though not until Conolly had incurred further slights from the warden.[85]

On other fronts, too, the relationship between the university and its professors grew strained. The proprietors wished to move to a system in which a professor's pay was directly proportional to the income he generated from his lectures. Initially, they had been forced to modify this plan in order to attract faculty to a new and untried enterprise, offering salary guarantees for the first three years of the university's existence. By the spring of 1830, however, financial difficulties were increasing as student numbers declined, and 'the University was eating up its capital at a rate of £1,000 a year.'[86] Rumours began to circulate that the council was contemplating an early end to the system of guaranteed salaries. A number of professors, Conolly among them, responded by laying out an alternative plan to rescue the institution's finances. They insisted that 'a salary should be secured for every professor in the event of his fees from pupils not attaining a certain amount', arguing that the institution was still too new for payment by results to work, and that the failure to provide such a guarantee would inhibit the professors' study of their subjects, since such activities would be 'unproductive of immediate pecuniary advantage'.[87] Some professors' lecture fees amounted to less than £100, of which the university proposed to take a third, and yet 'it is expected that the professor will subsist in the rank of a gentleman upon the balance'. To balance the budget, they proposed tailoring the length of courses to the convenience of students, since the university could not expect, 'for many years to come, to draw any considerable number of students from the upper ranks [of society]';[88] and *reducing* fees so as to attract additional students who would otherwise attend the cheaper courses given by such places as the Royal Institution and the London Institute. Finally, a great deal of money could be saved by abolishing the office of warden, with his salary of £1,200 a year (a suggestion scarcely inclined to endear its authors to Horner). These proposals were leaked to the press, and met by anonymous responses from the warden, a war of words that continued until 21 April, 1830, when the *Sun* reported that with some lecture rooms all but empty, the proprietors had decided to reduce the salary guarantees to the least successful professors.[89]

This news must have been a considerable blow to Conolly, for his financial situation had been precarious since his arrival in London. On the same day, he wrote to Horner declining to repeat the summer session lectures he had given the year before, partly because the number of students was likely to be small, rendering the course unremunerative; and also because 'I am under the necessity of employing some of the year in occupations unconnected, or not immediately connected, with my Professorship, which I could not possibly do if I were to lecture ten months out of twelve.'[90] During the 1829–30 session, his university salary declined from £300 to £272 15s., and before the year was out, he was forced to request an advance of '100 pounds on account' from the warden he detested[91] – a humiliation he was compelled to undergo twice more before he finally left London the following spring.[92]

Conolly could scarcely have viewed the prospect of a further decline in his guaranteed salary with equanimity, for, notwithstanding all his laborious preparation and his personal charm, his lectures 'were not great successes, if they were not in truth failures, [being] somewhat vague and diffuse, wanting in exact facts and practical information.'[93] Here, as elsewhere, in the judgement of one of his friends, 'the aid which Dr Conolly rendered to the diffusion of knowledge was not special or professional.'[94] Unfortunately, his efforts to augment his income from private practice were likewise unsuccessful. Conolly was blessed with considerable advantages which ought to have brought him patients: Lords Russell, Auckland, and Brougham provided aristocratic sponsorship; his university affiliation ought for once to have been an advantage; and he was amply provided with the necessary social graces.

> 'Though by nature passionate and impetuous, he had great command over his manner which was courteous in the extreme. Indeed he never failed to produce, by the suavity of his manner and the grace and ease of his address, the impression of great amiability, kindness, and unaffected simplicity; while his cheerful and vivacious disposition and his lively conversational powers rendered him an excellent social companion.'[95]

He sought to capitalize on these advantages, following the well-worn path of the aspiring London practitioner. He joined the Medical and Chirurgical Society of London, and became an active member of the Society for the Diffusion of Useful Knowledge. He took the examination of the Royal College of Physicians and became a licentiate. And he secured election to the staff of the London Fever Hospital. Notwithstanding all his efforts, however, 'practice did not come sufficiently quickly'.[96] On a larger stage, he suffered a repetition of his failures at Lewes and Chichester, and almost certainly for the same reasons: his own deficiencies in the investigation of disease, his evident lack of faith in the medicines he prescribed, and his dislike of the tasks medical practice imposed, coupled with his settled disposition 'to shrink from the disagreeable occasions of life, if it were possible, rather than encounter them with deliberate and settled resolution'.[97]

Unlike the deficiencies of some of his colleagues, at least Conolly's failures were not the focus of public attention. Granville Sharp Pattison, the Professor of Anatomy, was not so fortunate. Having been one of Conolly's teachers at Glasgow, he had subsequently emigrated to the United States to an appointment at the University of Maryland. Apparently his tenure there was less than an overwhelming success (he was attacked in a pamphlet published in Philadelphia as 'an adventurer with a tainted reputation'),[98] but he succeeded in securing one of the first chairs at the University of London, Conolly providing a testimonial in his behalf. The appointment proved to be a mistake. He neglected his work or performed it incompetently, giving superficial and perfunctory lectures when he bothered to attend. By contrast, J.R. Bennett, who had been appointed Demonstrator in Anatomy and had previously taught in Paris, 'was a competent and popular teacher, and came to feel a contempt for Pattison as an anatomist which he was at no pains to conceal'.[99] Conflict flared in the very first session and continued intermittently for more than two years. Pattison at first secured the support of many of his colleagues by alleging that Horner, whom they detested, was plotting his removal. But by the spring of 1830, student complaints about his performance grew more insistent, and the scandal surfaced in the medical press. A student memorial published in the *London Medical and Surgical Journal* 'charge[d] him with *unusual ignorance* of old notions, and *total ignorance of* and *disgusting indifference* to new anatomical views and researches ... he is ignorant, or, if not ignorant, indolent, careless, and slovenly, and above all, indifferent to the interests of science.'[100] Conolly remained one of Pattison's staunchest supporters. He complained to the Council that 'the most heartless and iniquitous persecution has been carried on against the Professor of Anatomy ... because his ruin would be convenient to the Warden's friends.'[101] And for a few months, Pattison managed to cling to his position. But when the new session opened in October 1830, student discontent grew increasingly unmanageable. Pattison's classes were periodically boycotted and routinely disorderly. By February 1831, the students had opted for open rebellion, and 'for over a month it was impossible to lecture. The scenes in the anatomy theatre reminded a contemporary reporter of Covent Garden during the O.P. [Old Price] riots.'[102] Conolly, too, began to lose control of some of his students, and on at least one occasion, nearly half of his class failed to attend his lecture.[103] Ultimately, the tumult subsided only after Horner abruptly relinquished his post and when Pattison was forced to resign.[104] By then Conolly, too, had left the university.

Pattison was not the only colleague of doubtful competence whom Conolly sought to defend. His intervention on behalf of John Gordon Smith proved similarly unavailing, perhaps not surprisingly in view of its maladroitness. Smith was a former army surgeon who had secured an appointment as Professor of Medical Jurisprudence. A knowledge of forensic medicine conferred few obvious advantages on those seeking to practise medicine, and Smith's prospects of attracting a sufficient number of students to his classes were not aided by his rambling and disjointed lecture style. 'Condensation ... is not a virtue of Dr Smith's' the *Morning Chronicle* commented on the occasion of his inaugural lecture,[105] and students voted with their feet not to listen to interminable stories of his wartime exploits. In early December 1830, while depressed and in his cups, he offered the council his resignation; then on sobering up, sought to withdraw it. Conolly's intervention can only have sealed his fate. He had been treating Smith, he informed them, for a periodic 'severe affection of the stomach' (most probably this was a side effect of Smith's heavy drinking). These episodes lasted for only a few days at a time, but

'on the decline of each attack, he is subject to a peculiar, but temporary, excitement of the nervous system which has once or twice, I believe, led to the interference of his friends. It was during one of these afflicting accessions that he lately conveyed to you his determination not to lecture in the University unless certain concessions were made to which he has ceased to attach any importance; and I know that he unfeignedly and extremely laments that he made such a communication to you.'[106]

Lament he might, for the Council, notwithstanding Conolly's warning that the loss of Smith's chair would be 'an irretrievable, perhaps a ruinous calamity to him',[107] gratefully accepted the opportunity to be rid of him. (Conolly, incidentally, proved a better prophet than advocate: within three years, Smith was dead, dying of alcoholism in a debtor's prison.)[108]

Conolly's manifold failures and disappointments made his resignation from the university not unexpected, but its manner and timing were nevertheless distinctly odd, lending weight to Maudsley's observation that he was 'apt to do serious things in an impulsive way'.[109] Only a few hours after sending a letter to the council begging them to ignore Smith's resignation, Conolly submitted his own. Bellot comments that 'the reasons for Conolly's resignation are obscure',[110] and Conolly himself, in requesting Horner 'to lay my resignation before the Council' added: 'I have not troubled them with a useless detail of all my motives, but I am anxious that they should not think that I resigned from any want of interest in the University'.[111] The penultimate paragraph of the same letter suggests that the Council's refusal to heed his pleas on Smith's behalf may have constituted the final straw. ('I am sorry to have to trouble the Council with a *second* communication on the same day, but Dr. Smith is so deeply concerned in my doing so that I hope it will be excused'); and there are hints that some of his colleagues may have been glad to see him go ('I cannot doubt that Dr. Thompson and Mr. Amos will approve of what I have done in this matter');[112] but finally, Conolly is content to express no more than a veiled hope that his successor will have 'a more favourable combination of circumstances than those in which I have endeavoured to perform [my duties]'.[113]

Characteristically, his valedictory address given at the end of the academic year offers little substance at great length. He acknowledges that others may be puzzled by his decision:

'Retiring as I do, from a station, none of the prospective advantages of which have altogether escaped my attention – from a station which I was, four years ago, ambitious to obtain, and to which I felt it a great honour to be appointed – retiring, too, without the excuse of years, or any consciousness of a growing incapacity for exertion – I feel that a few words of explanation may be thought necessary, addressed to those who have interested themselves in my success.'

Many words but no explanation then follow. He grants that 'It will be believed that powerful motives must exist which induce me to resign all these expectations, and when every previous hope has been sacrificed, to retire from a scene of public activity in which I might at least have continued without discredit.' He then adds, 'I think I could show that circumstances exist – have for some time existed – which so limit my usefulness here as to make it no less my duty, than it is my inclination, to withdraw from this institution.' But the nature of those 'circumstances' he glides over in silence, not wishing 'to carry with me any unpleasant recollection'.[114]

Whatever the precise reasons for his departure, the blow it constituted to his pride, to say nothing of his prospects, must have been staggering. Victorian medicine was marked by an enormous 'division between the prestigious and influential men at the top of the profession and the ordinary practitioners [beneath]'.[115] Having once had hopes of belonging to the elite, Conolly now appeared to be thrust back, all but irretrievably, into the ranks of provincial obscurity. As one who later confessed 'that he did not care for money, but that he very much liked the comfort and elegancies which money brings',[116] the prospect was scarcely inviting.

Placing his furniture in storage (where it was to remain for eighteen months until he could afford to rent a house large enough to contain it), he gathered his wife and four children (a third daughter, Anne Caroline, had been born in 1830) and removed once more to Stratford. But the attempt to pick up the threads of his old practice was a failure, and within a few weeks he felt compelled to uproot them all again, and move to the nearby town of Warwick. His one remaining tie to the metropolis was Thomas Coates, the secretary of the Society for the Diffusion of Useful Knowledge, now Horner's replacement at the university (though at a salary of £200 rather than £1,200); and the correspondence between them gives us what little insight we have into Conolly's existence over the next seven years.

Conolly at first feigned optimism. While complaining that the demands of practice, being 'unsettled as to house, and distracted at times with the noise of children', were interfering with his book on Ardent Spirits for the Society, he boasted that 'my practice [at Warwick] began at *once*, and the average thus far has equaled that of my best year before I left Warwickshire to be tormented "for some sin" in the University.' As for the future of 'that Institution ... much may be hoped from the timely (or *untimely*) death of some of the Council and Professors.'[117] Two weeks later, the attractions of the provincial backwater had begun to diminish. Conolly had begun a second book for the Society, a popularization for the lower classes of medical ideas about cholera, only to discover that 'this is a land when no books are to be borrowed or even stolen. The latest publication in the hands of any of my medical neighbours is a dissertation on the diseases which followed the Great Flood.' Perforce he had to order three or four from London, 'very unwillingly', because he could scarcely afford to purchase them. 'Since these are for a piece on Cholera for the Society', he wondered whether 'the publishers for the Society have the means of getting them more advantageously than I can do'.[118] In the future, he assured Coates, his financial position was bound to improve: 'I really begin to think that at last I shall become a prosperous man, for I find myself getting Jewish.'[119]

Such expectations were doomed to disappointment. In late December, he wrote an answer to Coates's 'kind inquiry about my proceedings here. I think I am *getting on* so as to have a hope in time, of struggling through many difficulties.'[120] But the difficulties were formidable. He finished the manuscript on cholera just before Christmas 1831,[121] but the small sum it earned him was swallowed up in the attempt to satisfy some of the creditors he had left behind in London: 'after the 15th, Mr Denies of 27 Princes Street Bank who is occasionally "paying off" things for me will call to receive the fifty pounds – to save you any trouble.' The companion volume on Ardent Spirits, first promised for December, then for January,[122] remained unwritten, though Conolly in each letter promised its imminent despatch.[123] Meanwhile, he proposed that he write other titles for the Society, only to have Coates decline them.[124]

By May of 1832, the burden of his past failures and the struggle to scratch an inadequate living from his practice began to show in his letters:

'I have been very busy lately, both in practice, and in lecturing to the Mechanics' Institution here, and in commemorating Shakespeare's birthday at Stratford. But I require constant task work to overcome a restlessness which what I suffered latterly in London has left in my brain and nervous system, which I sometimes fear will never leave me.'[125]

And his protestations that, except for the SDUK, 'I hardly regret having lost anything else that London contains'[126] sound increasingly hollow. After a long silence, he wrote plaintively to Coates, 'Once upon a time there was a professor of my name, where is he now? May I flatter myself that you sometimes wonderingly ask that question?' If Coates were to visit him in Warwick, 'You will find me a very rustic physician with some provincial fame, no doubt, but as my foolish friends say, *buried*.' Revealingly, he continued, 'I often wish I really were. . . . The London University has provided me for life with incurable care – but "what's that"! – I have learned that resignation is the best philosophy'.[127]

The 'incurable care' was not to be vanquished so easily, however. Less than two years later, Conolly wrote to Coates again begging for a commission to write a series of popular treatises for working men on diseases of the chest, stomach, brain, etc., to appear in the *Working Man's Companion*.

'It is but candid to say that I am in some degree driven to the idea of this industry by necessity . . . I have long been trying [?] to extricate myself from the ruin [sic] which London brought me . . . I am looking out for work. I am convinced I could prepare the little volumes of the Physician *one every three months*. Please think about it, and drop me a line soon – something I must set about and nothing takes my fancy more.'[128]

But nothing came of this proposal, and in 1838, still drowning in debt,[129] Conolly embarked on a desperate attempt to escape from his provincial exile. 'Not much encouraged thereto by his friends, who regarded such a step as the suicide of reputation and the confession of complete failure in life',[130] he applied for the vacant position of superintendent of the Middlesex County Lunatic Asylum, at Hanwell. At least this offered the security of a salary of £500 per annum, together with free living space and board for his family in the asylum; and he had, after all, a long-standing interest in the treatment of the insane, had written on insanity and served as inspector of the Warwickshire madhouses. To his dismay, however, his application was rejected, and in his stead the magistrates appointed J.R. Millingen, a retired army surgeon with no discernible background in the treatment of insanity.[131]

Conolly's humiliation was now complete. 'The outlook into the future as black as ever, family cares increasing', he once more uprooted his household and moved to Birmingham, to see whether, in a different setting, his luck would change.[132] At forty-two, this latest failure appeared to have permanently dashed all the hopes he had once nurtured 'of obtaining, through my exertions ... that reputation and those advantages of fortune, about which no reasonable man can, or ought to be indifferent'.[133] His fixed disposition to refuse 'to recognize or accept the painful necessities of life' meant that throughout his life, 'troubles, shirked at the time, were gathered up in the future, so as to demand at last some convulsive act of energy, in order to disperse them.'[134] But by this time, it must have seemed that even convulsive efforts would not suffice.

Ironically enough, Conolly was to be rescued from this depressing prospect by someone else's failures. The superintendency at Hanwell had originally fallen vacant when the Middlesex magistrates decided to experiment with a system of divided authority, allowing the superintendent to continue as the final arbiter of medical matters, but handing over administrative chores to a lay steward.[135] The arrangement proved unworkable, and exacerbated by Millingen's inexperience and quarrelsome disposition, conditions in the asylum degenerated until they verged upon anarchy. Finally the magistrates were forced to intervene, dismissing the steward, Mr Hunt, and accepting Millingen's resignation.[136] This time Conolly's application was successful. Less than a year after his initial rejection, a few lines appeared in *The Times* announcing that 'Dr Conolly, late of [Warwick], is appointed to the very important office of Resident Physician at the Hanwell Lunatic Asylum, Middlesex.'[137]

Quite unexpectedly, the stern critic of asylum treatment, a man apparently incapable of managing his own affairs with even a modest degree of success, turned out to be an able and effective administrator of what was already the largest and – because of its metropolitan location – the most visible English asylum. Within a few weeks, the magistrates cheerfully announced that a remarkable change for the better had already taken place in the discipline and order of the establishment.[138] Conolly had at last found something he could do well, and to his final days was to insist 'that if his life were to come over again, he should like nothing better than to be at the head of a large public asylum, in order to superintend its administration'.[139] All the doubts he had once expressed about the appropriateness of the asylum solution, all questions about the deleterious effects of institutional existence, were at once suppressed in his enthusiasm for his new task.

Thomas Bakewell, not many years before, had commented that 'the regular [medical] practitioner has little advantage either of reputation or profit to expect from the treatment of [insanity].'[140] But whatever the general merits of this proposition, in Conolly's case it was emphatically disconfirmed. His achievements at Hanwell brought him, in rapid succession, national attention, royal notice and favour, election to a fellowship of the Royal College of Physicians, and ultimately recognition as 'the most valuable consulting physician in mental disorders in Great Britain, and I suppose, in the world'.[141] In Maudsley's words, 'On the crest of the wave which he raised and rode he was carried to great fame and moderate prosperity.'[142]

The first half of the nineteenth century witnessed a long struggle to 'reform' the treatment of the mentally ill.[143] Indeed, Hanwell, like all other 'county asylums', was one product of this movement. It was the proud boast of the reformers that the adoption of their programme, based on the new system of moral treatment pioneered by the Tukes at the York Retreat, did away with the cruelties previously visited upon the insane, and replaced them with a regimen based on kindness and forbearance. Whips and chains, those traditional accoutrements of the madhouse, were, like the straw and stench that were their inevitable accompaniment, to be banished from the modern asylum. The most sanguine hopes of the reformers had their limits, though. In Samuel Tuke's own words,

'With regard to ... the necessity of coercion, I have no hesitation in saying, that it will diminish or increase, as the moral treatment of the patient is more or less judicious. We cannot, however, anticipate that the most enlightened and ingenious humanity, will ever be able entirely to supersede the necessity of personal restraint.'[144]

Yet it was precisely this extraordinary feat that Conolly claimed to have accomplished. Beginning with his very first report of Hanwell, he boldly asserted 'that the management of a large asylum is not only practicable without the application of bodily coercion to the patient, but that, after the total disuse of such a method of control, the whole character of the asylum undergoes a gradual and beneficial change.'[145] So far from being a regrettable necessity, or even a means of cure, restraint 'was in fact creative of many of the outrages and disorders to repress which its application was commonly deemed indispensable';[146] and to that extent 'restraints and neglect, may be considered as synonymous'.[147] In their place,

'we rely wholly upon constant superintendence, constant kindness, and firmness when required ... insanity, thus treated, undergoes great, if not unexpected modifications; and the wards of lunatic asylums no longer illustrate the harrowing description of their former state. Mania, not exasperated by severity, and melancholia, not deepened by the want of all ordinary consolations, lose the exaggerated character in which they were formerly beheld.'[148]

These were large and astonishing claims, and they were greeted in many quarters with scepticism, if not outright hostility. They were, sniffed 'Medicus' in the correspondence columns of *The Times*, 'a piece of contemptible quackery and a mere bait for the public ear'.[149] Millingen seized the opportunity to denounce his successor: 'Nothing can be more absurd, speculative, or peculative than the attempts of theoretic visionaries, or candidates for popular praise, to do away with all restraint. Desirable as such a management might be, it can never prevail without much danger to personal security, and a useless waste and dilapidation of property.'[150] Others went further still and reiterated the traditional medical claim that restraint was a form of therapy. Dr Samuel Hadwin, former house surgeon at the Lincoln Lunatic Asylum, wrote:

> 'Restraint forms the very basis and principle on which the sound treatment of lunatics is founded. The judicious and appropriate adaptation of the various modifications of this powerful means to the peculiarities of each case of insanity, comprises a large portion of the curative regimen of the scientific and rational practitioner; in his hands is a remedial agent of the first importance, and it appears to me that it is about as likely to be dispensed with, in the cure of mental diseases, as that the various articles of the materia medica will altogether be dispensed with in the cure of the bodily.'[151]

But while many medical men viewed non-restraint with extreme suspicion, the new system quickly attracted powerful support in other quarters. During the first month of 1840, the correspondence columns of the *Lancet* were opened impartially to both proponents and opponents of the new system, in an effort 'to contribute, in any way, to the solution of a question of so much importance'.[152] However, the strain of such uncharacteristic even-handedness eventually told on its editor, Thomas Wakley. Never one to abide by his own admonition to the disputants that 'Angry recrimination can do no good, and may do much evil,'[153] he soon switched to a fervent advocacy of the cause of reform, couched in his inimitable mixture of panegyric and vituperation.[154] More respectable opinion also rallied to Conolly's support. The venerable Samuel Tuke visited and bestowed his benediction ('Who can visit or contemplate the establishment of Hanwell, containing 800 insane persons, governed without any personal restraint, without gratitude or surprise?').[155] Lord Anthony Ashley Cooper, by now leader of the parliamentary forces seeking 'lunacy reform', saw non-restraint as the vindication and epitome of reform: he 'could not speak too highly either of the system itself, or of the manner in which it was carried out by the talented Superintendent, Dr Conolly'.[156] Meanwhile, the *Illustrated London News* brought Conolly's achievements to the notice of a still wider audience, extolling still another British contribution to the triumph of humanity.[157]

Perhaps the most important force in transforming Conolly into a national celebrity was, however, *The Times*. Beginning in late 1840, it devoted close and sympathetic attention to the progress of his experiment for a period of some four years.[158] Commenting on the 'very considerable opposition ... the attempt to obtain so desirable an object' had stirred up, it noted that such resistance had also surfaced within the institution, 'not simply on the part of several of the county magistrates, but even from many of the servants and officers of the asylum'. Fortunately, 'that humane gentleman', Dr Conolly, had, with the staunch support of another faction among the magistrates, vanquished the peculiar notion that there was 'more actual cruelty hidden under the show of humanity in the system of non-coercion than was openly displayed in muffs, strait-waistcoats, leg-locks, and coercion chairs'; and had successfully brought to fruition 'one of the greatest works that the dictates of the humane mind could suggest'.[159] Three weeks later, a report on the celebration of 'Old Year's Night' at Hanwell demonstrated for the paper's readers the happy effects of the salutary system of non-restraint. The furies of madness were thoroughly domesticated, and 'the utmost tranquility prevailed'. Indeed, when the 400 patients assembled for the commencement of the merriment, 'scarcely a word was to be heard and the effect produced was most striking and pleasing'.[160] Soon afterwards, non-restraint received the royal imprimatur: the Duke of Cambridge arrived and spent two and a half hours at 'this admirable institution', lunched with Conolly (presumably not on ordinary asylum fare), and left proclaiming himself 'highly delighted' with all he had seen.[161]

Basking in this unexpected praise and attention to one of their pauper institutions, the Middlesex magistrates at once issued Conolly's first four annual reports bound together in a single new edition. Professional recognition of his achievement also grew apace. At the third annual meeting of the new Association of Medical Officers of Asylums and Hospitals for the Insane,[162] Conolly was asked to take the chair. In 1844, he was elected a fellow of the Royal College of Physicians.[163] The 1844 report of the Metropolitan Commissioners in Lunacy, it is true, exhibited rather more ambivalence about the value of non-restraint,[164] but two years later, the new national Lunacy Commission had thrown aside such doubts, and non-restraint became the ruling orthodoxy of British asylumdom.

Conolly had thus become, in the eyes of his admirers, 'one of the most distinguished men of the age, and one whose name will pass down to posterity with those of the Howards, the Clarksons, the Father Mathews, and other great redressers of the wrongs, crimes, and miseries of mankind'.[165] Oxford University awarded him an honorary DCL; and his marble bust was executed by Benzoni.[166] In 1850, the Provincial Medical and Surgical Association fêted Conolly at their annual meeting at Hull.[167] And two years later, with Lord Shaftesbury presiding,[168] Conolly's achievements were again celebrated, and he was presented with a gift of a three-quarter-length portrait by Sir John Watson Gordon, RA, and an allegorical piece of silver plate standing two feet high and valued at £500, which illustrated mental patients with and without restraint, all surmounted by the god of healing.[169]

Such extraordinary praise and recognition suggests that Conolly's

achievement had a symbolic significance for the Victorian bourgeoisie that
extended far beyond its contribution to the welfare of the mad. Confronted
by the threats of Chartism and a militant working class; surrounded by the
all-but-inescapable evidence of the devastating impact of industrial capitalism on the social and physical landscape; and themselves the authors of a
new Poor Law assailed by its critics as the very embodiment of inhumanity
and meanness of spirit (most memorably in Dickens's *Oliver Twist*), the
Victorian governing classes could at least find a source of pride in the
generous and kindly treatment now accorded to the mad. In a wholly
practical way, the work of the lunacy reformers constituted a proof of their
society's progressive and humane character. (Hence the curious claim made
by Sir George Paget, that the Victorian asylum was 'the most blessed
manifestation of true civilization the world can present'.[170]

As the man who epitomized and had brought the new approach to
perfection, John Conolly had thus richly earned his audience's applause. The
paternal order he had established demonstrated that even the irrational and
raving could be reduced to docility, and by moral suasion and self-sacrifice
rather than force. Here, as he put it in the concluding lines of his panegyric
on the new asylum,

> 'Calmness will come; hope will revive; satisfaction will prevail. Some
> unmanageable tempers, some violent or sullen patients, there must always
> be; but much of the violence, much of the ill-humour, almost all the
> disposition to meditate mischievous or fatal revenge, or self-destruction
> will disappear ... cleanliness and decency will be maintained or restored;
> and despair itself will sometimes be found to give place to cheerfulness or
> secure tranquility... [The asylum is the place] where humanity, if
> anywhere on earth, shall reign supreme'[171]

A Potemkin village characterized by an absence of conflict and strife, it
constituted a veritable utopia wherein the lower orders of society could
coexist in harmony and tranquillity with their betters (personified by the
figure of a superintendent devoted to their welfare and content to 'sacrifice
... the ordinary comforts and conventionalities of life' for their sake).[172]

In celebrating Conolly's accomplishment, Victorians were thus simultaneously affirming the moral validity of their social order itself. And his
powerful friends, while acknowledging that he 'no doubt received important
assistance from fellow-labourers in the same field', now closed ranks around
the proposition that 'Dr Conolly himself put an end to the use of all forms of
mechanical restraint in our asylums.'[173] But such claims were, as Conolly
himself acknowledged,[174] at best a serious distortion. Non-restraint was
introduced, not by him, but by Robert Gardiner Hill, then a twenty-four-
year-old house surgeon at the provincial subscription asylum at Lincoln.
Hill had announced the system in a public lecture to the Lincoln Mechanics
Institute in 1838: 'I wish to complete that which Pinel began. I assert then in
plain and distinct terms, that in a properly constructed building, with a
sufficient number of suitable attendants, restraint is never necessary, never

justifiable, and always injurious, in all cases of lunacy whatever'.[175] For almost two years before Conolly assumed his duties at Hanwell, Hill had demonstrated in practice the feasibility of such an approach. And it was, in fact, a visit to Lincoln that prompted Conolly to try the new system.[176]

Yet Hill's obvious claims as the originator of non-restraint brought him little honour and scant reward of any other sort. Though bearing the brunt of the early assaults on the system as speculative and wildly misguided,[177] he was granted none of the subsequent recognition and social lionization so readily accorded to Conolly. On the contrary, machinations among the staff and governors at the Lincoln Asylum forced his resignation there,[178] and he found himself unable to obtain another asylum post. Ironically, a failure that must have been especially galling, he was even rejected when he sought the position of medical officer under Conolly at Hanwell,[179] and so was forced by default to enter general practice.[180] Though a decade later he became the proprietor of a private licensed mad-house, he never managed to obtain an appointment at another public asylum.

One can readily imagine the effects of this on someone as sensitive to questioning of his own merits as Hill was. The last straw seems to have been when he was present at the 1850 meeting of the Provincial Medical and Surgical Association, and heard Conolly praised as the author of *his* system. Though Conolly graciously indicated that the merit was not his alone, but was shared with Dr Charlesworth (the visiting physician at Lincoln), and though Charlesworth then indicated that 'the real honour belonged to Mr Hill',[181] he was not satisfied – not least, perhaps, because it was forcibly brought home to him how soon his claim to priority had been forgotten.[182]

He promptly sought to reassert his claims by writing to the medical press, only to be met by an attempt by his former enemies at Lincoln to claim the merit for Charlesworth.[183] And when Hill's supporters took up a collection for a testimonial to rival Conolly's, his opponents promptly erected a statue of Charlesworth, with a plaque on the base describing him as the originator of non-restraint, on the grounds of the Lincoln Asylum.[184] More seriously, Hill fell foul of Thomas Wakley's pen, and found himself traduced in the *Lancet*'s columns in the latter's typically unscrupulous fashion.[185]

Conolly's role in all of this was hardly innocent. With whatever motives, he consistently declined to give Hill his due. That he had borrowed the idea of non-restraint from Lincoln he could not deny; that the discovery was Hill's he sought constantly to obscure,[186] and when Hill in exasperation at length lashed out at his now deceased rival,[187] he succeeded only in alienating his audience and in further tarnishing his own reputation. Hill's shrill and strident claims of priority, his wearisome marshalling of minutiae to prove his own originality,[188] were 'not only boring, but repellent'.[189] As he proved chronically unable to grasp, one who exhibited such boorish and ungentlemanly qualities could never hope to be accorded a place of honour in a profession desperate to dissociate itself from all that smacked of lower-class, tradesman-like behaviour.

The elegant and socially graceful Conolly inflicted no such handicaps on himself, displaying 'a certain humility of manner, a degree of self-depreciation ... which failed not to attract men; it was nonetheless captivating because it might seem the form in which a considerable dash of self-consciousness declared itself.'[190] On the public stage which he had secured for himself at Hanwell, he took delight in the opportunity to display the liberal and paternalist instincts of the gentleman:

'His interest in the patients never seemed to flag. Even cases beyond all hope of recovery were still objects of his attention. He was always pleased to see them happy, and had a kind word for each. Simple things which vainer men with less wisdom would have disregarded or looked upon as too insignificant for their notice, arrested Dr. Conolly's attention, and supplied matter for remark and commendation – e.g., a face cleaner than usual, hair more carefully arranged, a neater cap, a new riband, clothes put on with greater neatness, and numerous little things of a like kind, enabled him to address his poor illiterate patients in gentle and loving accents, and thus woke up their feeble minds, caused sad faces to gleam with a smile, even though transient, and made his visits to the wards to be longed for and appreciated. Dr. Conolly rejoiced in acts of beneficence. To be poor and to be insane were conditions which at once endeared the sufferers to him; and when the insanity was removed, and when the patient left the asylum, he generally strove to obtain some pecuniary aid for her from the "Adelaide Fund" (a fund originated for the relief of discharged patients), and supplemented this very often indeed with liberal donations from his own purse.'[191]

Despite a patient population nearing a thousand, a 'monstrous multitude of diseased humanity'[192] crammed into buildings originally designed for half that number, and notwithstanding a dismally low cure rate, Conolly's Hanwell was widely regarded as a splendid advertisement for the merits of reform and non-restraint.[193] From time to time, he protested mildly that the asylum was too big,[194] and objected to the Middlesex magistrates' propensity to seek cheeseparing economies. But for the most part, he sought to exploit Hanwell's fame to persuade others of the advantages, indeed the necessity, of expanding the numbers of county asylums. Such endeavours acquired a new urgency in the wake of the passage of the 1845 Lunatic Asylums Act, for although public provision for the pauper insane was now made compulsory, magistrates in many parts of the country sought to delay or evade building asylums of their own. Accordingly, Conolly wrote a series of articles for the *Lancet* (republished the following year as a monograph)[195] extolling the humanity and economy of asylums devoted to the cure of the lunatic and urging their rapid construction. Ironically enough, his own role at Hanwell was by this time much diminished, and soon to end. His disengagement was not provoked by any disenchantment with administering an ever-larger warehouse for the unwanted; nor did it constitute a protest at the deficiencies of an overcrowded establishment later described as 'a vast and straggling building, in which the characteristics of a prison, a self-advertising charitable institution, and some ambitious piece of Poor Law architecture struggle for prominence'.[196] Instead, it derived from administrative changes that threatened his own authority and status.

The Middlesex magistrates had long exhibited a much greater disposition to interfere in the daily running of 'their' asylum than was to be found elsewhere. Their evident belief that non-medical administration could effect significant economies had already led them to a proposed reorganization of Hanwell that had provoked their first superintendent, Sir William Ellis, to resign. And they were apparently not dissuaded by the fact that their subsequent experiment with a system of divided authority had dismally failed, forcing the resignation of the physician and the dismissal of the steward, and thus indirectly bringing about Conolly's appointment. For when the Metropolitan Commissioners in Lunacy insisted that Hanwell's 'extreme magnitude' required more extensive supervision, the justices once more developed a scheme to place daily administration in lay hands. Conolly did not wait for the plan's implementation – in later years, he spoke of 'the absurdity – I could almost say the criminality, – of committing one of the most serious of human maladies to the charge of anyone uninstructed in medicine'[197] – but promptly offered his resignation.

This time, as had not been the case with Ellis, a compromise was arranged. Anxious to retain the connection with Conolly that had brought them so much favourable publicity, the magistrates offered him the post of 'visiting and consulting physician' at a reduced salary of £350, and he accepted. His duties now became 'to give his attendance for two days a week, and for six hours at every attendance'. At other times, medical matters were to be dealt with by the house surgeons who had formerly acted as his assistants.[198] Convinced that it was imperative to have a single resident officer exercising ultimate control over the asylum and its staff, and equally certain that medical men were fit neither by temperament nor by training to assume such a role, the magistrates announced the appointment of John Godwin, a retired army officer, to fill the position.[199]

Under the terms of the appointment, it was specified that 'The Governor has the power of suspending not only the servants but even the Medical Officers and Matron of the Asylum. He has, also, the entire control over the classification, employment, amusements, instruction, and general management of the patients ... subject only to the general control of the Visiting Justices.'[200] His superiority was reflected in the higher salary paid him; while the two resident medical officers received £200 each, the governor was paid £350 a year. In view of the range and scope of affairs in which his lay judgement was supposedly given precedence, there was a disingenuousness about the claim that 'in regulating his particular duties ... the Visiting Justices have endeavoured to reconcile his position as their officer whom they will vest with paramount authority to enforce all their orders and regulations, with the distinct responsibility of the Medical Officers in all that concerns the moral management as well as the strictly medical treatment of the Patients.'[201] For, in practice, to concede the doctors' right to direct the moral treatment of the patients would involve taking away from the governor the very areas of supervision where his authority was supposed to be paramount; while to refuse to concede it was to reduce the asylum physicians to mere decorative appendages. Conflict was, thus, unavoidable. The struggle reached swift conclusion. In August of 1844, just four months after his initial appointment, the justices cryptically announced, in two lines buried at the end of their report, that Godwin's resignation had been tendered and accepted.[202] In their next report, they indicated that 'After the retirement of the late Governor, the Visiting Justices resolved to defer filling up the vacancy for awhile, and to entrust the management of the Asylum to the ability and experience of the principal [i.e. medical] officers until they could determine what course for its future government it would be most advisable to adopt.'[203] Already, however, they were noting 'the progressive improvement in the order and discipline of the Establishment' since Godwin's departure.[204] Six months later, they conceded that under medical supervision, 'good management and order prevail . . . [and] that they have every reason to be satisfied with the way in which the Asylum continues to be conducted.'[205]

The idea of employing a lay administrator to direct the asylum's affairs was now quietly buried; but the attempt to implement it had already served to all but sever Conolly's connection with Hanwell, after less than four years on the job. 'Mutual trust between himself and the Justices was lost. He felt that they preferred the opinion of others and that his authority and system were eroded.'[206] He hung on to his visiting appointment until 1852 when he finally resigned, to the relief of the magistrates, to whom his departure now meant little more than saving the ratepayers some money.

Even before this final rupture, Conolly's situation was such that he was forced to seek some alternative means of earning his livelihood. At £500 per annum, his salary as resident officer at Hanwell had scarcely been munificent, but at least he was also provided with room and board, a not inconsiderable benefit. His visiting appointment, however, entailed not just a reduced salary, but also the loss of this hidden subsidy. His new-found eminence ought presumably to have allowed him to escape the penury he had endured until middle age. But the difficulty was to know how to earn a living, given that there were no defined alternative careers for alienists outside the burgeoning asylum system.

Almost fifty, Conolly had never possessed the qualities to succeed in single-handedly defining and developing a new form of specialist practice. Not until much later in the century, with the careers of men like his son-in-law, Henry Maudsley,[207] or Sir George Savage,[208] did the alternative of a practice based almost exclusively on the consulting room become possible. Conolly's fame did lead to his being called in as a consultant in difficult cases,[209] and he was also a frequently called expert witness in criminal cases where the insanity defence was raised.[210] But as in his earlier efforts at private practice, he scarcely distinguished himself in these spheres. His forensic testimony in the Pate case, for example, prompted the *Morning*

Chronicle to complain that 'Dr Conolly appears to have devoted his attention so exclusively to ... mental disease that ... he can apparently no longer distinguish where absolute madness begins and moral and legal responsibility ceases. There are very few of our fellow subjects, we suspect, who could get from Dr Conolly a certificate of perfect sanity.'[211]

Both lunacy inquisitions and criminal trials in which the insanity defence was invoked were highly charged occasions. While the latter was widely seen as a ruse to escape just punishment, a threat to the concept of responsibility and, thus, to the very foundation of criminal justice,[212] the former raised the spectre of wrongful confinement of the sane in asylums, 'a living death' which inspired periodic moral panics throughout the nineteenth century.[213] Large segments of the Victorian public seem to have questioned both the motives and the competence of alienists who claimed expertise in assessing madness, and Conolly's published opinions and his actions both helped to feed these suspicions. Before entering upon a career as an asylum doctor, he had insisted that not every case of unsound mind required incarceration in an asylum. Rather, there was a need for a careful assessment of each case to determine *'whether or not the departure from sound mind be of a nature to justify the confinement of the individual'*[214] and such enquiries were likely to disclose that 'complete restraint is very rarely required'.[215] A less discriminating approach posed a serious threat to individual freedom and peace of mind.[216]

Two decades later, these were almost precisely the fears his clear repudiation of his earlier views seemed calculated to arouse. In 1849, in the case of Nottidge v. Ripley, the Lord Chief Baron of the Court of the Exchequer, Sir Frederick Pollock, declared that in his opinion, 'no lunatic should be confined in an asylum unless dangerous to himself or others.'[217] Notwithstanding the fact that Conolly's own earlier opinions were the expressed authority for this decision,[218] he at once issued a lengthy remonstrance declaring Pollock's dictum 'both mistaken and mischievous'.[219] It transpired that he now believed that an extraordinary range of behaviours qualified one for the madhouse: 'excessive eccentricity', 'utter disregard of cleanliness and decency', 'perversions of the moral feelings and passions', a disposition 'to give away sums of money which they cannot afford to lose', indeed all cases where people's 'being at large is inconsistent with the comfort of society and their own welfare'.[220] Particularly in the young, incipient madness took on protean forms, and its cure required active and early intervention. Suitable cases for treatment included:

'young men, whose grossness of habits, immoderate love of drink, disregard of honesty, or general irregularity of conduct, bring disgrace and wretchedness on their relatives; and whose unsound state of mind, unless met by prompt and proper treatment, precedes the utter subversion of reason; – young women of ungovernable temper, subject, in fact, to paroxysms of real insanity; and at other times sullen, wayward, malicious, defying all domestic control; or who want that restraint over the passions without which the female character is lost. For these also such protection, seclusion, and order, and systematic treatment as can only be afforded in an asylum, are often indispensable. Without early attention and more careful superintendence than can be exercised at home, or in any private family ... [many] will become ungovernably mad, and remain so for life.'[221]

Conolly's eagerness to consign the morally perverse and socially inadequate to the asylum was widely shared by his colleagues,[222] but was seen in other quarters as a dangerous blurring of immorality and insanity.[223] In addition, many of the public were inclined to believe that alienists' willingness to define others as mad on such slender pretexts reflected their financial interests in expanding their pool of patients. Conolly's actions in the Ruck case served only to reinforce these suspicions. Ruck was an alcoholic whose wife had secured his commitment to a private asylum on certificates issued by Conolly and Dr Richard Barnett. Enforced abstinence brought about a rapid recovery, but several months passed before Ruck, at a cost of £1,100, secured an inquisition in lunacy, at which a jury found him sane by majority vote. He then sued Conolly and others for false imprisonment. At the trial which followed, Conolly was forced to make a series of damaging admissions. He had issued his certificate of Ruck's lunacy after a joint examination with Barnett, a clear violation of law; and, more seriously, he had received a fee from Moorcroft House, where he was the consulting physician, for referring Ruck. The jury was obviously not impressed with Conolly's disingenuous defence: 'I know the act says that a certificate should not be signed by any medical man connected with the establishment. I do not consider myself connected with the establishment, as I only send male patients to it'!'[224] As a result, he faced a swingeing judgement against him for £500 damages.

Subsequently, too, his transparent rationalizations, and the convenient congruence between his beliefs and his self-interest, were savagely burlesqued in Charles Reade's scurrilous best-seller, *Hard Cash*, where Conolly appears in thinly disguised form as the bumbling Dr Wycherly.[225] Wycherly, in the sardonic words of Reade's hero, Alfred Hardie, 'is the very soul of humanity', in whose asylum there are 'no tortures, no handcuffs, nor leg-locks, no brutality'.[226] But his 'vast benevolence of manner'[227] and the 'oleaginous periphrasis' of his conversation concealed a second-rate mind 'blinded by self interest' and apt to perceive insanity wherever he looked.[228] In Reade's savage caricature, Conolly/Wycherly's pretensions to gentlemanly status are mocked, and his vaunted psychological acumen exposed as a pious fraud. 'Bland and bald', this psychocerebral expert was 'a voluminous writer on certain medical subjects ... a man of large reading and the tact to make it subserve his interests';[229] a task in which he was greatly aided by his settled disposition 'to found facts on theories instead of theories on facts'.[230] As 'a collector of mad people ... whose turn of mind, cooperating with his instincts, led him to put down any man a lunatic, whose intellect was manifestly superior to his own',[231] he is easily duped into diagnosing a sane man as lunatic, and thereafter persists stubbornly in his opinion till the unfortunate inmate is willing to grant that 'Hamlet was mad'.[232] In the climactic courtroom scene that brings the melodrama to a close, Reade puts Wycherly on the witness stand and gives him for his lines Conolly's most damaging admissions in the Ruck case. Wycherly, like his alter ego, tries to bluster his way through by protesting that counsel's questions are an affront to his professional dignity – but to no avail. Question:

> '"Is it consistent with your dignity to tell us whether the keepers of private asylums pay you a commission for all the patients you consign to durance vile by your certificates?" Dr Wycherly fenced with the question, but the remorseless Colt only kept him longer under torture, and dragged out of him that he received fifteen per cent from the asylum keepers for every patient he wrote insane; and that he had an income of eight hundred pounds a year from that source alone.'[233]

Along with his sometimes embarrassing forays into the courtroom, and his moderately rewarding practice as a consultant, Conolly was forced to turn to the private 'trade in lunacy' as an additional source of income. His private residence, Lawn House, only a stone's throw from Hanwell,[234] was adapted to take a handful of female patients.[235] Subsequently, he acquired an interest in another small asylum at Wood End, and opened a third mad-house, Hayes Park, in partnership with his brother, William,[236] and in 1853 he became consulting physician to Moorcroft House Asylum from which he received both a salary and a percentage of the patients' fees.[237]

'A man', said Conolly a few years later, 'must live by his profession, and a physician who devotes himself to mental disorders has to deal with a very small portion of the population, and he generally adds to his consulting practice, the plan of having a place where the treatment of patients can be conducted entirely under his own observation.'[238] There can be no doubt, however, that trading in lunacy was at first distasteful to him. He had long argued that 'every lunatic asylum should be the property of the State, and should be controlled by public officers',[239] and during his time at Hanwell had become the leading spokesman for the new county asylums. Moreover, with its obvious overtones of 'trade' and its long-established unsavoury reputation (to which the writings of reformers like himself had in no small measure contributed), the business of running a private asylum was widely regarded as one of the most *déclassé* forms of medical practice; potentially lucrative, to be sure, but abhorrent to those of gentlemanly sensibilities.

But however repugnant, it was unavoidable. Conolly's income at Hanwell had been 'barely sufficient to maintain his family', even with accommodation and food provided. Thrown back entirely on his own resources, his difficulties were compounded by the fact that he was once more 'very liberal-minded in practice and otherwise, and gave little attention to financial matters'.[240] More seriously, however, his household remained a large, even a growing burden. His eldest daughter soon married a Chinese missionary;

but Sophia Jane did not marry until 1852, at the age of twenty-six;[241] and Anne Caroline not until 1866, at the age of thirty-five.[242]

Much the greatest source of concern, though, was his son, Edward Tennyson, who far exceeded even his father's youthful fecklessness, and displayed a remarkable inability to find any settled pursuit. When he was eighteen, his father's connections had secured him a position as part-time secretary to the Society for the Diffusion of Useful Knowledge. But in 1846, with the disbanding of the Society, this came to an end, and the elder Conolly's appeal to Lord Brougham for another patronage appointment for his son met with no response.[243] Five months later, Edward himself renewed the petition, asking specifically for an appointment with the new Railways Commission.[244] Spurned, he was not discouraged. Three years later, he sought Brougham's assistance to obtain a position as 'a Poor Law Inspector', urging his experience as 'one of the Guardians of the Poor for Brentford Union, [undertaken] in the absence of any more remunerative employment', as a qualification for the job.[245] He was no more successful on this occasion, and since he had now reached his late twenties, it seems at last to have occurred to him that further efforts of his own were required. An attempt to practise as a barrister brought no improvement: 'prospects of . . . business are anything but encouraging, and I am every year more desirous of doing something profitable in the world'. The upshot was still another appeal to Brougham: 'I venture to apply to your lordship to know whether there is likely to be any appointment connected with the new Charities Commission which I have any chance of obtaining'.[246] There was not.

Now married, he still remained almost entirely dependent on his father's largesse, a burden that was further augmented with the arrival of the first of a series of children. At thirty-three, he had 'been four years at the bar; . . . had hardly any practice' and decided to renew his entreaties: 'My Lord, I have been so often troublesome with applications that I am ashamed to make another'. Nevertheless, he did not let a little embarrassment stand in his way, this time seeking the vacant post of secretary to the Lunacy Commission.[247] But even the Conolly name could not secure this appointment, or a similar post with the Scottish Lunacy Commission, for which he applied some two years later.[248] As late as 1864, his father still did not know what was to become of him: 'Past forty – seven or eight children [sic] – no present means of educating them, nor of emigration where they might prosper – no friends whom he has continued to see – no prospects at the Bar, etc., etc.'[249] (In 1865, however, a year before his father's death, he finally adopted the favourite strategy for failed scions of the Victorian middle classes, and emigrated to New Zealand, where he became a Supreme Court judge.)[250]

Faced with these demands on his income, it is not surprising that John Conolly had to swallow his pride and seek financial reward where he could find it. But just as he had earlier turned from a sceptic about asylum treatment into an advocate of a greatly expanded asylum system, so he now publicly defended the private institutions he once anathematized. Repudiating his prior stance on domestic treatment, he contended that 'the management essential to recovery is impracticable in [the lunatic's] own house, or in any private family'.[251] Yet out of the strong desire to conceal the presence of insanity, the wealthy attempted to resort to these expedients, with the result that 'the whole house becomes a kind of asylum, but without the advantages of an asylum'.[252] The consequences were necessarily antitherapeutic: 'the alarm and even the affection of surrounding friends lead to hurtful concessions and indulgences, and to the withdrawal of all wholesome control; until the bodily disorder present in the first stages is increased, and the mind is much more irritated, thus making eventual recovery more difficult, and often altogether doubtful or impossible.'[253] Still less enviable was the situation of those placed 'in detached residences, where no other patient is received'. Gloom, solitude, and neglect, both physical and moral, were their lot, 'such, indeed, as to make the position of lunatics of wealthy families inferior to that of the lunatic pauper'.[254] Private asylums had once been notorious for similar abuse and neglect. But their current proprietors were, with few exceptions, men 'of high character and education'; and the institutions themselves 'are now so well conducted as to present every advantage adapted to the richer patients, and to secure all the care and comfort which the poorer patient enjoys in our admirable county asylums'; with the result that the patient's reception into the asylum 'is usually followed by an immediate alleviation of his malady, and he becomes at once surrounded by every circumstance and means favourable to cure'.[255]

This Panglossian portrait was far from universally admired. Bucknill dismissed private asylums as 'institutions for private imprisonment';[256] and the success of Charles Reade's *Hard Cash*, a story centring upon the improper confinement of its hero in a series of private mad-houses, suggests that Bucknill's opinion reflected a widespread public suspicion.[257] But Conolly's views certainly corresponded closely with the official mythology of the Victorian asylum system and were fitting for one who now ranked as the doyen of his profession.

The publication of his defence of private asylums represented Conolly's last significant public activity. By 1860, he lived 'in an elegant retirement' at Lawn House,[258] consulting occasionally in difficult cases, but for the most part concentrating upon *A Study of Hamlet*, an essay designed to show that the Prince was indeed mad.[259] His health steadily worsened until, on 4 March, 1866, he suffered a massive stroke. By the following day, he was dead. 'His name', as the *Journal of Mental Science* puts it, 'liveth forevermore.'[260]

John Conolly not only played a central role in the success of the Victorian lunacy reform movement, but the vicissitudes of his individual biography nicely illustrate some of the general sociological features that attended the constitution of Victorian alienism as a specialism.[261] His widely publicized work at Hanwell contributed significantly to the creation of a marketplace for the alienists' services and helped to legitimize medical monopolization of the treatment of lunacy. Both ideologically and practically, his activities consolidated the Victorian commitment to institutional 'solutions' to the

problems posed by the deviant and the dependent. Furthermore, notwithstanding his scepticism about the value of most medical remedies for
madness, and his own overt reliance upon and preference for moral suasion
and management in the treatment of his charges, he was most insistent on the
crucial importance of medical control over the treatment of the insane. Any
alternative to this professional monopoly he stigmatized as fatally misguided, almost 'criminal'. In this he echoed and lent the considerable weight
of his prestige to the opinions of his colleagues.[262]

As was generally true of Victorian alienists, it was his prerogatives as a
professional that Conolly defended most fiercely against outside threats.
Thus it was a proposal to limit the authority of the medical superintendent,
not such critical issues as the unwieldy size and organized monotony of the
Victorian asylum, that provoked his resignation from Hanwell – though size
and routine undoubtedly contributed the more powerfully to the transformation of the ideal of curative institutions into the reality of museums for
the collection of the unwanted.[263] So far from acquiescing in the dilution of
his authority, Conolly was among the first to insist that, for the alienist,
everything that occurred within the institution was relevant to cure, and in
consequence nothing could be safely delegated into lay hands. This claim, as
I have pointed out elsewhere,[264] was widely shared in the profession at this
time, reflecting the importance of monopolistic control of asylum administration as support for an otherwise shaky professional authority. Hence the
urgency with which alienists sought to persuade their employers that they
alone should have authority over the most minute details of day-to-day
activity in this 'special apparatus for the cure of lunacy'.[265]

As we have seen, Conolly's major concern, in the course of his writings on
insanity, was with the administrative aspects of the treatment of insanity,
and over the course of his career he evinced a declining interest in
contributing to the scientific understanding of the condition itself. Almost
certainly, this hierarchy of concerns accounts for a good measure of the
hostility that lurked only just beneath the surface of Henry Maudsley's
strikingly ambivalent 'Memoir' of his late father-in-law.[266] The markedly
different – almost diametrically opposed – priorities of these two men
(probably the leading figures of their respective generations of British
alienists), in turn mirror the sharp alteration of the context within which
the profession operated in the two periods: the movement from what came
to be seen as the naive optimism of the first half of the century, that medicine
possessed the means to diagnose and successfully treat insanity, to the
deepening pessimism of late Victorian psychiatry, with its sense that insanity
was all-but-incurable, the product of defective heredity and Morelian
degeneration.[267] For those adhering to the latter orthodoxy, the issue of
improving the treatment of the insane naturally lost some of its urgency, to
be replaced by the need to explain (or explain away) the profession's
apparent therapeutic impotence.

But even Conolly's own position underwent dramatic internal evolution
in the couse of his career. In his earliest writings on insanity, the product of a

period in which he was very much the outside critic of existing practices, he assailed the indiscriminate confinement of the insane, urged the elimination of the private, profit-making 'mad-houses', and touted the merits of domiciliary care. A decade later, on his appointment as superintendent of one of the largest of the existing county asylums, he became one of the most important and effective proselytizers for the expansion of the asylum system, and before long was railing against those who wanted to confine asylum admissions to lunatics dangerous to themselves or others. Towards the close of his career, at a period in which he had become one of the leading private specialists in the treatment of insanity, he exhibited yet another volte-face using the occasion of his second presidential address to the Medico-Psychological Association to issue a lengthy defence of the social utility – indeed indispensability – of the private asylum system.

It is possible, if one is charitably inclined, to view the evolution of his views as the product of greater experience and maturity. The inexperienced observer of his earlier years was disposed to promote impractical, if superficially attractive visionary schemes of non-asylum treatment. Later acquaintance with the realities of treating insanity and the therapeutic possibilities of asylum treatment forced him to revise his ideas, as did his subsequent experience of running a private asylum. Equally, of course, one may opt for a cynical interpretation of his intellectual 'progress'. As Conolly himself remarked, early on in his career, 'When men's interests depend upon an opinion, it is too much to expect that opinion always to be cautiously formed, or even in all cases honestly given.'[268] The close correspondence between the evolution of his ideas and the unfolding of his career is too marked to escape comment. And even in the nineteenth century, there were those who saw the parallels as more than coincidental. John Charles Bucknill, whose own intellectual development was in precisely the opposite direction to Conolly's, from an enthusiastic advocate to a scathing critic of the asylum system, both public and private,[269] was convinced that Conolly's judgement had been subverted by self-interest. Praising the positions Conolly had adopted in *The Indications of Insanity* ('Nothing which Dr Conolly ever wrote does more credit to his head and heart than these opinions'), he noted with sorrow his later repudiation of them. One could only regret that 'advancing years and personal interests had made him indulgent to the evils he had denounced'.[270]

The less moralistically inclined may prefer to adopt a rather different perspective on the internal evolution of Conolly's ideas. It is instructive to note how difficult it is for modern readers to portray his intellectual journey as 'progress'. For our generation has learned to view the asylum as an almost unmitigated disaster, a fatally mistaken approach to the problems of managing the mad, and one that cannot be too swiftly consigned to the dustbin of history. Viewed from this perspective, Conolly's changing views appear to mark an almost perverse shift *from* enlightenment *to* error. It is to his earliest work that our contemporaries turn, when they count him the author 'of principles of treatment that have scarcely been improved in all the succeeding epochs of vanguard practice'.[271] But for the Victorians, it was precisely this early critique of the asylum and advocacy of domiciliary care that was anomalous; and the abandonment of such aberrant opinions in favour of an elaborate defence of asylum treatment required no special explanation: it simply represented an acknowledgement of the findings of modern medical science. Here, as elsewhere, we observe how slippery the concept of 'scientific knowledge' is in the human sciences, and how profoundly dependent the content of that 'knowledge' is upon the nature of the larger social order.

Notes

I should like to acknowledge the helpful comments of Bennett Berger, Elaine Showalter, William Bynum, and Roy Porter on earlier drafts of this essay. A much briefer version previously appeared under the title 'A Brilliant Career? John Conolly and Victorian Psychiatry' in *Victorian Studies* 27 (1984): 203–35. I am grateful for permission to draw upon that earlier version here.

1 *The Lancet* 1 (1843–44); 71–2, quoting the *Morning Chronicle*.
2 *Report from the Select Committee of the House of Commons on Lunatics, with the Minutes of Evidence*, 1859. Evidence of Lord Shaftesbury, pp. 45–9.
3 Sir James Crichton-Browne, *Victorian Jottings* (London: 1926).
4 Sir Benjamin Ward Richardson, 'Medicine under Queen Victoria. The First Advancement: the Treatment of the Insane', *The Asclepiad* 4 (1877): 203–14.
5 An exception is Denis Leigh, *The Historical Development of British Psychiatry* (Oxford: Pergamon Press, 1961).
6 Richard Hunter and Ida MacAlpine, *Introduction* to *John Conolly, An Inquiry Concerning the Indications of Insanity* (London: Facsimile Edition, Dawsons, 1964), p. 1.
7 '[Conolly] originated a non-restraint movement which spread to all Europe and America. His follower, Robert Gardiner Hill (1811–1878), chief surgeon of the Lincoln Asylum ... wrote a good deal against any form of restraint.' Gregory Zilboorg, *A History of Medical Psychology* (New York: Norton, 1941), p. 387.
8 John Conolly, 'Autobiographical Sketch', reprinted in Leigh, *British Psychiatry*, pp. 211–15.
9 Henry Maudsley, 'Memoir of the Late John Conolly', *Journal of Mental Science* 12 (1866): 161.
10 Leigh, *British Psychiatry*, p. 216. Hunter and MacAlpine, *Introduction to John Conolly*, p. 4.
11 M. Jeanne Peterson, *The Medical Profession in Mid-Victorian London* (Berkeley: University of California Press, 1978).
12 Anthony Trollope, *The Vicar of Bullhampton*, cited in Peterson, *The Medical Profession*, p. 194.
13 Maudsley, 'Memoir', p. 164.
14 Leigh, *British Psychiatry* p. 216. Dugald Stewart (1753–1828), Professor of Moral Philosophy at the University of Edinburgh from 1785 to 1820, was profoundly interested in the processes of mind in mental disorders. His lectures

and writings were widely influential, among physicians as well as philosophers.

15 Alexander Crichton, John Haslam, and Thomas Arnold are among the best known of his predecessors.

16 Reminiscing at the end of his career, Conolly recalled:

'My interest in the insane, and my observation of the phenomena of mental disturbance, began early, and became increased as years advanced ... because the most active years of my life happened to be passed in a period signalised by an almost total change in the character of Lunatic Asylums. In the first year of my medical studies, my thoughts, which had previously and often been directed to metaphysical reading, were more consistently directed to mental phenomena, and especially to those of minds in a disordered state, by an accidental visit to the old Lunatic Asylum of Glasgow – from which visit it has happened that all my subsequent life has taken its colour.... The impression made in that and several other visits by the conversation of patients, and by the several forms and degrees of eccentricity and unreason there witnessed, has never been effaced.'

(John Conolly, 'Recollections of the Varieties of Insanity, Part I,' *Medical Times and Gazette* 10 (1860): 6–9)

17 On the importance of possessing either a family tradition of medical practice and/or the means to short-circuit the otherwise laborious and uncertain business of building a general practice by purchasing an existing one, see Peterson, *The Medical Profession*, passim, especially pp. 91 ff.

18 Peterson, *The Medical Profession*, pp. 24 ff.

19 *Edinburgh Medical and Surgical Journal* 75: 255.

20 In later years Forbes was appointed physician to the Queen's household. For his career, see *Lives of the Fellows of the Royal College of Physicians of London 1826–1925* (London: for the College, 1955), pp. 34–5, hereafter cited as *Munk's Roll*.

21 Maudsley, 'Memoir', p. 164.

22 Maudsley, 'Memoir', p. 172.

23 Compare Peterson, *The Medical Profession*.

24 On medical incomes in this period, compare Peterson, *The Medical Profession*, pp. 207 ff.

25 George Birkbeck (1776–1841), MD Edinburgh 1799, was a friend of Brougham's at Edinburgh, famous for his role as the founder of mechanics' institutes, including the London Mechanics' Institute (now Birkbeck College). College).

26 Lord Henry Brougham (1778–1868) was educated at Edinburgh University, and was one of the founders of the *Edinburgh Review*. A barrister, Whig politician, and law reformer, he later served as Lord Chancellor in the Lord Grey and Lord Melbourne administrations. Almost certainly, Conolly's Edinburgh connections helped to secure Brougham and Birkbeck's patronage.

27 H.H. Bellot, *University College London 1826–1926* (London: University of London Press, 1929), p. 37.

28 There were some famous names, however, including Charles Bell, A.T. Thomson, and D.D. Davis. For biographical details, see D.N.B.

29 Peterson, *The Medical Profession*, p. 161. See also I. Waddington, 'General Practitioners and Consultants in Early Nineteenth Century England: The Sociology of an Intraprofessional Conflict', *Bulletin of the Society for the Social History of Medicine* 17 (1976): 11–12.

30 John Conolly to Leonard Horner, 21 July, 1827, College collection, University College London Library.

31 John Conolly [to Messrs Longman], 21 July, 1827; 23 May, 1838. Wellcome Institute for the History of Medicine, London; see also John Conolly to Thomas Coates, 3 April, 1828, 'I cannot at present let anything draw my attention from my University duties.' Society for the Diffusion of Useful Knowledge Collection (hereafter SDUK Coll.), University College London.

32 John Conolly to Leonard Horner, 26 September, 1827; 7 November 1827. UCL Library.

33 He had been preceded by Charles Bell.

34 *Morning Chronicle*, 3 October, 1828, p. 3A; 4 October, 1828, p. 2D. See also *The Life and Times of Henry Brougham by Himself* (London, 1871), vol. 2, pp. 498–99.

35 John Conolly, *An Introductory Lecture Delivered in the University of London, October 2, 1828* (London: 1828), p. 23.

36 Conolly, *Introductory Lecture*, p. 16. See also University of London, *Second Statement by the Council of the University of London Explanatory of the Plan of Instruction* (London: Longman, 1828), p. 150.

37 Maudsley, 'Memoir', pp. 165–66.

38 John Conolly, *Introductory Lecture*, pp. 16–17.

39 Review of *An Inquiry into the Indications of Insanity*, in *Medicochirurgical Review* 13 (1830): 289–308.

40 On these developments, see generally Andrew Scull, *Museums of Madness* (London: Allen Lane, 1979), especially ch. 3.

41 Robert Gardiner Hill, *A Lecture on the Management of Lunatic Asylums, and the Treatment of the Insane* (London: Simpkin Marshall, 1839, pp. 4–5.

42 John Conolly, *An Inquiry Concerning the Indications of Insanity with Suggestions for the Better Protection and Care of the Insane* (London: Taylor, 1830), p. 9.

43 Conolly, *Inquiry*, p. 31.

44 Conolly, *Inquiry*, pp. 8–9.

45 Conolly, *Inquiry*, p. 6.

46 Conolly, *Inquiry*, p. 1.

47 Conolly, *Inquiry*, p. 28.

48 Conolly, *Inquiry*, p. 17.

49 Conolly, *Inquiry*, pp. 4–5.

50 Conolly, *Inquiry*, p. 2.

51 Conolly, *Inquiry*, p. 35, italics in the original.

52 Conolly, *Inquiry*, p. 25.

53 Conolly, *Inquiry*, p. 7.

54 Conolly, *Inquiry*, p. 17.

55 Conolly, *Inquiry*, pp. 17–18.

56 Conolly, *Inquiry*, pp. 30–31.

57 Michael Clark, 'Victorian Psychiatry and the Concept of Morbid Introspection' (unpublished paper, Oxford University, 1981).

58 Conolly, *Inquiry*, pp. 22–3.

59 Conolly, *Inquiry*, pp. 18.

60 Conolly, *Inquiry*, pp. 19–20.

61 Conolly, *Inquiry*, p. 20.

62 Conolly, *Inquiry*, p. 21.

63 Conolly, *Inquiry*, p. 31.
64 Conolly, *Inquiry*, p. 22.
65 Conolly, *Inquiry*, p. 29.
66 Conolly, *Inquiry*, p. 26.
67 Conolly, *Inquiry*, p. 23.
68 Conolly, *Inquiry*, pp. 29–30.
69 Conolly, *Inquiry*, p. 21.
70 Conolly, *Inquiry*, p. 483.
71 Conolly, *Inquiry*, pp. 13–14.
72 Conolly, *Inquiry*, pp. 7, 37–8.
73 *The Medicochirurgical Review* 13 (1830): 289–308.
74 The German alienist Maximillian Jacobi did object a few years later that 'Doctor Conolly takes occasion … to recommend the treatment of such persons in their own houses in far too unconditional a manner, and without any adequate consideration of the objections against', and insisted on the value of asylum treatment. Jacobi, *On the Construction and Management of Hospitals for the Insane* (London: Churchill, 1841), pp. 7–10. (The original German edition appeared in 1834.) But such direct attempts to refute Conolly's claims were otherwise notable by their absence.
75 Bellot, *University College London*, p. 191.
76 Bellot, *University College London* p. 191.
77 Bellot, *University College London*, pp. 193–96. Leonard Horner (1785–1864), was born and educated in Edinburgh. An active Whig politician with a notoriously great respect for 'people of station and property', he was, like his older brother Francis, one of Brougham's intimate circle – a fact which doubtless explains his appointment as warden. Following his resignation from that position, in March 1831, he was to achieve fame for his role as one of the chief inspectors under the Factories Act, a position he occupied until 1856. For details of his life, see Katherine M. Lyell (ed.), *Memoir of Leonard Horner, Edited by His Daughter*, 2 vols (London, 1890).
78 University College London, Minute-book of the Faculty of Medicine, Inaugural Meeting, 26 October, 1827.
79 John Conolly to Leonard Horner, 10 July, 1830, UCL.
80 Hunter and MacAlpine, *Introduction to John Conolly*, pp. 25–6.
81 John Conolly to Leonard Horner, 18 August, 1828, UCL.
82 John Conolly to the University Council, 5 May, 1830; see also John Hogg to L. Horner, 8 May, 1830, UCL.
83 Leonard Horner to John Conolly, 8 July, 1830, UCL.
84 John Conolly to Leonard Horner, 10 July, 1830, UCL.
85 John Conolly to Leonard Horner, 19 July, 1830, UCL.
86 Bellot, *University College London*, p. 177.
87 *A Letter to the Shareholders and Council of the University of London on the Present State of that Institution* (London, 1830), pp. 12–15.
88 *A Letter to the Shareholders and Council*, pp. 23, 28.
89 *The Sun*, 21 April, 1830, p. 4, column D.
90 John Conolly to Leonard Horner, 21 April, 1830, UCL.
91 John Conolly to Leonard Horner, 16 November, 1830, UCL.
92 John Conolly to Leonard Horner, 1 March, 1831; John Conolly to Leonard Horner, 28 April, 1831, UCL.
93 Maudsley, 'Memoir', p. 172.

94 Charles Knight, *Passages from a Working Life*, quoted in Leigh, *British Psychiatry*, p. 219. Hunter and MacAlpine (*Introduction to John Conolly*, p. 32) have disputed this negative verdict on Conolly's capacities as a lecturer, but it must be said that the four lectures he committed to print (John Conolly, *Four Lectures on the Study and Practice of Medicine* (London: Sherwood, Gilbert and Piper, 1832)) serve only to confirm the accuracy of Maudsley's claim that they were 'vague and discursive'.

95 Maudsley, 'Memoir', pp. 173–74.

96 Obituary of John Conolly, *Journal of Mental Science* 12 (1867): 148.

97 Maudsley, 'Memoir', pp. 172–73. Compare Sir George Thane's comments: 'In spite of the friendship of Lord Brougham, Lord John Russell, and other very influential men, John Conolly failed in practice as a London physician, nor does it appear that his duties were performed with any distinguished ability' (Thane, *Medical Biographies*, quoted in Kathleen Jones, *Lunacy, Law and Conscience* (London: Routledge and Kegan Paul, 1955), p. 154).

98 *Correspondence between Mr Granville Sharp-Pattison and Dr N. Chapman* (Philadelphia, 1820).

99 Bellot, *University College London*, pp. 198–99.

100 *London Medical and Surgical Journal* 5 (1 November, 1830): 443–48.

101 Quoted in Hunter and MacAlpine, *Introduction to John Conolly*, p. 29.

102 Bellot, *University College London*, pp. 207–08.

103 John Conolly to Leonard Horner, 30 March, 1831; 8 April, 1831, UCL.

104 For a fuller version of these events, see Bellot, *University College London*, ch. 6.

105 *Morning Chronicle*, 23 October, 1828, p. 3, column B.

106 John Conolly to the University Council, 4 December, 1830, UCL.

107 John Conolly to the University Council, 4 December, 1830, UCL.

108 He had previously been an unsuccessful candidate for the appointment as first superintendent at the new Hanwell Lunatic Asylum – ironically, a job John Conolly was to seek and obtain some years later.

109 Maudsley, 'Memoir', p. 161.

110 Bellot, *University College London*, pp. 250–51.

111 John Conolly to Leonard Horner, 4 December, 1830, UCL.

112 John Conolly to Leonard Horner, 4 December, 1830, UCL.

113 John Conolly to University Council, 4 December, 1830 – his official resignation.

114 John Conolly, 'Valedictory Lecture on Retiring from London University', *London Medical Gazette* 8 (1831): 161–62 et seq.

115 Peterson, *The Medical Profession*, p. 25. On the jealousies and tensions in the medical profession, and the split between the elite and the general practitioners, cf. also Ivan Waddington, 'The Development of Medical Ethics: A Sociological Analysis', *Medical History* 19 (1975); and S.W.F. Holloway, 'Medical Education in England (1830–58): A Sociological Analysis', *History* 49 (1964). For a fictional account of the vicissitudes of provincial practice, see Anthony Trollope, *Dr Thorne* (London: 1858).

116 Maudsley, 'Memoir', p. 173. As Maudsley waspishly commented, this was 'an amiable sentiment, which however, when closely analysed, might be made to resolve itself into a liking for enjoyment without a liking for paying the painful cost of it.'

117 John Conolly to Thomas Coates, 13 October, 1831, SDUK Coll., UCL.

118 John Conolly to Thomas Coates, 27 October, 1831, SDUK Coll., UCL.

119 John Conolly to Thomas Coates, 27 October, 1831, SDUK Coll., UCL.

120 John Conolly to Thomas Coates, 27 December, 1831, SDUK Coll., UCL.

121 John Conolly to Thomas Coates, 18 December, 1831, SDUK Coll., UCL.

122 John Conolly to Thomas Coates, 13 October, 1831, SDUK Coll., UCL.

123 See, for example, John Conolly to Thomas Coates, 14 February, 1832; 2 February, 1833 ('I venture to promise to *finish* forthwith my part of the *Book of Gin*'); 13 May, 1834 (it would be done in three weeks if he could but get rid of his patients); 14 January, 1836; till he finally abandoned the project later that year.

124 John Conolly to Thomas Coates, 17 January, 1832, SDUK Coll., UCL.

125 John Conolly to Thomas Coates, 7 May, 1832, SDUK Coll., UCL.

126 John Conolly to Thomas Coates, 2 February, 1833; see also 14 January, 1836.

127 John Conolly to Thomas Coates, 13 May, 1834, SDUK Coll., UCL.

128 John Conolly to Thomas Coates, 14 January, 1836, SDUK Coll., UCL.

129 Richard Hunter and Ida MacAlpine, *Introduction* to the Facsimile Edition of John Conolly, *The Treatment of the Insane without Mechanical Restraints* (London: Dawsons, 1973), p. xxxiv, speculate that by this period, to make matters worse, his wife may have gone mad and required confinement in an asylum. It must be noted, however, that the evidence for this assertion is slender indeed.

130 Maudsley, 'Memoir', p. 167. Compare Mortimer Granville's later comment: 'It is inconceivable that a man of position and culture would allow his family to have any connection with an asylum' (Granville, *The Care and Cure of the Insane* (London: Harwicke and Bogue, 1877), vol. 1, p. 99).

131 A year later, Conolly discovered that it was his progressive politics and association with efforts to educate the working classes that had cost him the job: 'I lost my election to Hanwell last year solely by my exceedingly moderate Northampton lecture; and I daresay nothing would give more annoyance to the Magistrates than my setting off to inflame county towns after the old fashion.' Suitably chastened, he declined Coates's invitation to lecture for the SDUK at Lewes: '[Though I continue to believe] that those who endeavour, however humbly, to advance the intellectual condition of the people are their truest benefactors, I feel my exertions in that direction are closed (John Conolly to Thomas Coates, 26 August, 1839, SDUK Coll., UCL).

132 Maudsley, 'Memoir', p. 167.

133 Conolly, 'Valedictory Lecture', p. 161.

134 Maudsley, 'Memoir', p. 173.

135 Hanwell County Lunatic Asylum Visitors' Reports, number 45, 1838, pp. 187–88. The existing superintendent, Sir William Ellis, resigned rather than submit to the change.

136 Hanwell County Lunatic Asylum Visitors' Reports, number 49, 1839, pp. 12–13.

137 *The Times*, 15 May, 1839, p. 3, column F.

138 Hanwell County Lunatic Asylum Visitors' Reports, number 50, 1839, p. 26.

139 Maudsley, 'Memoir', p. 172.

140 Thomas Bakewell, *The Domestic Guide in Cases of Insanity* (Newcastle, 1805), p. ix. Bakewell was perhaps the best known non-medical asylum proprietor of the early nineteenth century.

141 Edward Jarvis to Almira Jarvis, 31 May, 1860; 5 June, 1860, Jarvis Papers, Concord Free Public Library, Concord, Massachusetts. I am grateful to Gerald Grob for this reference.

142 Maudsley, 'Memoir', p. 169. I find the image of Conolly surfing his way to success at least mildly amusing.

143 Compare Scull, *Museums of Madness*; Jones, *Lunacy, Law and Conscience.*

144 Samuel Tuke, *Description of the Retreat* (York: Alexander, 1813), p. 163.

145 John Conolly quoted in Maudsley, 'Memoir', p. 169.

146 John Conolly quoted in Granville, *The Care and Cure of the Insane*, vol. 1, p. 111.

147 John Conolly, *Treatment of the Insane* p. 323.

148 John Conolly, quoted in Sir James Clark's *A Memoir of John Conolly*, M.D., D.C.L. (London: Murray, 1869), pp. 22, 28.

149 *The Times*, 10 December, 1840, p. 6, column A.

150 J.G. Millingen, *Aphorisms on the Treatment and Management of the Insane* (London: Churchill, 1840), p. 106.

151 *The Times*, 25 January, 1841. This was perhaps an unfortunate comparison, given the subsequent fate of the bulk of the nineteenth-century pharmacopoeia. For earlier versions of Hadwen's position, see William Cullen, *First Lines of the Practice of Physic* (Edinburgh: 1784), vol. 4, pp. 151–55; John Haslam, *Observations on Madness and Melancholy*, 2nd edn (London: Callow, 1809), pp. 280–91; George Man Burrows, *Commentaries on the Causes, Forms, Symptoms and Treatment of Insanity* (London: Underwood, 1828), p. 686 Alexander Morison sought to rally opposition to non-restraint by forming the Society for the Improvement of the Condition of the Insane.

152 Editorial, *The Lancet*, 4 April, 1840, p. 58. There were some fifty contributions of one sort or another to this debate during the first six months of 1840.

153 Editorial, *The Lancet*, 4 April, 1840. Compare his characteristic description of the elites who controlled the Royal Colleges of Physicians and of Surgery as 'crafty, intriguing, corrupt, avaricious, cowardly, plundering, rapacious, soul-betraying, dirty-minded BATS' (*The Lancet* 1 (1831–32): 2).

154 See *The Lancet*, 22 November, 1842, p. 326. See also *Hansard's Parliamentary Debates*, 3rd series, vol. 61, 17 March, 1842, cols. 803–04. On Wakley and his 'crusades', see S.S. Sprigge, *The Life and Times of Thomas Wakley* (London: Longman, Green, 1899); and Charles W. Brook, *Battling Surgeon* (Glasgow: Strickland, 1945).

155 Samuel Tuke, *Introduction* to Maximillian Jacobi, *On the Construction and Management of Hospitals for the Insane* (London: Churchill, 1841), p. xxxv.

156 *Hansard's Parliamentary Debates*, 3rd series, vol. 65, 16 July, 1842, column. 223.

157 *Illustrated London News*, 21 May, 1843; see also 15 January, 1848.

158 See for example *The Times*, 18 November, 1840, p. 6, column E; 10 December, 1840, p. 6, column E; 30 December, 1840, p. 3, column B; 8 December, 1841, p. 3, column A; 14 December, 1841, p. 3, column D; 5 January, 1842, p. 5, column F.

159 *The Times*, 8 December, 1841, p. 3, column A; 14 December, 1841, p. 3, column D.

160 *The Times*, 5 January, 1842, p. 5, column F. The praise may strike modern readers as misplaced, even itself bizarre, but the Victorians exhibited an unalloyed delight in the reduction of the vicious, the depraved, and the unruly to at least a simulacrum of order and decorum. Such practical demonstrations of the power of 'reason and morality' evidently possessed great symbolic power, and those who successfully staged them could count on widespread approval

and acclaim. I shall discuss the sources of this praise in a moment. On the changing meaning (and methods) of domesticating the mad, from the early eighteeenth to the mid-nineteenth century, see Andrew Scull, 'The Domestication of Madness', *Medical History* 27 (1983): 233–48.

161 *The Times*, 8 March, 1842, p. 13, column E.

162 The Association was founded in 1841, mainly through the efforts of Dr Samuel Hitch of the Gloucester Asylum. Intended to draw together the nascent specialty, and to protect the professional interests of its members, it drew its membership from the chief medical officers of both public and private asylums. In 1865, it was renamed the Medico-Psychological Association, and is now the Royal College of Psychiatry.

163 See *Munk's Roll*, vol. 4, p. 33.

164 *Report of the Metropolitan Commissioners in Lunacy* (London, 1844).

165 *Morning Chronicle*, 5 October, 1843.

166 Leigh, *British Psychiatry*, p. 227.

167 See *The Lancet*, 10 August, 1850, pp. 181–82; 17 August, 1850, p. 224.

168 Ashley, who had now succeeded to his father's title, remained one of Conolly's staunchest admirers, referring to his achievement before an 1859 select committee of the House of Commons as 'the greatest triumph of skill and humanity the world ever knew' (*Select Committee on the Care and Treatment of Lunatics*, 1859–60, London, pp. 45–49).

169 *The Lancet*, 3 April, 1852, p. 339; Clark, *Memoir*, pp. 44–51.

170 Sir G.E. Paget, *The Harveian Oration* (Cambridge: Deighton, Bell, 1866), pp. 34–5.

171 John Conolly, *On the Construction and Government of Lunatic Asylums* (London: Churchill, 1847), p. 143.

172 Conolly, *Construction and Government*. David Rothman has likewise argued that American alienists and others saw the asylum as a model for the proper functioning of the larger society, though he fails to make explicit the ideological resonance of these claims. See David Rothman, *The Discovery of the Asylum* (Boston, Mass.: Little, Brown, 1971).

173 Clark, *Memoir*, pp. vii–viii.

174 For example, Hanwell Lunatic Asylum Annual Report, 1840, p. 52; John Conolly, *Treatment of the Insane* pp. 177–78; John Conolly, 'President's Address', *Journal of Mental Science* 5 (1859): 74; Clark, *Memoir*, p. 49.

175 Hill, *Management of Lunatic Asylums*, p. 147.

176 He arrived in May 1839, with his brother William, proprietor of a licensed asylum at Cheltenham, and noted in the visitors' book, 'Having read Mr Hill's lecture ... we visited this asylum with feelings of unusual curiosity and interest; we have been deeply impressed', quoted in Hunter and MacAlpine, *Treatment of the Insane*, 1973, p. x.

177 See, for example *The Lancet*, 28 November, 1840, pp. 337–41; 9 January, 1841, pp. 532–40; 30 January, 1841, p. 659; 15 January, 1842, pp. 544–46.

178 Robert Gardiner Hill, *A Concise History of the Entire Abolition of Mechanical Restraint in the Treatment of the Insane* (London: Longman, 1857), pp. 13–14.

179 Alexander Walk, 'Lincoln and Non-Restraint', *British Journal of Psychiatry* 117 (1970): 481.

180 I have suggested elsewhere (Andrew Scull, 'From Madness to Mental Illness: Medical Men as Moral Entrepreneurs', *European Journal of Sociology* 16 (1975): 219–61) that the professional ostracism and abuse may in part have derived from

Hill's heretical insistence that 'in the treatment of the insane, medicine is of little avail.... *Moral treatment with a view to induce habits of self-control, is all and everything*' (Hill, *Management of Lunatic Asylums*, p. 45, italics in the original; also quoted in *The Lancet*, 6 July, 1839, p. 554, and in Hill, *Entire Abolition*, p. 72). Walk, 'Lincoln and Non-Restraint', p. 488, by contrast blames his acerbic temperament and unimpressive personality. Certainly, one must concede that Conolly's gentlemanly attributes and demeanour, to say nothing of his powerful friends, must have made him a far more suitable candidate for canonization than his unpolished, ill-educated, and obscure provincial rival. See the more extended discussion of this issue below.

181 *The Lancet*, 24 August, 1850, pp. 247–48.

182 For example, Dr Archibald Robertson, vice-president of the PMSA and physician to the Northampton Infirmary, wrote of Charlesworth's concession:

'The information made the greater impression on me, as it was perfectly new to *me*; so vague and imperfect was my knowledge as to the first discovery and practice of the "non-restraint system" prior to the Hull meeting, that I had thought the merit of it belonged to Dr. Conolly of Hanwell. Acting on this thought, I had ... contributed my mite towards a testimonial to Dr. Conolly; which had been suggested at a meeting in London presided over by Lord Ashley.'   (quoted in Hill, *Entire Abolition*, p. 225)

183 Charlesworth, who had been the most active of the three visiting physicians at Lincoln (see Walk, 'Lincoln and Non-Restraint'), but who had nevertheless freely acknowledged till now that the credit for the discovery belonged to Hill alone, henceforth maintained a studied silence on the issue.

184 Charlesworth had died before this occurred, on 20 February, 1853.

185 Compare Brook, *Battling Surgeon*, p. 149. Hill's claims were dismissed as 'the audacious assaults of envy', and his sanity was subsequently called into question (*The Lancet*, 4 March, 1854; 10 October, 1857, p. 365). Wakley's venom may in part have reflected his friendship with Conolly. It certainly also derived from the fact that Hill had the misfortune to have his cause adopted by the rival *Medical Circular*, a journal which attacked Wakley as a liar given to 'senile ranting', 'as insensible to evidence as he is to shame', a 'licensed reviler' who was 'an offense to professional nostrils' (*Medical Circular*, 11 August, 1852, p. 304). On Wakley's generally strained relations with the rest of the medical press, see Sprigge, *Thomas Wakley*, pp. 156–66; and compare, for example, his reception of the first issue of *The Medical Times and Gazette*: 'The *Medical Gazette*, whose special mission it was to crush ourselves, died of dulness and debility; the *Medical Times* of stupidity and infamy. A hybrid spectral illusion, commemorating the joint names of these two departed journals, and putting on, as its only hope, our outward form and semblance, is all that remains' (*The Lancet*, March 1854, p. 286).

186 Conolly's friends continued the process even after his death. See, for example, Clark, *Memoir*, p. 39. Andrew Wynter, otherwise as given to eulogizing Conolly as were most Victorians, was sharply critical of his behaviour on this point: Conolly's attempt to give a share of the credit to Charlesworth 'must be ascribed to a too partial friendship. Dr. Gardiner Hill is certainly not persuasive in his style, and for that reason has raised up many enemies to his assertions.' But his rightful claims should not thereby be rejected. Modern observers have not always been so kind about Conolly's motives. Frank, for example, while

John Conolly's Career 145

acknowledging that he and Charlesworth were 'very friendly', places more emphasis on the fact that 'Hill discredited entirely Conolly's role as a pioneer, at the same time reminding one and all that Conolly was older than he and was never influential until after Hill had made his notable Mechanics Institute speech' (Justin A. Frank, 'Non-Restraint and Robert Gardiner Hill', *Bulletin of the History of Medicine* 41 (1967): 157).

187 Robert Gardiner Hill, *Lunacy: Its Past and Present* (London: Longman, Green, 1870), p. 53.

188 Hill, *Entire Abolition*: Hill, *Lunacy*.

189 Walk, 'Lincoln and Non-Restraint', p. 494.

190 Maudsley, 'Memoir', p. 174. Conolly, said the American alienist, Edward Jarvis, was 'one of the most polished gentlemen I have met in England'. E. Jarvis to A. Jarvis, 8 July, 1860, Concord Free Public Library, Concord, Massachusetts.

191 John Hitchman, quoted in Clark, *Memoir*, pp. 40–3. Hitchman, later super-intendent of the Derby County Asylum, had begun his career under Conolly at Hanwell. See also [Andrew Wynter] 'Non-Restraint in the Treatment of the Insane', *Edinburgh Review* 131 (1870): 83.

192 Edward Jarvis to Almira Jarvis, 22 June, 1860, Jarvis Papers, Concord Free Public Library, Concord, Massachusetts.

193 In 1842, he even managed to gain permission to introduce the clinical teaching of medical students in the asylum, something he had originally proposed while at the University of London.

194 Conolly, *Construction and Government*, p. 10.

195 Conolly, *Construction and Government*.

196 Granville, *The Care and Cure of the Insane*, vol. 1, p. 154. See also Edward Jarvis to Almira Jarvis, 31 May, 1860, Concord Free Public Library, Concord, Massachusetts. Only in his declining years did Conolly vigorously protest the tendency of county asylums to be little more than 'museums for the collection of insanity' (Francis Scott, 'English County Asylums', *Fortnightly Review* 26 (1879): 114–43. See Conolly, 'President's Address', especially p. 75. John Conolly, *A Letter to Benjamin Rotch, Esquire, Chairman of the Committe of Visitors, on the Plan and Government of the Additional Lunatic Asylum ... about to be Erected at Colney Hatch* (London: Churchill, 1847), p. 18.

197 Conolly, *Letter to Benjamin Rotch*, p. 18.

198 Hanwell Lunatic Asylum, 69th Visitors' Report, 16 January, 1844, p. 4.

199 Hanwell Lunatic Asylum, 70th Visitors' Report, pp. 3–7.

200 Metropolitan Commissioners in Lunacy Report, 1844, p. 28, my italics.

201 Hanwell County Asylum, 69th Visitors' Report, 1844, p. 5.

202 Hanwell County Asylum, 72nd Visitors' Report, 1844, p. 13.

203 Hanwell County Asylum, 73rd Visitors' Report, 1845, p. 1.

204 Hanwell County Asylum, 73rd Visitors' Report, 1845, p. 1.

205 Hanwell County Asylum, 75th Visitors' Report, 1845, p. 3.

206 Hunter and MacAlpine, *The Treatment of the Insane*, p. xxxii.

207 Henry Maudsley (1835–1918), editor of the *Journal of Mental Science* (1862–78) and Professor of Medical Jurisprudence at University College London, was the leading alienist of his generation. On his life, see Aubrey Lewis, 'Henry Maudsley: His Works and Influence', *Journal of Mental Science* 97 (1951): 259–77; and Elaine Showalter, *Crazy Jane* (New York: Pantheon, 1985).

208 Sir George Savage (1842–1921), formerly physician superintendent of the Bethlem Royal Hospital, editor of the *Journal of Mental Science*, and President

of the Medico-Psychological Association and the Neurological Association, was one of the most fashionable consultants on mental diseases in late nineteenth-century London. For Savage's role in treating Virginia Woolf, see Stephen Trombley, '*All that Summer She Was Mad': Virginia Woolf and Her Doctors* (London: Junction Books, 1981).

209 For example, when the confinement of Lady Rosina Bulwer Lytton in a private asylum threatened to become a scandal of major proportions, her husband sought advice from 'the most experienced and able physicians' specializing in psychological medicine, choosing Conolly and Forbes Winslow. By a curious coincidence, Lady Lytton, whose sanity they confirmed, was an inmate in Robert Gardiner Hill's asylum, Wyke House (*The Times*, 19 July, 1858, p. 12, column E). Conolly also testified at such well-publicized commissions in lunacy as W.F. Windham, Sir Henry Meux, and Mrs Catherine Cummings.

210 For example, Robert Pate, Edward Oxford, Luigi Buranelli. On this aspect of Victorian psychiatric practice, see Roger Smith, *Trial by Medicine* (Edinburgh: Edinburgh University Press, 1981).

211 *The Morning Post*, quoted in Hunter and MacAlpine, *The Treatment of the Insane*, p. xxxvii. Robert Pate, a former cavalry officer, had struck Queen Victoria on the head with his walking stick. His defence, for which Conolly appeared as an expert witness, was that his conduct was the product of an irresistible impulse, itself caused by underlying mental derangement. This provoked a memorable response from the judge, Mr Baron Alderson: '*A man might say that he picked a pocket from some uncontrollable impulse, and in that case the law would have an uncontrollable impulse to punish him for it*' (reported in *Medical Times* 1 (1850): 66, emphasis in the original).

212 Compare Smith, *Trial by Medicine*.

213 Peter McCandless, 'Liberty and Lunacy: The Victorians and Wrongful Confinement', ch. 13 in Andrew Scull (ed.), *Madhouses, Mad-doctors, and Madmen: The Social History of Psychiatry in the Victorian Era* (Philadelphia, Pa.: University of Pennsylvania Press, 1981).

214 Conolly, *Inquiry*, p. 35, italics in the original.

215 Conolly, *Inquiry*, p. 386.

216 Conolly, *Inquiry*, pp. 8–9.

217 John Conolly, *A Remonstrance with the Lord Chief Baron Touching the Case Nottidge versus Ripley*, 3rd edn (London: Churchill, 1849), p. 3. For Conolly, the case of Louisa Nottidge precisely illustrated the dangers of 'leaving imbecile, visionary, and fanatical women at large'. A wealthy spinster, Miss Nottidge insisted on residing in the Agapemone, or Abode of Love, a millenial community in Somersetshire presided over by a former curate, where 'a mock religion and a boundless fanaticism sanction modes of worship which tend to destroy all sense of modesty'. Only confinement in an asylum, he commented, could protect her reputation and her property. Though cure might still prove elusive, 'the delusions might [then] have died away, and a sense of duty have returned; her habits would at least have been regulated, all excess avoided, all painful exposure prevented' Yet the court intervened to prohibit her commitment. 'Those who exult in her liberation from the asylum,' said Conolly sternly, 'are exulting over her ruin.' For further discussion of the Nottidge case, see Andrew Scull, 'The Theory and Practice of Civil Commitment', *Michigan Law Review* 82 (1984): 101–17.

218 T.T. Wingett, *The Law of Lunacy* (Dundee: 1849).

219 Conolly, *Remonstrance*, p. 3.
220 Conolly, *Remonstrance*, pp. 4–5.
221 Conolly, *Remonstrance*, pp. 6–7. 'Seclusion and systematic superintendence', were, he continued,

'strictly part of the medical treatment in such cases; and to censure those who resort to it is as utterly foolish as it could be to reprove a physician for checking an inflammation by bleeding and blistering before life was endangered, or a surgeon for preventing the progress of a disease of a joint before incurable disorganization rendered amputation necessary.'

222 McCandless, 'Liberty and Lunacy', pp. 350–56.
223 *Daily Telegraph*, 7 January, 1862; *The Times*, 7, 21, 31 January, 1862; *British Medical Journal*, 11 January, 8 February, 1862.
224 'Report on the Ruck Case', *Journal of Mental Science* (1858), p. 131.
225 Charles Reade, *Hard Cash: A Matter-of-Fact Romance* (London: Ward Lock, 1864).
226 Reade, *Hard Cash*, p. 335. The reference to non-restraint makes transparent who the target is, but Conolly's identity becomes still more blatantly obvious in later passages.
227 Reade, *Hard Cash*, p. 211.
228 Reade, *Hard Cash*, p. 208.
229 Reade, *Hard Cash*, pp. 203, 212.
230 Reade, *Hard Cash*, p. 335.
231 Reade, *Hard Cash*, p. 339.
232 Here, the reference to Conolly was unmistakable, for the latter's *A Study of Hamlet*, addressed to precisely this issue, had appeared but a few months earlier. Reade maliciously takes his vendetta a step further: Wycherly readily debates the sanity of Alfred Hardie, the man he has wrongly incarcerated,

'With a philosophical coolness, the young man admired, and found it hard to emulate; but this philosophical calmness deserted him the moment Hamlet's insanity was disputed, and the harder he was pressed, the angrier, the louder, the more confused the Psychological physician became; and presently he got furious, burst out of the anti-spasmodic or round-about style and called Alfred a d——d ungrateful, insolent puppy, and went stamping about the room; and, finally, to the young man's horror, fell down in a fit of an epileptic character, grinding his teeth and foaming at the mouth.'

Alfred, by now well acquainted with the face of lunacy, has discovered Wycherly's secret: he was himself a monomaniac! (Reade, *Hard Cash*, p. 340.)
233 Reade, *Hard Cash* p. 452. For someone with a powerful animus against the pretensions of Victorian alienists, Conolly was a tempting target, both because of his eminence and because of his general reputation as a great humanitarian; and in attacking him, Reade was at once ruthless, unscrupulous, and resourceful, not shrinking from quoting Conolly out of context, and putting his behaviour in the worst possible light. Not surprisingly, Conolly, his family, and friends (who included Charles Dickens, in whose *Household Words* Reade's novel had first appeared in serial form) were deeply distressed. On this last point, see Richard A. Hunter and Ida MacAlpine, 'Dickens and Conolly: An Embarrassed Editor's Disclaimer', *Times Literary Supplement*, 11 August, 1961, pp. 534–35.

234 Apparently, he could not bear to leave the site of his earlier triumphs:

> 'No longer residing in Hanwell Asylum, and no longer superintending it, or even visiting it, I continue to live within view of the building and its familiar trees and grounds. The sound of the bell that announces the hours of the patients' dinner still gives me pleasure, because I know that it summons the poorest creature there to a comfortable, well-prepared and sufficient meal; and the tone of the chapel bell, coming across the narrow valley of the Brent still reminds me, morning and evening, of the well-remembered and mingled congregation of the afflicted, and who were then assembling, humble, yet hopeful and not forgotten, and not spiritually deserted.'
>
> (Conolly, *Treatment of the Insane* pp. 341–42)

235 The annual reports of the Commissioners in Lunacy reveal an average of five or six present at any one time.

236 In 1859, he had to rescue this enterprise from bankruptcy.

237 Hunter and MacAlpine, *Treatment of the Insane*, pp. xxxv–xxxvi.

238 House of Commons Select Committee on the Care and Treatment of Lunatics p. 185.

239 Conolly, *Inquiry*, p. 481.

240 Maudsley, 'Memoir', p. 172.

241 To Thomas Harrington Tuke, one of Conolly's former pupils.

242 To Henry Maudsley, another alienist and former pupil.

243 John Conolly to Lord Brougham, 19 June, 1846, Brougham Collection, University College Library.

244 Edward Conolly to Lord Brougham, 10 November, 1846, a request he reiterated on 27 November, 1846.

245 Edward Conolly to Lord Brougham, 3 February, 1851, Brougham Collection, UCL.

246 Edward Conolly to Lord Brougham, 27 December, 1853.

247 Edward Conolly to Lord Brougham, 6 December, 1855, Brougham Collection, UCL.

248 Edward Conolly to Lord Brougham, 8 August, 1857, Brougham Collection, UCL. 'I do not know if I am asking too much.' He was.

249 John Conolly to Thomas Harrington Tuke, quoted in Hunter and MacAlpine, *Treatment of the Insane*, p. xxxvi.

250 Leigh, *British Psychiatry*, p. 227.

251 John Conolly, 'On Residences for the Insane', *Journal of Mental Science* 5 (1859): 412–13.

252 Conolly, 'On Residences for the Insane', p. 413.

253 Conolly, 'On Residences for the Insane', p. 412.

254 Conolly, 'On Residences for the Insane', pp. 415–17. It is instructive to compare these opinions with those voiced only a few years later by Charles Lockhart Robertson and John Charles Bucknill. Roberston and Bucknill had also relinquished the superintendencies of county asylums (Sussex and Devon), but both had subsequently become Chancery Visitors in Lunacy, in that capacity visiting rich lunatics in both asylum and domestic settings. Robertson confessed, 'I could not have believed that patients who were such confirmed lunatics could be treated in private families the way Chancery lunatics are, if I had not personally watched these cases' (*House of Commons Report of the Select*

Committee on the Operation of the Lunacy Law, 1877, pp. 53–5). And Bucknill went further still:

'The author's fullest and latest experience has convinced him that the curative influences of asylums have been vastly overrated, and that of isolated treatment in domestic care have been greatly undervalued.... It has long been the accepted doctrine [among alienists] that insanity can only be treated curatively in asylums.... A wider knowledge of insanity ... would have taught them that a very considerable number of cases of insanity run a short course and recover in domestic life with no great amount of treatment, and that perhaps not of a very scientific kind.'

(J.C. Bucknill, *The Care of the Insane and Their Legal Control* (London: Macmillan, 1880), p. 114)

255 Conolly, 'On Residences for the Insane', pp. 417–18.

256 Bucknill, *The Care of the Insane*, p. 128.

257 As Reade put it, 'The tenacity of a private lunatic asylum is unique. A little push behind your back and you slide into one; but to get out again is to scale a precipice with crumbling sides' (*Hard Cash*, p. 330).

258 Edward Jarvis to Almira Jarvis, 31 May, 1860, Jarvis papers, Concord Free Public Library, Concord, Massachusetts. 'Dr Conolly is apparently seventy or more [sic], yet hale and vigorous; very kind, bland, affectionate in his manners. Having ever cultivated the higher moral and intellectual [sic], he manifests a beautiful spirit. He has retired from active practice and devotes himself to study, writing, social enjoyment and some consultation practice.'

259 Compare John Conolly, *A Study of Hamlet* (London: Moxon, 1863). See also 'Hamlet on the Couch' by W.F. Bynum and Michael Neve, in this volume.

260 'Obituary of John Conolly', *Journal of Mental Science* 12 (1866): 146.

261 On the constitution of Victorian alienism, see my earlier essays: 'From Madness to Mental Illness'; and 'Mad-doctors and Magistrates: English Psychiatry's Struggle for Professional Autonomy in the Nineteenth Century', *European Journal of Sociology* 17 (1976): 279–305.

It would be useful to compare Conolly's career pattern with those of others within the emergent profession of alienism, and I would like briefly and tentatively to address that issue here. The uncertain and halting progress of Conolly's career bears some interesting similarities to that of his contemporary, James Cowles Prichard (see Denis Leigh, *British Psychiatry*); and it is equally apparent that by the time of Conolly's death, careers in alienism were developing on a wholly different and much more systematic basis. Instead of the haphazard patterns of recruitment and disparate background experiences that appear to characterize the first generation of nineteenth-century alienists, the growing size and number of public asylums created a substantial and growing number of entry level positions for assistant physicians. Increasingly, superintendents were recruited from the ranks of these experienced apprentices, in one sense signalling the maturation of the profession of alienism, and perhaps contributing to the growing conservatism and bureaucratic inertia that marked late nineteenth-century asylumdom.

Unfortunately, however, it is difficult to go beyond these generalities, since we lack any study of English alienism to compare with John Pitts's interesting PhD dissertation on their American counterparts, 'The Association of Medical Superintendents of American Institutions for the Insane, 1844–1892: A Case

Study of Specialism in American Medicine' (unpublished PhD thesis, University
of Pennsylvania, 1978). A detailed prosopographical study of the English
profession over the course of the nineteenth century would unquestionably be
most welcome.

262 Scull, 'Mad-doctors and Magistrates'.
263 Cf. Scull, *Museums of Madness*, esp. chs 3 and 6.
264 Scull, 'Mad-doctors and Magistrates', pp. 300 ff.
265 Granville, *The Care and Cure of the Insane*, vol. 1, p. 15.
266 'As a writer on insanity, he painted eloquently and pathetically the external
features of the disease, but the philosophical depths of mental phenomena he
never cared to sound, and the exact scientific investigation of mental disease he
never devoted himself to' (Maudsley, 'Memoir', p. 172).
267 See the chapter by Dowbiggin in this volume.
268 Conolly, *Inquiry*, p. 3.
269 Matching the development of his own career, from superintendent of the Devon
County Asylum, to an extra-asylum career as Chancellor's Visitor in Lunacy,
and private consultant.
270 Bucknill, *The Care of the Insane*, p. 60.
271 Peter Sedgwick, *Psychopolitics* (London: Pluto Press; New York: Harper and
Row, 1982), p. 141. For a critique of modern 'community care' see Andrew
Scull, *Decarceration*, 2nd ed (Oxford: Polity Press; New Brunswick, NJ:
Rutgers University Press, 1984).

CHAPTER SIX

Darwin and the face of madness

Janet Browne

A MADMAN, CLAIMED Charles Bell in 1806, is an outrageous maniac, little more than a savage animal, and like an animal he is usually kept confined for the safety of other inmates and the warders of his asylum (*Figure 6.1*). But do not let the chains distract you, he added. For Bell's real purpose lay in describing not just animality and madness, the loss of 'human' reason and a lapse into primitive, brutal behaviour, but the actual *expression* of insanity and what it was that distinguished the face of a deranged person from someone we might consider normal.[1] His illustration was merely one in a whole series of essays on the anatomy of facial expression, and was clearly not so much a contribution to psychiatry as it was a study in the ancient field of physiognomics, the art of discerning character and emotion in the face, or, for medical philosophers and doctors like Bell, a new science for diagnosing the patient's internal state of mind.

Physiognomy has always held a special sort of fascination for scholars, and Bell was no exception. It seemed to him the very essence of diagnosis that the exterior facade of an individual should display the signs and symptoms of inner bodily states, and that doctors, guided by an appropriate set of rules for deciphering the outer man, would be better able to understand his innards. Long after Lavater (1741–1801) had set out his idiosyncratic guidelines for reading the character behind eighteenth-century faces,[2] Bell was trying to establish his own rules for a new, medical, physiognomical science.

So his book, *Essays on the Anatomy of Expression*, was about faces rather than madness. His aim was to demonstrate the natural theological argument that man's place in nature was decidedly at the top, and that facial expressions were designed to show it. The creator had given us a whole range of feelings that animals could not share – the finer feelings like love, anguish, the artistic sensibilities – and had provided extra sets of muscles for their proper expression.[3] The question of lunacy was obviously critical here, for Bell, like many of his contemporaries, really did think the insane were somehow closer to animals than the rest of humanity, and this, by his own definition, meant that they ought to lack some essentially human quality in their faces. Eye muscles and eyebrows, he decided, which for him usually denoted 'mind', were completely inactive in the face of a madman.[4] They were not absent, for insane people were, after all, human, but they nevertheless remained unused, mimicking the fact that these were also muscles which were, he thought, missing in animals. This absence of any external sign of mental activity, coupled with an expression of animal rage around the mouth and lower half of the face, emphatically conveyed an idea of what Bell considered to be genuine insanity. Remove the signs of rationality and one found only an animal; take away the normal expression of thought in man, and there was the brute revealed. Like it or not, said Bell, the appearance of a lunatic was medically distinctive. Animality was written all over his face.

One wonders what Queen Charlotte and her six fastidious daughters made of all this animality when they asked Bell for a copy of his book to be sent to the Palace.[5] Probably, like Thomas Lawrence of the Royal Academy, they thought he displayed a 'total lack of temper, modesty and judgement', and ought not to be encouraged in his attempts to secure the chair of anatomy at the Royal Academy, once held by William Hunter.[6] But another famous reader thought rather differently. Coming across the first edition during a visit to his wife's family in Staffordshire, Charles Darwin was fascinated. He found Bell's arguments absorbing, and was deeply impressed by the author's comparative analysis of human and animal musculature and his excursions into the theory of art, anthropology, philosophy, and psychology.[7]

In particular, he was struck by the claim that insanity could be equated with raw animality. Darwin, after all, had set himself the task of demonstrating that species were descended from other species, that human beings were little more than glorified animals. The lunatic as beast revealed, the animal passions lurking behind a polite, Hanoverian facade, were ideas that must surely have intrigued him. Yet Darwin is not noted for his active participation in the world of medicine, even though his theories, introduced by younger contemporaries such as Henry Maudsley and John Hughlings Jackson, proved as decisive here as in other areas of nineteenth-century thought. His main interest in therapeutics, for example, as Ralph Colp and others have described, seems to have been looking after himself rather than following the latest medical debates at meetings and in journals.[8] So it comes as something of a surprise to learn that Darwin *did* actively engage in one particular branch of medicine, the philosophical study of the insane, and furthermore that he had very definite ideas about madness, about the possible existence of a beast in man, and about contemporary theories of psychiatric diagnosis. He carefully considered the mentally ill, deliberated over the external appearance of madness, and wrote about insanity, albeit in a somewhat specialized way. Taking his cue from Charles Bell's persuasive natural theology, he presented an alternative, evolutionary account of the actual face of insanity.

Most of Darwin's ideas in this area were written up in his book on the *Expression of the Emotions*, published in 1872, the year after the *Descent of*

Man, and intended to be a kind of illustrated sequel to that crucial, but rather inconclusive, evolutionary text.[9] He wanted to show how our faces were not, so to speak, our own, but were instead the complex product of 'descent with modification'. Although every human face is beguilingly different, the outward appearance of emotions such as anger or fear, embarrassment or joy, are obviously stereotyped and transcend the individual. It was probable, thought Darwin, that these expressions had evolved like any other part of the human frame and would reveal our animal origins in a particularly interesting way: even specifically human expressions like smiles, laughter, blushing, and tears were the result of adaptation and natural selection, not of God-given design. In a great finishing stroke to the arguments put forward in the *Descent*, the *Expression of the Emotions* was intended to show that even the most 'human' of human characteristics were derived from animals.[10]

But why, in Darwin's case, study the physiognomy of the insane? Quite simply, he believed their emotions were uncontrolled and intense, and that, rather like children, their faces would display their feelings in a pure, uncomplicated way, ideal for a scientific survey of expression. The passions would be more strongly accentuated and easier to identify; emotions less complex than in the sane. In particular, a study of lunacy would provide him with a much-needed opportunity to tackle some of the more philosophical issues that surrounded the origins and character of human beings, many of which had been left unresolved in the *Descent of Man*. Was rationality, for instance, lost in reverse order to the way in which Darwin believed civilized behaviour had been acquired? Did the insane have a sense of their own identity and were they able to blush, like ordinary people, when made to feel self-conscious? Armed with such detailed information, Darwin thought he would be well prepared to overturn Bell's widely disseminated thesis about insanity.

Having decided that he wanted to study the insane, Darwin did what he usually did in such circumstances and found himself an expert. He engineered an introduction to James Crichton Browne (1840–1938), one of the most distinguished psychiatrists of the later nineteenth-century, and at that time medical superintendent of the West Riding Lunatic Asylum, near Wakefield in Yorkshire. Not only Darwin, but other scientists and medical men such as Maudsley, consulted Crichton Browne concerning the most recent research on neurological pathology and mental diseases. At Wakefield, for example, he had initiated a programme of investigation on a scale not previously known in Britain and established both a pathological laboratory and a journal, the *West Riding Lunatic Asylum Medical Reports*, to publish the laboratory's findings. According to Sander Gilman, who has closely studied his correspondence with Darwin, Crichton Browne was also an amateur photographer and it was this more than anything that enticed Darwin to make his acquaintance.[11] In 1871 he invited Browne to supply photographs of the patients under his care and to describe, if he could, their usual behaviour and diagnosis, along with any other observations he might have on particularly striking aspects of insane behaviour, especially anything to do with the face.

When Darwin approached Crichton Browne to obtain photographs of the insane as well as help in understanding the nature of their expressions, he became involved in something of a medical tradition. As Charles Bell's work so clearly showed, it had long been understood that the mad generally possessed a distinctive physiognomy separating them from the sane. Such a belief was part and parcel of the intellectual baggage that surrounded other, more well-known nineteenth-century traditions that mental illness was very much a disease, a real biological malfunction that could be diagnosed by the appropriate external signs. The behaviour of the insane, their gestures, posture, and facial expressions were consequently useful indicators of some specific internal disorder. And over the century, from Esquirol to John Hughlings Jackson, as the so-called 'diseases' of the mind were progressively itemized, put into categories and classified, so the exterior signs of these diseases were also categorized and classified, to the point where John Conolly (1794–1866) or Alexander Morison (1779–1866) could claim there was a readily identifiable 'face' for every type of madness.[12] As the mind disappeared, so to speak, into the recesses of the head, so a system of external facial and behavioural clues became increasingly important for psychiatric science. Important, that is, for *written* psychiatry, because it remains much of a mystery whether these ideas genuinely altered the way in which patients were diagnosed or, indeed, their subsequent courses of treatment.

Such medical ideas were powerfully reinforced by more general theories of physiognomy, a set of assumptions about characters and faces that goes back way beyond Caspar Lavater to the world of ancient theatre. Originally, physiognomics was conceived as the art of reading personality in the face, and the important features were obviously the permanent traits, where an aquiline nose showed its bearer to be noble like an eagle, and the bovine face betrayed a placid disposition.[13] These comparisons, which were first illustrated in the sixteenth-century in Giambattista della Porta's *De humana physiognomonia* of 1586, undoubtedly relied on a reaction which most of us have experienced: we may quarrel whether cows look placid or not, depending on how you feel about cattle, but no one would easily deny that they have an 'expression' which an unfortunate man or woman may unwillingly share.

When the influential principles of animal physiognomics first came under fire in the eighteenth-century, its critics, notably William Hogarth and his commentator Georg Christoph Lichtenberg,[14] stressed that it was not the permanent traits which allow us to read a character but, more obviously, the fleeting expression of emotions. These mobile expressions, so they argued, gradually mould a face, and a person who is frequently worried will acquire a furrowed brow while a cheerful one will acquire a smiling face because the transient will pass into permanence. Hogarth, in other words, regarded the face in the same light as Locke regarded the mind: both were a *tabula rasa* before individual experiences wrote their story on to its surface. And although it is something of a dramatic leap from Locke to the early years of the nineteenth-century, it is, I suggest, this same principle that governed the surge of interest in medical physiognomics from Charles Bell onwards. A person's experiences, his or her disappointments in life, the setbacks, the successes, and of course, their mental disorders, would necessarily turn up on the face, especially after a lifetime of varied existence. In this way, it was thought, a nineteenth-century mental patient really could display the face of madness.

However, Lavater, in his *Physiognomische Fragmente* (1775), as well as early medical investigators such as Bell, relied more on various forms of artistic reproduction than on patients themselves as the basis of their interpretations. Not the individual, but the artist's interpretation of the individual stood as the foundation of their studies. The more sensitive among the early nineteenth-century psychiatrists such as Etienne Georget were aware of this problem and confronted it directly by insisting that only practical observation of the patient could lead to diagnoses and medical results with any meaning.[15] Yet most theorists dealing with the expression of the insane, such as Esquirol and Morison, commissioned artists to present what they naively assumed were accurate representations. Possibly, because they were interested in *categories* of insanity, it did not matter too much if their artists made everyone look much the same or succumbed to visual conventions of the kind that crept up on Bell. Esquirol, for instance, had been one of the first alienists to appreciate the advantages of physiognomic diagnosis, and his textbook, published in 1838 under the title *Des Maladies Mentales*, was illustrated by twenty-seven engraved portrait drawings of individual hospital cases. Discussing them in the text he emphasized that physiognomy was unsurpassed as a guide to the ideas and affections experienced by the mad. One day, he promised, he would publish more on this subject and would provide diagnostic illustrations for every one of his reformulated nosological categories.[16]

Most of Esquirol's drawings are either profile busts or unposed full-length studies depicting the patients in strait-jackets, restraining chairs, or against the background of a hospital interior. Ambrose Tardieu was the artist. *Figure 6.2* shows a victim of demonomania, and is exceptional in that the subject was the only patient mentioned by Esquirol as having posed willingly for the artist: apparently she believed her portrait would be given to the Archbishop of Paris. Through some bibliographical mistake in the various editions of his book, Esquirol mixed up the case history of this patient (case H) with another one, known as case L.[17] Curiously, the mistake was never discovered in Esquirol's lifetime, and only goes to show that contemporary readers, and even Esquirol himself, saw exactly what they were told to see, even if it was a description of another patient entirely. This mismatching of text with illustration has a lot to tell us about the psychology of perception.[18]

Esquirol never did publish his studies on physiognomy but the torch was

taken over by Alexander Morison whose book on the outward appearances
of mental disease is deservedly well known. Like Esquirol's work, however,
the representations of Morison's patients are virtually meaningless without
the case histories supplied next to every illustration; flicking through the
book, looking at the pictures alone, the most striking observation must
surely be that they all look precisely the same, and the question arises as to
how Morison or his readers could ever suggest there were distinguishing
features for each one of his written diagnoses. They are blank, sad,
depressing portraits. C.C. Bohme, who supplied the lithographs, was
nevertheless congratulated by Morison for displaying great anatomical skill,
'without individuality'; that is, without conveying any special sense of the
personality of the sitter beyond his diseased state of mind. It was evidently
the *illness*, the category of insanity, not the person, that Morison hoped to
capture.

One of Morison's illustrations shows a patient believed to have chronic
dementia, who had shot a man during his insanity. His symptoms were an
almost complete withdrawal from life and he sat for long periods with his
hands on his knees, unable to bring himself to speak (*Figure 6.3*).

Looking rather similar, but quite differently catalogued, the patient
depicted in *Figure 6.4* had 'religious insane pride'. Formerly he was a
chemist; now he believed himself to be God, and refused to shake hands
with anyone. His usual salutation was 'I am the warrior God of Heaven and
of Earth – I can strike you dead in a moment.'[19]

It is clear from the character of these drawings, and Morison's and
Esquirol's comments on them, that both physicians understood the problem
of portraying the patients solely as routine graphic documentation. The
French painter, Theodore Géricault, on the other hand, approached the
subject with acute sensitivity and, under Georget's direction at the Salpêtrière, created great works of art in fulfilment of his commission. Géricault,
in his paintings of Georget's patients, interpreted insanity not in terms of
behaviour, nor in terms of a disease category that transcends the individual,
but as a state of mind which, though disordered and clinically classifiable,
emphasized rather than obliterated individuality. The patients were painted
as if sitting for portraits, the genre most appropriate to the study of human
personality.[20]

There are only five portraits positively known to be of mentally ill sitters,
although attempts have been made to identify one or two undocumented
Géricaults as the rest of a set of ten supposed to have been painted in 1822 or
1823. They are all of monomanias of various kinds, one being *Monomanie
du commandement militaire* (*Figure 6.5*). The next, now in the Ghent
museum, is *Monomanie du vol*, a kleptomaniac, although persistently
referred to in the catalogues as the Mad Assassin (*Figure 6.6*). Two further
studies show *Monomanie du vol des enfants*, a kidnapper, and *Monomanie
de jeu*, a gambler. *Monomanie de l'envie* (*Figure 6.7*) is the only one of
the five troubled faces which shows any ferocity or violence, and even here it
is well within the expressive range of the normal face, and has a quite

different character from the delirium seen in either Bell's or Esquirol's contorted illustrations.

Yet Géricault's work was apparently disregarded, in Britain at least. What was wanted by the time of Darwin's *Origin of Species* was an *objective* study of insanity, not the sensitive subjective images of Géricault's portraiture. And it was only with the introduction of photography that a fully objective portrait seemed to be accessible. No more than twenty years old in the England of 1859, photography was thought to be the ultimate form of realistic portrayal and a new, empirical study of madness was proclaimed to be possible at last. The revitalized empiricism of the French psychiatric school can only have accentuated this surge of British enthusiasm for photographing the mad, and provided a complex double reinforcement of assumptions that were now becoming widely pervasive. Only with a belief in physical stigmata was there any point in looking at pictures; and conversely, pictures of the mentally ill encouraged physicians to look for physical signs of disease. John Conolly's work was pivotal in this respect, for he took every opportunity to stress that the photographer could provide the doctor with true representations of mental malady. The point was driven home in a major series of essays on the physiognomy of the insane in the *Medical Times and Gazette* of 1858 and 1859 where he described the different illnesses of patients photographed by Hugh Diamond. Photographs, he said, were virtual copies of nature, possessing a truthfulness, and preserving minutiae, which could not easily be perpetuated by any of the older methods.[21]

Unfortunately for Conolly, his argument was hardly enhanced by the fact that Diamond's originals could not be commercially printed, and his case notes were poorly illustrated with lithographs. B.A. Morel (1809–73), a convert to Conolly's point of view at least as far as physiognomy was concerned, found that he too was forced to illustrate his work on degeneration and congenital idiocy with lithographs taken from photographs of patients in the Salpêtrière.[22] Both these authors are however noted for their early attempts to use photography as a definite part of medicine, as an analytic guide to health and disease rather than an enhancement of the arts and sciences.

But although photographs could not, for commercial reasons, be put directly before the medical public, they reigned supreme in the backrooms of the asylums. In addition to using them as diagnostic tools – although, as already hinted, it is difficult to know exactly how much they were really used for diagnosis – physicians also attempted to use photographs in the medical treatment of patients. Hugh Diamond, for instance, showed his photographs to inmates of the Surrey Asylum hoping that the novelty of seeing themselves as others saw them would have a beneficial effect, and claimed to achieve one or two positive results.[23] The superintendent of the Chester County Asylum, Thomas Brushfield, also tried this technique with some success. Brushfield, however, was more interested in another function of psychiatric photography, already pointed out by Conolly and Diamond –

that is, using photographs for the improvement of medical records. Apart from the usual Victorian preoccupation with recording things for the sake of recording them, there was an additional persuasive reason for compiling a file of portrait photographs in this way. If any criminal lunatics escaped from Chester, Brushfield argued, they could be traced by sending their photographs to the police, who would then (he hoped) secure their return to the asylum.[24]

So a number of nineteenth-century trends combined to make psychiatric photography popular in the asylums at least. Questions of law and order, certain administrative advantages, rising medical empiricism and an emphasis on the individual and his personal case history, coupled with the attractions of the art of photography itself, encouraged doctors such as James Crichton Browne to believe they were at last approaching a true understanding of insanity. Browne's enthusiasm for photography spills over into his correspondence with Darwin, and it seems also that Darwin subscribed to some of the same general beliefs. Together, with the aid of Browne's photographs, they worked on the facial expression of madness.

Darwin first discussed the insane in a chapter on weeping in his *Expression of the Emotions*, citing two of Browne's cases of depression and melancholia: 'One melancholic girl wept for a whole day,' he wrote, 'and afterwards confessed to Dr Browne that it was because she remembered that she once shaved off her eyebrows to promote their growth.'[25] Later, Darwin again cited Crichton Browne concerning the expression of grief among the insane, referring to specific photographs sent to him by Browne:

> 'Dr Browne carefully observed for me during a considerable period three cases of hypochondria, in which the grief-muscles were persistently contracted. In one of these, a widow, aged 51, fancied that she had lost all her viscera, and that her whole body was empty. She wore an expression of great distress, and beat her semi-closed hands rhythmically together for hours. The grief-muscles were permanently contracted, and the upper eyelids arched.'

Privately, Darwin may have seen in this photograph (*Figure 6.8*) some kind of proof of the existence of exaggerated expressions in the insane – exaggerated even to the point of permanence.[26]

To suffer was not always to weep, as Darwin took pains to point out, and he was particularly keen to have examples of the facial movements of babies before they learnt to cry. Did the insane provide a parallel case, he tentatively enquired of Crichton Browne?

> 'You propose to send me a photograph of a case of "general paralysis of the insane," and I should be very glad to see it. I have been trying to get a London photographer to make one of a young baby screaming or crying badly; but I fear he will not succeed. I much want a woodcut of a baby in this state. I presume it will be hopeless, from the constant movement, to get an insane person photographed whilst crying bitterly?'[27]

Darwin certainly understood the practical difficulty of his request. After persevering for some months with an inadequate collection of pictures purchased from various London studios, he was delighted to report to Browne the discovery of Oscar Rejlander, perhaps London's most able photographer and certainly one of the most popular, who was both technically competent to carry out Darwin's special requests and willing to take an active part in the researches.[28] Rejlander, for example, took a picture of an infant screaming without the production of tears which, unlike Crichton Browne's photographs of melancholia, was reproduced in the *Expression* book (*Figure 6.9*) to illustrate the square outline of the mouth and pronounced furrows on the cheeks, seen also on the faces of Crichton Browne's depressed patients. Rejlander, who was, among other things, a retired oil painter and amateur actor, was also eager to pose personally for Darwin's photographs, and sent Darwin several studies of emotions simulated by himself or his wife. In *Figure 6.10* he is posing next to an enlarged version of the crying infant, on the left hand side simulating suffering, and on the right laughter, an idea of his own that he thought might help Darwin distinguish the key points between them.

On 3 April, 1871, Crichton Browne sent Darwin the photograph of the paretic he had requested. Browne, who had long had a special interest in general paralysis of the insane, contributed a short discussion of the subject to the *Journal of Mental Science*,[29] parts of which he forwarded to Darwin along with his photographs. Darwin was consequently better situated to judge Crichton Browne's argument than any of their medical contemporaries because, once again, the photographs could not be directly reproduced even in a journal like *Mental Science*. However, the pictures of paretics were, explained Browne, not very helpful:

> 'They are, I regret to say most unsuccessful and only indicate very imperfectly the labial tremor which I have described to you. The difficulty of photographing such shaky subjects is however immense and the artist a novice.... In all those whose photographs are now forwarded to you, the exalted extravagant profusive ideas have been well marked. They have given away millions daily.'[30]

Crichton Browne's interest in paralysis also led him into a prolonged study of what he called euphoria mania, where the contraction of the face into the semblance of a smile was so frequent that physiognomy could act as a primary means of diagnosis (*Figure 6.11*). Darwin wrote about these optimistic faces in his chapter on smiling.

Pride was another emotion among the mentally ill actually 'seen' by Darwin. He wrote:

> 'In some photographs of patients affected by a monomania of pride, sent me by Dr Crichton Browne, the head and body were held erect, and the mouth firmly closed. This latter action, expressive of decision, follows, I presume, from the proud man feeling perfect self-confidence in

himself. The whole expression of pride stands in direct antithesis to that of humility.'[31]

Darwin's chapter on anger, the classic sign of mania, also drew on Browne's comments on the angry scowl of an epileptic idiot under his care (*Figure 6.12*). In this context Darwin also cited Henry Maudsley's book on *Body and Mind* to the effect that the idiot is an arrested form of man at an earlier (and more primitive) stage of development.[32] Darwin's views on congenital insanity seem greatly influenced by Maudsley's formulation, and while it is clear that Darwin never subscribed to Maudsley's general view that *all* insanity is a form of reversion, it was certainly within his understanding of the expression of the emotions among the insane. The stigmata of insanity would be shown by the absence of 'civilized' standards of behaviour and a return to earlier modes of uncontrolled expression.

All in all, Crichton Browne supplied Darwin with forty-one photographs, each carefully labelled with his diagnosis, backed up with copious notes and descriptions of the patient's behaviour. Only one was reproduced in the *Expression of the Emotions*, an unexceptional figure who illustrated the rough, bristly nature of the hair of the insane. But Darwin was genuinely grateful for the photographs for all that, because they gave him an entry into a world previously very much unknown to him. Most of Crichton Browne's interpretations were incorporated into his book, and furthered Darwin's arguments in a way that he greatly appreciated. 'I have been making immense use almost every day of your manuscript,' wrote Darwin. The book, he said, ought to be called by Darwin *and* Browne.[33]

Such an extravagant compliment is, I believe, unique in the history of Darwin's long writing career: he depended on Crichton Browne's information and good judgement with a commitment that was rarely offered to scholars other than his closest friends. Browne was not a close friend of Darwin's, which makes it all the more remarkable. Everything that Darwin wrote on insanity was thus derived from Browne – or from some other medical authority like Maudsley or Paget. Darwin, one of the men who could have transformed the study of madness by bringing evolutionary theories to bear on problems of mental development, on the links between emotion and reason, and on the nature of mind itself, ducked the entire issue and remained utterly conventional. He took all his understanding of mental activity from prominent psychiatrists of the day, and relied on their expertise to substantiate the various ideas he was exploring concerning the topic of expression. It is a curious, perhaps paradoxical point that Darwin, whose theories did indeed transform psychiatric practice through the work of his younger contemporaries, had little of his own to contribute, beyond bringing the investigation of the mad into a general work on the behaviour of men and animals. Inveterately original, Darwin seems to have failed us here.

But this is undoubtedly overstating the case, for Darwin did make one remarkable contribution to psychiatry, one which went against the flow of mid-century research and which overturned much of the work put forward by Crichton Browne and others mentioned here. Unfortunately, it was also completely ignored. Unlike his medical contemporaries, Darwin did not believe in physiognomical rules and was unable to see the mental diseases described by Browne in the pictures that he sent him. One photograph was very like another, and the various conditions were indistinguishable without clues from the caption. Darwin saw only distress, a disturbed mind, distraction, and the ordinary expressions of rage, fear, and sorrow, albeit exaggerated with dramatic force. He completely failed to see the categories, the complex taxonomies that pervaded Browne's entire corpus and underpinned nineteenth-century theories of madness. Almost as if he was applying natural history concepts to the mentally ill, Darwin looked for evidence of 'species' of madness and could find none. As Michael Neve has astutely suggested, there were no dividing lines between taxonomic categories, no differences between species and varieties, no inbuilt property of, say, melancholia that could be defined without reference to some other state of mind.[34] Darwin's theory of evolution, of course, demanded that nature was a seamless web, that classificatory boxes or pigeon holes could not exist except in the mind of the observer, and he seems to have applied this idea to mental diseases just as readily as he used it in the study of orchids or barnacles. In the same way as he brought about the downfall of animal and plant classification schemes based on Cuvierian concepts of fixity and stability, Darwin here exploded the taxonomy of insanity that lay behind almost every psychiatric endeavour of the later nineteenth century. Though Sander Gilman is certainly right when he argues that Darwin studied the insane through the eyes of other, more knowledgeable people, and that Crichton Browne supplied his correspondent with conventional labels for the 'types' of madness he was to view, Gilman does seem to have overlooked one of the more intriguing aspects of Darwin's intellectual make-up – the tendency to consider all natural phenomena in a developmental, evolutionary way. Evidence for evolution – a preconceived motive just as persuasive as Crichton Browne's search for the taxonomy of insanity – was surely the overriding purpose of Darwin's foray into psychiatric photography, not the assessment of contemporary medical practice.[35] All Browne's attempts to provide a picture gallery of insane diseases were, in the end, apparently pointless, because Darwin simply could not *see* any differences.

And his book on the *Expression of the Emotions* reflected this particular kind of perception. By integrating the insane into a wide-ranging survey of expression, Darwin de-emphasized the category of insanity itself. There was no special chapter on mental disease, no sensationalist sequence of photographs, no particular emphasis on mad expressions as being something different. Darwin treated the insane as one of many interesting sources of behaviour, useful because of the intensity of their emotions, but part of a unified biological context for all that. The general effect of this thoughtful approach was to include – not exclude – the insane within conventional society. In particular, Darwin's work showed that there was no single distinguishing feature that separated the physiognomy of asylum patients from the rest of mankind: their anger was like our anger, their happy expressions the same as anybody else's. So the one significant contribution that Darwin – rather than his followers – made to nineteenth-century theories of psychiatry was the quirky, unrecognized fact that a specific physiognomy for the insane did not exist. For Darwin, there was no face of madness.

Notes

I would like to thank Michael Neve for his interest in this paper and the idea that physiognomy could perhaps be considered as the story of *blankness*, rather than expression. As always, Bill Bynum, Roy Porter, Christopher Lawrence, and Nick Browne have made helpful comments, and I am indebted to Professor Sander Gilman of Cornell University whose paper on Darwin and Crichton Browne has been an invaluable guide. Peter Gautrey and William Schupbach kindly provided illustrations which are reproduced with the permission of the Syndics of Cambridge University Library, and the Wellcome Trustees. The Museum voor Schone Kunsten, Ghent, the Musée des Beaux Arts, Lyon, and the Sammlung Oskar Reinhart am Römerholz in Winterthur generously forwarded photographs of their Géricault portraits with permission to publish. The work for this paper was carried out with the gratefully acknowledged aid of the Wellcome Trust.

1 Charles Bell, *Essays on the Anatomy of Expression in Painting* (London: Longman, 1806), pp. 153–55.
2 Johann Caspar Lavater, *Physiognomische Fragmente* (Leipzig: 1775–78), later translated by Thomas Holcroft, *Essays on Physiognomy* (London: Robinson, 1789). Two of the best recent studies of Lavater's work and impact are John Graham, 'Lavater's *Physiognomy* in England', *Journal of the History of Ideas* 22 (1961): 561–72, and G. Tytler, *Physiognomy in the European Novel: Faces and Fortunes* (Princeton, NJ: Princeton University Press, 1982).
3 Bell's theory of expression was inspired by natural theology and a belief that the muscles were there for a purpose: the human face had more muscles and was the most mobile of the animal kingdom because it was believed to express a greater range of thoughts and feelings. He attempted to arrange the passions in a system based on pain and pleasure, exertion and relaxation. All expressions were a combination of these. Such general opinions were widely shared by Bell's contemporaries and for this reason Darwin used the 1844 edition as an authoritative source against which he could evaluate his own researches. Bell, of course, held a view of expression directly opposite to that of Darwin:

'It is thus to observe how the muscles, by producing distinct expressions, afford a new occasion of distinguishing the tribes of animals; and, as signs of superior intelligence, become proofs of the higher endowments of man, and a demonstration of the peculiar frame and excellence of his nature.'
(Bell, *Essays on the Anatomy of Expression*, p. 101; see also pp. 89–96, 98)

The principal muscles peculiar to man were those running from the top of the nose to the eyebrows (corrugator supercilii), and from the base of the lower jaw to the corner of the mouth (depressor anguli oris and triangular oris). The corrugator supercilii 'knits the eyebrows with a peculiar and energetic meaning, which unaccountably, but irresistibly, conveys the idea of mind and sentiment' (p. 95); the others provide a 'combination of muscular actions of which animals are incapable' (p. 98).

4 Bell, *Essays on the Anatomy of Expression*, pp. 155–56.

5 Sir Gordon Gordon-Taylor and E.W. Walls, *Sir Charles Bell: His Life and Times* (Edinburgh: Livingstone, 1958), p. 21.

6 Royal Academy of Arts, Thomas Lawrence Papers 1: 202. It is not generally known that the first edition of Bell's book was intended to win him a chair at the Royal Academy (Royal Academy MS, Lawrence 1: 199–202, and 4: 310). Only later, having failed to secure a chair, did he turn to his more famous work on the nerves. Subsequent editions of the book were in effect manifestos for his particular interpretation of the nervous system, significant in the controversy with François Magendie over the discovery of the twin functions of spinal nerve roots, as described by Paul Cranefield in his elegant *The Way In and the Way Out: François Magendie, Charles Bell and the Roots of the Spinal Nerves* (New York: Futura, 1974). Bell explained some of the changes in his theories in the introduction to his second edition, revealingly retitled *Essays on the Anatomy and Philosophy of Expression* (London: Murray, 1824).

7 Darwin first came across Bell's *Essays on the Anatomy of Expression* at Maer Hall, Staffordshire, during a visit to his wife's father, Josiah Wedgwood (the second), and, according to his reading notebooks ('Catalogue of Books', Cambridge University Library, DAR 119), red it sometime between 10 June and 14 November, 1840. When the third, heavily revised, edition was issued in 1844, Emma Darwin presented her husband with a copy, and it is this book which served as the basis for Darwin's later studies. It is heavily annotated and in the Darwin Library at Cambridge University Library.

8 R. Colp, Jr., *To Be an Invalid* (Chicago: University of Chicago Press, 1977); R.S. Porter, 'The Descent of Genius: Charles Darwin's Brilliant Career', *History Today* 32 (1982): 16–22; L.A. Kohn, 'Charles Darwin's Chronic Ill Health', *Bulletin of the History of Medicine* 37 (1963): 239–56.

9 *The Descent of Man and Selection in Relation to Sex* (London: Murray, 1871), was, of course, undoubtedly the more important study, being his magnum opus on man, an answer to the crucial question left untouched by the *Origin of Species* (1859). The *Expression of the Emotions* is clearly a secondary book. It is easy to identify, for example, the places in *Descent of Man* where Darwin had intended to insert sections on expression. However, as the book progressed, Darwin decided that facial expressions were an inappropriate digression and thought it 'better to reserve my essay for separate publication' (Darwin, *Descent of Man*, vol. 1, p. 5). According to Darwin's 'Journal' the *Expression of the Emotions* was begun on 17 January, 1871, the last proof of the *Descent of Man* having been finished on 15 January. Much of the manuscript was actually written on the backs of the *Descent* folios (Cambridge University Library, DAR 17 (i)).

10 Janet Browne, 'Darwin and the Expression of the Emotions', in David Kohn (ed.), *The Darwinian Heritage* (Princeton, NJ: Princeton University Press).

11 Sander L. Gilman, 'Darwin sees the Insane', *Journal of the History of the Behavioral Sciences* 15 (1979): 253–62, and rewritten as 'Darwin's Influence on Seeing the Insane', ch. 15 in Gilman's excellent book *Seeing the Insane* (New York: Brunner, Mazel, 1982). See also W.F. Bynum, 'The Nervous Patient', in this volume.

12 John Conolly, 'On the Physiognomy of Insanity', *The Medical Times and Gazette* n.s. 16, 17, 18 (1858–59); Alexander Morison, *The Physiognomy of Mental Diseases* (London: Longman, 1838). Sander Gilman provides a detailed account in *Seeing the Insane*, pp. 91–100, 164–69.

13 E.C. Evans, 'Physiognomics in the Ancient World', *Transactions of the American Philosophical Society* n.s. 59, no. 5 (1969).

14 W. Hogarth, *The Analysis of Beauty Written with a View of Fixing the Fluctuating Ideas of Taste* (London: Reeves, 1753); G.C. Lichtenberg, 'Fragment von Schwänzen', *Baldingers Neues Magazin für Aerzte* 5 (1783), a satirical, physiognomic analysis of the devil's tail, extensively quoted in translation by Ernst Gombrich in 'On Physiognomic Perception', from *Meditations on a Hobby Horse and Other Essays on the Theory of Art* (London: Phaidon, 1978), pp. 45–55.

15 Etienne Georget, *De la Folie, ou aliénation mentale* (Paris: Bechet, 1823) (extract from *Dictionnaire de médecine* (Paris: Bechet, 1821–28)); and Gilman, *Seeing the Insane*, pp. 84–90.

16 Etienne Esquirol, *Des Maladies mentales, considérées sous les rapports médical, hygiénique et médico-légal* (Paris: 1838), vol. 2, p. 167.

17 A German translation and critical edition of Esquirol's collected papers had been published in 1827 under the title *Allgemeine und Specielle Pathologie und Therapie der Seelenstörungen* (Leipzig: 1827). I take my information from Margaret Miller, 'Géricault's Paintings of the Insane', *Journal of the Warburg and Courtauld Institute* 4 (1940–41): 151–63, p. 160.

18 See, for example, the studies of P. Ekman, W. Friesen, and P. Ellsworth, *Emotion in the Human Face* (Oxford: Pergamon Press, 1972) and Ekman's article in P. Ekman (ed.), *Darwin and Facial Expression* (New York: Academic Press, 1973). In a more historical context Jennifer Montague has described some of the inaccuracies in the captions to later versions of Charles Le Brun's 'designs for the passions' (1668) in her 'Charles Le Brun's *Conférence sur l'expression générale et particulière*' (University of London PhD thesis, 1959). Darwin himself confessed that if he had examined his research photographs without any explanation he would have been pressed to identify some of the expressions without written or verbal 'clues', e.g. Darwin, *Expression of the Emotions*, p. 14.

19 Morison, *Physiognomy of Mental Diseases*, facing plate 44.

20 Miller, 'Géricault's Paintings'.

21 Conolly, 'The Physiognomy of Insanity', *Medical Times and Gazette*, n.s. 16 (1858) p. 3. See also Sander L. Gilman, *The Face of Madness: Hugh W. Diamond and the Origin of Psychiatric Photography* (New York: Brunner, Mazel, 1976).

22 B.A. Morel, *Traité des dégénérescences physiques … accompagné d'une atlas* (Paris: Baillière, 1857).

23 Hugh W. Diamond, 'On the Application of Photography to the Physiognomic and Mental Phenomena of Insanity', unpublished paper presented to the Royal Society, 22 May, 1856 and reprinted in Gilman, *The Face of Madness*, pp. 17–24, p. 21.

24 T.N. Brushfield (1857) quoted from Gilman, *The Face of Madness*, p. 9.

25 Darwin, *Expression of the Emotions*, p. 155.

26 Darwin, *Expression of the Emotions*, p. 185. Darwin cites Browne as saying that 'the persistent lines or furrows, due to their habitual contraction, are characteristic of the physiognomy of the insane belonging to these two classes [melancholia and hypochondria]' (p. 185), and refers to the Frenchman Duchenne

(1806–75) who had studied expression rather more practically than other workers in the field by galvanizing muscles in the face of an old man whose skin was relatively insensitive, thereby producing various responses which were photographed on a large scale and published in his *Mécanisme de la physionomie humaine* (Paris: Renouard, 1862). Greatly impressed by these illustrations and Duchenne's meticulous analysis of the facial musculature, Darwin had a large number of Duchenne's photographs copied for his own researches and entered into a detailed correspondence with him, very little of which survives today. Duchenne's photographs are at the Ecole des Beaux Arts in Paris and his galvanizing equipment is in the Wellcome Museum of the History of Medicine at the Science Museum, London. See E. Bikaplan, 'Duchenne of Bologne and the *Physiologie des mouvements*', in S.R. Kagan (ed.), *Victor Robinson Memorial Volume* (New York: Froben, 1948), pp. 172–92.

27 8 June, 1870, quoted from Gilman, 'Darwin Sees the Insane', p. 258.

28 Rejlander was one of the key figures in nineteenth-century photography. Living and working in Wolverhampton, by 1872 he had gained an enviable reputation as a portraitist, genre worker and photographic artist; not content with photographing other people (mainly actors) at Darwin's suggestion, he also made several self-portraits illustrating various expressions, including disgust, defiance, surprise, shrugging, and helplessness, which appear in *Expression of the Emotions*, for example, facing p. 255. See also E.Y. Jones, *Father of Art Photography: O.G. Rejlander 1813–1875* (Newton Abbot: David and Charles, 1973). Rejlander's photographs are in Darwin's papers (seventy-three in total), Cambridge University Library, DAR 53 (i) and (ii).

29 First described in detail by A.L.J. Bayle (1799–1858) in 1822, general paralysis of the insane was well known by the 1870s as a frequent and often fatal complication in insanity. Crichton Browne believed it was a condition that followed in the wake of civilization, possibly even a disease *of* civilization, caused by the unceasing 'struggle for existence'. GPI could be arrested and treated, he suggested, by the application of counter-irritants to the head, and this programme had been carried out under his supervision at Wakefield Asylum. Browne was anxious to demonstrate that the first and most telling symptom of GPI was the trembling of one solitary cheek muscle, the zygomatic. If both cheek muscles trembled that was a sign of great emotion, not of encroaching paralysis. J. Crichton Browne, 'On General Paralysis of the Insane', *Journal of Mental Science* 17 (1871–2): 147–49, a short commentary on Robert Boyd's paper 'On General Paralysis of the Insane', *Journal of Mental Science* 17 (1871–72): 1–24.

30 3 April, 1871, quoted from Gilman, 'Darwin Sees the Insane', p. 259.

31 Darwin, *Expression of the Emotions*, p. 264.

32 Henry Maudsley, *Body and Mind: an Inquiry into their Connection and Mutual Influence, Specially in Reference to Mental Disorders* (London: 1870).

33 26 March, 1871, quoted from Gilman, 'Darwin Sees the Insane', p. 260.

34 M. Neve, 'The Construing of the Face', *Times Literary Supplement* 4146 (17 September, 1982): 991, an illuminating essay on the perception and non-perception of 'types' of people.

35 Gilman, 'Darwin Sees the Insane', p. 262.

CHAPTER SEVEN

Obsessional disorders during the nineteenth century: terminological and classificatory issues

G.E. Berrios

Introduction

NO EPISTEMOLOGICAL BREAK seems to have taken place in psycho-pathology since the early nineteenth century; at least no good case has so far been made for one. This makes this period – in spite of its complexities – a promising hunting ground for the humbler breed of clinical historians. Once the lions have left and the macro-concepts been dealt with, the historian of psychopathology must move in. One of the unglamorous tasks he must carry out is the detailed analysis of the transactional role played by clinical micro-concepts. He must be able to map the successive compromises reached between semiology and the behavioural dislocations it purports to describe.

Early nineteenth-century alienists inherited a set of molar categories (mania, melancholia, phrensy, lethargy, etc.), the semantic bounds of which were strongly determined by social variables. By the end of the century some of these categories had gone for good, others had been drastically refurbished and yet others created anew. More importantly, the semantic bounds of the new categories were now determined by empirical rules obtained directly from observation and counting.

This metamorphosis is in need of explanation and somehow the grand hypotheses do not seem to be doing the job; at least not to the satisfaction of the clinicians. It may be trite to say that complex philosophical, social, and empirical factors must have mediated this change but no model has yet been put forward which takes into consideration the influence of clinical observation or the constancy elements inherent in the biological aspects of the insanity phenomenon. In this regard a working model for clinicians has recently been suggested.[1]

What is known is that by the 1840s the old categories (apart, perhaps from delirium),[2] had all exploded. The analytical and correlational epistemology of the anatomo-clinical view of disease demanded the identification of surface markers, of signs of disease, which could represent the anatomical lesion. The behavioural fragments left behind by the destruction of the old categories were chosen as the new units of analysis.

The second half of the century witnessed a trend towards the formation of new clusters. The early stages of this process were carefree but soon longitudinal observation, biological markers, and statistics introduced a sense of discipline and order. By the time of Magnan and, certainly by the time of Kraepelin, few but robust clinical categories had been developed.

It would be incorrect to deny that this epistemological drama occurred in a larger scenario. Social and political factors no doubt will have the last word in the market of explanations. Fortunately these have exercised great minds in recent years and nothing that might be said in this chapter could improve upon their endeavours.

The brief

Terminological and taxonomic difficulties have bedevilled the obsessional disorders since their clinical inception.[3] Of interest to the historian is the manner in which terminology has shaped their development and the way in which the obsessional disorders related to generic categories such as neurosis and psychosis; both these issues are dealt with in this chapter.

Not less important to the development of the obsessional disorders have been other contextual factors such as volitional theories, the degeneration issue, faculty psychology and associationism; these have been dealt with elsewhere.[4] Recent historical accounts are not very helpful in this respect.[5]

Object and terms

'Obsessional states' are interloping fragments of behaviour characterized by inordinate repetition, anomalous content and resistance from the affected subject. Their iterative nature and offending content create individual uneasiness and cultural dissonance, and often fracture, and paralyse the flow of behaviour. 'Obsessional' forms of behaviour have been identified in most cultures and historical periods and cannot be said to be fictions created by nineteenth-century alienists.[6]

The technical meaning of terms such as 'obsession', 'compulsion', 'imperative idea', 'mental besetment', 'impulsion', 'contrary act', etc. developed only during the latter part of the nineteenth century. Before this period, however, these terms had had wide currency in ordinary language to name will-related mental acts.[7]

Terminological issues

Questions on the origin and development of classical psychiatric vocabulary and of its relevance to current taxonomic disputes have been neglected by historians. It is plausible to assume, however, that this area of study should provide mediating hypotheses to explain the effect of social variables on clinical definitions.

In general, it can be stated that nineteenth-century psychiatric terminology had three origins: classical terms inherited from Greek or Roman times (for example mania, melancholia, paranoia); words from the *sermo vulgaris* furnished with technical meanings (for example hallucination, obsession, stupor); and neologisms (for example lypemania, monomania).

Whatever their origin these terms underwent successive redefinitions as aetiological hypotheses changed and clinical boundaries were redrawn. Their original etymologies, however, often remained like familiar ghosts to influence usage and theory.

Although the origin of this psychiatric terminology is multinational, there is little doubt that France contributed to it the most.[8] The French psychiatric vocabulary was assimilated into most languages. French classifications and theoretical assumptions however, have been less influential. It is not surprising therefore that after World War I, France became isolated from the rest of the psychiatric world.[9]

German terminology

Krafft-Ebing coined in 1867 the term 'Zwangsvorstellung' to refer to irresistible thoughts.[10] 'Zwang', derived from the high German term 'dwang' ('twanc' during the middle high German period),[11] meant 'to compel, oppress';[12] its stem was the Sanskrit 'tvanźkti' ('he pulls together').[13] The term 'Vorstellung' (presentation or representation) had been introduced by Wolff one century earlier to refer to the Cartesian 'idea'.[14] It acquired currency in German psychology with Herbart.[15] Krafft-Ebing's term, therefore, is best rendered as 'forced representation'.[16]

Westphal[17] equated 'presentations' to 'ideas' and suggested that obsessional states resulted from a disorder of intellectual function. This intellectualistic interpretation remained influential. He also distinguished between 'presentations' as pure mental acts (obsessional ideas or ruminations) and 'presentations' as initiators of action (compulsions). Terms such as 'Zwangshandlung', 'Zwangsphänomenen', 'Zwangszustand' were subsequently coined to refer to iterative actions.[18]

'Zwang' qualifies both obsessional thoughts and actions and this ambiguity is of historical interest. 'Zwangsvorstellung' was translated as 'obsession' in Great Britain and as 'compulsion' in the United States; 'obsessive-compulsive disorder' emerged as a compromise.[19]

Griesinger[20] introduced a second root word, 'sucht'. Meaning 'disease, passion' it was the nineteenth-century version of the old high German 'suht', related to 'siech' (sick), and a cognate of the Armenian 'hiucanim' ('I am ill').[21] Griesinger's compound term 'Grübelnsucht' ('ruminatory or questioning illness') reflects well the clinical characteristics of the three cases he reported. The evocative force of 'Grübelnsucht' is also helped by the meaning of 'Grübeln', the old German word for 'racking one's brains'. The usage of 'sucht' in other medical areas such as 'Fallsucht' (epilepsy), 'Schwindsucht' (tuberculosis), and 'Giftsucht' (toxicomania) created classificatory confusion and led to its abandonment as a root word for the obsessional states.[22]

Donath in 1897 suggested a third root word, 'Anancasmus'.[23] This term lent itself to adjectival use and Schneider[24] coined the derivative 'anancastic personality'.[25] The French have, in general, disregarded the term anancasm.[26] Writers of psychodynamic persuasion occasionally consider the phobic states as a form of anancasm.[27]

The attempt by Ziehen[28] to incorporate the Latin term 'obsessio' into German psychiatry was unsuccessful.[29]

French terminology

Common names for the obsessional states during the nineteenth century were 'manie sans délire',[30] 'maladie du doute',[31] 'folie du doute avec délire de toucher',[32] 'folie lucide',[33] 'délire émotif,[34] and 'onomatomania'.[35]

The term 'obsession' gained medical currency during the 1880s. Littré[36] (1877) did not include a medical meaning under this word but Luys[37] referred to as 'obsessions pathologiques' all anomalous and repetitive, subjective events without external source. Until then the term had been mostly used in a 'transitive' sense, that is, to describe the action of an abstract, external agent, 'besieging' the individual.[38] Luy's usage was therefore a major departure in that he made 'obsessions' into an internal, private affair; the new usage was soon accepted.[39]

Other French terms carried related clinical meanings, for example 'idée fixe',[40] 'idée irrésistible',[41] and 'impulsion'.[42] The French rendition of the term 'Vorstellung' gave rise to some debate and no agreement seems to have been reached as to whether it should be 'représentation' or 'présentation'.[43]

English terminology

Terminology in the English language followed a similar path.[44] Tuke[45] referred to 'imperative ideas' and Mickle[46] to 'mental besetments'. The *Nomenclature of Diseases*, drawn up by the joint committee of the Royal College of Physicians in London (with George Savage and Percy Smith as the psychiatric members) included an 'obsessive insanity'.[47]

When translating Legrain's entry[48] for his *Dictionary*, Tuke anglicized the

French title to 'Obsession and Impulse', but in his own entry on the topic he prefers 'imperative ideas'.[49] The term 'obsession', however, was adopted by the main medical journals of the day.[50] When Shaw[51] published a review of these states he wrote as if the word 'obsession' had been in English psychopathology for a long time. The term also appears in American literature around this period.[52]

Literal translations of French and German categories such as 'doubting madness',[53] 'ononomatomania', 'insanity of doubt',[54] and 'reasoning mania' made only a fleeting appearance in the English and American literature.

Obsessional disorders and the insanity concept[55]

By classifying the obsessional phenomena of 'Mademoiselle F.' as a form of 'monomania' ('délire partiel', p. 70), Esquirol[56] initiated the view that the obsessional disorders were a form of insanity. Late nineteenth-century French writers were therefore right to consider Esquirol as the starting point for the nosological analysis of these phenomena.[57]

Esquirol[58] defined 'monomania' as 'a chronic disease of the brain, without fever, characterized by a partial lesion of the intellect, the emotions or the will'. Volitional monomania referred to involuntary, irresistible, and instinctive activity. Thus the subject is 'chained to actions that neither his reason nor emotion have originated, that his conscience rejects and his will cannot suppress. This is called 'monomanie sans délire' or "instinctive monomania".[59]

Monomania was a version of the 'partial insanity' concept,[60] and encompassed pathological states other than the obsessional disorders.[61]

Esquirol noticed that Mademoiselle F.'s circumscribed and repetitive symptoms fitted well into the intellectual monomania category; but he also noticed that she described them as 'irresistible' and hence seemed to have insight into her symptoms. Patients like Mademoiselle F. suffered from 'délire partiel' and 'carried out actions they considered as bizarre and absurd ... but were aware of their state, able to talk about it and longed to be rid of it'.[62] Esquirol surmised that this irresistibility was a manifestation of a secondary disorder of the volitional faculty.[63]

The view that the obsessional disorders were a form of partial insanity or monomania did not last long. The concept of monomania had never been popular and by the 1850s it was criticized on various grounds.[64] First it was said to result from the mechanical application of faculty psychology to insanity;[65] second, it was considered as incomplete due to the fact that it had been created during a period that still defined mental disorder in cross-sectional terms;[66] third, it was felt to encompass too many clinical states and had little or nothing to say about their individual phenomenology;[67] fourth, it was said to have no conceptual machinery to incorporate subjective symptomatology which, since the 1840s, had become an important aspect of the definition of mental disorder;[68] and fifth, it was observed to create legal difficulties as there was a tendency by psychiatrists to diagnose as volitional monomania almost any form of impulsive crime.[69]

Each point was hotly contested.[70] Even a new category, 'pseudomonomania', was created to account for cases of monomania who in the longitudinal observation proved to be suffering from 'diffuse insanity'.[71] In the event the category monomania burst open and the various clinical states it had uneasily contained had to find other diagnostic shelter. For example cases of lypemanie (i.e. *monomanie triste*) were reallocated to categories such as depression, melancholia, *folie circulaire*, and chronic delusional insanity.[72]

The disappearance of the monomania concept set asunder the obsessional states. Not surprisingly a number of the conceptual difficulties which had beset the monomania concept were inherited by this clinical state.

The transition

The collapse of the monomania concept did not lead to an immediate reclassification of the obsessional disorders as neurosis. This latter concept was undergoing redefinition and at the time there was no obvious clinical reason to bring together obsessions with disparate states such as hysteria, hypochondria, or neurasthenia.

The process of separating the insanities from the neuroses started during the third quarter of the nineteenth century and was carried out on speculative-aetiological rather than on clinical criteria.[73]

The key feature of the notion of insanity since Locke,[74] if not before, had been the disorder of thinking, and so it remained until the nineteenth century.[75] One of the perturbing legacies of the monomania concept, however, was that it recognized, at least theoretically, the existence of emotional and volitional insanity. This constituted a challenge to the 'intellectualist' view. Transitional concepts such as 'folie lucide', 'folie avec conscience', and 'folie raisonnante' (i.e. insanity accompanied by insight)[76] were created to deal with this difficulty. The obsessional phenomena became a member of the 'folie lucide' category. This was to be expected as insight had become a defining feature of 'obsessional thought' since Esquirol.[77] After the 1870s the transitional categories ceased to play a clinical role, mainly as a result of the decline of the intellectualistic view of insanity and the recreation of the paranoia concept that gathered under its wing all primary disorders of intellect.[78]

The boundaries between insanity and neurosis and dementia were also undermined by the 'degeneration hypothesis'.[79] There was also a growing awareness of the existence of mixed clinical states that combined obsessional with affective, organic, and hallucinatory disorders. This also led to a belief in the existence of a mechanism of transition which explained symptomatic transformations (for example obsessions into delusions).

As the notion of 'folie lucide' faded away it became necessary to decide on the nosological status of the obsessional states. Some, like Morel,[80] chose to enhance the emotional aspect of these disorders and to consider them as 'neuroses' in a narrow sense (i.e. as disorders of the autonomic nervous system). Others, like Legrand de Saulle, [81] preferred to consider the obsessional disorders as a separate form of mental illness.

These two options influenced not only the modern view of the obsessional states but had wider repercussions: (a) the emphasis on emotions provided a clinical criterion to separate neurosis from insanity (before Freud), and (b) the classification of the obsessional states as a form of neurosis reinstituted 'insight' as a pathognomonic feature of insanity and resolved the 'insanity with insight' anomaly.

Obsessional states and the concept of neurosis

Morel described obsessional states as a form of 'délire émotif';[82] this category he considered not as 'an insanity but as a neurosis, that is a disease of the emotions'.[83] He wrote: 'what I call "délire émotif" corresponds to a particular type of fixed idea and abnormal act whose existence, however, does not entail an involvement of intellectual faculties'.[84] Morel's emphasis on the 'emotional' aspects constituted a departure from previous 'intellectualistic' interpretations. He explained the psychomotor 'drive' that led to the compulsion as a 'heightened affective state'. Baruk[85] has called this emotional dimension the 'infernal circle of the obsession' and suggested that 'it was for this reason that Morel called this phenomenon "délire émotif"'.

Morel's use of 'délire' is unconventional, and he requested that the term should not be taken in the general sense of 'folie'.[86] Analysis of the seven cases he reports confirms his idiosyncratic use. They presented with vasomotor and digestive symptoms, phobias,[87] dysphoria, unmotivated fears, fixed ideas, impulsions, and absence of cognitive impairment. The clinical presentation of Morel's cases is in fact similar to Janet's 'psychasthenias'.[88]

Morel considered this constellation of symptoms as a 'neurosis'. In the medicine of his time complaints such as these were imputed to the autonomic nervous system.[89] But he emphasized the 'functional lesion' view: 'As a result of the failure of anatomopathological research [the aetiological] issue cannot yet be clarified. Nonetheless the response [of the patients] to therapy confirms our theoretical claim that "délire émotif" constitutes a neurosis of the ganglionic system.'[90]

Morel's reclassification of the obsessional states caught on rapidly in French psychiatry for two reasons: it provided an alternative to the rival German view that obsessional states were a disorder of thinking akin to paranoia[91] and it allowed for a rational classification of a number of somatic symptoms, nowadays considered as 'anxiety-equivalents'.[92]

Luys[93] elaborated upon Morel's hypothesis. He suggested that ideas, emotions, and actions had separate cortical localization and hence nervous excitation might, according to the locus involved, give rise to 'bizarre ideas', 'involuntary' emotions, or compulsive acts. He disagreed with Morel's view that all vegetative functions were localized in the ganglionic system and suggested that the functions impaired in the obsessional disorders might in fact be sited on the cortex.[94]

Luys' view was well received. Magnan, expanding upon the clinical application of the degeneration hypothesis, suggested that in brains congenitally ill-developed (for example hereditary degenerates) there was a marked loss of functional interdependence. The resulting functional anarchy (or disjunction) could explain why in the same individual there was a coexistence of bizarre obsessions and normal ideas.[95] Magnan's view of degeneration was less religious and more reductionist than Morel's. Magnan defined degeneration as a gradual loss of cerebral 'synergistic' activity secondary to a primary disruption of anatomical pathways.[96] In general terms Magnan's view reflects the subtle shift from 'feelings' to 'movements'[97] that can be detected in European psychiatry at the time and that was to culminate in the work of Wernicke. The net effect of this conceptual shift on the obsessional disorders was the increasing emphasis given to compulsions.[98]

The period of clinical autonomy

The obsessional disorders were once again in difficulty after the appearance of neurasthenia, a popular category which threatened to engulf the entire class of neuroses.[99] The obsessional disorders were rescued by the magnificent work of Janet,[100] Pitres and Régis,[101] and Freud, all of whom endeavoured to make the obsessional disorders independent.

Pitres and Régis's *Les obsessions et les impulsions*[102]

These authors defined obsessions as: 'A morbid syndrome characterised by the anxious experiencing of parasitical thoughts and feelings which force themselves upon the self and lead to a form of psychical dissociation whose final stage is a splitting of the conscious personality' (p. 16). Concerning aetiology they wrote: 'We do not hesitate to consider the emotion as the primitive and fundamental element of the obsession' (p. 8).

Pitres and Régis divided the obsessional disorders into 'phobic' and 'ideational' and each type, in turn, into 'diffuse' and 'specific' (p. 19). They defended the 'emotivist' view at the twelfth International Congress of Medicine in Moscow in 1897.[103]

Janet

Janet considered the obsessional disorders[104] as a dislocation of *function*.[105] There was, according to him, an 'engourdissement' of the mind which required no anatomical substratum.[106] He regarded 'obsessions' as the experiential or subjective concomitant of a 'feeling of incompletion' that resulted from a profound defect in the 'function of the real'. This hypothesis probably amounts to no more than a metaphorical redescription of what patients often say in relation to their inability to complete tasks.

Janet created the category 'psychasthenia' which he carved out of neurasthenia.[107] Psychasthenia, itself an over-inclusive category, contained *inter alia* the obsessional disorders and soon became the new 'giant of neuropathology'.[108] In *L'Automatisme psychologique*[109] Janet had considered obsessions as a type of *idée fixe* which, together with hallucinations, constituted 'simple and rudimentary forms of mental activity'. In his *Nevroses et idées fixes* (a transitional work as far as the concept of obsession is concerned)[110] he moved away from Morel's view and distinguished 'délire émotif' from 'obsessions et compulsions'.

In his crowning work of 1903 Janet defined 'psychasthenia' as:

'A Psychoneurosis characterized by a reduction of the level of those functions that serve to control the environment and perceive reality, and which may be substituted by lower functions which manifest themselves as doubting, agitation and anxiety and by obsessional ideas'.[111]

This definition, however, is an 'aetiological' one and provides no recognizable diagnostic criteria.[112] It relies on theoretical mechanisms such as 'reduction' in psychological tension[113] and the non-introspective process of 'incompletion' (*inachèvement*).[114] Schwartz was right in referring to Janet's psychasthenia as 'a cluster of symptoms artificially demarcated to which the predominance of a "typical (causal) mechanism" conferred a particular aspect'.[115] Indeed, analysis of the 236 cases he reported in his book shows that psychasthenia not only included the obsessional disorders but also panic, phobic and tic disorders, hypochondriacal and confusional states, and some forms of epilepsy.

Janet's psychological view, however, placed the obsessional states firmly in the new territory of the 'neuroses' which comprised at the time neurasthenia, hysteria, and psychasthenia.[116] By 1911 these were still being defined as 'conditions affecting the nervous system *without* appreciable organic lesion in terms of the available techniques'.[117] In an interesting departure from Janet's views Raymond considered psychasthenia as a 'primitive alteration of psychomotor activity' (p. 30) where the 'doubts' constituted an intellectual 'equivalent' of volitional hesitation and motor uncertainty.

From this period on, the main textbooks began to treat the obsessional disorders in a separate section. For example Bianchi defined obsessions as 'psychic facts with an esthenic or emotive basis'.[118] Kraepelin treated them as 'Zwangsneurose' in the 1915 edition of his *Lehrbuch*.[119] Bleuler did likewise.[120]

Freud

Freud wrote on obsession in 1896:

'I have found reason to set alongside hysteria the obsessional neurosis [Zwangsneurose] as a self-sufficient and independent disorder, although the majority of the authorities placed obsessions among the syndromes constituting mental degeneracy or confused them with neurasthenia.'[121]

He suggested that obsessions and phobias should be separated from each other for in 'true obsessions it is quite plain that the emotional state is the chief element, since this state persists unchanged while the idea associated with this varies'.

Freud (1895) believed that the 'motive' for this substitution was a 'defensive reaction [Abwehr] of the ego against the intolerable idea'.[122] In a paper in the same journal a year later he extended his sexual theory from hysteria to obsessions:[123] 'The obsessional neurosis arises from a specific cause closely analogous to hysteria. A premature sexual experience which has occurred before puberty ... there is only one difference ... in the obsessional neuroses we are concerned with an experience that was pleasurable'.[124] These early views (which Freud was to disown) were based upon analogical transpositions of content to aetiology; that is, the detection of guilt in the obsessional patient suggested the presence of hidden sources of guilt (over the enjoyment of early and forbidden sexual activity). Likewise the 'substitution hypothesis' which accompanied these views was excessively mechanistic.[125]

Freud's conception of obsession changed *pari passu* with his theory of neurosis. He was to put more emphasis on the obsessional personality structure than on the mechanical production of obsessional symptoms.[126] The resulting structural and topographic hypotheses of the 'obsessional neuroses', although complex and attractive, have however had limited therapeutic value, even within orthodox Freudian analysis.[127]

Freud's two early papers on obsessions (although published in a French journal) had little impact on French psychiatry.[128] This may have resulted, surprisingly enough, from the fact that his early ideas did not seem to depart considerably from contemporary views.[129] Concerning this Dalbiez has said that French alienists 'ascribed to him a theory of obsessions akin to that of Pitres and Régis'.[130] Janet's rival hypothesis on the obsessional disorders, supported by his towering reputation, constituted yet another obstacle to the spread of Freudian views.[131]

Summary and conclusions

This chapter has dealt with two specific aspects of the nineteenth-century history of the obsessional disorders: terminology and taxonomy.

It has been shown that (a) a number of terms were tried to refer to the forms of behaviour currently known as obsessional; and (b) these terms were not passive labels – in fact their residual etymology evoked images and metaphors which have influenced the clinical and causal analysis of the obsessional disorders.

Concerning taxonomy, it has been shown that there were three stages in the evolution of these disorders: (a) obsessions as a form of insanity (monomania); (b) a transitional period following the collapse of the monomania concept which set the obsessional disorders adrift; (c) obsessions as neurosis following the transformation of the concepts of psychoses and neuroses during the second half of the nineteenth century.

It has also been shown that this reclassification required two major conceptual changes: from the descriptive viewpoint obsessions had to be redefined as non-delusional; from the aetiological viewpoint they had to be considered as 'functional'. This latter process culminated in the work of Janet whose psychological theory still contains vestiges of the 'degeneration view' and in the work of Freud who separated obsessions from phobias (giving up degeneration as an explanatory concept) and reaffirmed the nosological independence of the syndrome.

Notes

1 G.E. Berrios, 'Descriptive Psychopathology: Conceptual and Historical Aspects', *Psychological Medicine* 14 (1984): 303–13.
2 G.E. Berrios, 'Delirium and Confusion in the Nineteenth Century: A Conceptual History', *British Journal of Psychiatry* 139 (1981): 439–49.
3 Berrios, 'Descriptive Psychopathology'.
4 G.E. Berrios, 'Descriptive and Aetiological Aspects of the Obsessional Disorders during the Nineteenth Century: A Conceptual History', unpublished manuscript.
5 Early historical work is more accurate than recent publications on the obsessional states: e.g. P.L. Ladame, 'La Folie du doute et le délire du toucher', *Annales médico-psychologiques* 12 (1890): 368–86; W. Warda, 'Zur Geschichte und Kritik der sogenannten psychischen Zwangszustände', *Archiv für Psychiatrie und Nervenkrankheiten* 39 (1905): 239–85, 533–85; K. Schneider, 'Die Lehre vom Zwangsdenken in den zwölf Jahren', *Zeitletztenschrift für die Gesamte Neurologie and Psychiatrie* 16 (1918): 113–251; W. de Boor, 'Die Lehre vom Zwang Sammelbericht über die Jahre 1981–1947', *Fortschriften für Neurologie und Psychiatrie* 17 (1949): 49–72.
   For example S.J. Rachman and R.J. Hodgson, *Obsessions and Compulsions* (Englewood Cliffs, NJ: Prentice-Hall, 1980) refer to three (mythical) stages: 'Religious, medical and psychological' and claim (wrongly): 'for a considerable period of time obsessions were regarded as manifestation of depression' (p. 24).
   A. Black, 'The Natural History of Obsessional Neurosis', in H.R. Beech (ed.), *Obsessional States* (London: Methuen, 1974), pp. 19–54, accepts uncritically A. Lewis's view, in 'Obsessional Illness', *Acta Neuropsiquiatrica Argenti-*

Figure 6.1 'Madness'. Taken from Charles Bell, *Essays on the Anatomy of Expression in Painting* (London: Longman, 1806), p. 153. Wellcome Institute Library, London.

Figure 6.2 'Dämonomanie'. Taken from J.E.D. Esquirol,
Des Maladies Mentales (Paris: Baillière, 1838), pl. 6.
Wellcome Institute Library, London.

Figure 6.4 'Religious insane pride'. Taken from Alexander Morison, *The Physiognomy of Mental Diseases* (London: Longman, 1843), pl. 44. Wellcome Instiute Library, London.

Figure 6.3 'Chronic dementia'. Taken from Alexander Morison, *The Physiognomy of Mental Diseases* (London: Longman, 1843), pl. 77. Wellcome Institute Library, London.

Figure 6.5 'Monomanie du commandement militaire', by Theodore Géricault. Reproduced with the permission of the Sammlung Oskar Reinhart, am Römerholz, Winterthur.

Figure 6.6 'Monomanie du vol', by Theodore Géricault. Reproduced with
the permission of the Museum voor Schone Kunsten, Ghent.

Figure 6.7 'Monomanie de l'envie', by Theodore Géricault. Reproduced with the permission of the Musée des Beaux Arts de Lyon.

Figure 6.8 'Melancholia'. Patient in the Wakefield Asylum; a photograph sent by James Crichton Browne to Darwin (Darwin Archive, Cambridge University Library). Reproduced with the permission of the Syndics of Cambridge University Library.

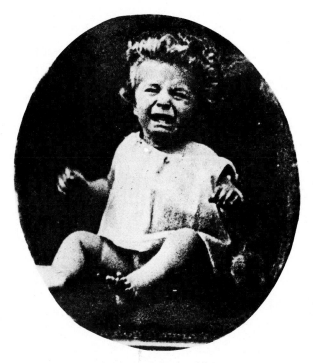

Figure 6.9 Child crying without weeping. Taken from C.R. Darwin, *The Expression of the Emotions in Man and Animals* (London: J. Murray, 1872), facing p. 148. Wellcome Institute Library, London.

Figure 6.10 Oskar Rejlander simulating suffering (on the left) and laughter (on the right) (Darwin Archive, Cambridge University Library). Reproduced with the permission of the Syndics of Cambridge University Library.

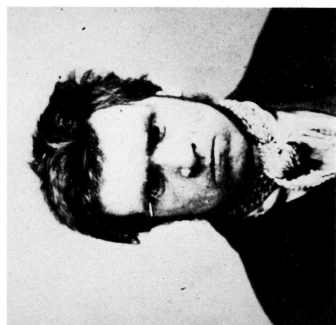

Figure 6.12 'Epileptic dementia'. Patient in the Wakefield Asylum; a photograph supplied by James Crichton Browne. Reproduced with the permission of the Syndics of Cambridge University Library.

Figure 6.11 'Euphoria mania'. Patient in the Wakefield Asylum; a photograph supplied by James Crichton Browne. Reproduced with the permission of the Syndics of Cambridge University Library.

na 3 (1957): 323–35, p. 20, that Janet had made the most 'authoritative' attempt to delineate the syndrome and (wrongly) considers Westphal as the first to give a 'comprehensive definition [of obsessions] as ideas which come to consciousness in spite of and contrary to the will of the patient'.

A. Carr, 'Compulsive Neurosis: A Review of the Literature', *Psychological Bulletin* 81 (1974): 311–18, (wrongly) claims 'it was not until 1925 that the first formal definition of a compulsion was proposed (Schneider)' (p. 311), thus ignoring at least seventy-five years of detailed work on 'impulsions', the term used to refer to this very phenomenon (H.Ey, 'Impulsions. Etude No. 11', in *Etudes Psychiatriques* (Paris: Desclée de Brouwer, 1950), vol. 2, pp. 163–212).

L. Salzman and F.H. Thaler, 'Obsessive-Compulsive Disorders', *American Journal of Psychiatry* 138 (1981): 286–96, do away with the most important period in the history of the obsessional disorders by taking an olympian leap from the 'earliest theories [that] involved the notion of possession' to 'the first dynamic and rational hypotheses developed by Freud' (p. 286). Although Freud contributed to the evolution of the notion of obsessional state it is inaccurate to attribute to him the first 'rational' theory.

A. Lewis, in 'Problems of Obsessional Illness', *Proceedings of the Royal Society of Medicine* 29 (1936): 325–36, p. 144, states that Bleuler 'considered obsessional neuroses to be latent schizophrenia'. What E. Bleuler, in *Textbook of Psychiatry* (New York: Macmillan, 1934), really said was: 'Obsessions occur temporarily in neurasthenic and melancholic states, in schizophrenia, and also as a special, and frequently very severe, disease, in people originally disposed to such abnormalities' (pp. 89–90).

Lewis, in 'Obsessional Illness', also states (without providing a reference) that Griesinger had identified in 1867 the relationship of obsessional disorders and manic depressive psychosis (p. 160). Although W. Griesinger did present a paper to the Medico-Psychological Association in Berlin on 23 March, 1868, on 'Über einen wenig bekannten psychopathischen Zustand' (three cases with obsessional features) (*Archiv für Psychiatrie und Nervenkrankheiten* 1 (1868): 626–35), he did not touch on the said association.

6 For example Robert Burton, *The Anatomy of Melancholy* (London: Chatto and Windus, 1883), (quoting Montanus) described an individual who

'dared not go over a bridge, come near a pool, rock, steep hill, lie in a chamber where cross beams were, for fear he be tempted to hang, drown or precipitate himself. If he [was] in a silent auditorium as at a sermon, he [was] afraid he shall speak aloud at unawares, something indecent, unfit to be said' (p. 253)

Bishop Moore of Norwich referred to those who are overwhelmed by 'naughty and sometimes blasphemous thoughts' which 'start in their minds while they are exercised in the Worship of God' (G. Mora, 'The Scrupulosity Syndrome', *International Journal of Clinical Psychology* 5 (1969): 163–74, p. 163). The word 'scruple' (small, sharp, or pointed stone) (C.T. Lewis and C. Short, *A Latin Dictionary* (Oxford: Clarendon Press, 1879)) was used during the seventeenth century to refer to repetitive thoughts of religious nature. Bishop J. Taylor, in *Ductor dubitantium, or the Rule of Conscience*, 2 vols (London: Royston, 1660), wrote: 'scruple is a great trouble of minde proceeding from a little motive, and a great indisposition, by which the conscience though sufficiently determined by proper arguments, dares not proceed to action, or if it doe, it cannot rest' (vol. 1, p. 208).

David Hartley, in *Observations on Man, His Frame, His Duty and His Expectations* (1749), 6th edn (London: Thomas Tegg and Son, 1834) described states of 'frequent recurrency of the same ideas':

'When a person applies himself to any particular study, so as to fix his attention deeply on ideas and terms belonging to it ... it is commonly observed, that he becomes narrow minded ... the perpetual recurrency of particular ideas and terms makes the vibrations belonging thereto become more than ordinarily vivid, converts associations into strong ones' (p. 249)

James Boswell, in *The Life of Dr Johnson* (1791), 2 vols (London: J.M. Dent, 1933), wrote of Johnson:

'He had another particularity ... it appeared to me some superstitious habit, which had contracted early ... this was his anxious care to go out or in at a door or passage, by a certain number of steps from a certain point, or at least so that either his right or his left foot (I am not certain which) should constantly make the first actual movement when he came close to the door or passage.'

See the essay by Roy Porter in this volume.

7 The popular view that the obsessional disorders may be volitional dysfunctions can be traced back to the adoption of these will-related terms as official clinical names.

8 Berrios, 'Descriptive Psychopathology'.

9 P. Pichot, 'The Diagnosis and Classification of Mental Disorders in French Speaking Countries', *Psychological Medicine* 12 (1982): 475–92.

10 R. Krafft-Ebing, 'Über Geistestörung durch Zwangsvorstellungen', *Allgemeine Zeitschrift für Psychiatrie* 35 (1879): 303–28.

11 M. O'C. Walshe, *A Concise German Etymological Dictionary* (London: Routledge and Kegan Paul, 1951), pp. 260–61.

12 B. Llopis, 'Translator's Note', in K. Schneider, *Las personalidades psicopáticas* (Barcelona: Editorial Cientifico-Medica, 1950), p. 104.

13 Walshe, *Concise German Etymological Dictionary*.

14 N. Abbagnano, *Dizionario di filosofia* (Turin: Unione Tipografico-Editrice, 1961).

15 Th. Ribot, *La Psychologie allemande contemporaine*, 2nd edn (Paris: Felix Alcan, 1885), pp. 21–5; B. Erdmann, 'Vorstellung', *Viertel-jarsch. für wissenschaftliche Philosophie* 10 (1886): 307–15.

16 S. Monserrat-Esteve, J.M. Costa Molinari, and C. Ballús (eds), 'Patología obsesiva', in *Ponencias de el xi Congreso Nacional de Neuro-psiquiatria* (Málaga: Graficasa, 1971).

17 K. Westphal, 'Über Zwangsvorstellungen', *Archiv für Psychiatrie and Nervenkrankheiten* 8 (1877): 734–50.

18 W. Bräutigam, 'Zwang', in Ch. Muller (ed.), *Lexicon der Psychiatrie* (Berlin: Springer, 1973), pp. 586–87.

19 S. Rado, 'Obsessive Behaviour', in S. Arieti (ed.), *American Handbook of Psychiatry* (New York: Basic Books, 1959), p. 324.

20 Griesinger, 'Über einen wenig bekannten psychopathischen Zustand'.

21 Walshe, *Concise German Etymological Dictionary*.

22 Monserrat-Esteve, Molinari, and Ballús, 'Patología Obsesiva'; P. Matussek, 'Zwang und Sucht', *Nervenarzt* 29 (1958): 452–56.

23 Julius Donath ('Zur Kenntniss des Anancasmus (psychische Zwangszustände)', *Archiv für Psychiatrie und Nervenkrankheiten* 29 (1897): 211–24 suggested in a lecture before the Royal Medical Society of Budapest in November 1895, that the term 'Anancasmus' (ἀναγχασκές = necessitas = das Zwingen) be used to name the condition that Thompsen, in 'Klinische Beiträge zur Lehre von den Zwangsvorstellungen und verwandten psychischen Zuständen', *Archiv für Psychiatrie und Nervenkrankheiten* 27 (1895): 319–85, had called 'idiopathic obsessional state'.

24 K. Schneider, *Las personalidades psicopáticas* (Barcelona: Editorial Científico-Médica, 1950), p. 40.

25 E. Kahn, 'Die anankastische Psychopathen', in O. Bumke (ed.), *Handbuch der Geisteskrankheiten* (Berlin: Springer, 1928), vol. 5, part 1; G. Skoog, 'The Anancastic Syndrome and Its Relation to Personality Attitude', *Acta Psychiatrica Scandinavica* 34 (1959) (Suppl. 134): 5–207; Th. Videbech, 'The Psychopathology of Anancastic Endogenous Depression', *Acta Psychiatrica Scandinavica* 52 (1975): 336–73; W. Blakenburg, 'Anankastische Psychopathie', in Ch. Muller (ed.), *Lexicon der Psychiatrie*; I.C.D. 9, *Mental Disorders: Glossary and Guide to Their Classification* (Geneva: World Health Organisation, 1978), p. 39.

26 A. Porot, *Manuel alphabétique de psychiatrie* (Paris: Presses Universitaires de France, 1975): A. Green, 'Obsessions et psychonévrose obsessionelle', in *Encyclopédie médico-chirurgical de psychiatrie* (Paris: Editions Techniques, 1965), vol. 3 (37370 A 10).

27 H.G. Richter, 'Some Observations on Anancasm', *American Journal of Psychiatry* 96 (1939): 1459–467.

28 Th. Ziehen, 'Zur Lehre von den psychopathischen Konstitutionen. (d) Zwangsvorstellungen und andere psychische Zwangsprozesse', *Charite-Annalen (Berlin)* 32 (1908): 113–32.

29 Schneider, *Las personalidades psicopáticas*.

30 Ph. Pinel, *Traité médico-philosophique sur l'aliénation mentale*, 2nd edn (Paris: J. Ant. Brosson, 1809).

31 J.P. Falret, *Des Maladies mentales et des asiles aliénés. Leçons cliniques et considérations générales* (Paris: J.B. Baillière, 1864), pp. 425–48.

32 H. Legrande du Saulle, *La Folie du doute (avec délire da toucher)* (Paris: Adrien Delahaye, 1875).

33 U. Trelat, *La Folie Lucide* (Paris, 1861).

34 B.A. Moyel, 'Du Délire émotif. Névrose du système nerveux ganglionaire viscéral', *Archives générales de médecine* vi^e séries 7 (1866): 385–402, 530–51, 700–07.

35 J.M. Charcot and V. Magnan, 'De l'Onomatomanie', *Archives de neurologie* 10 (1885): 157–68; J. Seglas, 'Des Troubles de la fonction da langage dans l'onomatomanie', *Médecine moderne* 2, no. 2 (1891): 845–47.

36 E. Littré, *Dictionnaire de la langue française* (Paris: Librairie Hachette, 1877), vol. 3, p. 784.

37 J. Luys, 'Des Obsessions pathologiques dans leurs rapports avec l'activité automatique des éléments nerveux', *L'Encéphale* 3 (1883): 20–61.

38 Littré, *Dictionnaire de la langue française*; J. Jastrow, 'Obsession', in J.M. Baldwin (ed.), *Dictionary of Philosophy and Psychology* (London: Macmillan, 1901), vol. 2, p. 198.

39 J. Falret, 'Obsessions intellectuelles et émotives', *Archives de Neurologie* 2 (1889): 274–93; B. Ball, 'Des Obsessions en pathologie mentale', *Annales de*

psychiatrie et d'hypnologie 2 (1892): 1–15; Van Eeden, 'Les Obsessions', *Revue de l'hypnotisme* 6 (1892): 5–14.

40 J.B. Parchappe, 'Symptomatologie de la folie', *Annales médico-psychologiques* 3 (1851): 62.

41 A. Brierre de Boismont, 'De l'Etat des facultés dans les délires partiels ou monomanies', *Annales médico-psychologiques* 5 (1853): 567–91.

42 M.H. Dagonet, 'Des Impulsions dans la folie et de la folie impulsive', *Annales médico-psychologiques* 4 (1870): 5–32, 215–59.

43 A. Lalande, *Vocabulaire technique et critique de la philosophie* (Paris: Presses Universitaires de France, 1976), pp. 820–21.

44 G.E. Berrios, 'Henri Ey, Jackson et les idées obsédantes', *L'Evolution psychiatrique* 12 (1977): 687–99.

45 D.H. Tuke, 'Imperative Ideas', in D.H. Tuke (ed.), *A Dictionary of Psychological Medicine* (London: J. and A. Churchill, 1892), vol. 1, pp. 678–81.

46 W.J. Mickle, 'Mental Besetments', *Journal of Mental Science* 42 (1896): 691–719.

47 Royal College of Physicians, *The Nomenclature of Diseases*, 4th edn (London: His Majesty's Stationery Office, 1906).

48 M. Legrain, 'Obsession and Impulse', in Tuke (ed.), *A Dictionary of Psychological Medicine*, vol. 1, pp. 866–68.

49 Tuke, 'Imperative Ideas'.

50 'Mental Obsession', editorial in *British Medical Journal* 2 (1901): 100; 'Obsessions and Morbid Impulses', editorial in *Lancet* 1 (1904): 1441.

51 J. Shaw, 'Obsessions', *Journal of Mental Science* 50 (1904): 234–49.

52 T. Diller, 'Obsessions; Fixed Ideas, Indecisions, Imperative Conceptions, Abulias, Phobias', *The Medical News* 81 (1902): 961–68.

53 H.L. Snow, 'Doubting Madness', *British Medical Journal* 2 (1878): 474.

54 P.C. Knapp, 'The Insanity of Doubt', *American Journal of Psychology* (Worcester) 3 (1890): 1–23.

55 The medical view of the obsessional disorders starts with the early nineteenth-century attempts to classify the phenomena as a disease. The fact, however, that during this period both the concepts of neurosis (J.M. Lopez Piñero, *Historical Origins of the Concept of Neurosis*, trans. D. Berrios (Cambridge: Cambridge University Press, 1983)) and psychosis (insanity) (J.J. Sauri, 'Las Significaciones del vocable psicosis', *Acta psiquiatrica psicologica de America latina* 18 (1972): 219–26; C. Masi, 'Histoire des psychoses endogènes', *L'Information psychiatrique* 57 (1981): 57–72) were undergoing major transformation creates severe difficulties for the historian. These categories only achieved a semantic steady state by the very end of the century.

56 E. Esquirol, *Des Maladies mentales considérées sous les rapports médical, hygiéniques et médico-légales*, 2 vols (Paris: Baillière, 1838).

57 Ladame, 'La Folie du doute'; A. Ritti, 'Folie du doute avec délire du toucher', in A. Dechambre (ed.), *Dictionnaire encyclopédique des sciences médicales* (Paris: Asselin 1876), pp. 339–48; A. Pitres and E. Régis, *Les Obsessions et les impulsions* (Paris: Octave Doin, 1902), p. 434.

Pinel has been considered, rather anachronistically, as the first to include 'obsessions', under the category of 'folie (manie) raisonnante' (Green, 'Obsessions et psychonévrose obsessionelle'; Ladame, 'La Folie du doute'). For this the only evidence presented is his report of a man who feared that 'his nose would become detached into his handkerchief if he blew it too strongly', and who also 'felt the compulsion of slashing his throat when shaving' (Pinel, *Traité médico-philosophique sur l'aliénation mentale*, p. 95). Pinel's intention, however, when including this clinical vignette, was to describe 'folie raisonnante' as a disorder in which 'judgement was preserved', for the 'patient could be shown to offer adequate answers in spite of his extravagant fears' (p. 93). It is beyond the scope of this chapter to analyse Pinel's taxonomy – for this see P. Bercherie, *Les Fondements de la clinique. Histoire et structure du savoir psychiatrique* (Paris: La Bibliothèque d'Ornicar, 1980); G. Swain, *Le Sujet de la folie. Naissance de la psychiatrie* (Paris: Privat, 1977); J.M. Lopez Piñero, 'Orígenes históricos del concepto de neurosis', *Cuadernos Valenciauos de historia de la medicina* (Valencia: Industrias Graficas, ELIR, 1963).

Warda, in 'Zur Geschichte und Kritik', in turn has claimed that Hoffbauer, *Die Psychologie in ihren Hauptanwendungen auf die Rechtspflege* (Halle, 1808), had already identified 'obsessional contrary-associations' as 'states of blind impulse to carry out specific acts' (p. 240).

58 Esquirol, *Des Maladies mentales*, vol. 2, p. 1.
59 Esquirol, *Des Maladies mentales*, vol. 2, p. 2.
60 Partial insanity was distinguished from general insanity before and during the nineteenth century (G.E. Berrios, 'The Two Manias', *British Journal of Psychiatry*, 139 (1981): 258–60; J. Kageyama, 'Sur l'Histoire de la monomanie', *L'Evolution psychiatrique* 49 (1984): 155–62) on the basis of four criteria: (1) symptom intensity; (2) extension of the personality involvement; (3) impairment of selective psychological functions; and (4) exclusiveness of the delusion.

Criteria one, two, and four were used in pre-nineteenth-century classifications (P. Zacchias, *Questione medico-légales* (Lugduni: Editio Nova, 1701); M. Casaubon, *A Treatise Concerning Enthusiasme ...* (London: Johnson, 1655), pp. 87–9). Criterion three was made possible only by the reintroduction during the early nineteenth century of faculty psychology, i.e. the view that the human mind could be operatively analysed into autonomous faculties. Kant and the Scottish philosophers were important in this context (F.M. Albrecht, 'A Reappraisal of Faculty Psychology', *Journal of the History of the Behavioral Sciences* 6 (1970): 36–40; G.P. Brooks, 'The Faculty Psychology of Thomas Reid', *Journal of the History of the Behavioral Sciences* 12 (1976): 65–77; E.R. Hilgard, 'The Trilogy of Mind: Cognition, Affection and Conation', *Journal of the History of the Behavioral Sciences* 16 (1980): 107–17.

The influence of faculty psychology is clearer in the work of Esquirol than in Pinel. For example, the difference between 'mania' and 'melancholia' in the work of the latter was not based on faculty psychology but on the pre-nineteenth-century criterion of a total versus a partial involvement of the intellectual faculty. Esquirol's classification of monomania, however, as an impairment of intellect, emotion, and will is based on faculty psychology (Esquirol, *Des Maladies mentales*; L.F. Calmeil, 'Monomanie', in *Dictionnaire de médecine ou repertoire général des sciences médicales considérées sous les rapports théoriques et pratiques*, 2nd edn (Paris: Bechet et Labé, 1839), vol. 20, pp. 138–68; E. Billod, 'Maladies de la volonté', *Annales médico-psychologiques* 10 (1847): 15–35, 170–202, 317–47; Brierre de Boismont, 'De l'Etat des facultés'). Likewise the affective faculty becomes relevant to the analysis and classification of melancholia only in the work of Esquirol (L.J.F. Delasiauve, 'Du Diagnostic differential de la lypémanie', *Annales médico-psychologiques* 3 (1851): 380–442; Berrios, 'Descriptive Psychopathology').

Esquirol's views however were not accepted by all his contemporaries. Falret Senior had opposed it in 1819 and so did his son forty years later (Falret, *Des Maladies mentales*). Both invoked the principle of 'mental solidarity' according to which no individual faculty could be independently impaired. Hence they concluded that 'folie raisonnante' and 'monomania' were not clinically possible (J. Falret, 'Discussion sur la folie raisonnante', *Annales médico-psychologiques* 24 (1866): 382–426). In spite of this dissenting view the notion of partial insanity held sway until the 1860s.

During the same period English alienists also considered the obsessional disorders as a form of partial insanity. For example J.C. Prichard, in *A Treatise on Insanity and Other Disorders Affecting the Mind* (London: Sherwood, Gilbert, and Piper, 1835), included a typical obsessive-compulsive disorder under the category of 'moral insanity' (case 1, p. 35).

61 Calmeil, 'Monomanie'; A. Linas, 'Monomanie', in A. Dechambre (ed.), *Dictionnaire encyclopédique des sciences médicales* (Paris: Asselin, 1871), 2nd series, vol. 5, pp. 146–95.
62 Esquirol, *Des Maladies mentales*, vol. 2, p. 70.
63 Billod, 'Maladies de la volonté'.
64 F. Winslow, 'On Monomania', *Journal of Psychological Medicine and Mental Pathology* 9 (1856): 501–21.
65 Falret, *Des Maladies Mentales*; Falret, 'Discussion sur la folie raisonnante'.
66 G.E. Berrios, 'Pseudodementia or Melancholic Dementia: A Nineteenth-Century View', *Journal of Neurology, Neurosurgery and Psychiatry* 48 (1985): 393–400.
67 Kageyama, 'Sur l'Histoire de la monomanie'.
68 G.E. Berrios, 'The Psychopathology of Affectivity: Conceptual and Historical Aspects', *Psychological Medicine* (in press, 1985).
69 R. de Saussure, 'The Influence of the Concept of Monomonia on French Medico-Legal Psychiatry (from 1825–1840)', *Journal of the History of Medicine* 1 (1946): 365–97.
70 The debate on monomania at the Societé Médico-Psychologique lasted ten sessions (S.M.P., 'Discussion sur la monomanie (minutes)', *Annales médico-psychologiques* 6 (1854): 99–118, 273–98, 464–74, 629–44) and dealt with three issues: (1) whether it was possible for mental faculties to break down independently (the solidarity v. autonomy question); (2) whether it made clinical sense to bring together disparate clinical states under one category (i.e. monomania); and (3) whether mental illness could be considered as an exaggeration of ordinary behaviour (continuity hypothesis) or whether it constituted a new state (discontinuity hypothesis).

The first issue as to the nature of mental faculties remained unresolved (A. Jacques, 'Facultés de l'âme', in M.A. Franck (ed.), *Dictionnaire des sciences philosophiques* (Paris: Hachette, 1875). The question on the usefulness of monomania was answered in the negative for it had given rise to many clinical (S.M.P., 'Discussion sur la monomanie') and legal problems (Saussure, 'Influence of the Concept of Monomania'); in the event it was dropped in spite of some spirited defence (Brierre de Boismont, 'De l'Etat des facultés'). The continuity v. discontinuity issue was partially resolved by suggesting a combination of the two.
71 Bercherie, 'Les Fondements de la clinique'.
72 Ch. Bardenat, 'Monomanie', in A. Porot (ed.), *Manuel alphabétique de psychiatrie* (Paris: Presses Universitaires de France, 1975); Linas, 'Monomanie'.

73 The word 'neurosis' evoked in many the image of hysteria and hypochondria
   and no longer the generic 'nervous affection of Cullen's nosology' (R.G. Mayne,
   *An Expository Lexicon of the Terms, Ancient and Modern, in Medical and
   General Science* (London: John Churchill, 1860)). In fact, the majority of
   conditions classified by Cullen as neuroses had already been separated off on the
   basis of a related anatomical lesion (Lopez Piñero, *Concept of Neurosis*).
       In clinical practice there was no general diagnostic picture for the neuroses.
   The 'functional lesion' view had become predominant: Neuroses were defined
   as: 'Affections of the nervous system occurring without material agent producing them without inflammation or any other constant structural change which
   can be detected in the nervous centres; in other words, functional affections of
   the nervous system' (P.W. Latham, 'Neuroses', in R. Quain (ed.), *A Dictionary
   of Medicine*, 2 vols (London: Longmans, Green, 1894). This definition offered
   little clinical help although it contributed to the separation of the neuroses from
   the psychoses.
74 J. Locke, *An Essay Concerning Human Understanding* (1690), collated and
   annotated by A.C. Fraser (New York: Dover, 1959).
75 Berrios, 'Pseudodementia'.
76 Trelat, *La Folie lucide*.
77 Esquirol, *Des Maladies mentales*.
78 E. Lanteri-Laura and M. Gros, 'La paranoia', in J. Postel and C. Quétel (eds),
   Nouvelle histoire de la psychiatrie (Paris: Privat, 1983), pp. 334–41; see also
   G.R.H. Génil-Perrin, *Les paranoiaques* (Paris: Maloine, 1926).
79 Since G.P.H. Génil-Perrin's important doctoral thesis ('Histoire des origines et
   de l'évolution de l'idée de dégénérescence en médecine mental', thesis (Paris:
   Alfred Leclerc, 1913)), scholarship on the degeneration theory has gradually
   accumulated (for references see R. Friedlander, *Bénédict-Augustin Morel and
   the Development of the Theory of Degenerescence (The Introduction of Anthropology into Psychiatry)* (doctoral thesis, San Francisco, University of California,
   1973)).
       The definitive study on B.A. Morel's total contribution to nineteenth-century
   psychiatry, however, is yet to be published. Born in Vienna, orphaned early and
   brought up by a priest in Luxembourg, Morel's first passion was the natural
   sciences. Claude Bernard, with whom he shared students' digs, put him in
   contact with Falret and through him with psychiatry. A complex intellectual
   figure, Morel's views brought together religion, creationism, Lamarckianism,
   and empirical observations (for example his work on cretins).
       His book on degeneration appeared in 1857 and became influential on
   psychiatry although its psychiatric sections are rather short and not specific. He
   reserved the term 'degeneration' for pathological processes and developed a
   longitudinal, trans-generational model of disease according to which the inherited disorder grows worse from father to son and to grandson. He identified as
   the principle of degeneration the original sin which had rendered man susceptible to the assaults of the environment. His Lamarckianism led him to put a
   great deal of emphasis on external events and this was of considerable importance
   to psychiatry. At the same time, and rather paradoxically, his view of degeneration as an internal process gave rise, as K. Jaspers noted (*General Psychopathology*, trans. J. Hoenig and M.W. Hamilton (Manchester: Manchester University
   Press, 1963)), to the notion of endogenicity in psychiatry. See the essay by
   Dowbiggin in this volume.
80 Morel, 'Du Délire émotif'.

81 Legrand du Saulle, *La Folie du doute*.

82 Morel, 'Du Délire émotif'. 'Délire émotif' has no adequate rendition in English. The term 'délire', in general, illustrates well the conceptual differences that separate psychiatry on both sides of the channel (B. Ball and E. Christian, 'Délire', in A. Dechambre (ed.), *Dictionnaire encyclopédique des sciences médicales* (1882), vol. 26, pp. 315–408; H. Ey, 'Groupe des psychoses schizophréniques et des psychoses délirantes chroniques', in L. Moreau (ed.), *Encyclopédie médico-chirurgicale de psychiatrie* (Paris: Editions Techniques, 1955), vol. 2 (37281 A10); H. Faure, *Les Appartenances du délirant* (Paris: Presses Universitaires de France, 1971); Pichot, 'Diagnosis and Classification'). The meaning of 'délire' is wider than 'delusion' but narrower than insanity (P. Marchais, *Les Processes psychopathologiques de l'adulte* (Paris: Privat, 1981)). Thus an old French psychiatric saying stated: 'si toute folie est un délire, tout délire n'est pas une folie' (Morel, 'Du Délire émotif', p. 386). In French psychopathology the word 'délire' has both descriptive and explanatory functions (J.M. Sutter, A. Tatossian, and J.C. Scotto, 'Les Délires chroniques', in *Encyclopédie médico-chirurgical de psychiatrie* (1981), vol. 3 (37299 A10)); it also suggests an involvement of the 'personality'; hence it has less intellectual allusions than the English word delusion (A.Z. Arthur, 'Theories and Explanations of Delusions: A Review', *American Journal of Psychiatry* 121 (1964): 105–15).
    In nineteenth-century French psychiatry terms such as 'délire émotif', 'délire de toucher' had wide currency. In all cases the important element was not the 'idées ou thèmes délirants' but the 'profound alteration of the psyche' (A. Porot, 'Délires (Généralités)', in Porot (ed.), *Manuel alphabétique de psychiatrie*). Legrand de Saulle referred to obsessions as 'idées délirantes' (*La Folie du doute*, p. 8). Ball agreed: 'Obsessionals know of their impulses; they are victims of a "délire", of a "délire avec conscience", of a "délire whose absurd nature they well realize"' ('Des Obsessions en pathologie mentale', p. 8).

83 Pitres and Régis, *Les Obsessions et les impulsions*, p. 2.

84 Morel, 'Du Délire émotif', p. 385.

85 H. Baruk, *Traité de psychiatrie*, 2 vols (Paris: Masson, 1959), p. 122.

86 Morel, 'Du Délire émotif', p. 705.

87 During the 1860s phobias were a symptom of 'délire émotif' and had no independent clinical or taxonomic pigeon-hole; their gradual separation started with Westphal (P. Errera, 'Some Historical Aspects of the Concept of Phobia', *Psychiatric Quarterly* 36 (1962): 325–36) and culminated with Eeden, 'Les Obsessions', and S. Freud, 'Obsessions et phobies', *Revue Neurologique* 3 (1895): 33–8.

88 P. Janet, *Les Obsessions et la psychasthénie* (Paris: Félix Alcan, 1911, first published 1903).

89 López Piñero, 'Orígenes históricos del concepto de neurosis'.

90 Morel, 'Du Délire émotif', p. 706.

91 A. Meyer, 'The Relation of Emotional and Intellectual Functions in Paranoia and in Obsessions', *Psychological Bulletin* 3 (1906): 255–74.

92 E. Doyen, 'Quelques considérations sur les terreurs morbides et le délire émotif en general', *L'Encéphale* 4 (1885): 418–38.

93 Luys, 'Des Obsessions pathologiques', p. 24.

94 R. Semelaigne, *Les Pionniers de la psychiatrie française (Après Pinel-suite)* (Paris: Baillière, 1932), vol. 2, p. 39.

95 Magnan's view on the 'disjunction' of anatomical structures was developed in various ways. For example Améline ('Considérations sur la psychophysiologie des obsessions et impulsions dégénératives', in IVe Congrès Internationale de Psychologie, *Comptes Rendus* (Paris: Félix Alcan, 1901), pp. 572–78) postulated, resorting to the law of thermodynamics, that the loss or absence of adequate connection in the degenerate brain prevented accumulation of 'generational entropy', leading to the eventual disappearance of that particular lineage.

96 Cl. Vurpas, 'Les Obsessions, les impulsions et les perversions sexuelles dans l'oeuvre de Magnan, *Annales médico-psychologiques* 93 (1935): 748–59, p. 757.

97 H. Hecaen and G. Lanteri-Laura, *Evolution des connaissances et des doctrines sur les localisations cérébrales* (Paris: Desclée de Brouwer, 1977).

98 Marchais, *Les Processes psychopathologiques*, p. 165.

99 T.D. Savill, *Clinical Lectures on Neurasthenia*, 3rd edn (London: Henry J. Glaisher, 1906); I.G. Cobb, *A Manual of Neurasthenia (Nervous Exhaustion)* (London: Baillière, Tindall, and Cox, 1920).

100 Cobb, in *Manual of Neurasthenia*, wrote that by creating the category of psychasthenia Janet had 'split off the mental symptoms of the exhaustion syndrome' (neurasthenia) (p. 352).

101 Pitres and Régis, *Les Obsessions et les impulsions*.

102 Published at the turn of the century, this book represents the culmination of a process started forty years before. Green, in 'Obsessions et psychoneurose obsessionelle', was right in calling it 'the swan song of the classical studies into obsessional pathology' (p. 1).

103 The debate was to continue in the Paris Medical Congress of 1900 when Haskovec ('Contribution à la connaissance des idées obsédantes', presented at XIIIᶜ Congrès International de Médecine, 1900, section de psychiatrie, Paris – 'Comptes rendus' (pp. 121–31) and *Revue Neurologique* 9 (1901): 341–49) defended the 'intellectualistic' hypothesis. A few years later Janet was to criticize the excessive associationistic view of Pitres and Régis.

104 Janet, *Les Obsessions et la psychasthénie*.

105 The process that led to the 'psychogenic' view of the neuroses started earlier in the century. Failure to find an anatomical lesion led to the search for a 'functional' impairment. To this explanatory shift the notions of spinal irritability and reflex action were important (Lopez Piñero, *Concept of Neurosis*).

The second stage in the process was to 'psychologize' the physiological notion of 'function' (which was still 'organic' in a real sense). This occurred gradually in the work of Charcot, the hypnotists, and Freud (J.M. Lopez Piñero and J.M. Morales Meseguer, *Neurosis y psicoterapia. Un estudio historico* (Madrid: Espasa-Calpe, 1970).

106 H. Baruk, *La Psychiatrie française de Pinel à nos jours* (Paris: Presses Universitaires de France, 1967), p. 98.

107 J.C. Chatel and R. Peel, 'The Concept of Neurasthenia', *International Journal of Psychiatry* 9 (1971): 76–9; Cobb, *Manual of Neurasthenia*.

108 P. Dubois, *Les Psychonévroses* (Paris: Masson, 1909), p. 241. Jaspers, in *General Psychopathology*, also made a similar comment: 'some of Janet's cases of psychasthenia are obviously, in part, schizophrenic' (p. 442). Janet can be forgiven, however, for this, as in 1903 the concept of schizophrenia had not yet been fully developed and that of 'dementia praecox' was finding some resistance in France (V. Parant, 'D'une Prétendre entité morbide dite démence précoce',

Annales médico-psychologiques 9:1 (1905): 229–41).

109 P. Janet, *L'Automatisme psychologique* (1889), 7th edn (Paris: Félix Alcan, 1911), p. 1.

110 F. Raymond and P. Janet, *Névroses et idées fixes* (1898) (Paris: Félix Alcan, 1908), vol. 2.

111 Janet, *Les Obsessions et la psychasthénie*, p. 756.

112 A. Hesnard, 'Psychasthénie', in Porot (ed.), *Manuel alphabétique de psychiatrie*, p. 525.

113 B. Sjövall, *Psychology of Tension. An Analysis of Pierre Janet's Concept of 'Tension Psychologique' together with an Historical Aspect* (Stockholm: Svenska Bökforlaget, 1967).

114 C.M. Prévost, *La Psycho-philosophie de Pierre Janet* (Paris: Payot, 1973).

115 L. Schwartz, *Les Névroses et la psychologie dynamique de Pierre Janet* (Paris: Presses Universitaires de France, 1955), p. 303.
    In spite of its overinclusiveness the notion of 'psychasthenia' received for a time international approval (viz. Dubois, *Les Psychonévroses*; E. Fernandez Sanz, *Las psiconeurosis* (Madrid: Calpe, 1921)). This was not to last (E. Minkowski, *Traité de psychopathologie* (Paris: Presses Universitaires de France, 1966)), and nowadays the term is used as a quaint synonym for 'constitutional psychic weakness' (H. Kind, 'Psychasthénie', in Ch. Müller (ed.), *Lexicon der Psychiatrie* (Berlin: Springer, 1973), p. 394) and 'asthenic psychopathy' (K. Schneider, *Clinical Psychopathology*, trans. M.W. Hamilton and E.W. Anderson (New York: Grune and Stratton, 1959), p. 27. Its speculative basis and clinical overinclusiveness have probably been the main cause of its failure. Efforts to reinterpret 'psychological tension' in terms of the 'cortical arousal' concept have not succeeded (B. Llopis, *Introducción a la psicopatologia* (Madrid: Ediciones Morata, 1970), p. 105).

116 Lopez Piñero and Morales Meseguer, *Neurosis y psicoterapia*.

117 F. Raymond, 'Névroses et psycho-névroses', in A. Marie (ed.), *Traité international de psychologie pathologique* (Paris: Alcan, 1911), vol. 2, pp. 1–59, p. 2.

118 L. Bianchi, *A Textbook of Psychiatry*, trans. J.H. MacDonald (London: Baillière, Tindall, and Cox, 1906), p. 620.

119 E. Kraepelin, *Klinische Psychiatrie. Ein Lehrbuch für Studierende und Ärzte* (Leipzig: Johann Ambrosius Barth, 1915), vol. 4, pp. 1823–1901.
    Kraepelin's concept of neurosis is also transitional. This, however, makes little difference to his attitude towards the obsessional disorders as he considered them as a separate group.

120 Bleuler, *Textbook of Psychiatry*.

121 S. Freud, 'L'Hérédité et l'étiologie des névroses', *Revue neurologique* 4 (1896): 47–62.

122 S. Freud, 'Obsessions et phobies, *Revue neurologique* 3 (1895): 33–8.

123 K. Levin, *Freud's Early Psychology of the Neuroses. A Historical Perspective* (Sussex: Harvester Press, 1978).

124 S. Freud, 'L'Hérédité et l'étiologie des névroses', *Revue neurologique* 4 (1896): 47–62.

125 Janet (*Les Obsessions et la psychasthénie*) claimed that Freud's 'substitution hypothesis' was a carbon copy of his own 'law of alternation of ideas' (p. 669).

126 J. Laplanche and J.B. Pontalis, *The Language of Psychoanalysis* (London: Hogarth Press, 1973).

127 Freud found obsessional symptoms more difficult to understand than hysteria,

in spite of the fact that obsessions did not involve, like hysteria, a leap 'from a mental process to a somatic innovation' (S. Freud, *Notes upon a Case of Obsessional Neurosis*, Collected Papers vol. 3 (London: Hogarth Press, 1925), pp. 293–383, p. 295). Freud's early views on obsessions 'excited nowhere near the number of comments his theories on hysteria aroused' (H.S. Decker, *Freud in Germany. Revolution and Reaction in Science 1893–1907*, Psychological Issues, Monograph 41 (New York: International Universities Press, 1977), p. 131). Decker suggests that this resulted from the fact that it was but a 'variation of the early theory of hysteria' and, to German physicians, 'hysterics posed a more pressing medical problem than did maladapted obsessional and compulsive people' (p. 131). Freud's views on obsessions were commented upon with varying degrees of disapproval by W. Strohmayer, 'Zur Charakteristik der Zwangsvorstellungen als Abwehrneurose', *Zentralblatt für Nervenheilkunde und Psychiatrie* 14 (1903): 317–25; L. Löwenfeld, *Die psychischen Zwangserscheinungen auf klinischer Grundlagedargestellt* (with chapter by S. Freud on 'Die Freudsche psychoanalysche Methode') (Wiesbaden: Bergmann, 1904); Moll and Oppenheim (Decker, *Freud in Germany*, p. 131); K. Bumke, *Was sind Zwangsvorgänge? Sammlung Zwangloser Abhandlung aus dem Gebiete der Nerven und Geisteskrankheiten* (Halle: Carl Marhold, 1906), Band 6, Heft 8, p. 45; and later by N. Skliar, 'Zur Kritik der Lehre Freuds über die Zwangszustände', *Zentralblatt für Nervenheilkunde und Psychiatrie* 32 (1909): 41–5; Kraepelin, *Klinische Psychiatrie*, pp. 1885–887; and Schneider, 'Die Lehre vom Zwangsdenken', pp. 136–46.

It is beyond the scope of this chapter to chronicle later psychoanalytical views on the obsessional disorders. See O. Fenichel, *The Psychoanalytic Theory of Neurosis* (London, Kegan Paul, Trench, Trubner, 1945), pp. 268–310; A. Green, 'Névrose obsessionelle et hystérie. Leurs relations chez Freud et depuis', *Revue française de psychoanalyse* 38 (1964): 679–716; W. Stekl, *Compulsion and Doubt*, trans. E. Gutheil, 2 vols (London: Peter Nevill, 1950); H. Nagera, *Obsessional Neuroses. Developmental Psychopathology* (New York: Jason Aronson, 1976); A. Freud, 'Obsessional Neurosis: A Summary of Psychoanalytic Views as Presented at the Congress', *International Journal of Psycho-analysis* 47 (1966): 116–22.

128 R. Dalbiez, *Psychoanalytic Method and the Doctrine of Freud*, trans. T.F. Lindsay, 2 vols (London: Longmans, Green, 1941), p. 269.

129 C.M. Prévost, *Janet, Freud et la psychologie clinique* (Paris: Bibliothèque Payot, 1973); A. Hesnard, *De Freud à Lacan* (Barcelona: Ediciones Martinez Roca, 1976); Green, 'Obsessions et psychonévrose obsessionelle'.

Freud in fact complained that 'of all European countries it was France that has shown itself most refractory to psychoanalysis' (see also Baruk, *La Psychiatrie française*; J.P. Mordier, *Les Débuts de la psychoanalyse en France 1895–1926* (Paris: Maspero, 1981)).

CHAPTER EIGHT

Degeneration and hereditarianism in French mental medicine 1840–90: psychiatric theory as ideological adaptation

Ian Dowbiggin

Introduction

THROUGHOUT THE LAST half of the nineteenth century the most important term in the French psychiatric vocabulary was mental degeneracy.[1] As a concept of psychological medicine, it had emerged during this period as an attempt to resolve the theoretical problem of the mind/body relationship based on what passed for medical understanding of the phenomenon of heredity.[2] At the same time, however, French mental pathologists commonly conflated it with the idea of hereditary predisposition itself.[3] This notion of hereditary degeneracy has been examined in terms of one or another of its many dimensions; yet, one dimension in particular has gone unexplored: the significance of hereditarian ideas for the French psychiatric profession in the nineteenth century.[4] I shall examine this feature of French psychiatric intellectual history by recounting the terms in which French mad-doctors perceived the incidence of morbid heredity in mental disorders. Clinicians essentially understood morbid heredity to be the organic transmission from parents to children of a neuropathic predisposition to mental disease. The period in question begins roughly with the publication of J.E.D. Esquirol's *Mental Maladies* in 1838 and ends with the appearance in print of Charles Féré's 1884 paper in the *Archives de neurologie* on the 'neuropathic family' and with the seminal discussions of the Société Medico-psychologique in 1885–86 on the physical, intellectual, and psychological signs of hereditary insanity. The 1880s marked the heyday of the degeneracy theory. By the turn of the century the notion of a class of the hereditarily insane ceased to be popular.[5] However, during the preceding fifty years the psychiatric conceptualization of morbid heredity had changed from its recognition as one cause among many other causes to an acceptance of its hegemony in the aetiology of mental and nervous illnesses. What seemed to impel this conceptual change was a growing conviction that the hereditary transmission of a disposition to disease constituted an irrefutable and ominous reality, though at no time did French psychiatrists agree on a formulation of heredity's laws and causal nature nor, with a few exceptions, did they characterize morbid heredity in anything more than general terms.[6]

I shall argue that the vague and imprecise terms in which it was perceived eased the acceptance of the theory[7] of morbid heredity by French psychiatrists. This factor combined with the vicissitudes of the French psychiatric community[8] to shape the process of theory-choice. Mid-nineteenth-century French psychiatrists were beset by all kinds of problems: the French public held them in very low repute, an attitude manifest in the press campaign waged against asylum doctors in the 1860s; the French magistracy openly derided medical claims to expertise in legal matters; the profession suffered from sharply defined divisions along theoretical lines; and the imperial government of Louis Napoleon passed legislation inimical to the interests of psychiatrists and generally created an intellectual environment uncongenial to their republican and anticlerical sympathies. The situation improved somewhat for mental pathology during the Third Republic, yet public attitudes softened little towards doctors of mental alienation. The conclusion here is that the psychiatric community, represented by the Parisian Société Médico-psychologique[9], reacted to these pressures[10] by undergoing a conceptual reorientation culminating in the acceptance of the theory of morbid heredity. This theory offered a loosely defined yet appealing cognitive model through which psychiatrists could terminate the theoretical conflicts dividing their profession and simultaneously counter their declining image, gain intellectual legitimacy through identification with more fashionable biological sciences, and accommodate themselves to a general pessimism that characterized nineteenth-century French currents of thought. In other words, the theory of morbid heredity enabled French psychiatrists to adapt to changing sociopolitical circumstances and quell internecine struggle. Thus, French mental pathologists in the second half of the nineteenth century responded to a hostile environment by revising the thematic content of their science in accordance with the life sciences and a salient feature of contemporaneous intellectual movements.[11] That it smoothed the process of shaping a professional consensus of sorts could only recommend it and reinforce its relevance to a beleaguered group of alienists.

The historiographic significance of this conclusion derives from its similarities to the cases of the Weimar acausal physics community and the seventeenth-century iatromechanist London College of Physicians.[12] In all three instances the pattern is roughly the same; scientific theory-choice was a function of a discrete scientific community or group that sought to undercut opposition from society through an adaptive appropriation of fashionable ideas, either from other scientific currents or from the wider

intellectual milieu. It is true that as a medical science psychiatry is different
from either physiology or physics in terms of its object of study –
psychopathology – and its experimental possibilities. Certainly, the lack of
firm knowledge of insanity's causes and somatic pathology distinguishes
psychological medicine from the other sciences.[13] Yet it is precisely this
feature of virtually permanent intellectual imprecision throughout the
nineteenth century that underlines French psychiatry's sociohistorical
kinship to Weimar physics and seventeenth-century British physiology, for
it left it vulnerable to conceptual shifts such as the one to heredity whenever
the conditions of its social and political environment grew threatening.
Hence, the comparison to other scientific groups or professions under attack
is more than apt; indeed, because of its chronic theoretical difficulties
psychiatry may illustrate most vividly the historical problem of philosophic
accommodation by the sciences.

To demonstrate this special significance of hereditarian ideas for
nineteenth-century French psychiatry, however, I must first review the
development of these ideas between about 1850 and the end of the century.

The rise of hereditarian ideas 1850–90

When Esquirol's *Mental Maladies* appeared in 1838, it represented the
culmination of forty years of work in diagnosing and treating what the
French called 'mental alienation'. Esquirol defined 'mental alienation' as a
'cerebral affection, ordinarily chronic, and with fever; characterised by
disorders of sensibility, understanding, intelligence, and will'.[14] For Esquirol the causes of mental alienation were 'as numerous, as its forms are
varied. They are general or special, physical or secondary, predisposing or
exciting.' He noted that:

> 'not only do climate, seasons, age, sex, temperament, profession, and
> mode of life, have an influence upon the frequency, character, duration,
> crises, and treatment of insanity; but this malady is still modified by laws,
> civilisation, morals, and the political condition of people.'[15]

While recognizing the frequency of hereditary pathological predisposition,
Esquirol saw it only as a 'remote cause'.[16]

By 1845, when Jacques Joseph Moreau (de Tours), one of Esquirol's
students, attacked him on the grounds that there was no error of judgement
in the insane and only a 'functional lesion', attention had still not shifted
perceptibly towards hereditary predisposition.[17] Moreau wrote that in the
organic process of mental illness there were myriad causes whose ultimate
nature remained unknown, 'those for example which hide and develop in the
secret depths of our tissues, which flow from one organism to another, so to
speak, and are transmitted by heredity'.[18] Because he believed that the 'basic
morbid psychocerebral factor' was an 'alteration' or 'modification' of the
thinking organ itself, he concentrated on the dysfunction of the brain rather

than on the many causes exhaustively enumerated already by Esquirol.[19]

However, there were indications that heredity was gaining prominence. In 1844 the psychiatrist Jules Baillarger published a paper on statistical research in the heredity of madness.[20] One of his more significant observations was that the study of insanity, better than any other illness, illustrated the 'general history of heredity' and its laws, since the insane were conveniently assembled in hospitals such as the Bicêtre and the Salpêtrière in Paris.[21] Baillarger continued to investigate the role of heredity in insanity and in 1849 maintained that madness was like other diseases such as chorea, pellagra, pulmonary tuberculosis, and rheumatism, because through heredity it could be transmitted in the form of a disposition to other disorders.[22]

The 1850s witnessed the emergence of heredity as a focal point of interest in the elucidation of mental and nervous pathology. Beginning with the appearance of the second volume of Prosper Lucas's *Philosophical and Physiological Treatise on Natural Heredity* in 1850, heredity was promoted to a hitherto unparalleled position of aetiological importance. Among those who were instrumental in effecting this change were members of the newly established Société Médico-psychologique (1852), such as Moreau and Lucas. These figures were fully aware that by championing morbid heredity they were breaking with the past in many respects. For E. Renaudin, the director of the asylum at Maréville, by the 1850s the long-term controversy over heredity had been more or less resolved. He wrote that 'today we possess numerous examples, not only of transmission but as well of hereditary accumulation of morbid predisposition', and concluded that there could no longer be any doubt that heredity was an essential causal condition of mental alienation.[23] In 1856 he wrote that 'heredity plays in the evolution of mental alienation a role that is best appreciated today, and which is perhaps even more important than it has been in any other era.'[24] His colleague Ulysée Trélat, a doctor at the Salpêtrière, also recorded his belief that while recognition of heredity's role in the genesis of insanity was hardly new, it was time for it to receive greater recognition: it was the irrefutable cause of causes.[25] According to Trélat, the emphasis on heredity was part and parcel of a philosophic shift from 'external' to 'internal' causes of mental alienation.[26] Environment was less important to him than the innate and idiosyncratic traits of the individual patient. He went on to publish his *Lucid Madness Studied and Considered from the Point of View of the Family and Society* in 1861 in which 'lucid madness' was seen as largely dominated by hereditary influences.[27]

The most significant impulses to a greater appreciation of morbid heredity were two treatises: B.A. Morel's *Treatise on the Physical, Intellectual, and Moral Degeneracy of the Human Race* of 1857 and Moreau's *Morbid Psychology and Its Relationship to the Philosophy of History* of 1859. Morel, chief physician at the St Yon asylum near Rouen, was born in Vienna in 1809. According to one psychiatrist writing on the hereditary illnesses of the nervous system in 1886, Morel's treatise was the most influential psychiatric text of the nineteenth century.[28] His theory of degeneracy was an anthropologico-psychiatric view of European civilization.[29] For Morel degeneracy was a 'morbid deviation from the primitive human type'.[30] Initially resulting from the pathogenic modern social environment and the unhealthy conditions of agrarian life, it became truly threatening because heredity tended to transmit the acquired pathological characteristics from one generation to another. Morel based his views on his own observations of families from industrial urban areas and isolated rural areas such as the valleys of the Tyrol. He claimed to have found that families that became 'tainted' through alcoholic abuse or poor nutrition became sterile and extinct after three generations of mental alienation, idiocy, and imbecility. Like Renaudin and Trélat he earmarked heredity as the salient element in degeneracy. The spectre of degeneracy made it all the more necessary, he wrote, to 'give to the word *heredity* a greater meaning than that assigned to it ordinarily'.[31]

Moreau was born in 1804, the son of a Napoleonic soldier and mathematician. His *Morbid Psychology* is largely overlooked now, although it was this work that established his contemporary fame. It is a lengthy medico-scientific critique of the world-view that held environment responsible for human character and pathology.[32] According to Moreau, this view disregarded the patent and innate inequality of minds and assumed the perfectibility of all under proper social conditions. Proponents of this world-view were normally identified as geniuses in Moreau's day, yet he hypothesized that their intellectual state was actually much closer to that which belonged to the insane.[33] He reasoned that their mental functioning was essentially morbid, the consequence of a cerebral condition seen often enough in families stigmatized by psychopathological heredity. This 'community of origin' for geniuses and the mad was a question of nervous heredity.[34] Thus Moreau was led to his equation of genius and madness as a 'fact of physiology', one of the most striking conjectures in the history of psychiatry.[35]

For Moreau as well the central fact was an unprecedented appreciation of heredity's magnitude. In fact, Moreau cited Trélat's 1856 paper from the *Annales médico-psychologiques* and Renaudin's own words of the same year to bear out his contention that heredity warranted the special attention of mental pathologists.[36] Echoing Trélat, Moreau warned against accepting simply outward appearances that diverted the physician's gaze from the real 'nature of the morbid fact': that is, 'the question of the heredity of the illnesses of the nervous system'.[37]

By the next decade there were signs that the Société Médico-psychologique had recognized how vital the hereditary issue was. At a meeting of the Société in 1860 Morel drew attention to Baillarger and Moreau, especially the latter's *Morbid Psychology*, for their contributions to understanding 'the classification of hereditary madness'. He also declared:

> 'I count on time, on the future studies of my younger contemporaries, to justify my creation of the classes of the hereditarily insane, which present to us the most varied morbid characteristics, as it were congenital, of

states of consciousness from those of apparently perfect reason to those of the most complete idiocy.'[38]

Morel's proclamation meant that he looked forward to a wide extension of Moreau's 'neuropathic family' rooted in the predisposing cause of heredity, for he had already suggested that the customary acceptance of 'direct' hereditary transmission of certain forms of insanity – that is, the transmission of a specific disease from parent to child – had to be expanded to include transformations in the kind of nervous disturbance or insanity as well as in the pattern of inheritance. In this context, the type of mental affliction was relegated to mere phenomenal status, secondary in importance to the hereditary mechanism responsible for its existence.

In the next thirty years hereditarianism evolved to the point where it dominated the interpretations of mental and nervous illnesses by French psychiatrists. The 1867–68 discussions at the Société Médico-psychologique marked the initial stage in this process. According to Auguste Voisin, one of the major participants in the debates, the hereditary issue had produced two basic positions among the members of the Société and a great deal of controversy befitting such a 'grave' problem.[39] Those who sided with Moreau held that there existed a 'solidarity' among epilepsy, other nervous disorders such as chorea and hysteria, and even certain 'general illnesses' such as tuberculosis, scrofula, alcoholism, meningitis, and typhoid fever.[40] The unifying element was hereditary predisposition since 'interrogating' the family members of epileptics had evinced evidence of mental alienation, neurosis, and other disturbances among the ancestors of epileptics. The other faction was willing to grant that epilepsy could be transmitted directly to progeny but would not go beyond those limited cases to an acknowledgement of a hereditary category itself.

Epilepsy was the key disease in these discussions because as a neurological disorder it had, like hysteria, many affinities with insanity.[41] To admit that epileptics were part of a general hereditary class whose stigmata characterized the mental and physical lives of certain families, it would be necessary to extend dramatically the influence of heredity in psycho- and neuropathology. Individuals such as Baillarger, Morel, and Moreau certainly thought that the time was ripe to follow this course of action. Hence, when the Société Médico-psychologique decided to formulate a 'precise programme' for investigating the role of heredity, the concerned parties accepted Charles Lasègue's proposition that they study the proportion in which heredity manifests itself in a family whose mother and father were epileptic.[42] When the discussions closed on 25 May, 1868, one of the *Société*'s members summed up the debate in these words:

'It is the natural history of the hereditary diatheses that we have just undertaken to study, beginning wisely and modestly with epilepsy. . . . By penetrating the mystery of the propagation of hereditary diatheses, and that of their genesis, medicine will have made the most difficult step towards purging the blood of races of living poisons.

> Such is ... the great and final mission of our science ... that is to say,
> ... going right to the causes, ... striking them at their roots, instead of
> wasting our energies with the innumerable multitudes of cease-
> lessly reappearing effects.'[43]

Perhaps the most important aspect of this speech is the ringing conviction
that a fundamental change in attitude, intention, and vision had just
occurred. The Société Médico-psychologique now deemed it profitable to
examine Moreau's theory of neuropathic heredity posed a decade earlier.
Clearly more minds were willing to entertain the possibility that morbid
heredity carried much more aetiological weight than previously thought. As
the most important association of French psychiatrists, the Sociéte provided
institutional confirmation of this change in psychiatric thinking.

The next time the Société Médico-psychologique turned its attention to
the hereditary issue was March 1885. This time the topic was 'the physical,
intellectual, and moral signs of hereditary insanity'. No fewer than nine
sessions were devoted to this problem, the last taking place on 22 June, 1886
– ample testimony to the transition in perception. Jules Falret opened the
discussions by noting that the question of special stigmata for hereditary
insanity recalled the discussions of 1867–68. Then, as in 1885, there were
two dissenting opinions on the subject. Some still believed that heredity
played a very great role in mental alienation but that it was only one cause
among several others and did not 'taint' the insane with any discernible
'stamp'.[44] Others, following Morel's earlier ideas, believed that certain
characteristics denoted the influence of heredity in alcoholism, hysteria,
epilepsy, and hypochondria.[45] Falret felt that Morel, who had died in 1873,
had shed new light during his career on 'the transformation of morbid
heredity'. He accordingly aligned himself with Morel's pupil Valentin
Magnan, doctor at the St Anne asylum and erstwhile intern under Prosper
Lucas. Falret included among the physical signs of hereditary insanity
asymmetry of the skull and face, strabism, facial tics, hare-lip, club-feet, and
hernias.[46] Physical stigmata were especially convenient for physicians, Falret
claimed, since they exposed the real '*aliénés*' during the deceptive periods of
lucidity and ostensibly normal mental activity.[47] He advocated further study
of those forms of insanity that particularly carried the signs of hereditary
taint, such as the 'insanity of reason' and the 'insanity of doubt'.[48]

If Falret had a disagreement with Magnan, and hence with Morel, it had to
do with the extent to which the latter wished to expand the domain of
hereditary insanity.[49] Others had more profound hesitations. Some thought
Magnan had widened the nosological category of '*folie héréditaire*' far too
much.[50] By so doing, it was argued, Magnan had obscured the very real
differences that existed between 'degenerates' and '*héréditaires*'. The former
group, as Morel had pointed out, frequently acquired their insanity through
alcoholism. A '*héréditaire*', however, was someone whose form of mental
alienation was purely and simply hereditary. One doctor asked: 'How then
do we separate hereditary transmission from an acquired illness?' Citing the

example of an alcoholic mother, he asserted that she not only transmitted to her children a morbid disposition to alcoholism, but exposed them as well to traumata from blows or falls. He concluded that the foetus was exposed to many different influences that could lead to degrees of idiocy in the child quite apart from the hereditary 'morbid germs' passed down from the parents.[51] Thus to group all '*aliénés*' under the heading of 'hereditary insanity' would erode the distinction between an acquired and an innate illness. Magnan's opponents seemed principally concerned with reinstating the 'individual side' of the degenerate, that oft-overlooked characteristic due to environmental influences.[52]

Magnan answered his critics in the final meeting of the Société on the issue of heredity. For his part, he saw no reason to separate degenerates from '*héréditaires*': if it appeared that degeneracy was sometimes the result of illnesses developed in the foetal stage, in most instances it was only one side of the greater question, one dominated by a specific hereditary predisposition to insanity.[53] His 'synthetic study' of degeneracy and morbid heredity, he stated, had the persuasive advantage of 'reuniting within the same frame of reference' the syndromes of different afflictions,

'all emanating, it must be recognised, from the same basis, and this common basis is nothing else than the mental state of the *héréditaire* already described by M. Falret, this disequilibrium [of the nervous system] which I was compelled to refer to in my first communication.'[54]

In reply to criticisms that the term 'hereditary' was misleading, Magnan countered that heredity was the best word available with which to comprehend the group of diseases founded on that distinctive 'mental state' observed so often in those tainted with heredity. Besides, he said, heredity was still the 'principal factor'.[55]

It would be misleading to ignore the consensus among members of the Société Médico-psychologique in 1886 by overemphasizing the disagreements over hereditary insanity. Magnan, for one, did not think that there was any great dispute; he closed the series of discussions by noting that:

'if we differ over the limits to be assigned to the aetiological conditions, the clinical side, that is, the constitution of the group of *héréditaires* or degenerates, is admitted by the greater number of us, and for my part, I am happy that in these new debates the Société Médico-psychologique has marked a great advance in the highly important study of mental degeneracy.'[56]

The unanimity was particularly evident to someone such as Jules Christian, a psychiatrist at the Charenton hospital in Paris, who contested Magnan's 'hereditary insanity'. Christian granted that the 'preponderance' of heredity as an aetiological factor was 'an opinion generally admitted' in 1886.[57] He described the dominant medico-scientific way of thinking during the 31 May, 1886 session:

'with the ideas that reign today in pathology, one is induced to make of heredity *the almost unique efficient cause of mental alienation*... The habit is to invoke a variety of causes that are only commonplace... If, however, these do come into play they can do so only by virtue of another cause, more essential and inherent in the constitution of the subject himself – that which is called *predisposition*.'[58]

Thus, between 1868 and 1886 the perception of morbid heredity within the Société Médico-psychologique changed fundamentally. By 1868 it was of interest primarily because of the pathfinding works of Moreau, Morel, Lucas, and Baillarger. If there were any consensus within the Société in 1868 it was only insofar as there was agreement that a 'precise programme' was necessary in order to set up guidelines for research, and that the study of epilepsy offered the best opportunities for illuminating the topic. Yet by 1886 it had been established in most minds that heredity was a viable enough concept to justify making it the foundation for an entire classification of mental disorders and diseases of the nervous system. The disagreements ought not to disguise the fact that important members such as Magnan and Falret were convinced that this was the correct course of action for mental pathologists or that many more members were inclined to sanction the project with or without qualifications. Thus between 1868 and 1886 the theory of morbid heredity received the professional endorsement of French psychiatry through the medium of the Société Médico-psychologique.

And it was in this setting that Charles Féré, another member of the Société, presented his theory of the 'neuropathic family' in the *Archives de neurologie* of 1884. Féré's 'neuropathic family' united the psychical, sensorial, and motor disturbances of the nervous system. These illnesses, Féré affirmed, constituted 'a family indissolubly united by the laws of heredity'.[59] He saw his studies as extending and improving upon the original discoveries of Lucas, Moreau, Morel, Wilhelm Griesinger, Charcot, Trélat, Baillarger, and Louis Delasiauve. He contended that his predecessors had been overly concerned with 'pathological states of mind' and had thus neglected the other nervous diseases. To redress the imbalance, he included the latter in the 'neuropathic family'. They comprised one of the two 'artificial' divisions of the 'family': the neuropathological in contrast to the psychopathological. The latter branch included the morbid psychical states and the neuroses most closely tied to them. The neuropathological branch embraced the organic diseases of the nervous system that affected sensibility and movement.[60] Among these he listed goitre, chorea, Parkinson's disease, migraine, and asthma.[61] Among the psychopathological diseases Féré listed 'suicidal mania' and alcoholism, as well as hysteria and epilepsy, the two neuroses with the closest similarities to the hereditary forms of insanity.[62]

The important point about Féré's paper is that he viewed his studies as both a continuation and amplification of Moreau's original insight that not just mental alienation alone is capable of engendering madness through heredity.[63] Moreau had earlier drawn connections between insanity on the one hand and hysteria, idiocy, epilepsy, paralysis, neuralgia, cerebral fever, apoplexy, and tics on the other. Féré hoped that his 'neuropathic family' brought together all these separate morbid classes, displaying in the process their common 'intimate parentage'.[64]

In a sense, then, Féré completed the programme outlined by Moreau roughly thirty years before. His 'neuropathic family' illustrated the malleability of symptoms in the illnesses of the nervous system. Each disease was capable of manifesting itself in progeny as a different disorder entirely, or even transforming itself in the same individual over time. The one constant, underlying, and indispensable factor was heredity, 'the primordial cause of nervous affections', according to Féré.[65] Along with Magnan, who can be seen as having completed Morel's programme, Féré bore witness through his own formulation of mental and nervous pathology to the great plausibility heredity had gained since the 1850s. Morbid heredity, it might be said, was to a large extent the late nineteenth-century prism for French psychiatrists and neurologists through which the images of pathology were refracted. The experimental psychologist Théodule Ribot, editor and founder of the *Revue philosophique* and an influential Third Republican thinker, lent credence to this conclusion in his *Heredity: A Psychological Study of its Phenomena, Laws, Causes, and Consequences* of 1873. Much of his book was devoted to morbid psychological heredity and was based on the writings of Morel, Moreau, Lucas, Alexandre Brierre de Boismont, and Magnus Huss. Ribot asked:

'Are the modes of mental life transmissable under their morbid, as they are under their normal form? Does the study of mental diseases contribute its quota of facts in favour of heredity? The answer must be in the affirmative. The transmission of all kinds of psychological anomalies – whether of passions and crimes ... or of hallucinations and insanity ... – is so frequent, and evidenced by such striking facts, that the most inattentive observers have been struck by it, and that morbid psychological heredity is admitted even by those who have no suspicion that this is only one aspect of a law which is far more general.'[66]

Even the 'sturdiest opponents of morbid heredity', Ribot wrote, concede the 'heredity of a disposition' to disease.[67] Ten years later a neurologist at the Salpêtrière echoed Ribot's comments when he declared that 'the hereditary transmission of the psychoses is a truth universally accepted today ... and it can be said today that insanity, whatever its forms, is always a hereditary affection.'[68]

However, if the evidence for heredity seemed adequate in the eyes of French mental pathologists, it had more to do with a deep-set psychological propensity to accept hereditary explanations than with the evidence itself. This conclusion is borne out by a consideration of what in fact constituted the evidence for morbid heredity. For example, despite the many psychiatric references to the biological phenomenon of heredity, it was patent to

Christian that this did not mean that his colleagues had a common and precise understanding of its laws. He told the Société Médico-psychologique that:

> 'heredity, I know, tends more and more to become the preponderant aetiological factor within the domain of the mental illnesses. However, we are far from a knowledge of its laws, and I wonder if an element so imperfectly understood, so capricious in its manifestations, can in sound logic serve as the basis for an entire doctrine. What we possess today is the intuition of heredity's laws much more than the laws themselves. I well know that in speaking in this way, I am running up against a generally admitted opinion.'[69]

Similarly, there existed the notion that heredity had to be 'accumulated' before it could manifest itself in a characteristic form.[70] This meant that in the case of an alcoholic the main cause of the malady was still morbid heredity, even if it could be shown that the ancestors or parents had never been truly afflicted with neurosis, psychosis, or motor dysfunction. It was sufficient that they had been highly excitable, 'inventive', or 'enthusiasts' of any sort for a physician to deduce hereditary taint. The psychiatric argument was that these ancestral syndromes were simply mild instances of a hereditary insanity that found its most virulent expression in the alcoholic descendant. Hence, it was thought that the hereditary disease had 'accumulated' almost imperceptibly over the course of several generations only to show its most malignant face in the unfortunate alcoholic. Another explanation of basically the same phenomenon was that morbid heredity could atavistically 'skip' a number of generations: a certain insane patient was seen as a reversion to a more or less remote ancestor.[71]

The 1885–86 debates at the Société Médico-psychologique revealed that most French psychiatrists preferred to cite inherent rather than acquired characteristics in their accounts of pathogenesis. This led to a sharp diminution in the significance attributed to accidental or traumatic causes, a view expressed by Féré in 1886:

> 'When no trace of degenerescence is discovered in the heredity of a subject, it does not follow that the nervous affection from which he suffers is accidental, arising from some purely fortuitous cause, such as a traumatism, or an infectious disease, etc. The patient may not have any hereditary taint but be the victim of a disturbance of evolution which may not break out until the development of the nervous system has reached its completion ...
>
> Hence, before we can admit the accidental origin of any nervous affection, it is necessary to eliminate not only the presence of any direct or indirect hereditary condition, whether similar or transformatory, but also that of any disturbance of evolution capable of bringing about a defective development of the nervous system.'[72]

So prevalent was the conviction that heredity was 'the primordial cause of nervous affections' that one writer could envisage a future in which acquired neuroses would dwindle substantially in number while the 'metamorphoses that they will submit to through the influence of descent' would present themselves more and more to clinicians.[73]

Yet, even a proponent of hereditary predisposition such as Wilhelm Griesinger had to recognize its shaky epistemological grounds. In the 1861 edition of his *Mental Pathology and Therapeutics* he cautioned his readers about the subtle differences between the 'aetiology' and 'pathogeny' of disease: the 'intimate connection' between cause and disease, that is, the way in which the latter develops from the former remained obscure in most cases. Aetiology, for Griesinger, was simply the empirical and statistical compilation of certain circumstances such as 'hereditary predisposition' which often coincided with or preceded insanity. 'Pathogeny' on the other hand explained the physiological connection between cause and effect or the 'mechanical act'.[74] Hereditary predisposition was founded merely on an empirical relationship between coincidental conditions of pathology and could not be legitimately assigned to the domain of more precise pathogeny though some doctors rather carelessly did so.

Nor, finally, was the hereditary lesion observable in many cases. Doctors such as L.F. Lélut and François Leuret in his *Moral Treatment of Madness* (1840) challenged mid-century psychiatrists with the fact that the brain of *aliénés* often revealed no lesion and concluded that insanity may be a purely psychological phenomenon involving nothing more than an 'aberration' of the faculty of intelligence. In reaction morbid heredity was conceived of as merely the transmission of a predisposition to disease and not a specific disease entity. The hereditary lesion that psychiatrists talked and wrote of freely after the mid-century often referred to a diffuse condition or 'disequilibrium' of the nervous system passed from parent to child. Its reality seemed to suffer not at all from the fact that it could not be detected at autopsy.

Thus the concept of morbid heredity adopted by French psychiatrists was vague and extremely flexible. Indeed, Ola Andersson, in her *Studies in the Prehistory of Psychoanalysis*, has claimed that this very inexactness of criteria of heredity made it so popular in late nineteenth-century psychiatry. It permitted a wide range of interpretations and was thus exceedingly suitable for uniting a wide variety of thinkers.[75]

Considering these features of the theory of morbid heredity, it is hardly surprising that therapeutic practice had little to do with the history of the theory's acceptance. Indeed, the period of the theory's popularity also witnessed a widespread absence of concern with questions of treatment. For example, in 1867 the outgoing president of the Société Médico-psychologique complained that since 1852 the *Annales* had included very few works on the cure of 'mental affections' in contrast to other issues such as the classification of mental diseases, the aetiology of insanity, or the connection between the illnesses of the mind and the 'diverse functional or organic lesions that characterised ordinary diseases'.[76] If the theory of morbid heredity had any relationship to treatment it would appear to have been as a rationalization for the continued use of therapeutic methods that considerably predated the theory itself.[77] Throughout the nineteenth century psychiatric therapy consisted of little more than a highly heterogeneous 'grab-bag' of techniques such as regimen, physical labour, travelling, tonics, narcotics, purgatives, hydrotherapy, electricity, discipline, music, and education. Even bleeding persisted to one degree or another, though its use fell off sharply after the mid-century.[78] 'Therapeutic eclecticism' was the expression used by the esteemed Salpêtrière physician J.P. Falret to describe the therapeutic orientation of most of his contemporaries.[79] The one method that enjoyed almost unqualified support from psychiatrists was 'isolation', the institutionalization of a disturbed individual in an asylum whose environment was allegedly free of the pathogenic influences of the domestic milieu.[80] When after the 1850s more and more emphasis was placed on the patient's moral and physical 'disposition' rather than his disordered ideas, 'isolation' was simply perceived as a longer procedure than imagined before; yet psychiatrists continued to stress the ameliorative effects of the asylum milieu that putatively counteracted and improved the mental state of the insane.[81] Thus, the theory of morbid heredity did not exclude the continued use of 'isolation'.

I have argued that the hereditarianism of post-1850 French psychiatry was in certain respects a paradigmatic phenomenon: mad-doctors exhibited a marked preference for hereditarian approaches to and explanations of insanity. None the less, it is clear that while hereditarianism constituted a discernible theoretical position for French psychiatrists, it was also characterized by inconsistencies and incongruities and was generally poorly defined. Moreover, it had little to contribute to progress in the treatment of lunacy, and hence to the 'normal science' of medico-psychological practice. The reasons for its popularity as a psychiatric way of thinking must therefore be sought in other circumstances influencing the intellectual history of mental medicine. The social demoralization and doctrinal divisiveness of the profession were two such sets of circumstances.

SOCIAL DEMORALIZATION AND INTELLECTUAL INSTABILITY 1843–77

As psychiatrists became more receptive to hereditarian approaches to the question of insanity, their professional community experienced a particularly insecure and doubt-ridden time, a chapter in its history demoralizing even for a branch of medicine like psychiatry that normally suffered from hostility and a lack of prestige.[82] Because of their republican and liberal leanings, the years 1843 to 1877 witnessed many difficulties for alienists. With Louis Napoleon's coup d'état of December 1851, the republican experiment begun in February 1848 ended abruptly. For the next nineteen years Napoleon ruled the Second Empire. His political regime was noted for its sympathies towards the Catholic Church. Consequently, clericalism pervaded the intellectual life of the country. The philosophic atmosphere proved to be inhospitable to any intellectual endeavours that could be construed as materialist or attacks on the reality of the 'soul' and the freedom of the will.[83] Jan Goldstein has shown that the imperial government intervened several times during the 1860s to suppress lectures at the Paris Faculty of Medicine or reject medical dissertations because of psychiatric writings on the delicate issue of the mind's relationship to cerebral anatomy and physiology.[84] Similarly, the imperial regime passed legislation that undermined French psychiatry's hard-won gains enshrined in the 1838 law which had set up the nationwide system of departmental mental institutions and had defined the process whereby patients were to be admitted to asylums.[85]

It might then be thought that with the establishment of the Third Republic in 1871 the political troubles of the psychiatric profession would be over. Yet the removal of the royalist threat to the Republic did not occur until the 1877 legislative elections and the resignation of President MacMahon. Until that date co-operation between Church and state persisted and even improved in the years immediately following the Commune and its anticlerical atrocities.[86] Indeed, Goldstein has termed the decade and a half before 1877 'a veritable time of troubles' for French mental pathologists.[87] They were badgered by government and the press, a campaign that began in the 1860s. Throughout the same decade the *Annales médico-psychologiques* were dotted with excerpts from the newspapers referring to violent crimes committed by the insane as well as with reports on complaints lodged with the French Senate and the Ministers of the Interior and Justice alleging unfair institutionalization by asylum doctors. Commissions were set up to investigate these claims; one commission report testified to the seriousness of the issue by stating that 'public attention since 1863 has turned to the legislation relating to the insane and the internal administration of asylums'.[88]

Jules Falret claimed during the 1868 discussions of the Société Médico-psychologique on the question of the 'dangerously insane' that psychiatrists had to sharpen their diagnostic criteria for determining which *aliéné* was curable and no threat to public order. Falret argued that public criticism of psychiatrists in the press, in 'political assemblies', in courts of law, and in the 'highest spheres of power', compelled pathologists to refine these criteria, or other professional interest groups like law would assume authority in decisions bearing on the question.[89]

Ludger Lunier spoke to the Academy of Medicine in April 1870 of the attack launched by the newspapers on the 1838 law.[90] Lunier complained that 'daily' reports of arbitrary sequestration of people suspected of insanity had fuelled a critique of the law that had spread to the *corps législatif*. Psychiatry's 'adversaries' were exploiting the situation, he said, in order to undermine the role of the doctor as expert in the placement of the mad in asylums. As a result, Lunier declared, 'the question of the insane is more than ever the order of the day'. In fact, Lunier was one of several pathologists singled out for public opprobrium with regard to this issue, and his fellow members of the Société Médico-psychologique were alarmed enough on his account to discuss the matter in a special meeting. Their concern was acute: as one of the members anxiously remarked: 'today M. Rousselin and M. Lunier are attacked: tomorrow it will be the turn of the other members of this society'.[91] Brierre de Boismont expressed the same concerns in his preface to Henry Bonnet's *The Insane According to Themselves, the Law, Legislation, Philosophic Systems, Society and the Family* of 1865.[92] Thus, psychiatry drew a great deal of public ire in the 1860s and well into the 1870s[93]. The doctors themselves were highly sensitive to it and were keen to remedy the situation by changing the public's low opinion of them.

The unpopularity and harassment of French psychiatry coincided with a crisis within the profession with regard to the administration of the asylum system. The overcrowding of the asylums, a chronic problem at the Bicêtre and Salpêtrière hospitals since the days of Pinel, had reached dire proportions by 1840.[94] Simultaneously, asylum doctors began to express real doubts about their ability to cure the majority of the asylum population, although cure-rates themselves provided no clear justification for such a change in attitude from the earlier therapeutic optimism of Pinel and Esquirol.[95] The widespread acceptance of incurability of the insane translated into a growing consensus on the chronic condition of mental illnesses and the perception by doctors that the mad were dangerous to public order.[96] As Marc Alexander has argued, the imperatives of the asylum changed from a 'ministering to' to an 'administration of' the insane: custodialism replaced an active and sanguine policy of treatment.[97]

By the 1860s the asylum's function was questioned seriously by psychiatrists and in 1865 the Société Médico-psychologique debated the issue of therapeutic and custodial assistance to the mentally ill. Psychiatrists noted that other professions like law and even some alienists advocated the abolition of the asylum and the repeal of the 1838 law.[98] Morel was particularly critical of the French asylum system, calling it 'congested' with patients and describing asylums as being in 'chaos, in which all the forms of mental degradation accumulate pell-mell, without any benefit to the sick or the doctors whose entire time is absorbed in writing monthly notes for the 900 patients that have to be treated'.[99] The profession managed to close ranks and endorse the efficacy of the asylum, yet it is undeniable that most psychiatrists were compelled to reevaluate their claims to authority and expertise in matters of treatment. If this process ended in a vote of confidence in the large institution with high doctor/patient ratios and alleged administrative and fiscal efficiency,[100] the fact remains that dissent from within and without the psychiatric community had helped to engender a crisis of confidence in the way practitioners perceived their responsibilities.

Problems in the interpretation of mental illness arose as well at mid-century. 1843 may seem arbitrary as the starting date for chronicling this process, yet there is at least one good reason for using it. The *Annales médico-psychologiques* began publishing in that year and the appearance of this journal was predicated on the unsatisfactory state of the science of mental pathology. Laurent Cerise, one of the two principal founders of the *Annales*, wrote in its first volume that the focus of attention for contributors to the journal would be 'the science of the relationship of body to mind'.[101] Unfortunately, Cerise wrote, this science had been hamstrung for too long by dogmatism, metaphysics, and an unfruitful 'diversity of doctrines' – a situation due in no small way to the presence of competing 'schools' such as the 'pathological anatomists', the 'psychologists', and the 'vitalists'. The first two were most important. The pathological anatomists attributed an illness such as monomania to a 'more or less deep organic alteration' of the brain, while the psychologists viewed madness as a disease of the 'soul' with no necessary organic lesion. Cerise wrote that the objective of the *Annales* was to eliminate this state of affairs by replacing it with a 'general doctrine of mental alienation' based on the study of the 'functional' operations of the nervous system. The *Annales* would provide the appropriate forum for the discussion of a wide variety of positions in a spirit of 'benevolent fraternity', a non-specialist journal that welcomed physicians, legislators, and politicians to contribute to the elucidation of the reciprocal influence of psychology and physiology as well as establish a 'tradition' guaranteeing the future of psychiatry while avoiding the obstacles that had impeded its development.

In the same issue Cerise vigorously attacked the purely 'physiological' school of Cabanis, Gall, Broussais, Bichat, and Georget.[102] Whether mental affections were traced to the 'excitation' of the viscera or the brain, the physiological argument failed to account for the undeniable influence of ideas on effective behaviour and thinking. Thus, Cerise found the writings of the most celebrated medical men such as Gall and Cabanis to be mostly 'vague' and 'confus[ing]'. He believed that only the view of the 'double nature of man' that accepted the reciprocal influence of the organism and spontaneous mind could reconcile the 'opposing doctrines'.

In condemning the 'physiological' school, Cerise was not reverting to 'psychologism'. Far from it: both he and the fledgling Société Médico-psychologique envisaged the study of the anatomy and physiology of the nervous system as a crucial part of the new medico-scientific approach.[103] It was felt that only a science devoted to the thorough investigation of both physical and mental features of vital existence could reconcile the 'materialists' and 'psychologists'.

Cerise's account of the conflicts within French psychiatry in the 1840s was confirmed by other writers. Jules Falret's father Jean Pierre, who had coined the term 'mental alienation' and had been Morel's mentor at the Salpêtrière in 1841, recounted in 1864 the extreme swings in taste that had characterized the preceding forty years in French psychiatry.[104] Falret confessed that his generation of Esquirol's students had begun by referring to pathological anatomy for the causes of mental disturbances. He and his colleagues Félix Voisin, Louis Calmeil, and Achille Foville followed Gall and looked only to the lesions of the brain's membranes for the 'seat' of insanity. Yet, dissatisfaction arose when doctors like Falret conceded that anatomical lesions were insufficient to explain the great diversity and many nuances of psychological phenomena accompanying mental disease. A reaction ensued and normative psychological standards were employed instead to distinguish insanity from non-pathological mental states. However, psychology also soon showed itself to be as sterile as its predecessor, pathological anatomy. Its sterility was conspicuous in therapy where a preoccupation with psychological symptoms led psychiatrists nowhere in their attempts to cure the insane. By the 1850s a 'third stage' had appeared, according to Falret. This was the 'clinical phase' which stressed careful observation of the chronological succession of complex psychological states in order to understand the correct aetiology, prognostics, and treatment.

Falret dubbed the years from 1840 to 1860 as a 'period of transition' or 'intermediate epoch' between the legacy of Pinel and Esquirol and the 'new doctrine', a 'scientific transformation' and 'renovation' of the old view which produced a new interpretation of mental life. Like Cerise, Falret looked towards a reconciliation of patho-anatomical somaticism and psychology as well as their representatives based on a 'dualistic' view of the organism. Both doctors admitted the distinct existence of body and mind, yet claimed that these two vital features were so 'intimately united' in morbid and normal states that every psychical phenomenon 'presupposes as an indispensable condition the cooperation of the brain'.

Renaudin echoed Falret's and Cerise's perceptions of a time of transition and conflict within French psychiatry. He too cited a 'divergence of opinions' between exponents of 'spiritualism' and 'materialism', a split which, though more acute in Germany, was strong enough in France to produce strife. Renaudin felt that since the beginning of the century 'too exclusive ideas' had been adopted one after another, and that this tendency had caused confusion by precipitating equally dogmatic ideas in reaction. By 1854, he claimed, the 'struggles' between the two schools had ceased and a 'marked tendency towards a unity of views and action' was operating to engender a commonly approved doctrine. This doctrine was the 'psychosomatic dualism' of mental life which, to Renaudin's mind, offered the best way to comprehend the 'reciprocal action of the mind and body' in insanity.[105] Neither affects nor physical lesions alone sufficed as causes; every psychical 'aberration' had to be linked to an unlocalized 'functional anomaly' of the body.[106] Renaudin argued that there occurred in the delirium of madness a 'lesion in the universality of psychological functions' involving the whole organism.[107] He hoped this notion, which he ascribed to Morel, would place the science of mental pathology on a secure footing and bridge the gap between the materialist and psychological schools.

Morel's impression of the tensions within the profession stemming from the exaggerated dichotomy of viewpoints was virtually the same as that of his colleagues at the Société Médico-psychologique, Cerise, Falret, and Renaudin. Morel's hope was for conciliation since the variety of pronounced viewpoints only served to fuel 'interminable discussions'. Like Cerise,

Falret, and Renaudin he granted that the brain was the 'material substratum' and 'indispensable condition' of all thought, but he denied that the material organization of the brain was the sole cause of morbid or normal psychical phenomena. To declare that the brain produced thought was as inadmissible as declaring that light was produced by the substance of the eye. For Morel, it was necessary to postulate an 'immaterial' force in intellectual activity such as the 'soul' no less objectively real than was electricity in physics.[108] This force underlined the 'incontestable influence of ideas on the organism', a fact, Morel observed, that Cerise had also pointed out.[109] Morel's intention was to show that the brain was the 'seat' of mental disease although its cause was sometimes not found in that organ.[110] In any case, the entire search for physical or psychological causes was in his eyes falsely dichotomous. In a sense, the search for physical or psychological causes was a 'privilege' for doctors that ought not to detract from the equally important obligation to provide treatment and care for the mentally ill.[111]

These responses to the mid-century troubles show that psychiatrists were very conscious of the unsatisfying sectarianism; most were confident that a new and more edifying consensus was either imminent or had already taken shape. Some like Foville and Morel thought the conflicts had arisen because the question of the link between body and mind had simply been posed incorrectly.[112] Yet, whatever the diagnosis, it was generally agreed that pathological anatomy had failed to supply evidence of cerebral lesions in the large number of mental disorders without dementia; hence, the materialist view was no longer tenable. It, like 'psychologism', had to be modified to comply with the facts derived from autopsy. Insanity was now seen as a morbid manifestation of intelligence, characterized by a diffuse functional lesion of the nervous system, entailing the pathology of the entire animal economy and obviating any firm separation of mind and body. As Morel put it: 'we have established sufficiently that mental alienation taken in its most general meaning is only the expression of pathological conditions that establish themselves between the diseased organism and the intelligence'.[113] Yet, at the same time the mind was viewed as a distinctly active and spontaneous element that could not be reduced to the material organization of the brain; mental life was neither independent from the operations of the organism nor a mere epiphenomemon of somatic structure.[114]

Thus a new and somewhat contradictory medico-psychological consensus was significantly forming while the psychiatric profession was under attack from the government, press, and other interest groups and was divided along theoretical lines. In the next section the relevance of the theory of morbid heredity to this change in conceptualization will be explored.

THE THEORY OF MORBID HEREDITY AS CORNERSTONE FOR THE NEW CONSENSUS

What is not yet clear is how the theory of morbid heredity fits the transition in psychiatric orientation. Indeed, at first glance it might seem that a theory postulating the transmission of an organic disposition to mental, neurological, or physical disorders would not be compatible with an interpretation of mental function authorizing the existence of an immaterial 'soul'. Nevertheless, the manner in which French mental pathologists understood morbid heredity not only corresponded to the new psychiatric viewpoint, but also made the latter palatable to both psychogenically and somatically oriented and religiously inclined doctors.

Everything hinged on the new concept of a 'lesion' in mental medicine, and it is not surprising that it was the work of Morel that best illustrates the issue. In his *Treatise on Mental Diseases* of 1860 Morel explicitly recognized the challenge to his 'physiologico-psychological interpretation' posed by the absence of cerebral lesions in autopsies performed on the insane. He confessed that post-mortem examinations had in some cases of mental illness furnished no palpable evidence of injury or disease. Yet he was reluctant to conclude that the nervous system had not been modified pathologically. He argued instead that in these instances of 'madness without lesion' what probably had occurred was similar to the process undergone in cramps, contractures, and paraplegia: paraphrasing Griesinger, Morel contended that even when inflammation of the spinal cord was not verified in autopsy, this phenomenon was still a result of an affection of that organ. In cerebral disorders the situation was the same: in certain cases, hyperemia had disturbed the brain yet the traces had evidently disappeared after the early and acute stages of the disease.[115]

Morel was loath to draw the 'antiphysiological' conclusions of the psychologists from the patho-anatomical data.[116] Instead he revised the standard anatomical definition of a 'lesion'. The lesion no longer referred to a localized injury to an organ discernible in autopsy. It now indicated a functional injury, an often temporary physiological condition leaving no trace of its presence. Thus he dismissed both the purely psychological perspective and the notion of organ specificity and proposed a much more dynamic and physiological understanding of a lesion.[117] And it is here that morbid heredity became crucial. For example, Morel wrote in 1860 that:

> 'it is in another order of functional cerebral lesions that it will be necessary to search for the pathological element in the great number of circumstances. This element is nothing else than the degeneracy with which hereditarily tainted individuals are invariably stricken in the normal development of their nervous systems.'[118]

The usual patho-anatomical signs found in advanced cases of dementia – such as darkening or thickening of the arachnoidal membrane of the brain, softening of the encephalon, and adhesions of the meninges – did not appear in *post-mortem* examinations of this class of *aliénés héréditaires*. Morel maintained that the clinician's eyes ought to be trained instead on 'certain vices of structure' or physiognomic stigmata that indicated an internal flaw.[119] This flaw was an 'organic lesion' whose meaning for Morel had to be broadened considerably to account for the anomalies of pathological anatomy. The lesion could still be viewed as 'material', for Morel identified it with a hereditary condition that produced 'troubles in the functions of the animal economy'. In order to understand 'the state of consecutive degeneracy' that distinguished so many of the insane, Morel went on, 'it is important to dispense for an instant with the common sense notion attributed to the word *lesion*, and to enter into the real significance of the word *heredity* in a very particular manner'.[120] In other words, heredity became the new reference point and conceptual basis for the modified interpretation of a psychiatric lesion.

The change in the meaning of a lesion from a localized organic injury to a diffuse functional state of the nervous system was consistent with Morel's emphasis on affective causes. For example, he argued that 'troubles of an intellectual and moral order' were as crucial as toxic agents or improper nutrition in creating lesions that produced degeneracy. Heredity was simply the somatic basis for the lesion associated with these causes.[121]

Accordingly, Morel believed that volitional activity would effectively alter the conditions responsible for the tide of degeneracy by changing the pathogenic 'moral' environment. By so doing, one could minimize the effects of exposure to 'immoral' ideas or faulty education, experiences that could produce physiological disorders just as easily as the toxic properties of an industrial milieu. It is understandable, then, how patho-physiological considerations and an adherence to a scientifically acceptable free will could coexist within the Morelian theory of degeneracy: a lesion that was psychosomatically as well as physiologically engendered and whose somatic reality was redeemed by heredity allowed for a wide variety of persuasions and approaches. Heredity was the indispensable somatic element and reference point, according to which mental doctors could indulge their fondness for cataloguing any number of physical or psychological causes depending on individual taste.[122]

Even a somaticist like Moreau found the new orientation to his liking. Since the beginning of his career Moreau had been intrigued by the body/mind problem and had favoured consistently the organicist position.[123] In the 1850s his attention turned for the first time to the hereditary issue. In his 1859 *Morbid Psychology* he rejected the phrenology of Gall that had flourished in the early July Monarchy, though he still eschewed the equally outmoded 'psychologism'.[124] His interest had now centred on the question of mental aptitude. This property depended on 'organization', yet Moreau conceded that thought could not be reduced to the material organization of the brain, nor was an organic disposition accessible to the senses. Reluctant like Morel to question its objective and material reality, Moreau as a good somaticist attributed the organic disposition that he felt dominated the psychology of the insane to a dynamic hereditary state of the nervous system. The indistinct nature of this neuropathic heredity can be understood better if it is contrasted with the other conditions that Moreau claimed could not account for the anomalies of intelligence in mental pathology: education, physiology, and comparative physiology. Indeed, its indeterminate nature was characterized as 'extraphysiological' by Achille Foville who reviewed Moreau's book for the *Annales médico-psychologiques*.[125] It is clear, therefore, that morbid heredity, conventionally thought of as a physical cause, denoted to Moreau a rather diffuse pathological state of the nervous system characterized by 'disequilibrium' and functional disturbances of vital nervous force and represented by certain modes of thinking and morbid ideas. As such it could be used to neutralize the awkward problem of the non-empirical status of many lesions of insanity and sustain the confidence that the pathological condition of lunacy was somatic. Morel evidently saw matters in the same light.

Thus, the consensus based on morbid heredity is best illustrated by the way in which the somaticist Moreau and the devoutly Catholic Morel responded to the challenge to mental medicine posed by the shortcomings of pathological anatomy. By reducing all phenomena of the nervous system to a hereditarily produced lesion and not to an anatomical injury, they could be either organicist or psychological without appearing to be less scientific or medical for abandoning pathological anatomy. Morel referred to a hereditary lesion so diffuse that it could derive from psychosomatic sources. Moreau for his part referred to an equally imperceptible 'neuropathic diathesis' as the origin for the 'nervous dynamism' responsible for the 'morbid modifications' of the nervous system.[126] These characterizations make it manifest why the factor of a hereditary transmission of an organic system like the nervous system was compatible with a dualistic view of body and mind; neither exclusively mentalist nor physical, heredity was a concept of physiological psychology that stressed the mutual influence of mind and body, a principle that explained the seemingly contradictory notion of an integrated organism which nevertheless featured a mental force that could not be reduced to material organisation.[126a] The problems presented by the anomalies of pathological anatomy were solved neatly by the hypothesis of morbid heredity: a pathologist like Morel could place the somatic and aetiological onus on organic heredity and thus salvage the assurance that it was the body that was diseased, while still associating great importance with psychogenic factors. Heredity in the Morelian sense was elastic enough to accommodate psycho- and neuropathological considerations, for it did not specify either the material or mental basis for the automatism underlying the involuntary character of madness. It is understandable, then, that Erwin Ackerknecht should have described the theory of hereditary degeneracy as 'pseudosomaticist': faced with the growing failure to discover structural brain damage and reluctant to jettison the somaticism that tied them to mainstream medicine and assured their credibility as medical scientists, psychiatrists referred to hereditary 'facts' and hence skirted the problem of unverifiable organic lesions.[127]

These concerns that psychiatry might lose its ties to the rest of medicine were voiced not only in the articles of the *Annales médico-psychologiques* dealing with 'the relations between the mental affections and the diverse functional or organic lesions that characterised the ordinary diseases' such as the neuroses and general paralysis;[128] they were also voiced by doctors such as Henry Bonnet, a member of the Société Médico-psychologique and asylum physician at Maréville. Quoting Leuret, Bonnet complained that the failures of pathological anatomy meant that insanity could be interpreted as a disorder unlike 'the common illnesses characterised by physical symptoms' and ruled by 'an order of phenomena completely foreign to the general laws of matter'.[129] The implications for mental pathologists were calamitous; as Albert Lemoine, a professor of philosophy, wrote in his *The Insane from the Perspective of Philosophy, Morality and Society* of 1862, if madness were simply a case of a mind being in error and thus fundamentally dissimilar to a syndrome like cerebral fever, then the doctor had no special claim to the treatment and cure of insanity because as a professional he was essentially a 'healer of the corporeal machine'. Any non-doctor could pose as the healer of mental illness if it could be shown to be a disorder distinct from the other maladies treated by medicine. It is little wonder, therefore, that heredity was a convenient alternative to the insufficient lesion of pathological anatomy: it re-established to the satisfaction of many French psychiatrists the belief that the insane patient was 'always a diseased body whose reason had become unhinged as a consequence of the general and close union of the body and soul' and whose cure was still the domain of the mental pathologist by virtue of this fact, whether physical or 'moral' methods were employed.[130] Scientific credibility was at issue: to view insanity as an illness whose causes belonged to 'an order of phenomena that has nothing to do with the laws of matter' was to run the risk of losing touch with the corporeal body. 'If this is admitted', Bonnet wrote, 'organic heredity and the organism in general will be passed over lightly' much to the detriment of the doctor's professional status.[131]

Like Morel, Lemoine saw no inconsistency between his firm conviction that insanity was a disease of the body and his allowance for the 'concurrent' influence of psychological and physical causes of mental alienation.[132] Monist in his interpretation of the organism as a complex unity of body and mind, Lemoine resembled contemporaries such as Moreau, Cerise, Renaudin, and Falret in his inability to discard dualist terminology when he described the phenomena of insanity. After all, to have dropped dualism would have meant dispensing with affective phenomena and thus forfeiting their uniqueness as pathological symptoms. The virtue of morbid heredity lay in its capacity as a monist biological principle to accommodate dualistic approaches.[133]

THE THEORY OF MORBID HEREDITY AS ADAPTATION TO SCIENTIFIC MILIEU

Facing socio-political hostility and severe intellectual problems stemming from the difficulties of maintaining the physicalist orientation of their profession, French psychiatrists were understandably concerned with sustaining their image as an accredited branch of mainstream medicine. Here, too, the theory of morbid heredity served a crucial purpose as an intellectual weapon in alienism's struggle to assert its medico-scientific respectability; by citing the role of heredity in mental illness psychiatrists echoed themes not only of general medicine but the biological sciences as well.

The transition from pathological anatomy to a new consensus based on a primarily functional lesion of the nervous system whose origin was hereditary coincided with a transition stage in French medicine. As Ackerknecht has written, the 'Paris school' of clinical medicine had reached a 'dead end' by the 1840s.[134] Despite great advances in pathology, the mid-1830s witnessed the beginnings of a self-critical movement in French medicine. While certain observers detected 'sterility' and 'dead routine' gradually overtaking the enthusiasm that had animated Parisian doctors since the early years of the century, it was becoming increasingly obvious to others that Germany was replacing France as the leader of European medicine. It was felt that localism and pathological anatomy had diverted pathologists from therapeutics and from detailed studies of morbid causes.[135]

There is evidence to suggest that the primary professional objective of French psychiatry was to align itself with general medicine both during these crucial years and earlier in the century. J.P. Falret confessed that he and his colleagues in mental medicine had become pathological anatomists initially because of the 'general tendency' of medicine in the 1820s and 1830s to look for anatomical lesions in autopsy.[136] Morel also testified to psychiatry's close ties to mainstream medicine. He addressed his *Treatise on Mental Diseases* of 1860 especially to 'non-alienist doctors', and wrote in his *Treatise on Degeneracy* three years earlier that his 'dominant idea' was to 'link mental alienation to general medicine more strongly than has been done until now'.[137] This desire to be identified with the rest of medicine was reinforced and amplified in the goal set by the Société Médico-psychologique in 1852: 'the *rapprochement* of the natural and psychological sciences'.[138] The idea was still very much alive in 1867 when the president of the Société, Robert-Hippolyte Brochin, reminded other members that, in order to contribute to the progress of medicine, psychiatrists had to break out of their 'isolation' and maintain constant touch with movements in philosophy, economics, and law as well as in anatomy, physiology, pathology, and 'medical methods of study', 'Psychiatry', Brochin declared, was 'intimately tied ... by the nature of its subject to the various sciences'.[139]

As a profession, then, French psychiatry seemed anxious to identify itself with the biomedical sciences in the 1850s and 1860s: retrenchment and isolation were definitely not its aims. Therefore, it seems that the psychiatric rejection of pathological anatomy stemmed less from the empirical development of its own clinical studies than from the example provided by the Paris School of Medicine. After all, since Pinel's and Esquirol's day psychiatrists had been aware of pathological anatomy's prominent shortcomings in mental pathology.[140] That doctors should have ignored the teachings of these venerable authorities until the time the Paris School rejected pathological anatomy speaks worlds about the deference psychiatry paid to the 'tendencies' of general medicine in the nineteenth century in keeping with its status as a sub-speciality of medicine whose lineage by mid-nineteenth century was unimpressive and whose subject matter – morbid mental phenomena – was often deemed unscientific. By following the lead of the Paris School in rejecting pathological anatomy and adopting the physiological notion of a lesion, psychiatry was merely conforming to the feature of its post-Pinel history that Richard H. Shryock identified: that is, its 'continuous effort to employ the concepts and methods of contemporary somatic medicine'.[141]

Did the theory of morbid heredity make this endeavour realistic? In the eyes of some mental pathologists it constituted a common ground on which psychiatry could ally itself with other branches of medicine and science. Speaking to the Parisian Academy of Medicine on 15 December, 1851, Moreau borrowed 'certain zoological facts' to contend that 'constant' and 'invariable laws' rule the manner in which the 'organization' of parents affects that of their children and that 'isolated traits' are not what constitute hereditary transmission; rather, it was 'large series of organs' such as the nervous system which were passed down during the act of 'generation'.[142] Achille Foville wrote of 'the great fact of heredity that dominates with all its prominence so many important medical questions'.[143] Another author wrote in the *Annales médico-psychologiques* in 1864 that 'the hereditary transmission of diseases or the tendency to contract them, has attracted much more attention recently than previously; the treatises of medicine have grown richer in this respect because of numerous and scholarly works of research'.[144] The general idea of heredity also became particularly current in the era of evolutionary biology.[145] For example, Charcot's pupil Jules Dejerine noted how heredity of the nervous system was a biological force that governed all morbid or normal affective behaviour.[146] Ribot, too, cited heredity as the fundamental aspect of evolution, a principle that accounted for the entire spectrum of psychological and physiological features of life. He went even further and stated that 'heredity is but one form of that ultimate law which by physicists is called the conservation of energy and by metaphysicians universal causality'.[147]

Achille Foville pointed to the studies conducted by physiologist C.E. Brown-Séquard on the hereditary transmission in animals of 'morbid states caused in one or other of their parents by some injury to the nervous system'.[148] Foville even drew attention to the young science of anthropology and the Société d'Anthropologie, founded in 1859. He noted how its membership was primarily made up of doctors, a fact which proved how anthropology's 'importance was appreciated by the medical community'. He also cited the work of the natural historian Armand de Quatrefages, who in 1868 held the only chair in France in anthropology and who had demonstrated 'what modifications had been imposed successively on the primitive type [of the species] by the combined influences of heredity and the environment, so that a considerable number of different races can be derived from them'.[149]

A good example of the way in which the psychiatric use of the hereditary concept can be traced to developments in biology and other medical disciplines was an 1868 paper in the *Annales médico-psychologiques* on 'the mania of reason', its aetiology and its pathogeny. Its author, a Dr Campagne from the asylum of Montdevergues in the Vaucluse, saw heredity not as a cause but as a 'means' through which 'natural selection' – the 'real cause' of the 'mania of reason' – could exercise its influence. Natural selection was an 'infallible biological law' according to Campagne, that determined the proportion of pathological offspring in the crossings between parents of the same species. Yet heredity was equally important and he cited Quatrefages's 'hereditary force' whose persistence was often 'troubled' by unwise marriages between individuals with medically dubious ancestors. Psychiatric disorders were no less susceptible to these biological facts; hence, Campagne observed how 'psychical force' could remain latent only to appear 'in all its energy' at one moment because of a relatively insignificant precipitating cause. Mental pathology provided frequent examples of this 'atavism', a hereditary phenomenon, Campagne added, 'unanimously acknowledged in the biological sciences'.[150] From Campagne's remarks about heredity and those of some of his colleagues in psychiatry it can be seen how these doctors were able to draw connections between themselves and other sciences such as biology, neurology, and physiology on the basis of their adherence to the theory of morbid heredity.

Moreover, it is unlikely that the appearance at roughly the same time of the psychiatric theory of morbid heredity, cellular patho-physiology, and the germ theory of infectious diseases was historically fortuitous. Louis Pasteur's attack on spontaneous generation in the 1860s coincided with the rise to prominence of the theory of morbid heredity. In so far as Pasteur refused to concede that matter could organize itself without pre-existing parental germs or organisms, he lent credence to the general notion that mere matter was not responsible by itself for vital phenomena.[151] Similarly, Rudolf Virchow and Claude Bernard avoided reducing organic processes to physico-chemical molecular forces. The vital force characterizing complex cell organization was better explained by cell continuity than by the laws of physics and chemistry; hence, Virchow's doctrine of cell pathology: *omnis cellula a cellula*.[152]

Psychiatrists exploited these ideas with alacrity in reference to morbid heredity. One French neuropsychiatrist saw the congruence between cellular patho-physiology and heredity when he wrote that heredity transmitted a 'nervous cell' which acted as the germ for a later neurological disorder.[153] Renaudin and Campagne were just two of the many who cited a 'pathological germ' developing progressively as it was passed from one generation to another.[154] Indeed, it is remarkable how often the word 'germ' was employed loosely by psychiatrists in the 1850s and 1860s in a hereditary context, in light of the fact that insanity was considered to be a chronic rather than an acute or infectious disease.

Finally, the 'explosive march' towards scientific autonomy and eminence of experimental physiology[155] did not go unnoticed by French mental pathologists. The similarities between the functional interpretation of a lesion as 'the measuring unit of physiological investigation' and the way in which a doctor like Morel conceived of a cerebro-spinal lesion have already been noted. Morel in particular was conscious of the importance of physiology to his theory of degeneracy in another respect: several times he cited Claude Bernard's experimental studies of toxic substances,[156] and indicated the relationship between Bernard's experimental physiology and 'the question of degeneracy' in his preface to the *Treatise on Degeneracy*.[157] Thus, Morel was expressing the readiness of French psychiatry to borrow ideas from or establish contact with the other scientific currents. And, in as much as the profession was simultaneously undergoing a period of self-questioning and attack from several different angles, it is certainly conceivable that the psychiatric community was endeavouring to bolster its faltering image of expertise in mental medicine by taking every opportunity to indicate its close cognitive correspondence to medicine and the biological and physical sciences. By employing the theory of morbid heredity to account for the origin of the neurophysical lesion that had superseded the lesion of pathological anatomy, psychiatry could keep abreast of conceptual shifts in the biomedical sciences and also associate itself with the experimental science of physiology which, particularly after the publication of Bernard's *An Introduction to the Study of Experimental Medicine* in 1865, enjoyed a special place of honour within the French scientific establishment.[158] At bottom was the great fear of mental pathologists that the recent advances in pathological anatomy had called into question their own science by casting doubts on its status as a legitimate branch of somatic medicine.

THE THEORY OF MORBID HEREDITY AS IDEOLOGICAL ACCOMMODATION

Thus, the emergence of the theory of morbid heredity after 1850 was symptomatic of the low estate of French psychiatry in two respects: first, it served as an intellectual means for healing the troubling rift between somaticists and psychologists; and second, it enhanced the scientific image and credentials of doctors of mental medicine by drawing attention to the shared ideas of mental pathology and the other biomedical sciences. Yet the hereditarian theory was also useful to psychiatrists in another – and perhaps more crucial – way. For no matter how important was the influence exerted by developments in the rest of medicine and the question of psychiatry's scientific status, the abruptly changed intellectual climate of the 1850s and 1860s was no less influential in shaping the process of theory-choice.

As noted earlier, the theological orientation of the imperial regime of Louis Napoleon meant that the erstwhile 'physiology' ran the risk of censure since it smacked of materialism and undermined the notion of a 'free will' or 'soul'. Indeed, materialism, republicanism, and atheism were normally conflated during the Napoleonic Second Empire. Within this changed socio-political and religious environment, it would be surprising if French Psychiatry, customarily identified with the earlier 'materialist' physiology, had not attempted to adapt its philosophical position to the acceptable ideology in order to avoid incurring the hostility of the government.

An example of psychiatry's response to the new political circumstances was the Société Médico-psychologique which gave every indication to the imperial government that its intentions and metaphysical persuasions did not challenge sanctioned ideas. Originally set to open in March 1848, the Société had not received ministerial approbation because of the outbreak of the February revolution, and the resulting disruption in administrative procedure.[159] Its opening was postponed until March 1852, significantly enough in the wake of the December 1851 Napoleonic coup d'état. The Société's new statute of 1852 proclaimed the antagonism between institutional science and revolutionary disturbances: 'the sciences have an essential need for peace and stability; agitation and upheavals are its very cruel enemies.' In the 'Report on the Modifications to Introduce into the Project of a New Statute', the commissioners appointed to draw up the new statute claimed that the original preamble to the 1848 statute had overemphasized 'physiology'; as a consequence 'empirical psychology' had been unfairly overshadowed. In fact, the commissioners stated, psychology had been in danger of being 'absorb[ed]' into 'encephalic physiology': in other words, reduced to the structure and function of the brain. Only the progress attained by the study of the physiology and pathology of the nervous system would ensure that 'the active or voluntary element ... whose mysterious alliance with cerebral organisation' warranted more scrutiny, received the attention it deserved from medical science. And, as a further illustration of the timeliness of the body/mind issue, the new regulations of the Société included a goal that had not appeared in the 1848 statute: the development of 'the science of the relationship of the physical body to the psyche'.[160]

In eschewing 'encephalic physiology', the commissioners rejected the materialist cerebral physiology of Gall; by recommending the further examination of the pathology and physiology of the nervous system they hoped to discover a new and firmer basis for the understanding of the distinct yet ultimately inseparable sides to the individual organism: the mind and the body. Only in this way, the commissioners reasoned, would the 'facts of a superior order' associated with intellectual life be rescued from the neglect they had endured in the heyday of brain physiology and pathological anatomy.

If there were any doubt exactly what the new statute referred to by citing 'facts of a superior order', Philippe Buchez made it plain in his paper entitled 'Several Words on Philosophy with Respect to Mental Alienation', read to the Société Médico-psychologique on July 26, 1852. Buchez was a former Saint-Simonian who had served as deputy mayor of Paris and president of the Constituent Assembly during the Second Republic. He and Cerise had been arrested in December 1851 by the authors of the coup. Buchez had also played a decisive role in founding the Société; indeed, many of his followers and friends were members, including Morel, Cerise, and Édouard Carrière, one of the three commissioners entrusted to draw up the revised 1852 statute.[161] Hence, it is no exaggeration to say that the early Société had a distinctly Buchezian flavour. In his lecture to the Société he argued that 'free will' was a property of life and the organism and attacked 'vulgar physiology' for teaching that thought was instead an inherent property of matter or a mere product of material organization. Buchez's intention was to demonstrate the faculty of 'free will' that constituted one side of the 'double nature' of human beings and whose domination of the organism was proof of 'an active principle of a spiritual nature'. Madness resulted when the dysfunctioning of the organism deceived the patient with illusions and thus paralysed the exercise of his reason and 'moral liberty'.[162] In other words, Buchez hoped to verify scientifically the spiritual side of the human species. His attack on materialism was a welcome endorsement of the religious instinct for officials who had just authorized the establishment of the Société. Buchez's anxiety to show his allegiance to the new regime is understandable in light of his personal involvement in the 1848 revolution; as well, it betokened the Société's willingness to reject its seditious and liberal past since some of its members, like Buchez, Trélat, and Félix Voisin were noted republicans.[163] For example, Louis Delasiauve, a doctor who had run unsuccessfully for the legislature in 1849, was almost obsequious in his 1857 account of the early history of the Société. Obviously conscious of the expediency in removing the stigma of association, since the freedom to hold meetings had been curtailed seriously during the Second Empire,[164] he made the connection between religious orthodoxy and the legitimacy of a scientific society quite clear:

> '"When some", Jesus Christ said, "are gathered in my name, I shall be among them." Associations have been feared for a long time, yet within the domain of charity and science, experience had proved the injustice of this precaution. The Divine Master could not have been lying; men of good will do not fail. The Société Médico-psychologique is a salient example; pure intentions and a prolific zeal animate its members'[165]

Delasiauve claimed that medicine could progress only through the efforts of scientific associations such as the Société. Yet his more basic purpose was to make the existence of the Société compatible with prevailing religious notions; to do so, he implied strongly that the Société was inspired by decidedly Christian values. He would only have done so, it goes without saying, if a psychiatric association had been cause for suspicion in the first place.

Plainly, French psychiatry was anxious to demonstrate its religious orthodoxy and comply with the metaphysical principles enjoying the sanction of a pro-Catholic administration. The question, then, is: what did the theory of morbid heredity have to do with this reaction of the

psychiatric profession to a new sociopolitical environment? Did it authorize
the notion of a 'free will' despite its determinist overtones?

Just as the theory of morbid heredity enabled psychiatrists to adapt to the
post-1840 trend in the Paris school of medicine and to forge a somatic/
psychological compromise, so its vague and imprecise conceptualization
allowed them to leaven their discourses on insanity with spiritual considerations. It must be remembered that the devoutly Catholic Morel saw no
contradiction between a belief in the 'spontaneity and liberty of the soul' and
a dramatic widening of morbid heredity's influence. Quite the contrary; it
has been argued here that it was precisely his espousal of heredity in mental
pathogenesis that enabled Morel to revise the definition of a psychiatric
lesion and hence validate psychosomatic causes. In fact, he cited the Catholic
Buchez frequently as the source for his insights into the mechanisms of
heredity.[166] For the most part, other pathologists seemed untroubled by the
implications for the freedom of the will of an organic hereditary predisposition. However, this was attributable to the way in which they conceived of
its operation. Bonnet quoted Moreau in this respect: 'heredity makes itself
felt much more often in the morbid state than in the healthy state'.[167] Thus,
Bonnet and Moreau were making a crucial distinction between heredity in
disease and heredity in the state of health, a distinction that assumes
particular importance in the study of the mind since heredity's consequential
role in mental pathology did not necessarily have anything to do with the
normal, healthy exercise of the power of reason, though later writers like
Ribot would extend heredity's significance to the domain of normal
psychology. Buchez reinforced the idea of heredity's restriction to pathological matters of the mind by making moral freedom and insanity mutually
exclusive: the fact that the latter was the mental state corresponding to
certain organic conditions simply meant that the former lay outside the
realm of pathology and that the morbid state revealed nothing substantial
about the operation of moral liberty.

Most mental pathologistis seemed relieved that the hypothesis of a
hereditary transmission of a distinctive state of the nervous system rein-
troduced the somatic element into discussions of insanity that had
threatended to degenerate into purely psychological disquisitions. And yet,
because the hereditary lesion was so non-specific and unlocalized it was still
possible to accommodate the notion of a 'soul'. This was Brierre de
Boismont's position: the acceptance of a hereditary 'physical condition' of
the nervous system as the indispensable, 'solid foundation' of psychological
phenomena was simply recognition that the nervous system was 'the
instrument of the soul'.[168] Bonnet agreed; though he wrote that 'to account
properly for heredity one must above all be an organicist', it was quite
another thing to 'treat disdainfully the affairs of the soul'.[169] Simply because
matter was 'intimately tied' to the mental functioning of the intelligence and
the exercise of morality, there was no reason to deny the capacity for
spontaneous moral decisions. By invoking a functional lesion of the nervous
system whose origin was hereditary, psychiatrists were able to silence

doubts of the somatic reality of their views of insanity while referring a contentious issue to a principle of physiological science that appeared to endorse religious themes and avoid the stigma of materialism.[170]

Thus, the atmosphere of political insecurity reinforced the sense of professional instability during the Second Empire. The theory of morbid heredity can now be understood as a creative intellectual response to a period of socio-political pressure, cognitive disorientation, and crisis within the profession. It has already been noted that the concept of a functional, hereditary lesion had explicitly acknowledged similarities to the lesions of pathophysiology, and that the general idea of heredity enjoyed a particular resonance in the age of evolutionary biology. It is undeniable that this scientific milieu after the mid-century made the theory of morbid heredity all the more acceptable as a way of improving psychiatry's desperately poor image and neutralizing public enmity, while it helped to heal the divisions within the professional community. Yet there is still another reason for the emergence of this culturally palatable theory: further to ease the pressure exerted by a hostile political regime and popular press on the psychiatric community, alienists adopted an ideological feature of general cultural appeal. And, here, too, the hereditarian theory proved to be beneficial as a culturally consonant idea. It is in this capacity that the final reason is found for psychiatry's intellectual attraction to the theory of morbid heredity.

The post-1848 period in France not only witnessed the acceptance of hereditarian explanations in insanity; as well, it was marked by an acute disillusionment among many intellectuals stemming from the political failures between 1848 and 1851.[171] This sentiment was expressed most often by liberals or members of the French left whose exposure to the events of popular insurrection in 1848 had caused them to lower their estimations of the masses and labouring classes. Still, the post-1848 reaction was just another stage in a steadily growing and century-long disenchantment that characterized French liberalism.[172] The dashed hopes of 1848 for political emancipation and social regeneration often translated into an elitist and antipopulist attitude on the part of intellectuals based on the belief in the 'congenital democractic immaturity of the Latin peoples'.[173] Thinkers such as Alexis de Tocqueville, Ernest Renan, and Hippolyte Taine contributed to the gradual revision of the original spirit of bourgeois liberalism by ascribing more and more importance to innate inequalities among races and social classes. French liberalism became more intent on preserving its heritage as a class and its intellectual leadership than honouring its radical commitment to civil liberty and freedom enunciated in 1789.[174] The French liberal became conservative instead, and in so doing came to respect heredity as a biomedical fact that explained fitness to govern and social adaptability.[175]

However, it would be a mistake to depict this pessimism as a purely bourgeois intellectual phenomenon. In fact, it crossed all political party boundaries. While it is true that the Second Empire deprived many liberal intellectuals of influence enjoyed during the July Monarchy, imprisoned some, and forced others into exile, 'one would greatly underestimate the significance of the new pessimism by merely regarding it as a form of political propaganda of men of letters against a detested regime. A mood of despondency was also common among writers who were politically indifferent or even in sympathy with the Empire.... Not only political pamphleteers but also clear-headed scholars ... and profound philosophers ... expressed their misgivings about the trends of their times.'[176]

In other words, 'traditionalists' as well as 'progressive thinkers' subscribed to this profound scepticism of France's democratic future. It was a common intellectual stance for *savants* of all political persuasions and tastes.

It is remarkable how well psychiatric writings on morbid heredity conformed to this pervasive sociopolitical pessimism.[177] For instance, the subject of 'great social commotions' often surfaced in conjunction with considerations of hereditary degeneracy. Morel and Moreau were the leaders in this enterprise, yet they were certainly not the only ones to address the problem. The many references to the pathological heredity of the social classes responsible for civil disorder strengthened the connection between the labouring masses and the innate instinct for deviant behaviour exhibited by the insane. For example, in his obituary article on Morel in 1874, Brierre de Boismont acknowledged the former's contributions to the study of heredity's role in the outbreak of revolution and the exacerbation of the morbid conditions among the 'dangerous classes'. These conditions gave rise to the *'fous démocratiques'* who threatened the existence of all social institutions and cherished ideals.[178]

It was especially in the wake of the Franco-Prussian War and the Paris Commune that the correlation between morbid heredity and social revolution hardened in the minds of psychiatrists. One work that seemed to distil the mood of the profession was J.V. Laborde's *Insurrectionary Men and Acts in Paris in Terms of Morbid Psychology*: *Letters to Doctor Moreau (de Tours)*. As the title indicates, Laborde dedicated his book to Moreau who presented it to the Société Médico-psychologique on January 15, 1872.[179] Laborde also acknowledged his debt to Morel, Baillarger, Renaudin, and Lunier, all of whom had argued for the importance of hereditary predisposition in insanity. For Laborde, French society was 'sick in body and mind'. The affliction was essentially hereditary and had produced a large number of individuals congenitally disposed to 'collective madness'.[180] This 'instinctive illness' was found mostly among the 'popular and working classes' who had been responsible during the last half-century for 'the political and social commotions' that had plagued French life.[181] Laborde quoted from Moreau's own *Morbid Psychology* to illustrate how hereditarily weakened men and women could be manipulated to commit horrendous political acts.[182] Other treatments of the subject such as Henri Legrand du Saulle's 'The Mental State of Parisians during the Events of 1870–71' made the same connection between mentally predisposed neuropaths and revolution.[183] The neuropathic heredity caused by alcoholism was also cited as the reason for 'the physical and moral decadence' that had putatively led to France's defeat at the hands of the Prussians and the events of the Paris Commune.[184] In all these accounts, the influence of Morel's and Moreau's original speculations stood out.

These examples of psychiatric characterizations of social disorder or cultural decline from the standpoint of morbid heredity could be multiplied substantially, yet the truth is that French psychiatrists spent a great deal of time and energy writing on the question of France's decline and offering interpretations from mental medicine. It is small wonder that the issue surfaced so often: the profession publicly announced its openness to extra-scientific ideas, most notably when the Société Médico-psychologique welcomed into its ranks in 1852 'philosophers', 'historians', 'moralists', 'poets', and 'ministers of religion'.[185] In addition, the Société admitted that the study of mental pathology gave rise within the domain of medicine to 'the gravest problems of social science and philosophy'.[186] Noting in 1867 that 'general medical science' had grown closer over the years to law, economics, public hygiene, psychology, and the 'moral sciences', Brochin also contended that psychiatry had become a richer science through its treatment of 'social and philosophic questions' since 1852; similarly, mental pathologists were encouraged to look towards 'history' for insights into morbid psychical phenomena.[187]

Morel underscored the receptiveness of French psychiatry to the exchange of ideas between the social and medical sciences when he wrote in 1860 that 'the historian who will want to study the origin of all the doctrines conceived to explain the nature of insanity will have to refer of necessity to the influence of the various philosophic doctrines' of the nineteenth century.[188] But it was Buchez who came closest to acknowledging the debt owed by psychiatry to philosophy. In his review of Morel's *Treatise of Degeneracy* he discussed favourably the theory of degeneracy, noting how as a bio-anthropological view it necessarily attracted the attention of 'men of state' and constituted a 'governmental science'.[189] He stated that to obtain a 'rigorous definition' and assess the significance of 'the question of degeneracies of the human race', one had to refer to 'the philosophy of history', a view of man's past that focused on both the 'degradation' and the 'perfectibility' of the species. Morel's treatment of the 'possibility of anthropological progress' was, according to Buchez, one that other doctors ought to read carefully since it dealt with a topic whose elucidation could only enhance psychiatry and 'place our science in the superior rank that the provident and educational professions occupy in the social domain'.[190] In addressing the Société Médico-psychologique, Buchez was clearly pointing out the professional benefits to be accrued by psychiatrists if they were to pursue the study of hereditary degeneracy. Furthermore, by drawing attention to the relevance of the 'philosophy of history' to a theory of mental medicine such as degeneracy, he confirmed that the theory of morbid heredity paralleled a broad interpretation of history which accentuated the rise and fall of the race. Indeed, in his characterization of human beings as the mouthpieces, so to speak, of powerful ideas,[191] Buchez hypothesized that scientific thinkers were basically the exponents of a *Zeitgeist* rather than disinterested medical scientists.

Thus, according to Buchez's own testimony, the example of the theory of degeneracy shows that French psychiatrists were quite eager to adopt ideas from outside the profession that improved the status of their science, attested to their political and religious orthodoxy, and confirmed their ideological conformity. In this regard, the theory of morbid heredity was ideal: it recycled contemporaneous intellectual currents into medico-scientific 'truths' that purported to explain the socio-scientific problems of revolution and national decline. It was an effective mediation between a swelling disappointment among French thinkers with respect to the democratic capacity of the urban lower classes and a state of cognitive dissonance among members of the psychiatric community. By deriving political dysfunction and decline from the virtually epidemiological mental state of the labouring classes that owed its virulence to heredity, doctors in effect brought their thinking into line with that of the major exponents of cultural pessimism. In the process they demonstrated their desire to win the approbation of the social world for their beleaguered profession.

Conclusion

It has been argued that the hereditarianism espoused by French psychiatrists between the mid-century and the 1890s thrived because it was a broadly defined, free-ranging, and culturally resonant concept which helped to disguise the confusion surrounding claims to psychiatric knowledge and to refurbish the scientific image of medical psychologists in the eyes of their non-alienist colleagues, society, and law. This process in recognizable in the early history of the Société Médico-psychologique and its journal, the *Annales Médico-psychologiques*. It was precipitated by a complex *conjoncture* of antipsychiatric medical, social, political, and religious forces during the middle third of the nineteenth century. The confluence of these elements created what might be called a psychiatric 'state of siege mentality'. Mental pathologists sought to counteract this attitude and neutralize hostility by embracing a concept of great political, social, and religious currency. Thus, French psychiatrists co-opted the social forces antagonistic to their profession through ideological adaptation. The results, if not unqualified, were at least positive enough to prompt Legrand du Saulle to comment in 1876 that psychiatry had gained a significant measure of social and medico-legal credibility during the previous forty years.[192] Yet, whatever the extent of the victory French medical psychologists imagined they had achieved by the 1880s, psychiatry's position within medicine and society remains somewhat insecure to this day.[193] As long as it is obliged to deal with the apparently insoluble mind/body question, and as long as psychopathology is explicitly and implicitly infused with normative behavioural and moral criteria, psychiatry will be vulnerable to the kind of social criticism and professional disorientation experienced by French mad-doctors in the mid-nineteenth century.

Notes

1 Georges Genil-Perrin, *Histoire des origines et de l'évolution de l'idée de dégénérescence en médecine mentale* (Paris: Leclerc, 1913), p. 9.

2 Genil-Perrin, *Histoire des origines*, pp. 11–12.

3 Paul Sérieux, *Valentin Magnan: Sa Vie et son oeuvre 1835–1916* (Paris: Masson, 1918), p. 62.

4 Besides Genil-Perrin, *Histoire des origines*, there is now a considerable literature on degeneracy theory; see Annemarie Wettley, 'Zur Problemgeschichte der "Dégénérescence"', *Sudhoffs Archiv.* 43 (1959): 193–212; Peter Burgener, *Die Einflüsse des Zeitgenössischen Denkens in Morels Begriff der 'Dégénérescence'* (Zurich, 1964); Milton Gold, 'The Early Psychiatrists on Degeneracy and Genius', *Psychoanalysis and the Psychoanalytical Rev.* 47 (1960–61): 37–55; Ruth Friedlander, 'B.A. Morel and the Theory of Degenerescence: The Introduction of Anthropology into Psychiatry' (University of California, San Francisco, Ph.D. thesis, 1973); François Bing, 'La Théorie de la dégénérescence', in Jacques Postel and Claude Quetel (eds), *Nouvelle histoire de la psychiatrie* (Toulouse: Privat, 1983), pp. 351–56; A. Zaloszyc, 'Les dégénérescences: une préhistoire?', Supplément aux *Confrontations psychiatriques* 16 (1978): 1–11; for the prevalence of hereditarian ideas in nineteenth-century science and society, see Jean Borie, *Mythologies de l'hérédité au XIXe siècle* (Paris: Editions Galilées, 1981); Larry Stewart, 'Freud before Oedipus: Race and Heredity in the Origins of Psychoanalysis', *Journal of the History of Biology* 9 (1977): 215–28; Charles Rosenberg, 'The Bitter Fruit: Heredity, Disease, and Social Thought in Nineteenth-Century America', in Rosenberg, *No Other Gods: On Science and American Social Thought* (Baltimore: Johns Hopkins Press, 1976), pp. 25–53. For the history of French psychiatry in general, see Henri Baruk, *La Psychiatrie française de Pinel à nos jours* (Paris: Presses Universitaires de France, 1967); Robert Castel, *L'Ordre psychiatrique: L'Âge d'or de l'aliénisme* (Paris: Editions de Minuit, 1976), G. Lanteri-Laura, 'Chronicité dans la psychiatrie française moderne', *Annales E.S.C.* 27 (1972): 548–68; Mark Daniel Alexander, 'The Administration of Madness and Attitudes Towards the Insane in Nineteenth-Century Paris' (Johns Hopkins University, Ph.D. thesis, 1976). Jan Goldstein has dealt with the relationship between professionalism in French psychiatry and medical theory-choice at an earlier stage in the history of French mental medicine in her 'French Psychiatry in Social and Political Context: The Formation of a New Profession 1820–60' (Columbia University, Ph.D. thesis, 1978).

5 Genil-Perrin, *Histoire des origines* pp. 266, 273–75, 279.

6 Heredity remained basically a mystery to biologists and medical men throughout the nineteenth century. For example, see Ch. Letourneau, 'Hérédité', *Dictionnaire encyclopédique des sciences médicales* (Paris: 1888), vol. 13, p. 592. For an earlier reference to the confusion and wide differences of opinion

surrounding the action, forms, and limits of hereditary transmission, see Prosper Lucas, *Traité philosophique et physiologique de l'hérédité naturelle dans les états de santé et de maladie du système nerveux*, 2 vols (Paris: Baillière, 1847–50), vol. 1, p. xi. This testimony matches what Rosenberg has written of the American context, 'Bitter Fruit', p. 45.

7 The word 'theory', though it will be used in this paper to describe the general psychiatric view of morbid heredity, is essentially a misnomer: as will become apparent, there was no rigorous formulation of heredity's influence on madness adopted by all doctors. Nevertheless, in as much as French psychiatrists referred to a theory of hereditary degeneracy, it is legitimate to use the term.

8 Of course, there are problems in assuming that all French psychiatrists (or 'alienists' as they often called themselves) formed a tightly-knit group of medical men with identical interests and beliefs. They were dispersed throughout the country, with only between one-third and one-fourth working in Paris. J. Baillarger, 'Association des médecins des hospices d'aliénés', *Annales médico-psychologiques* 1 (1843): 181. They obtained different kinds of employment in both private *maisons de santé* and public asylums. Also, the glut of doctors meant that there was much in-fighting for a comparatively small pool of potential clients. However, the majority did work in state-funded public facilities (Goldstein, 'French Psychiatry', p. 307), and the professional imperatives of a fledgling specialty of medicine eager to make its mark in society and science were powerful forces operating to unify this group of state functionaries into a more or less cohesive community.

9 The Société Médico-psychologique testified to the influence of the centralizating tendencies within French psychiatry and justified the use of the word 'community' to describe its members. The Société included virtually all the leading psychiatrists of the 1850–1900 period and was the sole association of French mad-doctors during these years. (The *Caisse d'Assistance Mutuelle des Médecins Aliénistes*, an off-shoot of the *Société*, had been formed in 1865, yet it was basically an organization to provide disability pensions for asylum doctors, their widows and orphans.) Moreover, the *Annales médico-psychologiques* was the most important psychiatric journal during these years, and was only rivalled between 1860 and 1870 by Louis Delasiauve's *Journal de médecine mentale*. See Castel, *L'Ordre psychiatrique*, p. 27 n. for confirmation of the thesis that the *Société* was representative of French psychiatry in general.

10 It must be conceded that these were not the only forces shaping the psychiatric acceptance of hereditarian ideas. French medical psychologists were equally concerned with reaffirming their professional privileges to administer medical therapy and oversee the moral management of the insane in the face of radical, non-medical endorsements of a purely psychogenic 'moral treatment'. To do this, they had to show that insanity was a certifiable disease of the organ of thought: the brain. Heredity constituted the somatic element that was necessary to legitimize the exclusive rights of psychiatry to treat the mad, and hence to redeem its medical status. For references to 'physicalism' as a means to 'entrench and enhance ... professional prerogatives' in nineteenth-century English psychiatry, see L.S. Jacyna, 'Somatic Theories of Mind and the Interests of Medicine in Britain 1850–1879', *Medical History*, 26 (1982): 258; and Andrew Scull, *Museums of Madness: The Social Organization of Insanity in Nineteenth-Century England* (London: Allen Lane, 1979), p. 161.

11 It is impossible to say exactly how unconscious or intentional this process of

theory-choice was. However, mental doctors for the most part seem to have been successful in deceiving themselves about the real advantages of hereditarianism. Genil-Perrin's account was most likely typical: he viewed the psychiatric adherence to degeneracy theory as a victory for positivism and as a concrete step in the progress of human thought. Genil-Perrin, *Histoire des origines*, p. 12.

12 See Paul Forman, 'Weimar Culture, Causality, and Quantum Theory 1918–1927: Adaptation by German Physicists and Mathematicians to a Hostile Intellectual Environment', *Historical Studies in the Physical Sciences* 3 (1971): 1–115; Theodore M. Brown, 'The College of Physicians and the Acceptance of Iatromechanism in England 1665–1695', *Bulletin of the History of Medicine* 44 (1970): 12–30; and 'The Rise of Baconianism in Seventeenth-Century England', *Science and History: Studies in Honour of Edward Rosen* 16 (1978), pp. 501–22.

13 For confirmation of this lack of knowledge of insanity's causes and somatic pathology, see John Romano, 'American Psychiatry: Past, Present, and Future', in G. Kriegman, R.D. Gardner, and D.W. Abse (eds), *American Psychiatry: Past, Present, and Future* (Charlottesville: University Press of Virginia, 1975), p. 29; Charles E. Rosenberg, 'The Crisis in Psychiatric Legitimacy: Reflections on Psychiatry, Medicine, and Public Policy', in Kriegman *et al.*, *American Psychiatry*, p. 137; Richard Hunter and Ida MacAlpine (eds), *Three Hundred Years of Psychiatry 1535–1860* (London: Oxford University Press, 1963), p. vii; Richard H. Shryock, *The Development of Modern Medicine: An Interpretation of the Social and Scientific Factors Involved* (Madison: University of Wisconsin Press, 1979), p. 361. For a nineteenth-century acknowledgement of this state of affairs, see J. Cotard, 'Folie', *Dictionnaire encyclopédique des sciences médicales* (Paris: 1879), vol. 3. pp. 304–05; also see Henri Dagonet, *Nouveau Traité des maladies mentales* (Paris: Baillière, 1876), p. 1.

14 J.E.D. Esquirol, *Mental Maladies: A Treatise on Insanity*, trans. E.K. Hunt (Philadelphia: Lea & Blanchard, 1845), p. 21.

15 Esquirol, *Mental Maladies*, p. 30.

16 Esquirol, *Mental Maladies*, p. 49.

17 J.J. Moreau (de Tours), *Hashish and Mental Illness*, ed. Helene Peters and Gabriel G. Nahas, trans. Gordon J. Barnett (New York: Raven Press, trans. of 1845 French edn, 1973), p. 209.

18 Moreau, *Hashish*, p. 209.

19 Moreau, *Hashish*, pp. 198–99.

20 Jules Baillarger, 'Recherches statistiques sur l'hérédité de la folie', *Annales médico-psychologiques* 3 (1844): 328–29.

21 Baillarger, 'Recherches', p. 337.

22 Jules Baillarger, 'De la paralysie générale chez les pellagreux', *Annales médico-psychologiques* 1 (1849): 329.

23 E. Renaudin, *Études médico-psychologiques sur l'aliénation mentale* (Paris: Baillière, 1854), pp. 33–4.

24 E. Renaudin, 'Observations sur les recherches statistiques relatives à l'aliénation mentale', *Annales médico-psychologiques* 2 (1856): 356.

25 U. Trélat, 'Des Causes de la folie', *Annales médico-psychologiques* 2 (1856): 21.

26 Trélat, 'Des Causes', p. 10.

27 Cited in Th. Ribot, *Heredity: A Psychological Study of its Phenomena, Laws, Causes, and Consequences*, no trans. (New York: Appleton, 1875), p. 131.

28 J. Dejerine, *L'Hérédité dans les maladies du système nerveux* (Paris: Asselin and

Houzeau, 1886), pp. 28–9.

29 Genil-Perrin, *Histoire des origines*, p. 50; see also Friedlander, 'B.A. Morel'.

30 B.A. Morel, *Traité des dégénérescences physiques, intellectuelles, et morales de l'espèce humaine* (Paris: Baillière, 1857), p. 5.

31 Morel, *Traité*, p. 565, his italics.

32 J.J. Moreau (de Tours), *La Psychologie morbide dans ses rapports avec la philosophie de l'histoire: ou de l'influence des névropathies sur le dynamisme intellectuel* (Paris: Masson, 1859), p. vii.

33 Moreau, *Psychologie*, p. 26.

34 Moreau, *Psychologie*, p. 60–1.

35 Moreau, *Psychologie*, p. 467.

36 Moreau, *Psychologie*, p. 117.

37 Moreau, *Psychologie*, pp. 60–1.

38 26 November, 1860, *séance* of the Société Médico-Psychologique. *Annales médico-psychologiques* 7 (1861): 176.

39 *Annales médico-psychologiques* 11 (1868): 278.

40 *Annales médico-psychologiques* 12 (1868): 116.

41 Ch. Féré, 'La Famille névropathique', *Archives de neurologie* no. 19, 7 (1884): 9.

42 *Annales médico-psychologiques* 11 (1868): 274.

43 *Annales médico-psychologiques* 12 (1868): 288.

44 *Annales médico-psychologiques* 3 (1886): 83.

45 *Annales médico-psychologiques* 3 (1886): 91.

46 *Annales médico-psychologiques* 3 (1886): 85.

47 *Annales médico-psychologiques* 3 (1886): 86.

48 *Annales médico-psychologiques* 3 (1886): 87.

49 *Annales médico-psychologiques* 3 (1886): 277.

50 *Annales médico-psychologiques* 3 (1886): 96.

51 *Annales médico-psychologiques* 3 (1886): 97.

52 *Annales médico-psychologiques* 3 (1886): 101.

53 *Annales médico-psychologiques* 4 (1886): 283.

54 *Annales médico-psychologiques* 4 (1886): 271–72.

55 *Annales médico-psychologiques* 4 (1886): 276.

56 *Annales médico-psychologiques* 4 (1886): 284.

57 *Annales médico-psychologiques* 4 (1886): 258.

58 *Annales médico-psychologiques* 4 (1886): 258; my italics.

59 Charles Féré, 'La Famille névropathique', p. 1.

60 Charles Féré, 'La Famille névropathique', p. 2.

61 Charles Féré, 'La Famille névropathique', pp. 24–5.

62 Charles Féré, 'La Famille névropathique', p. 9.

63 Charles Féré, 'La Famille névropathique', p. 22.

64 Charles Féré, 'La Famille névropathique', p. 23.

65 Charles Féré, 'Nerve Troubles as Foreshadowed in the Child', *Brain* 8 (1885): 231.

66 Ribot, *Heredity*, p. 119.

67 Ribot, *Heredity*, p. 10.

68 Dejerine, *L'Hérédité*, p. 41.

69 *Annales médico-psychologiques* 4 (1886): 255.

70 Charles Féré, 'La Famille névropathique', p. 7.

71 Charles Féré, 'Morbid Heredity', *Popular Science Monthly* 47 (1895): 396.

72 Charles Féré, 'Nerve Troubles', p. 231.

73 Dejerine, *L'Hérédité*, pp. xiv–xv.

74 W. Griesinger, *Mental Pathology and Therapeutics*, trans. C. Lockhart Robertson and James Rutherford (New York: Hafner, reprint of 1867 London trans. of German second edn, 1965), p. 127.

75 Ola Andersson, *Studies in the Prehistory of Psychoanalysis*, (Nortedts: Bokförlaget, 1962), p. 37 n. This is also Charles E. Rosenberg's conclusion about nineteenth-century American hereditarianism: since theories of heredity were 'devoid of verifiable content', Rosenberg has written, they were also 'usable in a wide variety of social contexts'; Rosenberg, 'Bitter Fruit', p. 49.

76 *Annales médico-psychologiques*, 11 (1868): 277–78.

77 This is Erwin H. Ackerknecht's conclusion about the relationship of medical theory to therapeutics in general. See his *Therapeutics: From the Primitives to the Twentieth Century* (New York: Hafner, 1973), p. 3. The same held true for pathological anatomy: French writers pointed out that it contributed little to therapeutic insight. Expressing a widely-held view, Jules Christian observed in 1876 that even if it were possible to demonstrate through pathological anatomy that a specific cerebral lesion corresponded to an equally specific variety of insanity, 'this proof . . . would only have a mediocre importance for treatment.' *Annales médico-psychologiques* 16 (1876): 148.

78 For an example of the recommendation of bleeding, see A. Brierre de Boismont, *Hallucinations: Or, The Rational History of Apparitions, Visions, Dreams, Ecstasy, Magnetism, and Somnambulism* (Philadelphia: first US ed. from second enlarged and French ed., Lindsay & Blackiston 1853): no trans., p. 496.

79 J.P. Falret, *Maladies mentales et des asiles d'aliénés* (Paris: Baillière, 1864), p. 680.

80 Ludger Lunier, 'De l'Isolement des aliénés considéré comme moyen de traitement et comme mésure d'ordre public', *Annales médico-psychologiques* 5, (1871): pp. 31–2.

81 Falret, *Maladies mentales*, pp. liii–liv; Renaudin, *Études médico-psychologiques*, p. 6.

82 Erwin H. Ackerknecht, *A Short History of Psychiatry*, trans. Sula Wolff, (New York: Hafner, 1965): p. viii.

83 Th. Ribot, 'Philosophy in France', *Mind*, 2, (1877), p. 368.

84 Jan Ellen Goldstein, 'The Hysteria Diagnosis and the Politics of Anti-Clericalism in late nineteenth-century France', *Journal of Modern History*, 54, (1982): 209–39, especially pp. 221–30.

85 The Imperial decree of 25 March 1852 was particularly galling to French psychiatrists: the full powers of appointment to provincial asylums were taken from the Minister of the Interior and returned to the departmental Prefects who had held them before 1838, thereby decentralizing the asylum system – another source of frustration to psychiatrists – and politicizing the appointment process. See Constans, Lunier and Dumesnil, *Rapport général à M. Le Ministre de l'Intérieur sur le service des aliénés en 1874* (Paris: Imprimerie Nationale, 1878), p. 56. For strife between local Prefects and doctors, see Goldstein, 'French psychiatry in Social and Political Context'. During this same period, psychiatrists seemed to be getting little co-operation from the government; administrators were so perfunctory in providing public assistance to the insane in France that Robert Castel referred to their efforts as the 'pseudo-application' of the 1838 Law. The same could be said of the new asylums recommended by the 1838 Law; although this was the era in which the first large-scale, modern public

asylums were built in France, progress was very slow and by 1874 only 40 out of 88 *départements* had special mental hospitals. For a recent treatment of nineteenth-century French asylum building following the 1838 Law, see Gérard Bléandonu and Guy Le Gaufey, 'The Creation of the Insane Asylums of Auxerre and Paris', in *Deviants and the Abandoned in French Society. Selections from the Annales Economies, Sociétés, Civilisations*, IV, ed. Robert Forster and Orest Ranum, trans. Elborg Forster and Patricia M. Ranum (Baltimore and London: Johns Hopkins University Press, 1978): pp. 180–212; also, Castel, pp. 233–41.

86 Adrien Dansette, *Religious History of Modern France*, 2 vòls., trans. John Dingle (New York: Herder and Herder, 1961), i, p. 315.

87 Goldstein, 'The Hysteria Diagnosis', p. 224. Even after 1877 things did not improve dramatically. When the government of the Third Republic authorized a chair in mental pathology at the Paris Faculty of Medicine in 1877 for the first time since 1822, the *universitaire* Benjamin Ball was chosen over the asylum doctor Valentin Magnan. Castel, p. 283n.

88 *Annales médico-psychologiques* 1 (1869): 363–66.

89 *Ibid.*, pp. 86–7, 88. Th. Rousel wrote that during the 1860s antipsychiatric campaign the 'medical competence' of mental pathologists was at stake. Th. Roussel, *Notes et documents concernant la législation française et les législations étrangères sur les aliénés. Rapport au Sénat de la commission relative à la révision de la loi du 30 Juin 1838*, Sénat; Session 1884. No. 157, I, (Paris: 1884), p. 212. Goldstein has noted that at least for the first half of the nineteenth century, French judges displayed a conventional 'condescension' towards and low opinion of medicolegal 'experts' (Goldstein, 'French Psychiatry' pp. 62–4). In his *Traité de la médecine légale des aliénés* (Paris: Masson, 1866), Morel suggested that these bad feeling persisted well after midcentury. Morel, pp. i–iv.

90 Lunier, 'De l'Isolement des aliénés', pp. 27–41.

91 *Annales médico-psychologiques* 3 (1870): 487–91. It was equally unsettling for psychiatrists to observe that newspapers of both the political Left *and* Right participated in the antipsychiatric movement. See Roussel, *Notes et documents*, p. 250 n, for the comments of Dr Collineau in his report to the *Société médico-pratique* in 1870. See also H. Dagonet, 'Loi de Juin 1838; Asiles d'aliénés', *Annales médico-psychologiques* 5 (1865): 216.

92 Henry Bonnet, *L'Aliéné devant lui-même, l'appréciation légale, la législation, les systèmes, la société, et la famille* (Paris: Masson, 1865), pp. viii–xvi.

93 For the temporarily successful attempt by the Prefect of the Seine to close down public clinical lectures delivered by Magnan and Prosper Lucas, see Réné Semelaigne, *Les Pionniers de la psychiatrie française avant et après Pinel*, 2 vols., (Paris: Baillière, 1930–32), 1, p. 235; 2, pp. 212–13. See also *Annales médico-psychologiques* 12 (1874): 270–72.

94 See Castel, p. 236 for the 'surencombrement' of asylums; also Alexander, 'The Administration of Madness', p. 292.

95 Alexander, p. 65.

96 G. Lanteri-Laura, 'Chronicité', pp. 548–68.

97 Alexander, 'The Administration of Madness', p. v.

98 Alexander, pp. 239–47.

99 *Annales médico-psychologiques* 2 (1869): 282–83.

100 Alexander, 'The Administration of Madness', p. 281.

101 *Annales médico-psychologiques* 1 (1843): i–xxvii.

102 *Annales médico-psychologiques* 1 (1843): 1–21.

103 'Société Médico-psychologique: Règlement', *Annales médico-psychologiques* 11, (1848): pp. 1–8.

104 J.P. Falret, *Maladies mentales*, pp. i-iv.

105 Renaudin, *Études médico-psychologiques*, pp. 2–3, 9.

106 Renaudin, *Études médico-psychologiques*, p. 15.

107 Renaudin, *Études médico-psychologiques*, p. 595.

108 B.A. Morel, *Traité des maladies mentales* (Paris: Masson, 1860): pp. 71–5.

109 B.A. Morel, *Traité des maladies mentales* (Paris: Masson, 1860): pp. 511–12.

110 Morel, *Traité des maladies mentales*, p. 75.

111 Morel, *Traité des maladies mentales*, p. 512.

112 Morel, *Traité des maladies mentales*, p. 73.

113 Morel, *Traité des maladies mentales*, p. 75.

114 Despite claims by mental pathologists later in the century that their orientation was thoroughly somatic, their view was that insanity always corresponded to a material alteration of the brain, but was not simply a mere product of that organ. Doctors preferred to leave discussions of an immaterial 'soul' out of their diagnoses, yet this in no way denied its reality or meant that they thought only in terms of organic causes. For example, see J. Luys, *Traité clinique et pratique des maladies mentales* (Paris: A. Delahaye and E. Lecrosnier, 1881), p. 229; Henri Dagonet, *Traité des maladies mentales*, (Paris: Baillière, 1894), p. 130; Benjamin Ball, *Leçons sur les maladies mentales*, second ed. (Paris: Asselin, 1890): p. 400.

115 Morel, *Traité des maladies mentales*, p. 509.

116 Morel, *Traité des maladies mentales*, p. 510.

117 Morel, *Traité des maladies mentales*, pp. 53, 332.

118 Morel, *Traité des maladies mentales*, p. 585.

119 Morel, *Traité des maladies mentales*, p. 586.

120 Morel, *Traité des dégénérescences*, p. 322.

121 Morel, *Traité des dégénérescences*, p. 340.

122 Morel himself complained of this 'habitual' psychiatric tendency of favouring one or the other category of causes. *Traité des maladies mentales*, p. 77; Goldstein has also pointed out the great imprecision of mental doctors when it came to formulating aetiologies of insanity (Goldstein, 'French Psychiatry' pp. 5–6). At least one French psychiatrist thought that ascribing long lists of causes to mental disorders was proof of the medical failure to discover their nature. Dagonet, *Traité des maladies mentales* (1894), p. 110.

123 Antoine Ritti, *Histoire des travaux de la Société Médico-psychologique et éloges de ses membres*, 2 vols. (Paris: Masson, 1913–14), 1, pp. 272, 310.

124 Achille Foville, review of Moreau's *Morbid Psychology*, *Annales médico-psychologiques* 6 (1860): 151–62.

125 Foville, review of Moreau's *Morbid Psychology*, p. 157.

126 J.J. Moreau (de Tours), 'De la Prédisposition héréditaire aux affections cérébrales. Existe-t-il des signes particuliers auxquels on puisse reconnaître cette prédisposition?', *Annales medico-psychologiques* 4 (1852): 451. The noted German chemist Justus von Liebig, for one, was distinctly suspicious of biomedical use of terms such as 'functional' and 'dynamic' to describe organic lesions: see John Charles Bucknill and Daniel H. Tuke, *A Manual of Psychological Medicine* (New York: Hafner facsimile of 1858 Philadelphia ed., 1968), pp. 346–47.

126a For some other nineteenth-century functional concepts of physiological psychology that cannot be considered as reductionist, see Roger Smith, 'The Background of Physiological Psychology in Natural Philosophy', *History of Science*, 11 (1973): 75–123. It was this trait of heredity that Brierre de Boismont cited approvingly in his review of Ribot's *Heredity*. See A. Brierre de Boismont, 'L'Hérédité au point de vue de la médecine légale et de l'hygiène', *Annales d'hygiène publique et de médecine légale*, 43 (1875): 193–94.

127 Erwin H. Ackerknecht, *Medicine at the Paris Hospital 1794–1848* (Baltimore: Johns Hopkins University Press, 1967), p. 171; see also his *Short History of Psychiatry*, p. 54. And yet, much like phrenology, hereditarianism did not necessarily discourage autopsical research. See Roger Cooter, 'Phrenology and British Alienists ca. 1825–1845', in Andrew Scull (ed.), *Madhouses, Maddoctors, and Madmen: The Social History of Psychiatry in the Victorian Era*, (Philadelphia: University of Pennsylvania Press, 1981), pp. 83–4; also P.A. Piorry, *De l'Hérédité dans les maladies* (Paris: Bury, 1840), p. 147.

128 *Annales médico-psychologiques* 11 (1868): 277–78.

129 Bonnet, *L'Aliéné* p. 133.

130 Albert Lemoine, *L'Aliéné devant la philosophie, la morale, et la société* (Paris: Didier et Cie., 1862), pp. 28–9.

131 Bonnet, *L'Aliéné*, pp. 133–34.

132 Lemoine, *L'Aliéné*, p. 32.

133 For psychiatric recognition of the danger of being incorporated into 'cerebral pathology', see Jules Falret's introduction to Griesinger's 'La Pathologie mentale au point de vue de L'École somatique allemande', *Annales médico-psychologiques* 5 (1865): 4. For more on this monist/dualist tendency in the history of psychiatry, see Theodore M. Brown's 'Descartes, dualism, and psychosomatic medicine' in this volume.

134 Ackerknecht, *Medicine at the Paris Hospital*, Ch. 10.

135 Ackerknecht, *Medicine at the Paris Hospital*, p. 129.

136 Falret, *Maladies mentales*, p. v.

137 Morel, *Traité des maladies mentales*, p. i; *Traité des dégénérescences*, p. xii.

138 'Rapport sur les modifications à introduire dans le projet de règlement de la Société Médico-psychologique', *Annales médico-psychologiques* 4, (1852): 227.

139 *Annales médico-psychologiques* 11, (1868): 276.

140 Esquirol, *Maladies mentales*, pp. 69, 396–97; Philippe Pinel, *A Treatise on Insanity*, trans. D.D. Davis (New York: 1962 Hafner reprint of 1806 translation of 1801 ed.); pp. 110–11.

141 Shryock, *The Development of Modern Medicine*, pp. 357–58.

142 J.J. Moreau (de Tours), 'De la prédisposition héréditaire aux affections cérébrales', *Annales médico-psychologiques* 4 (1852): 119–20.

143 Achille Foville, review of Moreau's *Morbid Psychology*, p. 155.

144 Hugh Grainger-Steward, 'De la Folie héréditaire', trans. E. Dumesnil, *Annales médico-psychologiques* 4 (1864): 356. There is much truth to this statement: by mid-century there existed a considerable body of medical literature on heredity in French. For a review of this literature and its history, see J. Luys, *Des Maladies héréditaires* (Paris: Medical Thesis, Faculty of Medicine, 1863). P.A. Piorry also remarked on the propensity of medical writers as well as recent authors of *Faculté* theses to exaggerate the influence of heredity in disease. Piorry, *De l'Hérédité dans les maladies* (Paris; Bury, 1840), pp. 31–2.

145 William Coleman, *Biology in the Nineteenth Century* (New York: John Wiley,

1971), p. 161. For a reference to how 'biological facts' had determined that for every mental state there was a corresponding 'nervous state' whose nature was hereditary, see A. Brierre de Boismont, 'L'Hérédité au point de vue de la médecine légale et de l'hygiène', pp. 193–94.

146 Dejerine, *L'Hérédité*, p. 27.

147 Ribot, *Heredity*, p. 391.

148 27 January *séance* of *Société médico-psychologique*, 1868, *Annales médico-psychologiques*, 11 (1868): 205. See C.E. Brown-Séquard, 'On the Hereditary Transmission of Effects of Certain Injuries to the Nervous System', *Lancet*, 1 (1875): pp. 7–8; Brown-Séquard's studies were also cited by Henri Legrand du Saulle in his *La Folie héréditaire: Leçons professées à l'École pratique* (Paris: Adrien Delahaye 1873), p. 15.

149 Achille Foville, rev. of de Quatrefages's *Rapport sur le progrès de l'Anthropologie depuis vingt ans, Annales médico-psychologiques*, 11 (1868): 474–80.

150 Dr Campagne, 'Manie raisonnante: Étiologie et pathogénie', *Annales médico-psychologiques* 12 (1868): 1–34; 207–34. For references to insanity as a biological failure of adaptation, see Luys, *Traité clinique et pratique des maladies mentales*, p. xv; also, Paul Jacoby, *Études sur la selection dans ses rapports avec l'hérédité chez l'homme* (Paris: G. Baillière, 1881); Jacoby wrote reviews of Russian medico-psychological literature for the *Annales médico-psychologiques*.

151 John Farley and Gerald L. Geison, 'Science, Politics, and Spontaneous Generation in Nineteenth-Century France: The Pasteur-Pouchet Debate', *Bulletin of the History of Medicine* 48 (1974): 161–98.

152 Everett Mendelsohn, 'Cell Theory and the Development of General Physiology', *Archives Internationales de l'Histoire des Sciences* (1963): 419–29.

153 Dejerine, *L'Hérédité*, p. 21.

154 Renaudin, 'Observations sur les recherches statistiques rélatives à l'aliénation mentale', pp. 264–65; Campagne, 'Manie raisonnante', p. 27. See also Prosper Lucas's reference to the physiologist J.F. Burdach's definition of a germ as an 'internal disposition to a determinate development' in the former's *Traité philosophique et physiologique de l'hérédité naturelle*, II, pp. 584–85. Lucas used this definition in his attempt to specify what he meant by 'heredity'.

155 J. Schiller, 'Physiology's Struggle for Independence in the first half of the Nineteenth Century', *History of Science* 7 (1968): 64–89.

156 Morel, *Traité des dégénérescences*, pp. 282–83n., 313–34n.

157 Morel, *Traité des dégénérescences*, p. xiii.

158 Schiller, 'Physiology's Struggle', p. 85.

159 'Centenaire de la Société médico-psychologique', *Annales médico-psychologiques* 2 (1952): 45.

160 *Annales médico-psychologiques* 4 (1852): 226–34.

161 'Centenaire', p. 53.

162 *Annales médico-psychologiques* 4 (1852): 509–19.

163 For an authoritative description of the Republican sentiments of the *Société médico-psychologique*'s doctors, see Alfred Maury, *Souvenirs d'un homme de lettres*, Bibliothèque de l'Institut de France, Ms. 2650, 5, p. 21. Maury (1817–92) was a founding member of the *Société* and a frequent contributor to the *Annales médico-psychologiques*.

164 Dansette, *Religious History of Modern France*, I, p. 314; for the historical background to the stigma of 'associationism' (Goldstein, 'French Psychiatry',

pp. 342–50).

165 'Société Médico-psychologique: Ses phases, ses travaux', *Gazette hebdomadaire de médecine et de chirurgie*, 4 (1857): 545.

166 For example, see Morel, *Traité des dégénérescences*, pp. 322–23. Buchez's treatment of heredity is in his *Essai d'un traité complet de philosophie du point de vue de catholicisme et du progrès*, 3 vols. (Paris: Eveillard, 1838–40), 3, p. 546.

167 Bonnet, *L'Aliéné*, p. 131.

168 Brierre de Boismont, 'L'Hérédité', pp. 193–94.

169 Bonnet, *L'Aliéné*, p. 134. Léon Rostan, Professor of clinical medicine at the Parisian Faculty of Medicine and a leading exponent of organicism, argued for the compatibility of an 'organicist' position in medicine and a belief in a 'pure' and 'immaterial' soul. See Rostan, *Exposition des principes de l'organicisme précedée de réflexions sur l'incrédulité en matière de médecine* (Paris: Asselin, 1864), pp. 160–70.

Rostan's explanation of organicism illustrates how medicine could come to terms with religious orthodoxy without sacrificing therapeutic territoriality; indeed, if anything, professions of faith in the reality of a spiritual soul solidified the medical claim to exclusive treatment of the mad. By agreeing that the soul could never be sick, yet at the same time maintaining that the body was always modified in some way during insanity, there would be no reason to call in philosophers, priests, or psychologists in cases of mental derangement.

170 The fact that the concept of morbid heredity authorized a belief in the freedom of the will and the soul links it to that other religiously controversial issue of the Second Empire, spontaneous generation. See Farley and Geison, 'The Pasteur–Pouchet Debate'. Religious considerations seem to have also influenced the French reception of Darwinism with its materialist overtones. See John Farley, 'The Initial Reactions of French Biologists to Darwin's *Origin of Species*', *Journal of the History of Biology* 7 (1974). While accepting the principle of natural selection, Campagne for one was careful to distinguish adherence to Darwinism from adherence to 'the law of selection' in hereditary matters. Campagne, 'Manie raisonnante', p. 214n. In Morel's eyes, there was no conflict between his theory of degeneracy and religion: a human product of degeneration was a regression from an ideal type that he identified with the original Adam. Morel, *Traité des dégénérescences*, p. 2.

171 Koenraad W. Swart, *The Sense of Decadence in Nineteenth-Century France* (The Hague: Nijhoff, 1964), especially ch. iv, 'The Great Disillusionment'.

172 Borie, *Mythologies de l'hérédite*, p. 180.

173 Borie, *Mythologies de l'hérédité*, p. 180.

174 Borie, *Mythologies de l'hérédité*, pp. 11, 13, 17, 206.

175 Borie, *Mythologies de l'hérédité*, pp. 180–82. A good example of this intellectual transition was Alfred Maury; as revolution followed revolution throughout the nineteenth century, Maury became increasingly suspicious of the political behaviour of the lower classes, often using concepts from mental pathology as terms of reference. He, too, was interested in the questions of degeneracy and morbid heredity. See his *Souvenirs*, Ms. 2649, 3, pp. 395–96; also, 'Les Dégénérescences de l'espèce humaine', *Revue des deux mondes*, 25, (1860): 75–102.

176 Swart, *The Sense of Decadence*, pp. 116–17.

177 For the congruence between hereditarianism and cultural pessimism, see Ch.

Letourneau, 'Hérédité', pp. 602–05; Letourneau noted how the ideas of racial rise and fall espoused by authors like Jacoby gladdened the hearts of the 'disciples of Schopenhauer and Hartmann' (pp. 602–03).

178 A. Brierre de Boismont, 'Morel: Fragments de son oeuvre en aliénation mentale, l'hérédité morbide, les dégénérescences', *L'Union médicale*, 7 July 1874, pp. 25–35, especially p. 34; 'Exposé des travaux du docteur Morel sur la médecine légale des aliénés', *Annales d'hygiène publique et de médecine légale*, 41, (1874): 184–97.

179 *Annales médico-psychologiques* 7 (1872): 257.

180 J.V. Laborde, *Les Hommes et les actes de l'insurrection de Paris devant la psychologie morbide: Lettres à M. le docteur Moreau (de Tours)* (Paris: Germer-Baillière, 1872), pp. iii, 2–3.

181 Laborde, *Les Hommes et les actes*, p. 72.

182 Laborde, *Les Hommes et les actes*, p. 89.

183 *Annales médico-psychologiques* 6 (1871): 222–41.

184 H. Taguet, 'De l'hérédité dans l'alcoolisme', *Annales médico-psychologiques* 18 (1877): 5–17. The relevance of psychopathological concepts to crowd psychology, social deviance, and political insurrection has been explored in Susanna Barrows, *Distorting Mirrors: Visions of the Crowd in Late Nineteenth-Century France* (New Haven: Yale University Press, 1981); Robert A. Nye, *The Origins of Crowd Psychology: Gustave Le Bon and the Crisis of Mass Democracy in the Third Republic* (London: Sage, 1975); and Ruth Harris, 'Murder Under Hypnosis' in the companion volume.

185 Maury was an excellent example of the kind of *savant* who exercised influence in the early *Société médico-psychologique*. He was a bibliophile, historian, and archaeologist and had training in both law and medicine. In the 1860s he was Louis Napoleon's librarian at the Tuileries and helped to edit the latter's *La Vie de César*. See 'Centenaire', pp. 51–2; also Maurice Paz, 'Alfred Maury, Membre de l'Institut, chroniqueur de Napoléon III, et du Second Empire', *Académie des sciences morales et politiques. Revue des travaux de l'Académie*, 117th year, 4th series (1964): 248–61.

186 Annales médico-psychologiques 4 (1852): 28–9.

187 *Annales médico-psychologiques* 11 (1868): 276–77.

188 Morel, *Traité des maladies mentales*, p. 65. Morel was not alone in making this observation. In 1888 Antoine Ritti cited Benjamin Ball's statement that it was psychiatry's 'eternal destiny and honour' to follow the 'fluctuations' of 'contemporary philosophy'. *Annales médico-psychologiques* 8 (1888): 192. It is worth noting that French philosophy was undergoing a 'crisis' at the same time as mental medicine. See Th. Ribot, 'Philosophy in France', *Mind* 2 (1877): 366–86; also Paul Janet, 'La Crise philosophique et les idées spiritualistes', *Revue des deux mondes*, 52, (1864), pp. 459–90. Janet was Pierre Janet's uncle and was president of the Société Médico-psychologique in 1867.

189 Philippe Buchez, 'Rapport fait à la Société médico-psychologique sur le *Traité des dégénérescences physiques, intellectuelles, et morales de l'espèce humaine et des causes qui les produisent*', *Annales médico-psychologiques* 3 (1857): 455–67; 460.

190 *Annales médico-psychologiques* 3 (1857): 461.

191 *Annales médico-psychologiques* 3 (1857): 458.

192 'Les Signes physiques des folies raisonnantes', *Annales médico-psychologiques* 15 (1876): 433.

193 For example, see the American psychiatrist John Romano's characterization of
the problems of US mental medicine in the last fifty years in his 'American
Psychiatry: Past, Present, and Future', in Kriegman *et al.*, American Psychiatry,
pp. 28–44, and 'Requiem or Reveille: Psychiatry's Choice', *Bulletin of the New
York Academy of Medicine*, 53 (1977): 787–805.

CHAPTER NINE

Psychical research and psychiatry in late Victorian Britain: trance as ecstasy or trance as insanity

J.P. Williams

WHEN A SPIRITUALIST medium enters trance, she will often start to speak with a different voice and use different turns of phrase, revealing knowledge she does not normally possess; in short, a different personality is shown. Even those who are not fully developed mediums can sometimes get a similar result without entering a trance simply by setting pencil to paper and letting their attention wander. They find that their hand moves, seemingly of itself, to produce connected writing; if questions are asked aloud, the hand will reply. Sometimes this 'automatic writing' is produced by fixing the pencil to a planchette, a small trolley with castors, on which one or more people rest a finger.

Automatism such as this has been interpreted by different people in very different ways. For spiritualists, from the beginnings of spiritualism in the 1850s, trance speaking or automatic writing was authentic communication from the spirits of the departed. The appeal of spiritualism was diverse (women could turn the traditional feminine ideal to their advantage by becoming mediums, healers, and lecturers; working-class spiritualists could avoid submission to the dominant culture and control their own religion and education; upper-class Christians could find support for beleaguered religious beliefs),[1] but in all parts of society the basis of the appeal was in spiritualist phenomena: evident practical demonstrations of the power and worth of the human spirit, existing beyond the repressive limitations of objectified material life, even beyond death. To experience trance speaking or automatic writing was therefore to be in a glorious and uplifted state.

To Victorian medical men, however, automatism meant loss of conscious control, representing a state of virtual insanity. For example, Henry Rayner, lecturer on mental disorders at St Thomas's Hospital, wrote in 1893:

'A state of automatism, every psychologist will admit, is a reduction of mental function to the plane which obtains in the lower developments of animal life, and an enduring reduction to this state in man, as seen more or less completely in some forms of insanity, confirms this view. I regard this condition, therefore, as a devolution of function which will, if frequently repeated, produce injurious results. On this ground I have always opposed the extensive use of hypnotism, and now oppose the self-induced automatic habit. ... The risk of mental deterioration by the frequent induction of states of incomplete consciousness, hypnotic or other, should ... be distinctly taught, and the habit for those of the neurotic diathesis labelled, "Dangerous – this way madness lies".'[2]

Victorian medical men saw automatism and hypnotism as conditions akin to insanity, therefore subjects on which they were entitled to pronounce. Pathological mental conditions were generally explained in physiological terms, so the apparently intelligent behaviour spiritualists attributed to the influence of discarnate spirits was attributed by most British doctors to the mechanisms of the nervous system, operating free from conscious control.

A third interpretation was proposed by Frederic Myers and Edmund Gurney, leading members of the Society for Psychical Research. They attributed the trance speaking or automatic writing of a medium to a part of her own mind of which she was unconscious. They took a psychological instead of a physiological view of automatism, hypnotism, and the clinical conditions of multiple personality and hysteria, as did some continental doctors such as Pierre Janet. In opposition to the medical men, both British and continental, they denied that such conditions of altered consciousness were essentially pathological.

This article is about the way in which Myers and Gurney came to develop their view of conditions of altered consciousness, and how it differed from the prevailing British medical view. This subject is linked to several different areas of historical interest. Myers developed a theory of the 'subliminal self', a part of the personality normally submerged beneath the threshold of consciousness, which makes him part of the history of 'the discovery of the unconscious' in the late nineteenth century.[3] The isolation of Myers and Gurney in adopting their psychological approach illustrates how British medical psychology was dominated by physiological approaches[4] – the acquisition of scientific status through a basis in physiological science having been a long-standing preoccupation in both medicine and psychology. More generally, the interest of Myers and Gurney in problems of the mind is an example of responses to the Victorian crisis of faith or 'the rise of scientific naturalism'. The different interpretations of conditions of altered consciousness illustrate how the mind became a disputed subject in late Victorian Britain, as the intellectual world ceased to have a shared complex of religious and philosophical ideas, and words such as 'mind' and 'soul' were used in incompatible ways by different groups with different purposes in increasingly specialized and isolated disciplines.[5] The work of Myers and Gurney played a major part in establishing the activity of psychical research, though most internal histories of the subject have tended to concentrate on their investigations of exotic subjects such as telepathy and poltergeists, failing to notice the extent of their work on conditions of altered consciousness, with which the dispute was not over their existence but over their interpretation and significance.[6] Finally, the intellectually elitist brand of psychical research promoted by Myers and Gurney had an uneasy relationship with the spiritualist popular movement – a subject with which I have dealt elsewhere.[7]

Though linked to all these historical areas, this article is presented mainly as a case-study of how mental conditions are interpreted, particularly how their pathology is determined. If the spiritualist interpretation was rejected, there were two basic questions posed by conditions of altered consciousness: whether they were to be considered physiologically or psychologically, and whether they were pathological or not. By seeing how Myers and Gurney came to different answers to most British doctors, we can begin to see how the pathology could be disputed: how, for instance, Hack Tuke could characterize the hypnotic trance as 'artificial insanity', while Myers could maintain that 'for some uneducated subjects it has been the highest mental condition which they have ever entered'.[8]

The first section will explain how Myers and Gurney came to be involved in psychical research and how they came to be interested in hypnotism, hallucinations, automatic writing, and various clinical cases reported in the French psychiatric literature. The second section will examine the medical views of these conditions, and the third will describe the research of Myers and Gurney and the development of their ideas. The concluding section will consider the origin of the two different interpretations.

Frederic Myers was born in 1843 into an evangelical household; his father was a parson at Keswick, and his mother came from the wealthy flax-spinning Marshall family. He was a sensitive and emotional child, moved almost to ecstasy by small things such as a flower, a bright moon, the lakeland scenery. He went to Cheltenham College, and at seventeen, already writing poetry extensively, he went up to Trinity College Cambridge. As an undergraduate he was egotistic and arrogant, sometimes referring to himself as a latter-day Virgil. In 1866, by then a fellow of Trinity, he came under the sway of the beautiful and fervently evangelical Josephine Butler; 'She introduced me to Christianity, so to say, by an inner door; not to its encumbering forms and dogmas, but to its heart of fire.' After a few years however, that fire died; science and history were speaking against the reality of the Christian miracles, and Myers became an unhappy agnostic. His anxiety was increased by a love-affair with Annie Marshall, the wife of a cousin. Their relationship was passionate but (on the surface at least) unsexual; they did not have sex together, which Myers later regarded as a spiritual and moral triumph, though he could no longer see any clear reason why they should not have done so. The affair was given further poignancy by her husband's commitment to Ticehurst Asylum, and her own suicide in 1876.[9]

Edmund Gurney, another junior fellow of Trinity, also came from a clerical family. His major interest in early life was music, and he once had hopes of a career as a performer and composer; however, becoming aware of his inadequate ability, he abandoned these ambitions in the 1870s. Instead, he wrote a theoretical book, *The Power of Sound*, dealing not with the acoustics or the physiology of aesthetics but attempting to place the actual phenomena of musical experience on a scientific basis. His aim was to prove that the faculty of musical appreciation was universal and independent of the intellectual, moral, or social conditions of the hearer, and that therefore music was capable of bringing a little joy and beauty to the dull and tedious lives of poor city dwellers; he wanted to see a large orchestra playing music nightly in the East End of London.[10] He began medical training in 1877, but had to abandon hopes of a medical career too, as he found he could not endure the anguish of hospital conditions. He had a great sympathetic sensitivity to pain, and was acutely aware of how much unmerited suffering there was in the world; having rejected the dogmatic Christianity in which he had been brought up, he rested, like Myers, in an unhappy agnosticism, unable to take comfort from the natural religion of the positivists.[11]

They sought the aid of another Trinity don, Henry Sidgwick, the moral philosopher; after his schooldays in the high-minded idealistic atmosphere of Rugby, Sidgwick too had lost his Christian faith under the consciousness-raising influence of the Apostles, John Stuart Mill's philosophy, and biblical criticism.[12] Though Sidgwick, Myers, and Gurney suffered the Victorian 'crisis of faith', they all retained their deep belief in – we still have no better word – 'spiritual' values such as duty, art, and love. The moments when they felt themselves to live most fully, with which they identified themselves most completely, were moments of noble self-sacrifice, aesthetic transport in poetry or music, or loving relationships unsullied by carnal desire. Once they had regarded these feelings as divine and eternal, but without God and immortality they were no longer confident of their reality. Conflating ontological materialism (rejection of the existence of a spiritual substance) with value materialism (rejection of spiritual values), they could not conceive of spiritual values without a spiritual universe to act as their vehicle.[13] Christianity's traditional doctrine was dubious, intuitive feeling was only personal, and metaphysical philosophy was too speculative; but they wondered whether there was still hope in the empirical method: the scientific study of ghosts, spirits, whatever.[14] In 1874, the year of three particularly aggressive statements of materialism,[15] Sidgwick, Myers, and Gurney gathered an informal group for the investigation of spiritualism.

The Sidgwick group attended seances with most of the major mediums of the time, including Florence and Katie Cook, Mrs Guppy, Henry Slade and William Eglinton; under whatever conditions of control the mediums would allow, they witnessed raps, movements of furniture, slate writing, materializations. Sometimes there were strong indications of fraud, but generally the results were inconclusive and discouraging, and their investigations petered out.[16]

In 1876, however, while public controversy over spiritualism was at a height, William Barrett, Professor of Physics at the Royal College of Science in Dublin, read a paper to the British Association on experiments in mesmerism which he had made in 1867. He reported that subjects in trance seemed to taste substances placed in the operator's mouth and feel pains inflicted on his body; they could also read the operator's thoughts. Community of sensation and thought-reading were traditional aspects of the mesmeric rapport – the alleged special relationship between operator and subject – but Barrett claimed to have demonstrated their existence under experimental conditions, taking adequate precautions to exclude the possibility of normal explanations.[17] Barrett subsequently wrote to the papers, appealing to the public for reports of apparent thought transference, and Myers and Gurney joined him in following up the replies with correspondence, interviews and experiments. In 1881, the Rev. A.M. Creery of Buxton wrote that his daughters and a maidservant could reliably produce thought-reading in the normal state, without any mesmeric trance. Barrett, Myers, and Gurney performed trials of their own with the girls, and reported their experimental demonstration of thought-transference in *Nature* and the *Nineteenth Century*.[18]

At the end of 1881, Edmund Dawson Rogers, a leading London spiritualist, suggested to Barrett the formation of a new society that would attract those 'many persons of culture and of good social position' who were interested in spiritualism but repelled by its disreputable public image.[19] Myers and Gurney agreed to give their support, but only on condition that Sidgwick became president. If the society was to include both the confirmed spiritualist and the interested but uncommitted investigator, it would need a president who could support that breadth of opinion and prevent it from becoming yet another spiritualist society; Sidgwick, one of the 'university liberals'[20] and whose powers of toleration and suspense of judgement were legendary, seemed the ideal person. After a number of meetings at the headquarters of the British National Association of Spiritualists, the Society for Psychical Research (SPR) was formally constituted and held its first general meeting on 17 July, 1882. After only a few years, however, many spiritualists rebelled, feeling that the SPR was actively hostile to their point of view and that they were not getting a proper hearing.[21] A number of leading spiritualists resigned, and the Sidgwick group, whose prolific research output had from the start dominated the Society, were left in undisputed control of the SPR.

Barrett's investigations had changed their centre of interest. They began to draw a distinction between the physical phenomena of spiritualism (raps, movements of furniture, matter-through-matter, materialization) and the mental phenomena (apparitions, trance, possession). The existence of thought-transference – or 'telepathy', to use the broader term coined by Myers – had been proved to their satisfaction, and in telepathy lay the promise of an empirical account of the soul and its nature, and an objective proof of the reality of spiritual values.[22] Though they maintained an interest in physical phenomena, from 1881 the Sidgwick group's confidence and hopes were more bound up with mental phenomena such as telepathy and mesmerism.

Gurney and Myers originally expected their investigation of mesmerism to concentrate on phenomena that were distinctively mesmeric and could not be explained by medically-accepted hypnotism: phenomena that suggested a fluid flow, or 'some specific influence or effluence', between operator and subject.[23] Increasingly however they regarded the mesmeric rapport as due not to a quasi-physical effluence but to mental telepathy;[24] they were particularly impressed by the apparent success of Janet and Gibert's experiments in putting a patient named Léonie into trance at will from a distance of up to a mile, where the long range seemed to rule out the action of any mesmeric effluence.[25] They continued to defend the possible action of an effluence at short range, implied by experiments where a randomly chosen finger of the subject was anaesthetized by mesmeric passes out of his sight,[26] but their attention moved away from the mesmeric phenomena and telepathy associated with trance. The bulk of Gurney's writing on hypnotism was about the trance itself.

Gurney and Myers were working just at the time of the explosion in hypnotism literature on the continent, especially in France, and thus they were led to the contemporary psychiatric literature, for hypnotism was recognized as being related to several clinical conditions. One was somnambulism – hypnotism was still commonly called 'induced somnambulism' – but in spite of its great prominence in literary culture there were few detailed clinical studies. There was better documentation for 'multiple personality' – also called 'alternating personality' or 'double consciousness'. The third related clinical condition was hysteria, and, following the work of J.-M. Charcot and his school at the Salpêtrière Asylum in Paris, this became the most important.[27] Arthur Myers, Fred's younger brother, who was a doctor, helped them find their way into this literature, and undoubtedly heightened and coloured their interest in conditions of altered consciousness by himself being an epileptic. He had suffered his first *haut mal* in 1874 at the time he was undergoing medical training, and from 1887 he began to have extended periods of automatism after an attack. His reports of his own case for Hughlings Jackson show special interest in the attendant mental conditions, such as the 'aura' which precedes a *petit mal*.[28] While Myers and Gurney were studying conditions of abnormal consciousness, therefore, they had a brother and a friend who knew them from the inside.

Their study of telepathy led them to the reports of spontaneous thought-transference collected by the Literary Committee of the SPR. In many of these, the percipient mysteriously heard a friend's voice or had a feeling that they were in danger, and later discovered them to have been seriously ill or in some state of crisis at the time; by extension, Myers and Gurney took apparitions of a dying friend or relative to be cases of spontaneous telepathy, and not real objective ghostly presences.[29] If apparitions were objective phenomena, one needed to postulate not merely astral bodies but astral clothes as well. From the first, they were confident in regarding apparitions as subjective phenomena, as hallucinations.[30]

Finally, Myers had access to a number of automatic writing scripts. Though the scribes had produced them with spirit communication in mind, other interpretations were possible, and they were the origin of a series of papers by Myers.

Having seen how Myers and Gurney came to be concerned with hypnotism, multiple personality, hallucinations, and automatic writing, the next section will outline the existing medical views of those conditions.

The British view was that mental disorder always had a basis in bodily disorder. Michael Clark has recently described how a dualist-interactionist or parallelist picture of mind and body was retained for speaking of mental health, where the conscious will had a firm control over the body, and sense perception reliably and accurately presented the outside world to the mind; but for mental illness, an epiphenomenalist picture was adopted, the mind having lost its autonomy, and its operations becoming increasingly perverted by the diseased state of the body.[31] A consequence of this view was that physiology and pathology became linked; a description in physiological language implied that free will had been suspended and that mental events were being determined by body events – an intrinsically pathological state. The prevailing descriptions of hypnotism, automatism, and hallucinations were in physiological terms, so that these conditions were inevitably pathological.

The linkage is clear in W.B. Carpenter's standard textbook *Mental Physiology*. Like all contemporary medical writers, he utilized James Braid's concept of hypnotism as the only genuine part of mesmerism. The trance was real, and so was the subject's deference to the suggestions of the operator, but it was only a physiological reaction on the part of the subject; it could be brought on by making him squint upwards at a bright light, so there was no need for mesmeric passes, and there was no mesmeric fluid, no rapport. Carpenter also invoked his theory of cerebral reflex action – extending the concept of a reflex from the more familiar settings of the spine and brain stem; he attributed to it that large part of normal mental life which is unconscious (that is to say, without awareness or volitional control). Normally, the cerebrum's neural mechanism was under the control of the Will, an irreducibly psychic entity, which through training could build up automatic systems for habitual actions such as speech or walking, allowing these actions to be performed without detailed volition for each individual muscular contraction. In the hypnotic trance, as in insanity or intoxication, the Will's control was removed, so that the subject lost control over his thoughts and actions, becoming a thinking automaton at the mercy of an operator's suggestion, since any suggested idea would dominate his mind.[32] The pathological nature of the hypnotic trance was self-evident.[33]

A similar view of trance was put forward by the neurologist Rudolf Heidenhain of Breslau, whose influence in Britain is indicated by Daniel

Hack Tuke's appreciative though critical endorsement of his work, and the fact that the entry on 'Animal Magnetism' in the ninth edition of the *Encyclopaedia Britannica* was almost entirely based on Heidenhain's book. He disputed Carpenter's claim that the trance state was caused by a decreased supply of blood to the brain; giving experimental examples of stimulation producing an inhibition of motor nerves, he attributed it instead to the inhibition of the higher regions of the nervous system associated with consciousness, which produced a cerebral short-circuit from optic thalami to corpora striata, from sensory centre to motor centre.[34] Though differing over the cause of the trance, Heidenhain and Carpenter agreed that it consisted of automatic sensori-motor reflex behaviour. Likewise, Hack Tuke, the principal medical advocate of hypnotism in Britain at this time, argued that though 'there must be a certain functional activity of the cerebral cortex', 'the will is suspended; in other words we have ... reflex cerebral action'.[35] The kinship of the trance with hysteria and other nervous disorders was confidently maintained by Sir Henry Holland and Horatio Donkin, and Charcot's paradigmatic exposition of this view was also influential, as is indicated by the articles by him and his collaborators in Hack Tuke's *Dictionary of Psychological Medicine*.[36]

The rival French school, of Hippolyte Bernheim at Nancy, was less influential in Britain. They emphasized the continuity with normal behaviour such as sleep and deference to persuasive authority and denied that only hysterical people could be hypnotized. They maintained, however, that the subject was a pure automaton, and therefore not responsible for crimes committed under a hypnotic suggestion. (See Ruth Harris, 'Murder under Hypnosis' in Volume II.)

French psychiatry also supplied much of the clinical data on multiple personality, the most famous case being that of Félida X, a patient of Eugène Azam of Bordeaux, on whom he reported at intervals between 1858 and 1893. She was a sullen, taciturn girl, suffering from several nervous symptoms, but she would regularly fall into a lethargic state from which she awakened into a different personality, lively and elated, and free from symptoms; this condition would last several hours, then she would return to her previous personality. Her secondary personality had knowledge of her life in her primary personality, but not vice versa. Azam always called her primary personality the 'normal' one, even though the periods of secondary personality eventually predominated.[37] Another striking case was that of Louis Vivé. In 1877, aged fourteen, he had been frightened by a viper and developed epilepsy and paralysis; after he had been in the Bonneval asylum for a couple of months, he had an epileptic attack, from which he awoke with no memory since the viper incident and a completely different character, violent and greedy. After escaping from Bonneval, he eventually turned up at the Rochefort asylum, where they found that he could be switched between different states of personality and symptoms by the application of metals to his body. Louis Vivé was reckoned to have at least six distinct states, none of which could be regarded as wholly normal.[38]

Hallucinations, as usually conceived, were by their very nature abnormal and pathological; they were perversions of sensation. For a large class of hallucinations, the somatic basis was evident: those produced by intoxication through alcohol, hashish, opium, or other drugs, those due to severe physical exhaustion, and the delirium of fever; for instance, Maudsley attributed their origin to 'a deranged sensory ganglion', and Carpenter to imperfect nutrition of the brain, or poisoning of the blood.[39] But Maudsley distinguished another class of hallucinations, which could be referred to an exceptionally vivid idea, so vivid as to produce a perception.[40] This process was not in itself pathological, for Maudsley used the example of Isaac Newton, who could allegedly hallucinate a spectrum in a dark room, and Henry Holland pointed out that it was related to the normal and rational process by which a recollected image is brought before consciousness;[41] the pathology lay in the hallucination being involuntary, and being confused with reality. Holland, Maudsley, and Carpenter[42] all drew a contrast between the early stages of a person's intoxication or insanity, when the morbid idea is known to be abnormal and the illusions to be imaginary, and the advanced stages, where the morbid ideas 'come at last to acquire a complete mastery over him; and his Will, his Common Sense, and his Moral Sense, at last succumb to their domination';[43] where 'spectral images or illusions . . . come unbidden into the mind'; the stages of 'insubordination to the will'.[44] As with hypnotism, it was the removal or subordination of the will that left the subject powerless to dispel the illusion and marked hallucinations as pathological, and as this subordination was conceived as the result of a disordered brain condition, even the class of morbid hallucinations originating in an idea was ultimately somatic.

The absence of voluntary control similarly marked automatism as pathological and basically physiological. Carpenter took it as a prime example of 'unconscious cerebration', reflex action of the cerebrum, which without the control of the will could produce intelligent behaviour, answering questions, utilizing consciously forgotten knowledge; this explained automatic writing, table tilting and pendulum divining which were otherwise attributed to spirits or discounted as fraudulent.[45] The medical agreement on this explanation is illustrated by a series of articles and letters on automatic writing in the *British Medical Journal* in 1893. Henry Rayner's outspoken contribution has already been quoted (pp. 233–34). All the authors agreed that it was 'unnecessary to introduce a 'spiritual' element to explain these phenomena, because they can be explained on a strictly physio-pathological basis',[46] and with one exception they regarded the condition as morbid and cautioned against the practice. The original editorial article for instance said: 'we are inclined . . . to think that this removal of higher control may be cultivated, but that there is danger in thus yielding up the reins'. J. Wiglesworth noted the

'analogy with some of the milder forms of mania, and epileptic states, the leading factors in which conditions are the throwing out of gear of the highest controlling faculties of the brain, and the consequent springing into greater prominence and automatic working of lower centres.... I am not surprised to hear that many mediums have become in all reality permanent monomaniacs, and I agree that the game is a dangerous one. The constant placing of the brain in a pathological condition has a tendency to produce permanent mental derangement.'

The medical view therefore placed automatism alongside the manifestations of 'the insane, the epileptic, the sexually irritated, the neurasthenic generally' as a neurally determined pathological somatic condition.[47]

The next section will describe the investigations of Myers and Gurney, and how their ideas about hypnotism and related clinical conditions, hallucinations and automatism departed from the prevailing medical views.

I have already suggested that Myers and Gurney were preoccupied with inner psychological experience, and that they came to psychical research looking for objective evidence for spiritual action, for the reality of the spiritual values associated with poetry, music, inspiration, duty, and love. Given this, it is not surprising that Gurney should have been interested in the psychology of the hypnotic trance rather than its physiology. From his first paper in 1884, he rejected the three-stage division of the trance proclaimed by Charcot and the Salpêtrière school, a division based on essentially somatic criteria, different muscle states. The muscular states were real enough, but they could be found coexisting with a whole range of mental states, and therefore as far as Gurney was concerned did not constitute distinct stages of hypnotism. He proposed instead a psychological criterion: memory. The 'deep' state of trance had its own train of memory, so that events which took place during the 'deep' state could not be recalled in the 'alert' state or on waking, but were remembered on re-hypnotization to the 'deep' state.[48] Gurney performed a series of experiments explicitly to demonstrate these distinct trains of memory. In the different states, the subject was told about different fictitious events in Brighton; transcripts of the ensuing conversation showed that these memories were exclusive, and that the subject interpreted an ambiguous remark by the knowledge appropriate to whichever state he was in at the time.[49]

Gurney argued strongly against the interpretation of trance as sensori-motor reflex behaviour. He claimed that subjects retained memory of their trance in almost all cases, even if it was only recoverable on re-hypnotization, which told against Heidenhain's view that there was no consciousness during trance. Against Carpenter's view that the Will was absent, he cited a familiar hypnotic experiment in which the subject has his arm made rigid and is then offered a sovereign if he can reach out to take it. Gurney argued that the subject does not lose his will, for he is not passively acquiescent with his inability to move his arm but is full of incredulity and rage, struggling till he goes red and the sweat runs down his face (Gurney's sovereign being absolutely safe). In so far as the reflex analogy was appropriate, Gurney claimed, it had to be a conscious or psychic reflex.[50]

Later he dropped the reflex analogy totally, and regarded the hypnotic trance as the manifestation of a normally hidden secondary intelligence, with its own train of memory. He found that this secondary intelligence could be allowed to express itself while the subject was awake through automatic writing with a planchette. In a series of experiments, the subject was given some intellectual problem while in trance and then immediately awakened; though he could not recall what he had been told to do (he was offered a sovereign if he could do so), in due course his hand would unconsciously write out an answer to the problem, thus implying that the answer had been worked out independently of the waking consciousness. Typical problems were complicated addition sums, spelling backwards, completing a rhyming couplet – sufficiently complex to suggest that automatic neural function was not an adequate explanation, but that there was genuine psychological action. A variation was to give a command to be executed a certain length of time after waking, or when Gurney had coughed a certain number of times; here the planchette reported how time was passing or how many coughs there had been, and the counting operation Gurney held to imply intelligence.[51]

Even within the SPR, there were those who took the orthodox view that the trance was a dangerous pathological state. An associate commented in a letter to the *Journal* that there seemed to be a real risk of hypnotism weakening the will of the hypnotized subject. Another anonymous correspondent who signed himself 'M.B.' (almost certainly his medical degree, not his initials) interpreted Gurney's hypnotic experiments as revealing lower, more easily influenced strata of the mind which could not be reached when the will was active; he compared the trance state to hysteria and brain or nervous disease, and wondered whether it was really desirable for any sane person to have himself put into that condition.[52]

Gurney and Myers, however, explicitly and emphatically denied the morbidity of the trance. For instance, when discussing definitions of the hypnotic state, Gurney insisted on the necessity of distinguishing it from morbid affections. He reported that his experiments, which had all been done on normal healthy subjects, showed no ill effects. It was a weakness of the French experiments that they were almost all performed on mental patients; indeed Charcot's school at the Salpêtrière maintained that only those with at least a disposition to hysteria could be hypnotized. Myers felt it necessary to protest continually against this claim and the assumption of morbidity; 'to call hypnotism a *névrose* seems to me about as reasonable as to call the act of dreaming a *névrose*, or the habit of hard study'.[53]

Myers continually extolled the possibilities of hypnotism as an anaesthetic, for 'moralization' through the cure of addictions (alcoholism, for instance), and for the treatment of recalcitrant mental patients. He and Gurney often referred approvingly to the 'suggestive therapeutics' of Auguste Voisin at the Salpêtrière and Bernheim and Liébeault at Nancy, whom they visited in 1885.[54] In a short article in *The Practitioner* and the entry on the history of hypnotism for Hack Tuke's *Dictionary*, Arthur Myers lamented the scant attention paid in England to hypnotism and emphasized possible therapeutic applications.[55] Two medical members of the SPR, J. Milne Bramwell and Charles Lloyd Tuckey, used hypnotism frequently in their own practice, and Bramwell's *Hypnotism: Its History, Practice and Theory* argued strongly for its wider use. His picture of the trance, like that of Myers and Gurney, and like that of the Nancy school, stressed the continuity with normal states; however he repeatedly denied the Nancy school's claim that a subject was a complete automaton and could be made to perform abhorrent actions, even crimes. This denial was a recurrent theme in SPR writings on hypnotism. Gurney insisted that his experiments, on *healthy* subjects, implied that they could not be made to perform actions opposed to their character; nor was there any sign of decrease in their power of resistance.[56] The trance was not intrinsically dangerous or pathological if it was interpreted in terms of a secondary intelligence.

Myers found support for that interpretation in Pierre Janet's work on hysteria. Under hypnosis, his patient Léonie manifested a different personality, whom they called Léontine. She could be made to do things while Léonie was awake, for instance untying her apron (perhaps one should say *their* apron); like Gurney's planchette experiments, this showed that the personalities existed simultaneously. In very deep trance, a third personality, Léonore, appeared; she could manifest herself to Léontine (the normal trance personality) as a hallucinatory voice.[57] However, whereas Janet presented such cases as wholly pathological distintegrations of the personality, Myers always emphasized their positive aspects. Lucie had a hypnotic personality called Adrienne who was in some ways less ill than Lucie; Adrienne had an unimpaired muscle-sense the 'normal' Lucie lacked; Lucie had an overwhelming fear she could not explain, but Adrienne could remember the trauma which had given rise to it (when she was seven, two men had hidden behind a curtain to surprise her); further, Adrienne and this recollection of hers were actually part of the process of cure.[58] Azam's patient Félida X was even better evidence for Myers's claim that a secondary personality was not necessarily pathological; Félida in her second so-called 'abnormal' state was free from symptoms, more lively, more caring and affectionate, intellectually more brilliant; it was her 'normal' state that was morbid.[59]

> 'We have no right', said Myers, 'to go a whit beyond actual observed facts in any judgment which we may pass as to the relative superiority or "normality" of any of man's different states. I refuse to call my actual waking state "normal" or "natural" in any sense except that of habitual or ordinary.'[60]

Paralleling this, Gurney and Myers refused to regard 'normal' perception as necessarily superior to hallucination. An apparition of a dying friend or relative was a hallucination since they were not really present, but in a sense the hallucination told the truth for it was linked to a real distant event, the death of that person; it was a 'veridical' not a morbid hallucination. The existence of veridical hallucinations implied the existence of telepathy.[61]

There were several weak links in the argument, which Gurney and Myers tried to strengthen. One was the possibility of chance coincidence between hallucination and death; to eliminate this they used an elaborate statistical argument and conducted a census to show the very low incidence of hallucinations among people in normal health. (However, one could still object, as did Janet, that anyone who suffered a hallucination was thereby not in a normal condition.)[62] Another problem was to explain the relationship between veridical and morbid hallucinations. To do this, Gurney took a parallelist view of mind and body, correlating a vivid idea (possibly subconscious) with a concentration of nervous energy in the cortex, and a hallucination with this energy bursting out and activating the visual centre of the brain; this eruption of a nervous impulse might be caused either by a morbid brain state or a telepathic impact.[63] A third weakness was that the analogy with experimental thought-transference was strained; no identifiable thought or image was transferred from mind to mind. To overcome this difficulty, Myers coined the word 'telepathy'[64] for the broader concept of distant mental action, and suggested that telepathy was a largely unconscious process; the dying person would produce telepathically the idea of himself in the mind of the percipient, an idea at first latent and subconscious, subsequently externalized as an associated hallucination. This would account for hallucinations that took symbolic form, for instance a coffin as an emblem of death.[65]

From their study of hypnotism and related clinical conditions, Myers and Gurney drew the idea of secondary intelligence or personality, always present just outside normal waking consciousness. From their study of thought-transference or telepathy and apparitions of the dying, they drew the idea that telepathy was associated with just such a subconscious part of the mind. Myers combined both ideas in his articles on automatic writing.

In his first article, he discussed the scripts produced by an anonymous friend, Mr A, in which the writing identity gave its name as Clelia. Mr A was very startled by the way in which Clelia kept up a dialogue and wrote quite unexpected answers to his verbal questions, sometimes replying in anagrams which took him much time and effort to solve. Myers took the view that there was no evidence that there was a discarnate spirit communicating, but that this case could barely be explained by Carpenter's purely physiological unconscious cerebration.[66] In his second paper, he discussed the scripts produced by the wife of the Rev. P.H. Newnham in 1871 during what had begun as simple experiments in thought-transference; the rector wrote down questions, and his wife, sitting out of sight, produced answers automatically with a planchette. The repeated relevance of the answers showed that Mrs Newnham was telepathically receiving the questions, together with background information previously unknown to her. For example, when the rector asked questions about Masonic rituals, the answers were plausible but incorrect, or partially incorrect, or incorporated material related to the correct answer; this suggested that the answers were unconsciously concocted by Mrs Newnham.[67] Myers now attributed the Clelia and

Newnham scripts to a 'secondary self', a distinct focus of psychical action or of cerebral energy (he used both phrases) capable of possessing an individuality and purposive activity of its own.[68] He was later able to support this interpretation with the case of Janet's patient Lucie, whose hypnotic personality Adrienne could be manifested through a planchette while Lucie was awake; here the automatic writing was of known origin, coming from a submerged part of Lucie's personality, a part of which she was unconscious.[69]

The manifestations of the 'secondary self' were linked, by the Newnham scripts, to telepathy, so they could not be regarded as purely pathological; Myers suggested that they might be not merely abnormal but 'supernormal', showing the operation of 'higher laws', 'apparently belonging to a more advanced stage of evolution'. Paralleling Gurney's argument about morbid and veridical hallucinations, Myers undertook to explain the relationship between abnormal and supernormal manifestations of the 'secondary self'. He conceived it as existing apart from the body and manifesting itself through the nervous system, tending to take the easiest 'path of externalisation'; the disintegrations of disease revealed the paths of 'low resistance', so supernormal manifestations were likely to resemble the abnormal, though not being in themselves morbid. Myers drew parallels between various forms of automatic writing and trance speaking and the disorders of the aphasia family, as classed by Charcot. A tendency of automatists to produce mirror-writing he compared to certain clinical cases, suggesting that it might correspond to the action of the subordinate cerebral hemisphere.[70] Hallucinatory voices among the insane had their parallels in cases where there was (said Myers) no question of madness; 'It is Socrates and Joan [of Arc] who should be our types of sanity'.[71]

Myers was not primarily concerned with the sick mind but the normal mind, the ordinary human personality, and by 1888 he had developed, from his studies of hypnotism, clinical cases, hallucinations, and automatism, a new account of its nature. The only major subsequent change he made was in terminology.[72] Till 1892, he tended to call his conception the 'unconscious secondary self', which was unclear because of the ambiguity of the word 'unconscious'. Physiologically, it meant a nerve impulse too weak to break into consciousness; psychologically, as intended by Myers, it meant simply outside normal waking consciousness. In his later papers and his posthumous book, Myers called his conception the 'subliminal self'.[73]

> 'The word *subliminal*, – meaning "beneath [the] threshold [of consciousness]," – has already been used to define those sensations which are too feeble to be individually recognised. I propose to extend the meaning of the term, so as to make it cover *all* that takes place beneath the ordinary threshold, or say, if preferred, outside the ordinary margin of consciousness; – not only those faint stimulations whose very faintness keeps them submerged, but much else which psychology as yet scarcely recognises; sensations, thoughts, emotions, which may be strong, definite, and

independent, but which, by the original constitution of our being, seldom emerge into that *supraliminal* current of consciousness which we habitually identify with *ourselves*'.[74]

So Myers and Gurney came to oppose orthodox British medical knowledge in three ways. First, they denied the common-sense view of the mind (identified with consciousness) as a unity; human nature, they argued, was multiplex. Second, they denied that conditions of altered consciousness could be adequately explained in terms of automatic deterministic neural mechanisms. Third, they denied that such conditions were in themselves necessarily pathological. The subliminal self was revealed in genius as well as multiple personality, in telepathy as well as hysteria.

A comparison of the theories of Myers and Gurney with those of orthodox British medicine reveals the contingency of the interpretations;[75] there was no 'right' answer determined simply by evidence and logic. The medical writers started from the usual Victorian middle-class idea of proper normal behaviour: an individual exercising responsible control over his thoughts and actions. To them, the most evident feature of conditions of altered consciousness was the lack of control, which made it imperative to label them as deviant. In conformity with the physiological bias of medical psychology, they took nervous reflex action as a model for their explanations, and the use of physiological language emphasized the absence of voluntary control and marked the conditions as pathological. Myers and Gurney were looking for a vehicle for spiritual values, and the most evident feature of conditions of altered consciousness to them was the analogy with inspiration or ecstasy, thoughts mysteriously emerging into consciousness; thinking of something spiritual and beautiful, they insisted on the use of psychological language and the absence of any essential pathology in these conditions.

Though this account has been given in terms of the cognitive psychology of individuals, as a conflict between different interpretations rather than different social groups,[76] some of its ingredients have obvious class affinities. Myers and Gurney's conceptions of duty, music, poetry, inspiration, and love were those of an affluent social elite, products of the liberal (and unpractical) education of the English public schools and Cambridge University, with the leisure to develop and enjoy intellectual interests. It was the spiritual values of their own culture which they promoted, as if it was the civilized ideal for all of society. Gurney saw the power of classical music as a great agency for brightening the lives of the uncultivated and ignorant working class; Myers scarcely troubled to conceal his irritation at Lombroso's claim that genius was a species of insanity, or Janet's remark that falling in love was like falling ill during a state of physical and moral debilitation.[77] Striving to uphold their own values, they wrote the signature of their social class into the theory of the subliminal self.

This may be one reason why the theory never had much currency outside the SPR; it appealed to a very restricted set of people.[78] Those who wanted reassurance about the existence of the soul would usually prefer more conventional religion (or spiritualism) which identified 'soul' with 'ego'; the theory of the subliminal self actually denigrated normal consciousness. Those who wanted a psychological approach to conditions of altered consciousness could turn to Janet and Freud, whose theories were more definitely psychiatric, carrying a strong implication of pathology. The psychiatric view, psychological or physiological, chimed in well with the conventional middle-class picture of orderly behaviour and moral respectability, and it is the one that has dominated down to the present day. Its triumph is illustrated by the setting in which I have been resurrecting the theories of Myers and Gurney: a volume of articles on the history of *psychiatry*.

Notes

I am very grateful to John Gabbay and Andrew Cunningham for their comments on earlier versions of this paper; also to Peter Searby, Logie Barrow, German Berrios, Alex Owen, and Jill Rubinstein for helpful and inspiring conversations. My special thanks go to John Cerullo and Janet Oppenheim and their publishers for allowing me to see their books in manuscript.

Abbreviations: *Proceedings = Proceedings of the Society for Psychical Research; Journal = Journal of the Society for Psychical Research.*

1 Alex Owen, 'Women and the Nineteenth Century Spiritualist Movement' (University of Sussex, D.Phil. thesis, forthcoming 1985; London: Virago Press, forthcoming); 'Women and Nineteenth Century Spiritualism: Strategies in the Subversion of Femininity', in Jim Obelkevitch, Lyndal Roper, and Raphael Samuel (eds), *Religion and Society* (London: Routledge and Kegan Paul, forthcoming 1985); 'The Other Voice: Women, Children, and Nineteenth Century Spiritualism', in Carolyn Steedman and Valerie Walkerdine (eds), *Language Gender Childhood* (London: Routledge and Kegan Paul, forthcoming 1985); Logie Barrow, 'Socialism in Eternity: The Ideology of Plebeian Spiritualists 1853–1913', *History Workshop Journal* no. 9 (Spring 1980): 37–63; 'Democratic Epistemology: Mid-19th-Century Plebeian Medicine', *Society for the Social History of Medicine Bulletin* 29 (December 1981): 25–9; Janet Oppenheim, *The Other World: Spiritualism and Psychical Research in England 1850–1914* (New York: Cambridge University Press, 1985). See also R. Laurence Moore, *In Search of White Crows: Spiritualism, Parapsychology and American Culture* (New York: Oxford University Press, 1977); Geoffrey K. Nelson, *Spiritualism and Society* (London: Routledge and Kegan Paul, 1969).
2 *British Medical Journal* (1893): 2, 1338.
3 Henri F. Ellenberger, *The Discovery of the Unconscious: The History and Evolution of Dynamic Psychiatry* (New York: Basic Books, and London: Allen Lane, 1970), ch. 3; Thomas Hardy Leahey, *A History of Psychology: Main Currents in Psychological Thought* (Englewood Cliffs, NJ: Prentice-Hall, 1980), pp. 162–63.

4 Michael J. Clark, 'The Rejection of Psychological Approaches to Mental Disorder in Late Nineteenth-Century British Psychiatry', in Andrew Scull (ed.), *Madhouses, Mad-Doctors, and Madmen: The Social History of Psychiatry in the Victorian Era* (Philadelphia, Pa.: University of Pennsylvania Press, 1981), pp. 271–312; L.S. Jacyna, 'The Physiology of Mind, the Unity of Nature, and the Moral Order in Victorian Thought', *British Journal for the History of Science* 14 (1981): 109–32.

5 Frank Miller Turner, *Between Science and Religion: The Reaction to Scientific Naturalism in Late Victorian England* (New Haven, Conn. and London: Yale University Press, 1974) studies six Victorians (including Sidgwick, Myers, and Alfred Russel Wallace) who rejected both orthodox religion and scientific naturalism; psychical research or spiritualism appears as part of their attempt to exist 'between science and religion'. On the scientists of the period, see also Ruth Barton, 'The X Club: Science, Religion, and Social Change in Victorian England' (unpublished Ph.D. Thesis, University of Pennsylvania, 1976); Frank M. Turner, 'The Victorian Conflict Between Science and Religion: A Professional Dimension', *Isis* 69 (1978): 356–76, and 'Public Science in Britain, 1880–1919', *Isis*, 71 (1980): 589–608. On the fragmentation of the intellectual world, see Robert M. Young, 'Natural Theology, Victorian Periodicals and the Fragmentation of a Common Context', in Colin Chant and John Fauvel (eds), *Darwin to Einstein: Historical Studies on Science and Belief* (Harlow, Essex: Longman in association with The Open University Press, 1980), pp. 69–107; Susan Faye Cannon, *Science in Culture: The Early Victorian Period* (New York: Science History Publications, 1978), chs 1, 9; Walter E. Houghton, *The Victorian Frame of Mind 1830–1870* (New Haven, Conn. and London: Yale University Press, 1957), ch. 1.

6 This is because many of these 'histories' have been written as extended arguments either for or against the existence of psychic phenomena. For an example of the former, see Brian Inglis, *Natural and Supernatural: A History of the Paranormal from Earliest Times to 1914*, pbk edn (London: Sphere Books, 1979; 1st edn, 1977); of the second is Ruth Brandon, *The Spiritualists: The Passion for the Occult in the Nineteenth and Twentieth Centuries* (London: Weidenfeld and Nicolson, 1983). Somewhat more balanced and less polemical studies are Alan Gauld, *The Founders of Psychical Research* (London: Routledge and Kegan Paul, 1968), and Eric J. Dingwall (ed.), *Abnormal Hypnotic Phenomena: A Survey of Nineteenth-Century Cases*, 4 vols (London: J. and A. Churchill, 1967–68). It seems to require professional historians or sociologists to break away from the tiresome question of the reality or otherwise of paranormal phenomena. See Turner, *Between Science and Religion* and the works cited in note 1, of which Oppenheim, *The Other World*, offers the best and most comprehensive guide to the Victorian period, though marred by a rather simplistic science-versus-religion framework. John J. Cerullo, *The Secularization of the Soul: Psychical Research in Modern Britain* (Philadelphia, Pa.: Institute for the Study of Human Issues, 1982) deals with the appeal and career of Myers's conception of the subliminal self but only briefly with its origin, and does not connect psychical research with the contemporary medical scene. Seymour H. Mauskopf and Michael R. McVaugh, *The Elusive Science: Origins of Experimental Psychical Research* (Baltimore, Md. and London: Johns Hopkins University Press, 1980) is an excellent history of parapsychology in the era dominated by J.B. Rhine (the 1930s onwards). H.M. Collins and T.J. Pinch, *Frames of Meaning: The Social Construction of Extraordinary Science* (London: Routledge and Kegan Paul, 1982), is a sociologically-

informed account of their own investigation of paranormal metal bending.

7 J.P. Williams, 'The Making of Victorian Psychical Research: An Intellectual Elite's Approach to the Spiritual World' (unpublished Ph.D. thesis, University of Cambridge, 1984), ch. 8.

8 Frederic W.H. Myers, 'Multiplex Personality', *Proceedings* 4 (1886–87): 507 (also in *Nineteenth Century* 20 (1886): 659); Daniel Hack Tuke, 'Artificial Insanity, Chiefly in Relation to Mental Pathology', *Journal of Mental Science* 11(1865–66): 56–66, 174–90.

9 Biographical information on Myers from Gauld, *Founders of Psychical Research*, pp. 38–44, 89–104, and *passim* (Gauld discusses extensively Myers's relationship with Annie Marshall); Turner, *Between Science and Religion*, ch. 5; Myers's autobiographical pamphlet *Fragments of Inner Life*, published by the SPR in 1961 (quoted passage from p. 13), printed with major omissions as the introduction to Myers, *Fragments of Prose and Poetry*, ed. Eveleen Myers (London: Longmans, Green, 1904). The MS of 'Fragments of Inner Life', containing much unpublished material, is in the library of Trinity College, Cambridge (Myers 26⁶³). See, also the essay by Charlotte Mackenzie in Volume II.

10 *The Power of Sound* (London: Smith, Elder, 1880), especially pp. vi–vii, ch. 17, p. 422; 'A Permanent Band for the East-End', in *Tertium Quid: Chapters on Various Disputed Questions*, 2 vols (London: Kegan Paul, Trench, 1887), vol. 2, pp. 96–118.

11 Gurney, *Tertium Quid*. Biographical information from Gauld, *Founders of Psychical Research*, pp. 154–60 and *passim*; Cerullo, *The Secularization of the Soul*, pp. 50–4; Trevor H. Hall, *The Strange Case of Edmund Gurney* (London: Duckworth, 1964), but see criticism of Hall's claims in Gauld, *Founders*, pp. 174–82. Gurney died in 1888; suicide is a possibility.

12 Biographical information on Sidgwick from A.S[idgwick] and E.M.S[idgwick], *Henry Sidgwick: A Memoir* (London: Macmillan, 1906); Turner, *Between Science and Religion*, ch. 3; Gauld, *Founders*, pp. 47–57 and *passim*; J.B. Schneewind, *Sidgwick's Ethics and Victorian Moral Philosophy* (Oxford: Oxford University Press, 1977); D.G. James, *Henry Sidgwick: Science and Faith in Victorian England* (London: Oxford University Press, 1970).

13 Williams, 'The Making of Victorian Psychical Research', ch. 5. I cannot here quote material to support this interpretation. It is based on a reading of Myers's *Fragments of Inner Life*, his letters to George Eliot, his introduction to *Phantasms of the Living*, 2 vols (London: Trübner, 1886), and sections of his *Human Personality and its Survival of Bodily Death*, 2 vols (London: Longmans, Green, 1903); Gurney's *Power of Sound* and *Tertium Quid*; Sidgwick's early letters (in the *Memoir*), his Apostles paper on prayer, and his article on Arthur Hugh Clough. I received some valuable hints from Cerullo's discussion in *The Secularization of the Soul*.

14 Myers, 'In Memory of Henry Sidgwick', *Proceedings* 15 (1900): 454.

15 T.H. Huxley, 'On the Hypothesis that Animals are Automata, and Its History', *Fortnightly Review*, 2nd series, 16 (1874): 555–80; John Tyndall, 'The Belfast Address', in *Fragments of Science*, 6th edn, 2 vols (London: Longmans, Green, 1879) vol. 2, pp. 137–203; W.K. Clifford, 'Body and Mind', *Fortnightly Review*, 2nd series, 16 (1874): 714–36.

16 For details of the investigations, see Gauld, *Founders of Psychical Research*, chs. 4, 5. Evidence for their discouragement comes from the manuscript of Myers's 'Fragments of Inner Life', and Sidgwick's letter of 24 June, 1878 to Roden Noel (*Memoir*, p. 336).

17 Barrett's paper, 'On Some Phenomena Associated with Abnormal Conditions of Mind', is reprinted with alterations in *Proceedings* 1 (1882–83): 238–44 (it was never published by the BA). Other information comes from Barrett, 'Appendix to the Report on Thought-Reading', *Proceedings* 1 (1882–83): 47–9.

18 Barrett, Gurney, and Myers, 'Thought-Reading', *Nineteenth Century* 11 (1882): 890–900; Barrett, 'Mind-Reading versus Muscle-Reading', *Nature* 24 (1881): 212, 236.

19 E.D. Rogers, *Light* 13 (1893): 429–30.

20 See Christopher Harvie, *The Lights of Liberalism: University Liberals and the Challenge of Democracy 1860–1886* (London: Allen Lane, 1976).

21 Williams, 'The Making of Victorian Psychical Research', ch. 8.

22 Williams, 'The Making of Victorian Psychical Research', pp. 162–79.

23 Barrett, Gurney and Myers, 'First Report of the Committee on Mesmerism', *Proceedings* 1 (1882–83): 220.

24 See Dingwall (ed.), *Abnormal Hypnotic Phenomena*, vol. 4, pp. 128–51. A mesmeric fluid, or some sort of 'ether' was of course a more obvious and more popular vehicle for spiritual values, especially amongst physicists. See note 76.

25 Janet's two papers are translated by Bert S. Kopell in 'Pierre Janet's Description of Hypnotic Sleep Provoked from a Distance', *Journal of the History of the Behavioral Sciences* 4 (1968): 119–31, 258–67; see Ellenberger, *Discovery of the Unconscious*, pp. 337–39. Myer's response was 'On Telepathic Hynotism and Its Relation to Other Forms of Hypnotic Suggestion', *Proceedings* 4 (1886–87): 127–88. Gurney's was 'Further Problems of Hypnotism', *Mind* 12 (1887): 212–32, 397–422; this was reprinted with alterations as 'Hypnotism and Telepathy', *Proceedings* 5 (1888–89): 216–59.

26 These experiments are reported in Gurney and Myers, 'Second Report of the Committee on Mesmerism', *Proceedings* 1 (1882–83): 257–60; Gurney, 'An Account of Some Experiments in Mesmerism', *Proceedings* 2 (1883–84): 201–05; 'Local Anaesthesia Induced in the Normal State by Mesmeric Passes', *Proceedings* 3 (1885): 453–59. They are discussed in Dingwall (ed.), *Abnormal Hypnotic Phenomena*, vol. 4, pp. 132–33.

27 Ellenberger, *Discovery of the Unconscious*, pp. 121–45.

28 I am indebted to German Berrios for directing me to David C. Taylor and Susan M. Marsh, 'Hughlings Jackson's Dr Z: The Paradigm of Temporal Lobe Epilepsy Revealed', *Journal of Neurology, Neurosurgery, and Psychiatry* 43 (1980): 758–67. The Jackson papers are 'On a Particular Variety of Epilepsy ("Intellectual Aura") . . .', *Brain* 11 (1888–89): 179–207; and, with Walter S. Colman, 'Case of Epilepsy with Tasting Movements and "Dreamy State" . . .', *Brain* 21 (1898): 580–90.

29 Gurney and Myers, 'Report of the Literary Committee', *Proceedings* 1 (1882–83): 116–55; see Sidgwick, presidential address, *Proceedings* 5 (1888–89): 274.

30 Myers, *Phantasms of the Living*, vol. 2, pp. 278–79; 'Second Report of the Literary Committee', *Proceedings* 2 (1883–84): 48.

31 Clark, 'The Rejection of Psychological Approaches to Mental Disorder'.

32 W.B. Carpenter, *Principles of Mental Physiology*, 4th edn (London: Henry S. King, 1876; 1st edn, 1874), chs 1, 14.

33 It was also an essential part of Carpenter's opposition to Huxley's claim that will or consciousness was *never* causally efficacious and was really redundant; he argued that while Huxley's evidence came from decerebrate frogs, brain-damaged soldiers and hypnotic subjects, his conclusions could not be applied to normal health (*Mental Physiology*, pp. xiii–xxx).

34 D. Hack Tuke, 'Hypnosis Redivivus', *Journal of Mental Science* 26 (1880–81): 531–51; Rudolf Heidenhain, *Der sogenannte thierische Magnetismus; Physiologische Beobachtungen*, 4th edn (Leipzig: Druck und Verlag von Breitkopf und Kärtel, 1880), translated by L.C. Wooldridge as *Animal Magnetism: Physiological Observations* (London: C. Kegan Paul, 1880); J.G. McKendrick, s.v. 'Magnetism, Animal', in *Encyclopaedia Britannica*, 9th edn, 24 vols (Edinburgh: Adam and Charles Black, 1875–89), vol. 15, pp. 277–83.

35 D. Hack Tuke, 'On the Mental Condition in Hypnotism', *Journal of Mental Science* 29 (1883–84): 78.

36 D. Hack Tuke, *A Dictionary of Psychological Medicine*, 2 vols (London: J. and A. Churchill, 1892). J.M. Charcot and Gilles de la Tourette, s.v. 'Hypnotism in the Hysterical', vol. 1, pp. 606–10; H.B. Donkin, s.v. 'Hysteria', vol. 1, pp. 618–27; J.M. Charcot and Pierre Marie, s.v. 'Hysteria: Mainly Hystero-Epilepsy', vol. 1, pp. 627–41.

37 Ellenberger, *Discovery of the Unconscious*, pp. 136–38.

38 Myers, appendix to 'Human Personality in the Light of Hypnotic Suggestion', *Proceedings* 4 (1886–87): 20–4; 'Multiplex Personality', pp. 497–500 (also in *Nineteenth Century* 20 (1886): 649–52); A.T. Myers, 'Psychological Retrospect: The Life-History of a Case of Double or Multiple Personality', *Journal of Mental Science* 31 (1885–86): 596–605.

39 Henry Maudsley, *The Pathology of Mind* (London: Macmillan, 1879), p. 375; Carpenter, *Mental Physiology*, pp. 653–56.

40 Maudsley, *Natural Causes and Supernatural Seemings* (London: Kegan Paul, Trench, 1886); pt II, chs 2 and 3 cover the two classes.

41 Maudsley, *Natural Causes and Supernatural Seemings*, p. 193; Henry Holland, *Chapters on Mental Physiology* (London: Longman, Brown, Green, and Longman, 1852), p. 115.

42 Holland, *Mental Physiology*, pp. 123–25; Maudsley, *Pathology of Mind*, pp. 371–75; Carpenter, *Mental Physiology*, pp. 672–74.

43 Carpenter, *Mental Physiology*, p. 673.

44 Holland, *Mental Physiology*, pp. 115, 118.

45 Carpenter, *Mental Physiology*, chs 13, 16.

46 *British Medical Journal* (1893): 2, 1225–226 (article unsigned).

47 The editorial was on an article in the *Pall Mall Gazette* for 30 October, 1893 about the automatic writing reported in two issues of W.T. Stead's *Borderland*. *British Medical Journal* (1893): 2, 1015, 1389–390, 1226. The letters continued till 27 January, 1894; see also Lloyd Tuckey in the notes section of the 10 February, 1894 issue.

48 Gurney, 'The Stages of Hypnotism', *Proceedings* 2 (1883–84): 61–72 (also in *Mind* 9 (1884): 110–21).

49 Gurney, 'Stages of Hypnotic Memory', *Proceedings* 4 (1886–87): 515–31.

50 Gurney, 'The Problems of Hypnotism', *Mind* 9 (1884): 477–508.

51 Gurney, 'Peculiarities of Certain Post-Hypnotic States', *Proceedings* 4 (1886–87): 268–323.

52 'An Associate', *Journal* 4 (1889–90): 24–5; 'M.B.', *Journal*, 3 (1887–88): 318–19. 'M.B.' refers to his observations of consumption, and none of the members or associates with initials M.B. seem likely possibilities.

53 Gurney, 'Further Problems of Hypnotism', p. 212; 'Peculiarities of Certain Post-Hypnotic States', pp. 268–69; Myers, 'Automatic Writing III', *Proceedings* 4 (1886–87): 245.

54 Myers, *Journal* 2 (1885–86): 450–53; Myers, 'Multiplex Personality', pp. 505–07 *The Nineteenth Century*, pp. 656–58; Gurney and Myers, 'Some Higher Aspects of Mesmerism', *Proceedings* 3 (1885): 423; Myers, 'Human Personality in the Light of Hypnotic Suggestion', pp. 16–19. Also in *Fortnightly Review*, 2nd series 38 (1885): 651–54.

55 *The Practitioner* 44 (1890): 196–206; s.v. 'Hypnotism, History of', in Tuke (ed.), *Dictionary of Psychological Medicine*, vol. 1, pp. 603–06.

56 Gurney, 'Peculiarities of Certain Post-Hypnotic States', pp. 268–69.

57 Myers, 'French Experiments on Strata of Personality', *Proceedings* 5 (1888–89): 374–97; Janet, 'Les Actes inconscients et la mémoire pendant le somnambulisme', *Revue Philosophique* 25 (1888): 238–79. Later Janet numbered the personalities Léonie I, II, and III.

58 Myers, 'Automatic Writing III', pp. 245–46; Janet, 'Les actes inconscients et la dédoublement de la personnalité pendant le somnambulisme provoqué', *Revue Philosophique* 22 (1886): 577–92.

59 Myers, 'Multiplex Personality', p. 503 (*Nineteenth Century*, pp. 654–55).

60 Myers, 'Professor Pierre Janet's "Automatisme Psychologique"', *Proceedings* 7 (1889–90): 190.

61 Myers, 'Second Report of the Literary Committee', pp. 48–9; Gurney and Myers, 'A Theory of Apparitions II', *Proceedings* (1883–84): 167–68 (*Nineteenth Century*, 16 (1884), pp. 77–8).

62 The SPR later did a more extensive census under the aegis of the first International Congress of Experimental Psychology. See Gauld, *Founders of Psychical Research*, pp. 167–68, pp. 182–85; *Congrès international de psychologie physiologique* (Paris: Bureau des Revues, 1890; reprinted Nendeln/Lichtenstein: Kraus-Thomson Organization, 1974), pp. 44–8; Janet's objection is on p. 46.

63 Gurney and Myers, 'A Theory of Apparitions II', pp. 167–70 (*Nineteenth Century*, pp. 77–80); *Phantasms of the Living*, vol. 1, pp. 484–95.

64 'Report of the Literary Committee', *Proceedings* 1 (1882–83): 147. His standard definition was 'the communication of impressions of any kind from one mind to another, independently of the recognised channels of sense' (glossary to *Human Personality*, vol. 1, p. xxii).

65 Further, some cases suggested a 'partial externalization', the image being seen in the mind's eye or as if projected onto a curtain or window. Gurney and Myers, 'A Theory of Apparitions', pp. 109–36, 157–86 (*Nineteenth Century*, 15 (1884) 791–815; *Nineteenth Century* 16 (1884): 68–95). Myers came to doubt the adequacy of this theory, which could account only with difficulty for apparitions perceived by several people; see his extended 'Note' in *Phantasms of the Living*, vol. 2, pp. 277–316.

66 'On a Telepathic Explanation of Some So-called Spiritualistic Phenomena', *Proceedings* 2 (1883–84): 217–37.

67 'Automatic Writing II', *Proceedings* 3 (1885): 6–23.

68 'Automatic Writing II', pp. 27, 30.

69 'Automatic Writing III', pp. 237–46.

70 'Automatic Writing II', pp. 30–61; appendix to 'Human Personality', *Proceedings* 4 (1886–87): 20–4.

71 'Automatic Writing IV', *Proceedings* 5 (1888–89): 546.

72 Myers *added* to the theory, especially after 1889 when he became converted to spiritualism, but he did not change its basic structure.

73 'Subliminal', unfortunately, is almost as ambiguous as 'unconscious'. Myers

contemplated for a time the alternatives 'transliminal' and 'extramarginal', and it was the latter that William James used in *The Varieties of Religious Experience* (London: Longman, Green, 1902).

74 Myers, *Human Personality*, vol. 1, p. 14.

75 It is particularly striking to see Carpenter quoting very similar evidence to Myers and Gurney, but to support an opposite conclusion.

76 For an attempt to capture psychical research in sociological terms, see Brian Wynne, 'Physics and Psychics: Science, Symbolic Action, and Social Control in Late Victorian England', in Barry Barnes and Steven Shapin (eds), *Natural Order: Historical Studies of Scientific Culture* (Beverly Hills, Calif. and London: Sage Publications, 1979), pp. 167–86. Wynne identifies a network of Cambridge intellectuals, physicists, and psychical researchers, and argues that their interest in the spiritual world and in the ether was an instance of 'conservative thought', an upper-class group's reaction to the threat from the naturalistic cosmology and demands for social reform of professional scientists and the rising industrial middle class. Though his discussion at the level of ideas is convincing, I have argued elsewhere ('The Making of Victorian Psychical Research', pp. 101–06) that his sociological analysis is seriously flawed, at least when applied to the psychical research side of the network, because he offers no satisfactory criteria to distinguish his upper-class and middle-class groups; the criteria he does offer (landed interest, advocation of a clerisy, supporting university reform, meritocratic liberalism) put either Sidgwick, Myers, and Gurney or the professional scientists into the wrong group.

77 Gurney, works cited note 10. Myers, *Human Personality*, vol. 1, pp. 71, 91–2; 'Janet's "Automatisme Psychologique"', pp. 196–97.

78 Restricted in number, not in type. Cerullo (*Secularization of the Soul*, ch. 6) has made biographical studies of a diverse assortment of SPR members in the period after 1900.

CHAPTER TEN

Contracting the disease of love: authority and freedom in the origins of psychoanalysis

John Forrester

IN HIS INTERESTING and thought-provoking diatribe against psycho-analysis, *Le psychanalysme*, Robert Castel bases his critique on the follow-ing considerations:

> 'The whole of psychoanalysis is determined by the framework of a contract. If I am not mistaken, no one has paid attention to the implications that this fundamental structure has: rules of protocol, the role of money, etc. As if this contract were a simple framework which surrounds something else, something essential. However, the problem is not to open up the packet to see what there is inside, because the contractual structure is not a framework, it is the fertile matrix of all psychoanalytic effects. Through it, emotion itself is contractualized.'[1]

Thirty pages on, he writes: 'The analytic relation represents the liberal assumption, its epiphany: free choice, free contract, free associations, free-floating attention, etc. – it is only the libidinal charges which are fixed.'[2] I will not be following Castel in his diatribe, but I think this perception of the analytic relation is essentially correct, and is a deep one. Not only can the twin notions of contract and the liberal ideal of freedom be claimed to pervade the western liberal societies in which psychoanalysis originated and in which it has come to occupy a privileged if restricted corner of public mythology, these ideals and the limited realities to which they cling can also be seen to determine the very nature of the psychoanalytic situation.

However, the psychoanalytic situation is defined by a contract that is proper to the professions. Maurice's (1838) definition of the professions, to be found in the OED, runs as follows: 'Profession ... is expressly that kind of business which deals primarily with men as men, and is thus distinguished from a Trade, which provides for the external wants or occasions of men.' Taking this interesting definition as our starting-point, we may ask: what does a professional contract yield to the parties? The naive answer, 'professional advice', may well be of use; the professional offers advice, instruction, esoteric knowledge – that blend of knowledge and authoritative support that Foucault called *savoir-pouvoir*. The relations that generate it are, in the ideal case, contracts between free men, not produced by occasional need, but concerned with something like the 'soul', whether it be the social, religious, or medical soul. What the professional contract is above all meant to preserve is the freedom of the contracting parties, enshrined in the notion, concomitant upon the idea of professional advice, that the parties are free to act upon that advice and free to ignore it. As likely as not, one paid for the advice, and the payment ensured the freedom to ignore it. What distinguished the prescription from the command was the interposition of the contractual dimension: the prescription was a command couched in terms of an 'opinion'.

What happened when the doctor's speech became the *materia medica*? The practice of hypnotism arose within the medical profession as a scientistic development which raised crucial questions of authority, freedom, and knowledge. Psychoanalysis inherited these questions from hypnotism and provided a novel form of rapprochement between the increasingly dominant ideal of knowledge as power, and the professional ideal of freedom. Hypnotism acted as a recasting of the ancient conception of medicine as both science and art, and set the scene for the twentieth-century embodiment of the doctor as 'artistic' healer – the psychoanalyst. Yet the question of 'art' – of a technique suited to the unique individual – was raised in the form of a technique of control and persuasion, and revealed the contradictions of the contract, rather than fulfilling it. Psychoanalysis was a response to this crisis of the medical contract as revealed by hypnosis – and aimed at supplying an auto-critique of itself as subject to the general laws of contract. Psychoanalysis was thus always a borderline case, subject to the power relations of the medical contract, but aiming at examining this contractual dimension itself as a fantasy.

The golden age of medical hypnotism lasted roughly twenty years, from 1875 to 1895.[3] Three features of this episode in medical history will retain our attention. First, the therapeutic zeal of those practitioners who took up the defence of hypnotism, a zeal that was in marked contrast with the therapeutic nihilism of the teaching hospitals. Second, arguments concerning hypnotism raised issues regarding the fundamental basis of all medical therapeutics – what we might well call an early theory of the placebo effect. A modern medical authority has defined the placebo effect as 'what all treatments have in common'.[4] The concept of suggestion elaborated in connection with the effects of hypnotism was an antecedent of such attempts to define what all treatments have in common. Third, the therapeutic effects of hypnotism revealed to the practitioners themselves features of power and authority upon which their livelihoods depended.

In defending the therapeutic uses of hypnotism, Freud drew variously upon these three factors. Both those who attacked and those who defended hypnotism argued that, while hypnotism may be new, suggestion has been employed by doctors since time immemorial. One of Freud's developments of this point was: ' "we are all constantly giving suggestions", [opponents] say; and in fact a physician – even a non-hypnotist – is never better satisfied than when he has repressed a symptom from a patient's attention by the power of his personality and the influence of his words – and his authority.'[5] Hence the fact that hypnotists use suggestion cannot legitimately be used to criticize it – such a criticism would bring down the House of Medicine together with the pillars of suggestion. The authority of medicine is already at issue – and it is only medical bad faith which will accuse hypnotism of being an abuse of such authority:

> 'It is quite interesting to find the most positive determinists suddenly defending the imperilled "personal free-will", and to hear psychiatrists who are in the habit of suffocating the "freely aspiring mental activity" of their patients with large doses of bromide, morphine and chloral, arraigning suggestive influence as something degrading to both parties.'[6]

However, despite his delightful piece of rhetoric, Freud was perhaps missing his own point. It was not the dubious moral side-effects that troubled these organic determinists, but rather the recognition, abundantly clear to Freud, that hypnotism implicated the doctor's authority, as well as his drugs, in any causal account of medical success. In an ideal world of drugs and surgery, the doctor's authority is conferred on him by his knowledge and skill. In hypnotism, his therapeutic success stands exposed naked, is *seen* to be dependent upon a system of authority relations. The fear of the more astute of those who attacked hypnotism was not that it was ineffective, nor that it was immoral; rather, they anticipated that the success of a psychology of hypnotism would reveal that the doctor was *always* only effective in so far as he was immoral, in so far as the real drug that was being prescribed was he himself, in one of his social incarnations.[7] Morphia and chloral would be revealed as the doctor's alibis, rather than his sacraments. According to these critics – and to Freud – it was not so much that the hypnotic state of sleep rendered the doctor that much more powerful, as that the hypnotic state of sleep allowed the doctor to take advantage of his patient and employ his full authority, without rendering it decent by dressing it up as a drug, a rest cure, or a spasm of electricity.

What of the social context of these relations of power that Freud and others recognized as consequent upon the uses of hypotism? On the one hand, the great discoveries of hypnotism, those of Charcot and Bernheim, were made in the wards and lecture theatres of large hospitals for the poor. Bringing hypnotism home to a private medical practice in Vienna was to transplant it, from the theatrical atmosphere of Charcot's weekly display to expectant students and a vast public of the arts of nosology and clinical description, to a private world in which the most prominent expectations of both doctor and patient alike were neither a thirst for melodrama nor a reward for servile obedience, but rather sceptical hostility and therapeutic pessimism.[8] Bernheim confessed to Freud that his private patients did not respond to hypnotism in anything like the eager and dramatic manner that the charity patients did. The picture of the venerable country doctor, Liébeault, the university professor Bernheim's pastoral mentor, hypnotizing the poor of his parish one after the other, under each other's gazes, in a large barn at the back of his house, could not offer a more poignant contrast with the hushed, heavily carpeted private world of bourgeois front rooms and bedrooms in which Freud practised his art.

Yet it is not easy to tease a social history out of these facts. However, the one lengthy case history that Freud published of a case cured by hypnotism does reveal the ambiguous social fabric out of which his cures based on the magisterial exercise of medical charisma were woven – yet it is (already) a family affair. A young woman with whom Freud had been acquainted since she (and he) were children, found herself unable to breast-feed her child, despite her wish to do so. To her astonishment, she would vomit her food and could not sleep. Her physicians 'saw to it that I was brought in professionally to employ hypnotic suggestion, since I was already personally acquainted with the patient.'[9] Two vigorous bouts of suggestion sufficed to correct the state of affairs, and the woman breast-fed her baby for eight months. Freud noted, 'I found it hard to understand, however, as well as annoying, that no reference was ever made to my remarkable achievement.'[10] A year later, with another baby, the patient again found it impossible to breast-feed. Freud repeated his spectacular treatment, and this was rewarded with the patient's explanation of her ungrateful behaviour: ' "I felt ashamed that a thing like hypnosis should be successful where I myself, with all my will-power, was helpless." '[11] Her family had colluded in ensuring that the hypnotist was no more than a near-invisible, ghostly adjunct to her exercise in free will in overcoming her 'inhibition'.

Of course, it was Freud's distinction as an observer and writer to be able to display the ambiguous relations between sick patient, host family, and self-confident doctor – though Freud's pique at not being recognized indicates that his confidence was not that unshakeable. He was able to weigh the shame this woman felt in the scales of the prognosis and possibility of cure. Then, in following Breuer's example, he realized that what the patient had to *say* about the symptoms – her confession of shame – as well as what the doctor could impose on her from without, might well establish the conditions for removing the symptom. The patient's will-power was not simply something that was to be overridden by the superior authority and wisdom of the hypnotist, even though Freud recognized that hypnotism was founded on the existence of this authority. Right from the start, Freud recognized that hypnotism in particular, and psychotherapy in general, involved a battle of wills, not just the physiologically vouchsafed appropriation by the physician of his natural position of command over the hearts, minds, and bodies of his flock, the procedure which had led to Liébeault's near-miraculous cures. In 1890, describing the basis of 'psychical treatment', Freud emphasized that the profound influence exerted by the hypnotist 'lies in the hypnotic subject's attitude to his hypnotist'.[12] This relation, or *rapport*, as the hypnotists called it, was distinguished by its exclusivity: the patient would obey *only* the doctor. And, Freud went on to note, it was in this respect similar both to a child's relation to its parents and to a lover's relation to the loved one – a benign mixture of 'exclusive attachment and credulous obedience'.[13] Hence:

> 'Hypnotism endows the physician with an authority such as was probably never possessed by the priest or the miracle man, since it concentrates the subject's whole interest upon the figure of the physician; it does away with the autocratic power of the patient's mind, which, as we have seen, interferes so capriciously with the influence of the mind over the body'.[14]

Once again the term 'authority' moves centre stage – with the complicating factor of being set in competition with the 'autocratic' power of the patient's mind over his body. This latter view, commonplace enough, takes on a new importance once the mental autocracy is articulated with the *social* autocracy of the doctor–patient relationship. The preconditions that might lead to the hypnotist's gaining enormous power over the patient included one interesting claim: 'if the right of a patient to make a free choice of his doctor were suspended, an important precondition for influencing him mentally would be abolished'.[15] Implicit here is the notion that a *contract* between doctor and patient, freely entered into rather than arranged by a higher authority, imposes obligations on the patient that he finds difficult to shrug off. It is along this line of thought that we should view the contract to speak freely about everything (the fundamental rule of psychoanalysis).

We thus see that, via the topics of hypnotism and suggestion, three themes that were to assume great importance in psychoanalysis were brought to the fore: love (of the hypnotist), freedom (of contract, of the will) and authority (over the body, over another). In the ideal case, hypnotism worked best by the patient exercising his or her free choice in deciding upon the doctor to whom he or she would submit, in an obedience wrought out of emotions akin to love and awe. Why, then, did hypnotism often fail? Precisely because the actual, day-to-day practice of hypnotism revealed that the doctor's authority was strictly limited. Once the authority card had been played, further treatment by other methods, if necessary, was made much more difficult. In addition, if hypnotic treatment were continued for too long, the patient would simply become addicted to the doctor's treatment, exactly as he might have done if morphine were the treatment of choice. More revealingly, Freud's personal difficulties with the technique led him to remark, in 1892, that 'in the long run neither the doctor nor the patient can tolerate the contradiction between the decided denial of the ailment in the suggestion and the necessary recognition of it outside the suggestion'.[16] From the doctor's point of view, this amounted to a subjective confession of scepticism as to the extent of his own authority – a 'perhaps' has crept into the doctor's mind, alongside the imperatives he voices to the subject.

Freud gave up hypnotism partly through his own inadequacies as a hypnotist – one might say through his inadequate incarnation of the idea of medical authority – and partly through the implicit logic of the cathartic cure that he borrowed from Breuer. The cathartic cure was created when Anna O., Breuer's severely disturbed patient, insisted that he listen to *her*, rather than that *she* listen and meekly obey *him*. Employing this technique, the kaleidoscope pattern of authority relations slowly began to shift: Freud's authority as doctor was still the motor that kept the stories of traumas flowing from the patient, but it was authority in the service of an insistence that the patient knew something which the doctor did not know, something which would help him in elucidating what the symptoms meant. To be sure, the crucial shift was from the doctor telling the patient *what to do*, to the patient telling *stories* that in some magical way dispelled the symptoms. The doctor, however, still provided the framework of authority: firstly, in putting the patient into an appropriate mental state in which memory was facilitated. This manoeuvre, initially achieved by hypnosis, later by more subtle methods, amounted to the doctor taking command of the patient's storehouse of memories. Whereas in hypnotism the doctor's authority had been confined to forbidding the patient specific feelings, ideas, bodily expressions, and so forth, or commanding these, in the new cathartic technique the doctor demanded that the patient make of him the repository of all his experiences and memories – as expressed in words. The aptly named 'pressure technique', an intermediary stage in the development of Freud's method, consisted in the doctor placing his hand on the patient's head and assuring him that he *will* discover the appropriate idea or image as soon as the pressure of the hand is removed. The next step was the fundamental rule – say whatever comes into your head, without regard to relevance, to importance, to politeness or good taste.

While we have arrived, with this rule, at a paradigm of freedom of speech, unparalleled before or since, it might still be argued that this extreme liberalism is simply a cloak for a more insidiously intrusive domination of the patient – the incessant demand to say more, until the story makes sense – to the doctor.[17] The demand for obedience has transmuted into a demand for comprehensibility. But the difference can be delineated more subtly.

The chief novelty introduced by hypnotism was its great reliance on words. Take a case of hysteria. One physician may write down in the case-notes; 'Diagnosis: Hysteria. Treatment; Chloral'. Such a medical practice matches an ideal of clinical medicine in which a statement about the natural world (the patient's body) unequivocally corresponds to a specific pharmacological action. Another physician – let us call him Charcot, for convenience's sake – may also diagnose hysteria. And he may also agree with the first physician in meaning by this statement a specific physiological state of the nervous system. But his therapy is different. He says – rather than writes, gives, or prescribes – 'You do *not* have hysteria – when you wake up you will no longer have your nervous cough'. The means by which this therapy is put into action is speech. More specifically, however, its form is that of a command expressed in speech – necessarily so, since one cannot command without speech. The therapy consists in an explicit mobilization of authority in speech. And, of course, there is a straightforward means of refusing this authority – you can retain the symptom. When the hysteric's symptom persists, the doctor's authority has been weakened in a way that a failure of chloral therapy never occasions. The reason for this lies in the nature of the different speech-acts involved. The speech-act of the command goes hand-in-hand with the speaker's taking up a position of authority. In refusing to obey, the subject is not saying that it is a false command, is thus not providing what a positivistic observer would take to be refutation of the truth of the command. Commands are neither true nor false. Rather, the patient is implying that the speaker of the command is not in a position to command him or her. It is the utterer, not the bare 'factual' content (if such could be said to exist), which has been made to fail. In other circumstances, with someone else, the patient might obey the command – such, at least, might be the fear or fantasy of the rebuffed physician. Whereas within the medical conception of chloral's action, it is assumed that it is not the doctor prescribing it who is the source of its efficacy: the prescription of chloral is not a speech-act implicating the doctor as authority.

Now turn to the psychoanalytic physician. The doctor diagnoses hysteria. He then says to the patient: 'Say whatever comes into your head'. Even if the patient takes this to be a command, whatever response he gives is appropriate – even if he says, 'There is nothing in my head,' he will be seen to be obeying the rule – seen (eventually) even by himself to be so doing. In this way, psychoanalysis amounts to a discovery of a new form of discourse, in which whatever is said complies with the wish (or the rules) of the doctor, and whatever is said implicitly bolsters his authority, in so far as saying anything falls within the domain of what the doctor ordered, thus reinforcing his position as utterer of that speech-act. Even if the patient says, 'I find your rule politically suspect – I refuse to obey it,' he is obeying it, thus crystallizing an authority relation between the two speaking subjects – an authority relation constituted by the demand for speech. As long as he keeps talking, the doctor's authority remains intact, and, indeed, is confirmed.

My argument so far has centred on the idea that the use of hypnotism with hysterical patients exposed the authority relations underlying doctor–patient relationships. Psychoanalysis was one answer to the crisis of medical self-confidence which could and did emerge as a consequence; it was an answer which both reinforced and displaced the authority of the doctor – a double movement to which we will return. Another index of this crisis was the debate over malingering. The basic issue, from our point of view, was as follows. Although malingering was originally a matter of concern principally to the army and navy, in their attempts to distinguish genuine from false physical complaints, by the end of the nineteenth century civil doctors were themselves attempting to exclude false diseases from their hospitals and practices. In as much as hysteria and malingering both exhibited symptoms that did not follow the medical laws of the possible as defined by anatomy, physiology, and pathology, they were both indicative of the influence of the patient's mind over the body. The key distinction was that in malingering the patient retained responsibility for the symptoms, whereas the hysteric did not. The malingerer's 'pathology' lay primarily in his will. Hence any attempt to cure the symptoms would expose the doctor to ridicule: the central medical transaction, in which the doctor graciously accepts the gift of the symptom, and takes responsibility for it, is rendered void, since the malingering patient never surrenders control of the symptom. Malingering thus signposts the fact that medical power is bounded by the patient's will. Just as the limitations of medical authority were revealed by the success and failure of hypnotism, so the doctor's impotence in the face of the patient's *responsibility* for his illness was pinpointed by malingering. In becoming pressing problems for the medical profession at the end of the century, malingering and hypnotism prompted the question: who is responsible for the failure of the treatment – the patient? the doctor? – or someone else?

Freud's invention of psychoanalysis provided a novel answer to this question, and I will turn now to a famous moment in the early history of psychoanalysis, when the issue, 'who is responsible?', became intertwined with Freud's early investigations of sexuality: the moment is the interpretation of the dream of Irma's injection, to which chapter 2 of *The Interpretation of Dreams* is devoted. I can give only a brief account of the ramifications of this founding dream and its interpretation; for a more detailed analysis I can refer the reader to my forthcoming book, *The Dream of Psychoanalysis*.[18] Briefly, in July 1895, Freud dreamed of a young woman patient of his, Irma, a hysteric, whose treatment was giving him problems. In the dream he examined her throat, and called in a senior colleague, who made foolish remarks about dysentery; it then became clear that another colleague had given Irma an injection with a dirty syringe, and at the end of the dream, Freud saw clearly a chemical formula in bold type – trimethylamine.

Freud's associations indicated that he was comparing Irma with two other women patients who would not have been so recalcitrant – that is, they would have allowed themselves to be cured by Freud more quickly. The various references to other doctors and colleagues in the dream had as their aim both to ridicule alternative theories as to the nature of Irma's ailments and to shift the medical responsibility for the difficulties of the treatment from Freud's shoulders to someone else's. Freud thus discovered that the main theme of the dream was a self-justification in answer to the question: who is responsible for the absence of an adequate cure?

On the one hand, he could point to another doctor who used a dirty syringe in the dream – it's not me, it's him; on the other hand, Freud had three alternative arguments proving that it was certainly not *him* (that is, Freud) who was responsible. First, if Irma's illness were an organic nervous disease, it was clear why psychotherapy did not work, and why Freud was not responsible for the persistence of her pains. Second, her symptoms were the result of sexual frustration resulting from her widowhood – yet again, it was clear that Freud was not the guilty party. Third, if she really were a hysteric, then it was her own fault that the cure did not progress, since she never opened her mouth properly, she never told him of the traumatic events that lay hidden behind her symptoms. She refused to obey the fundamental rule to say everything – so it was her own fault if she remained ill. Such recalcitrance on her part seemed to Freud very much like malingering; yet it is a much more manageable form of malingering when conceived of as Irma disobeying the fundamental rule of psychoanalysis, then when it is her symptoms that are the emblems of her defiant will.

When we leave behind us the account that Freud gave in his book, the story gets a little more complicated. What did Freud expect to hear from Irma, what did he expect her to tell him which would cure her of her illness? At the time of the dream, in 1895, he was developing the seduction theory: the hypothesis that hysteria results from sexual seductions experienced by the patient when a child, the seducer usually being the father. The seducers characteristically abused their position of authority in order to colour the relation of love between child and parent with a sexual gloss that the child could neither accept nor repudiate.[19] What Freud was asking his patients to do was to indict their parents of such abuses. In the name of an authority granted him by the hope for a cure, as embodied in the fundamental rule, Freud was inciting his patients to put in doubt and bring to judgement the first authority of their lives. No wonder, we might reflect, his patients were reluctant to tell him their stories – a reluctance that he took as good evidence of their veracity.[20] From the very first, Freud was clear that the authority of his cure was set in opposition to family authority and consisted in revealing an abuse of such authority.

If you cannot trust your father not to seduce you, whom can you trust? The fundamental rule – say anything – asked Freud's patients to place trust in an extended, contractually determined relation of medical confidence and confidences. Yet, underlying the Irma dream, as he admitted in a letter written in 1908, was another theme, in counterpoint with that confidence: 'Sexual megalomania is hidden behind it, the three women, Mathilde, Sophie, Anna, are my daughters' three god-mothers, and I have them all! There would be one simple therapy for widowhood, of course.'[21] Recall the second assumption of the dream: if Irma (in reality, Anna) and patients like her are neurotic because they are widows, there is a simple therapy – they should come to Dr Freud's consulting room for something other than telling him tales of being seduced. But if we align Freud's confession of sexual desire with the third assumption, that Irma was not obeying the fundamental rule, then the pieces fall into place in a slightly different manner. What Freud expected and hoped to *hear* were stories of paternal seduction – and this is what Irma was withholding. It looks remarkably as if Freud's desires, as expressed in the dream, match perfectly the seductions that he assumed had already taken place in his patients' childhoods: Freud's sexual desires to 'have' his patients mirrored perfectly a veiled desire to 'have' his daughters, the girls named after his three patients. The father (doctor) abuses his authority for sexual ends. One might say that he expected them to tell him a story whose content was what he wished, namely that they fantasized a seduction, but his wish would be recast in the form of a memory from the distant past, with the father figuring in the place of Freud. And, with the rejection of the seduction theory a couple of years later, the accent did come to fall on fantasy. And, again, it is remarkable how, in the run-up to this crisis in the development of his theory, his dream-life was intertwined with his patients' narratives. In a letter to Fliess, when discussing a dream in which he had been overtly over-affectionate towards one of his own daughters, he concluded: 'The dream of course fulfils my wish to pin down a father as the originator of neurosis and put an end to my persistent doubts.'[22] We find it difficult to answer the following question: is the dream-wish a wish that his *theory* be true, or is it a wish that is intended to deny that it could be someone other than the patient's father, some other male, threatening to abuse the authority relations between man and woman, parent and child, doctor and patient?

At the same time as Freud was elaborating the seduction theory and demonstrating that all dreams are wish fulfilments, he made the fundamental discovery concerning the practice of psychoanalysis. Towards the end of the *Studies on Hysteria*,[23] written in March 1895, Freud recounted how the chief obstacle to the patient obeying the fundamental rule occurred when her thoughts concerned the doctor – it was then that she was most likely to be tempted into silence. He gave an example, when a patient thought of receiving a kiss from him, a thought that she could not bring herself to confess. Once he had extracted this 'thought' from her, she then remembered an exactly parallel situation from the past, when she had desired to be kissed and had repudiated the thought. Freud called this phenomenon the transference: when thoughts that in reality belonged to a forgotten event in the past were transferred on to the person of the doctor. Even at this early date, while his technique was still primitive, Freud thought that the therapeutic work could just as easily be carried out in terms of the thoughts and feelings concerning the doctor as in terms of the 'true' source of these thoughts and feelings – the repressed past. Within the framework of the transference, then, Freud would *expect* his patients to fall in love with him, instead of telling him about the lost loves of the past – they would offer themselves to him, seduce him, repeating with him what had been thought or experienced in the past. These seductions, revengeful acts, accusations, would be welcome, because they were a form of remembering. And thus much of what Freud learnt about his patients' pasts was derived from the events of the transference: the exact strategies of pleading, hostility, revenge, and yearning employed by the patient with the doctor gave vital information about the past events. On the one hand, then, we find the patient, silent, replete with fantasies of the analyst seducing her; on the other hand, the analyst, urging her to tell him these fantasies (or memories). Alongside, as it were, is the shadowy figure of a man, struggling with unknown desires for his patients and daughters, and the urgent desire to inculpate the father.

The ruling theme is clearly seduction. And the question: who is seducing whom? Who is responsible for, who is initiating this seduction? Seduction as the primal trauma – seduction of the patient by the beneficent authority – the aim of the treatment is to seduce her into revealing the traumatic event, either in the form of a memory or in her attempts to seduce the doctor. Let us turn to a consideration of the logic of seduction, to try and find our bearings in this new scheme of medical intervention.[24] The first step in a seductive manoeuvre might be summed up as: 'I know what you're thinking.' Whether the seductive desire is aroused by a knowing glint in the other's eyes, or whether it is generated by some accident that betrays an unforeseen opening in the bland world of objects (what is commonly known as love at first sight, the *coup de foudre*), the impulse of the seducer is predicated upon a blind conviction of the accessibility of the other. 'I know what you're thinking.' Putting it in this succinct form reveals, firstly, the assumption of authority that seduction requires. And yet seduction is to be distinguished from sexual tyranny, as it might appear in rape, through the fact that the seducer sets great store upon the speech of the other, in particular upon the 'No' of the other. However, this respect for the judgement of the other is peculiar, for the seducer will never hear a 'No' as meaning 'No'; there is no final 'No'. Following each repeated 'No', he engages in further stratagems, in accordance with his fluctuating conception of the desire of the other. One stratagem consists in setting himself up as the midwife of the other's desire;[25] alternatively, he may believe in the contagion theory of desire, as Kierkegaard conceives of Don Giovanni: offering mystery to all, with more than enough to go round.[26] Whichever theory he subscribes to and puts into action, his aim will be to transform the 'No' into 'Yes'. Yet, in the very act of so doing, a doubt will arise: 'Is this a true Yes? If I did not trust the other's No, why should I trust his Yes, especially since I believe myself to have been so instrumental in engendering it?' Hence the seducer will always be prey to doubt as to the status of the other's consent, so that a seduction that is viewed from the standpoint of a questioning of the status of the consent will always be confused with rape, just as rape in which any ignorance as to the nature of the victim's desire is admitted will be deemed to have been seduction, in retrospect.

It is the authority of a subject *vis-à-vis* their own desires which is brought to the fore in this discussion of rape and seduction. Yet, as Freud had already recognized in hypnosis, love may well lead to a self-abasing respect for the authority of the loved one. In a later paper on transference (1915), Freud recognized this form of love as one of the primary features of psychoanalytic practice: the analyst will 'feel certain that [the patient's] docility, her acceptance of the analytic explanations, her remarkable comprehension and the high degree of intelligence she showed were to be attributed to' her affectionate transference.[27] Inevitably, this affection turns into something more insistently demanding: it becomes an 'endeavour to assure herself of her irresistibility, to destroy the doctor's authority by bringing him down to the level of a lover'.[28] Here Freud maps out two consecutive stratagems of seduction: first, docility and respect for authority in the hope that unforeseen advantages may accrue from this collusion with the loved one; second, a frontal assault on authority, in order to gain the fruits of love from the domination of the object, by securing its status as an appendage to the desire of the subject. But he was quite clear, both in 1895 and in 1915, that opting for the therapy for widowhood that his dream had suggested to him would not result in a cure. Rather, he would find himself in the position of the priest who, in hoping to convert the free-thinking insurance salesman on his deathbed, failed in securing the other's soul for God, and instead came away insured.[29]

What is both amusing and tragic in the story of the priest and the insurance salesman, or the patient and the analyst, is the breach of contract. If the priest is willing to insure his life, in all fairness shouldn't the salesman allow the priest to insure his death for him, by witnessing his contract with God? Similarly, in all fairness, shouldn't the psychoanalyst be expected to take seriously the seductions of the patient? Instead, he reminds her that it is not part of the contract for him to *believe* what she says, or, even if he does believe her, to act on these statements. Such an unseemly breach of the expectations of the seducer, who calculates that the other will pay more than lip-service to the charity conditions – the principles by which, according to analytic philosophers, all honest communication is generated – leads to a crisis, and it is then that the patient begins to employ speech in the mode of a command, just like a hypnotist. And this is where the different positioning of the authority relations in psychoanalysis and hypnosis is most clearly revealed: the psychoanalyst now appears as the guardian of speech which has no object or aim, for when the patient's demands appear in the guise of commands, he subsumes his authority within the fundamental rule, in so far as it is an implicit feature of that rule that no action shall be taken on the basis of what is said. The tables have truly been turned. Where the authority of the doctor's position as speaking subject was put on the line and weakened by the refusal of the hypnotized patient to get better, the authority of speech in general is first promoted and then radically questioned by the analyst's initial willingness to elicit any and every confession, followed by his refusal to recognize and act upon the patient's passionate declarations. It is as if the fundamental rule included a hidden clause: 'Say whatever comes into your head, but you cannot *then* expect me to place any faith in what you say, or take anything you say at face value.' The transference is characterized by the patient making a declaration that must be taken at its face value for it to have its full meaning; yet it is exactly at that moment that the analyst refuses just that. Perhaps I can clarify this with an analogy.

Suppose two people are getting married. As they stand before the officiator, one of them replies to the question with: 'I do'. As Austin pointed out,[30] it makes no sense to suppose that the person is lying at that moment, or that the statement is false – though the statement may 'misfire' for various reasons, for example if the utterer is already married. But the saying of the words 'I do' *is* the act of marrying. Now imagine that one of the parties to the marriage contract has already said 'I do', but when the other is asked to reply to the question, he or she, for reasons unknown, refuses to do so. The psychoanalytic dialogue reproduces this comedy of errors, in which, on the basis of a *prior* contract, one of the parties honestly enters into promises, pledges, commands, and indictments of this sort, known to philosophers as performatives. The other party, however, resolutely refuses to honour these performatives, and the means of evasion are easily described. He refuses to obey commands; he remains sceptical as to the future realization of those events conjured into existence by promises; he declines to sign on the dotted line; he declines to plead when accused; and so on. Instead, he hides behind the iron law of free speech. As Freud put it when a patient pleaded with him to be excused from following the fundamental rule when he had broached a certain delicate topic: 'I could not grant him something which was beyond my power. He might just as well ask me to give him the moon. The overcoming of resistances was a law of the treatment.'[31]

In following the fundamental rule, which offers him free speech, the patient encounters certain forms of speech that are not effective without the co-operation of the person addressed. Our misfired marriage is a humorous instance. And many other important instances are found in the spheres of love, hate, and authority. We have seen how seduction implies this dependence upon the other's 'Yes' and 'No'. One might even hazard the hypothesis that masturbation figures so prominently in psychoanalytic discourse not only because of the latter's heritage of moralistic medical intervention, but also because masturbation and rape, in an ideal world, do not require the consent of the other. Masturbation would certainly change its social status if it became normal practice for a practitioner to ask permission, or require a collective decision, before indulging. Be that as it may, in obeying the fundamental rule, one is bound to discover sooner or later that certain speech acts are not 'free', since they require the other's willingness to comply with the categories of first and second persons invoked by them.

Hence my logico-historical account runs as follows. As soon as the doctor began to dispense his speech, in place of a drug, as happened in hypnosis, the implicit relations of co-operation and co-option underlying medical practice became liable to breakdown. Freud's failure as a hypnotist, and his readiness to recognize failure, forced him to concentrate his energies on the speech relations involved in *any* talking cure: commands, confessions, pleas, seductions, rebukes. With the fundamental rule and the accompanying concept of the transference, he found the ideal vehicle for turning the tables on his patients, obliging *them* to encounter the obstacle to their cure in the social relations implied by the rules their specific discourses invoked, rather than him encountering the insuperable obstacle of a failure of medical authority in a confrontation with the patient's will, his 'responsibility' for the symptoms. Freud's innovation deflected the authority that patients wished to flaunt from being that of the doctor to being the authority of language itself. As he cannily put it in 1922: 'In psychoanalysis the suggestive influence which is inevitably exercised by the physician is diverted on to the task assigned to the patient of overcoming his resistances'.[32] That is, the analyst collaborates *with* the patient in combating the resistances represented by language – the watchword is always, 'Keep talking!'

So, in psychoanalysis, we find an uncannily modern commitment to a free speech that never achieves anything, that can never render its contracts valid. What is even more striking is that this commitment also supplies its own autocritique. Two examples will illustrate. Every psychoanalyst knows the patient who is a firm believer in psychoanalysis. He will offer his convictions and rationales as to the truth and importance of psychoanalysis as part of his free associations; these will receive the same neutrally evasive responses as any other discourse of belief and conviction. Psychoanalysis leaves the truth-status of all discourses in abeyance, in order to highlight whatever seductive or evangelical functions they may perform. But psychoanalysis not only treats all discursive systems as equal, equal before the law of free speech, ready to have their rules broken down and exposed by being submitted to the technique of 'take nothing at face value', it also demands access to *all* discourses. It is the most comprehensive of the invasive discursive apparatuses discussed by Foucault in *The History of Sexuality*, vol. 1. To illustrate, one last passage from Freud: 'It is very remarkable how the task of analysis becomes impossible if a reservation is allowed at any single place. . . . I once treated a high official who was bound by his oath of office not to communicate certain things because they were state secrets, and the analysis came to grief as a consequence of this'.[33] This remarkable anecdote captures much of what I have been trying to describe: the opposition between the obligatory freedom of speech demanded by the fundamental rule and any other discursive authority, as symbolized by the conflicting demands of the state and the liberal ideal of freedom of speech; the conviction that a 'No' that is allowed to subsist outside of the framework of the fundamental rule is equivalent to a residue of the 'feudal' relations between hypnotist and patient, or an element of the doctor–patient relationship that still upholds the myth of the 'No' of seduction. We can also gain a sense of how it is that the ideal of free speech can become the most arduous of all demands, to which all authority and relations of intimacy may be sacrificed, as the pledges and commands that make them up are rendered empty, in the name of a higher authority – that of speech itself.

To conclude: a hint of a further argument. One important theme I have omitted discussing is that of money. Psychoanalysis treats money as if it truly were the universal means of exchange, and patients do behave as if they can buy love. As has often been pointed out, the economic relations entered into in psychoanalysis are ones consonant with the social relations of the bourgeoisie: the professional is handsomely paid, but strictly for his services. Yet analysis, the youngest profession, also has close affinities with the prebourgeois, oldest profession. Money is intended to dissolve any obligations other than those of a contract entered into and fulfilled – on both sides. Such is the distillation of the liberal, *laissez-faire* ethos: a contract between free agents, honoured and paid for, whose means of accomplishment is the free speech whereby one of the parties will contract the disease of love that the other will cure by treating the precious, seductive words offered to him as if they were simply the universal means of exchange.

Notes

1 Robert Castel, *Le psychanalysme* (Paris: UGE Collection 10/18, 1976), p. 55.
2 Castel, *Le psychanalysme*, p. 87.
3 On the history of these aspects of hypnotism, see Georges Didi-Huberman, *Invention de l'hystérie. Charcot et l'iconographie photographique de la Salpêtrière*, (Paris: Editions Macula, 1982); Henri F. Ellenberger, *The Discovery of the Unconscious. The History and Evolution of Dynamic Psychiatry* (London: Allen Lane, 1970).
4 W. Modell, *The Relief of Symptoms* (Philadelphia, Pa.: W.B. Saunders, 1955) p. 55, cited in Howard Brody, *Placebos and the Philosophy of Medicine* (Chicago and London: University of Chicago Press, 1977), p. 37.
5 Sigmund Freud, 'Review of August Forel's *Der Hypnotismus*' (1889a), in *The Standard Edition of the Complete Psychological Works of Sigmund Freud*, under the general editorship of James Strachey in collaboration with Anna Freud, assisted by Alix Strachey and Alan Tyson (London: The Hogarth Press and the Institute of Psycho-analysis, 1953–74), vol. 1 (hereafter abbreviated as follows: SE, vol. 1), p. 94.
6 Freud, 'Review of August Forel's *Der Hypnotismus*', p. 94.
7 The idea of doctor as drug is discussed at illuminating length in Michael Balint, *The Doctor, His Patient and the Illness* (London: Pitman Medical, 1957).
8 See William Murray Johnson, *The Austrian Mind; an Intellectual and Social History, 1848–1938* (Berkeley, Calif.: University of California Press, 1972); Erna Lesky, *Die Wiener Medizinische Schule im 19. Jahrhundert* (Graz-Köln: Böhlau, 1965).
9 S. Freud, 'A Case of Successful Treatment by Hypnotism' (1892–93), in SE, vol. 1, p. 119.
10 Freud, 'A Case of Successful Treatment', in SE, vol. 1, p. 120.
11 Freud, 'A Case of Successful Treatment', in SE, vol. 1, p. 120.
12 S. Freud, 'Psychical (or Mental) Treatment' (1890a), in SE, vol. 7, p. 295.
13 Freud, 'Psychical (or Mental) Treatment', in SE, vol. 7, p. 296.
14 Freud, 'Psychical (or Mental) Treatment', in SE, vol. 7, p. 298.
15 Freud, 'Psychical (or Mental) Treatment', in SE, vol. 7, p. 293.
16 S. Freud, 'Preface and Footnotes to the Translation of Charcot's *Leçons du mardi*' (1892–94), in SE, vol. 1, p. 141.
17 See Michel Foucault, *The History of Sexuality*, vol. 1 (London: Allen Lane, 1979).
18 The literature on this dream is by now voluminous. The following are most useful: the text itself, with Freud's discussion, in S. Freud, *The Interpretation of Dreams* (1900a), in SE, vol. 4, pp. 106–21; for its place in Freud's self-analysis, Didier Anzieu, *L'Auto-analyse de Freud* (Paris: PUF, 1975); on additional previously unpublished important background material, Max Schur, 'Some Additional "Day Residues" of the "Specimen Dream of Psychoanalysis"',

in R. Loewenstein, L.M. Newman, M. Schur, and A.J. Solnit (eds), *Psychoanalysis – A General Psychology* (New York: International Universities Press, 1966), pp. 45–85. For interesting, controlled speculation, Michel Schneider, *Blessures de mémoire* (Paris: Gallimard, 1980), pp. 31–135; Serge Cottet, *Freud et le désir du psychanalyste* (Paris: Navarin, 1982); Frank R. Hartman, 'A Reappraisal of the Emma Episode and the Specimen Dream', *Journal of the American Psychoanalytic Association* 31, no. 3 (1983): 555–85. Controversial and dubious claims, with some new material, are to be found in J.M. Masson, *The Assault on Truth; Freud's Suppression of the Seduction Theory* (London: Faber and Faber, 1984).

19 S. Freud, 'The Aetiology of Hysteria' (1896c), in SE, vol. 3, pp. 202 ff.
20 Freud, 'The Aetiology of Hysteria', in SE, vol. 3, p. 204.
21 S. Freud and K. Abraham, *A Psycho-analytic Dialogue. The Letters of Sigmund Freud and Karl Abraham, 1907–1926*, eds Hilda C. Abraham and Ernst L. Freud (London: The Hogarth Press and the Institute of Psycho-analysis, 1965), p. 20 (letter dated 9 January, 1908).
22 S. Freud, *The Origins of Psycho-analysis. Letters to Wilhelm Fliess, Drafts and Notes, 1887–1902* (London: Imago, 1954), p. 206 (letter 64, dated 31 May, 1897).
23 J. Breuer and S. Freud, *Studies on Hysteria* (1895d), in SE, vol. 2, pp. 301–04.
24 See John Forrester, 'Rape, Seduction, Discourse', in *Rape: A Collection of Essays*, eds Roy Porter and Sylvana Tomaselli (Oxford: Basil Blackwell, forthcoming).
25 Jean Giraudoux, *Amphitryon 38*, in Jean Giraudoux, *Théâtre*, 4 vols (Paris: Bernard Grasset, 1958), vol. 1, p. 128: 'The main problem, with honourable women, isn't seducing them, it's to get them behind closed doors. Their virtue consists in open doors.'
26 S. Kierkegaard, *Either/Or*, 2 vols (Princeton, NJ: Princeton University Press, 1959), vol. 1, p. 100.
27 S. Freud, 'Observations on Transference-Love' (1915a), in SE, vol. 12, p. 162.
28 Freud, 'Observations on Transference-Love', in SE, vol. 12, p. 163.
29 Freud, 'Observations on Transference-Love', in SE, vol. 12, p. 165.
30 J.L. Austin, *How to Do Things with Words* (Oxford: OUP, 1962), pp. 13 ff.
31 S. Freud, 'Notes upon a Case of Obsessional Neurosis' (1909d), in SE, vol. 10, p. 166.
32 S. Freud, 'Two Encyclopaedia Articles' (1923a), in SE vol. 18, pp. 250–51.
33 S. Freud, 'On Beginning the Treatment' (1913c), in SE, vol. 12, p. 136.

CHAPTER ELEVEN

Freud's cases: the clinical basis of psychoanalysis

Anthony Clare

Introduction

THE SUCCESS OR otherwise of psychoanalysis as a method of psychological treatment cannot be taken to validate or invalidate it as a procedure for the investigation of mental processes believed to be inaccessible to other forms of enquiry or as a theory of psychological functioning. However, the evidence derived from a historical assessment of the efficacy of psychoanalytic therapy is hardly irrelevant to any discussion of its claim to be the investigative psychological theory par excellence.[1] From the outset, Freud constructed his theoretical structure out of the case material explored in the clinical setting and to this day, while psychoanalysts do point to other sources of evidence such as anthropological and biographical data or, more rarely, to experimental data, it is largely from within the clinical field of psychiatry and psychopathology that they claim to unearth their most substantial support. For this reason it would seem timely, eighty years on from the onset of Freud's single-minded feat, to subject the therapeutic status of his creation to scrutiny.

Psychoanalysis as treatment

It might be taken, perhaps, as a sign of a growing disenchantment with psychoanalysis as therapy, that so many practising analysts insist that from the outset Sigmund Freud was most cautious concerning the therapeutic potency of his theoretical formulations. Unbridled therapeutic zeal, it is argued, has largely contributed to a situation wherein more is expected from the techniques and procedures than its originator ever claimed. In support of this argument, Freud's somewhat pessimistic views during the latter years of his life are quoted, but it needs to be remembered that at no time in his life did Freud unequivocally disavow a role, and an important role at that, for psychoanalysis in the elucidation and treatment of the psychoneuroses and character disorders. It is, of course, true that on a number of occasions Freud expressed greater interest in the theory of psychoanalysis than in its applications. In *The Question of Lay Analysis* (1926), he admitted:

> 'I have never really been a doctor in the proper sense. ... I have no knowledge of having had any craving in early childhood to help suffering humanity. In my youth I felt an overpowering need to understand something of the riddles of the world in which we live and even perhaps contribute something to their solution.'[2]

However, in general Freud did not qualify the substantial therapeutic claims made on behalf of his theories. From the outset he boldly pronounced on their value. In 1910, in an address on the future prospects of psychoanalytic therapy, he observed that there was hardly anything like his treatment in medicine, 'although in fairy tales you hear of evil spirits whose power is broken as soon as you can tell them their name – the name which they have kept secret.'[3]

Six years later, he opened the first of a series of introductory lectures with an unequivocal statement to the effect that 'psychoanalysis is a procedure for the medical treatment of neurotic patients', went on to point out in the sixth lecture (on the technique of interpretation) that the whole purpose of psychoanalysis is what is sought for in all scientific work, namely, 'to understand the phenomena, to establish a correlation between them and, in the latter end, to enlarge our power over them', and then, in the sixteenth lecture (devoted to a consideration of the relationship between psychoanalysis and psychiatry), appeared to grasp the nettle of the possible therapeutic failure of his theories and the consequences of such a failure, only to let it slip:

> 'Even if psychoanalysis showed itself as unsuccessful in every other form of nervous and physical disease, as it does in delusions, it would still remain completely justified as an irreplaceable instrument of scientific research. It is true that in that case we should not be in a position to practise it. The human material on which we seek to learn, which lives, has its own will and needs its motives for co-operating in our work, would hold back from us. Let me therefore end my remarks today by informing you that there are extensive groups of nervous disorders in which the transformation of our better understanding into therapeutic power has actually taken place, and that in these illnesses, which are difficult of access by any other means, we achieve under favourable conditions successes which are second to no others in the field of internal medicine.'[4]

In 1918, he reasserted his confidence in the potency of pure psychoanalysis in a celebrated and characteristically pugnacious address in Budapest when he considered the growing tendency to introduce psychoanalysis to a wider and wider public and the corresponding tendency to dilute it:

'It is very probable too that the large-scale application of our therapy will compel us to alloy the pure gold of analysis with the copper of direct suggestion; and hypnotic suggestion, too, might find a place in it again as it has in the treatment of the war neuroses. But whatever form this psychotherapy for the people may take, whatever the elements out of which it is compounded, its most effective and most important ingredients will assuredly remain those borrowed from strict and untendentious psychoanalysis.'[5]

It is of course perfectly true that Freud expressed doubts continually about the universal applicability of psychoanalytic theory and techniques. As early as 1905, he outlined a series of remarkably restrictive criteria defining patient suitability for psychoanalysis which indicated that the most suitable patient would be a young adult of good intelligence, reasonably educated, well motivated, and of reliable character.[6] He expressed the view then, which he was to repeat thereafter, that certain disorders, most notably serious psychotic illnesses such as schizophrenia, manic-depressive psychoses, organic psychoses, and states of confusion, were unsuitable; and in 1930 he prophetically argued in a letter to Marie Bonaparte that the main hope for sufferers from severe mental illnesses lay in organic chemistry and endocrinology. It is also true that in one of his most thorough discussions of treatment, namely his essay *Analysis Terminable and Interminable*, published in 1937 just two years before his death, he expressed himself with considerable caution, even uncertainty, declaring:

'One has the impression that one ought not to be surprised if it should turn out in the end that the difference between a person who has not been analysed and the behaviour of a person after he has been analysed is not so thorough-going as we aim at making it and as we expect and maintain it to be ... analysis in claiming to cure neuroses by ensuring control over instinct is always right in theory but not always right in practice.'[7]

He constantly drew attention to the difficulties of practising psychoanalysis, and he relied on an analogy with surgery, pointing out that just as the surgeon needed a suitable room, good lighting, properly trained assistants, and the exclusion of relatives from the scene of the action, so too the analyst needed to practise his art in optimum circumstances and, in particular, free from the potentially intrusive and distorting influence of the patient's family.

But Freud never quite withdrew the claim for therapeutic efficacy as is clear from his comments in one of the second series of introductory lectures on psychoanalysis which he wrote in 1932 and 1933 and which, while never delivered as lectures, were subsequently published. While acknowledging that he was never a therapeutic enthusiast and that psychoanalysis, like any other treatments, has 'its triumphs and its defeats, its difficulties, its limitations, its indications', compared with the other psychotherapeutic procedures 'psychoanalysis is beyond doubt the most powerful'. As a method of treatment 'it is one among many though, to be sure, primus inter pares'.[8]

Freud's clinical material

At this point, it is probably helpful to recall the important ingredients in psychoanalysis which justified this pride of place in the pantheon of the psychotherapies. Psychoanalytic therapy, as developed by Freud and elaborated upon by his successors, essentially consisted of instructing and assisting the patient to employ the technique of free association. Such free associations as they emerged were interpreted, and any obstacles the patient encountered in attempting to freely associate, as well as the patient's feelings and attitudes towards the therapist, were also explored and interpreted. The crucial defining concepts upon which these techniques rested included the notion of the *unconscious*, that is to say the idea that there exists mental activity of which the subject is unaware but which, nevertheless, exercises a dynamic effect upon his behaviour; the idea of *resistance*, namely that consciousness resists the emergence of unconscious tendencies into consciousness and does so by the use of mental mechanisms or *defences*; and the concept of *transference*, whereby the patient displaces on to the analyst feelings, ideas, and attitudes which are derived from past relationships and, in particular, from those involving one or both of his parents.

Freud's main support for these concepts came from his clinical material. Yet when attempts have been made to examine in any detail the case material upon which he relied researchers have been struck by how few were the cases reported by Freud. The most thorough analysis of Freud's published case-load[9] produced only 12 major cases and 133 minor ones. The major category included all cases where there were several pages of discussion and some statement of the patient's circumstances that could serve as a vehicle for discussion, while the minor cases included every other case mentioned by Freud. This total emerges after a thorough analysis of 114 papers and the 22 books written by Freud. Freud undoubtedly saw more patients than these so that it is difficult to disagree with the observation of Fisher and Greenberg to the effect that 'it is perhaps a tribute to Freud's persuasiveness that in spite of the selectivity of his presentations, his conclusions have been so widely adopted and advocated by others'.[10]

The earliest cases, four of which are described in *Studies in Hysteria*, written by Freud in collaboration with Breuer between 1893 and 1895, have little to do with psychoanalysis as a treatment, involving as they did such procedures as hypnosis, pressing on the head, suggestion, and simple conversation. There are, in fact, only six extended accounts written by Freud undergoing psychoanalytic treatment. These six cases are *the Schreber case*, the case of *Little Hans*, the case of *Dora*, the case of the *Rat Man*, the case of the *Wolf Man*, and an unnamed case of female homosexuality. Of these six cases, two were not actually treated at first hand by Freud, namely the Schreber case and the case of Little Hans.

Daniel Schreber was a German magistrate of high intelligence and ability who spent ten years in a mental hospital on account of a severe mental illness characterized by elaborate paranoid hallucinations and delusions and fears of homosexuality. After his discharge from hospital, Schreber published an account of his illness which formed the basis of Freud's psychoanalysis. Freud based much of his theory that repressed homosexuality underlay paranoia on the Schreber account, despite the fact that the account lacked any substantial information about the man's family, childhood, and history before admission. Since Freud's analysis, there have been other attempts, equally plausible and convincing, to explain the nature of Schreber's illness.[11] The Schreber case does not cast any light on Freud's actual clinical technique or efficacy and more properly belongs to the second-hand analyses of long-dead figures or fictional characters which Freud undertook from time to time and which included the seventeenth-century painter Christoph Haizmann, Dostoevski, Moses, Leonardo da Vinci, and Hamlet.[12]

The case of Little Hans is of more central concern. In 1909, Freud published *The Analysis of a Phobia in a Five-Year Old Boy*.[13] It was the first published account of a child analysis and Freud believed that it provided a direct demonstration of the essential role of sexual urges in the development of phobias. Glover[14] referred to it as a 'remarkable achievement', 'one of the most valued records in psychoanalytical archives', and believed it provided crucial support for notions such as the Oedipal complex, castration anxiety, and repression. The case material on which Freud based his analysis was collected by the father of Little Hans. Indeed so important was the father to the whole enterprise that in the introduction to the published account, Freud declared that:

> 'The special knowledge by means of which he [the father] was able to interpret the remarks made by his five year old son was indispensable and without it the technical difficulties in the way of conducting a psycho-analysis upon so young a child would have been insuperable.'

In early January, 1908, the father wrote to Freud that Hans had developed 'a nervous disorder' characterized by fear of going into the street, depression in the evening, and a fear that a horse would bite him in the street. His father went on to suggest that 'the ground was prepared by sexual over-excitement due to his mother's tenderness' and that the fear of the horses 'seems somehow to be connected with his having been frightened by a large penis'. Prior to the development of this fear, Hans had shown a lively interest in the portion of his body which he used to describe as his widdler. Aged three and a half, he was found by his mother with his hand on his penis and she allegedly threatened him as follows: 'If you do that I shall send for Dr A. to cut off your widdler.'

Once, around the same time, Hans saw his mother naked and was curious about her genitalia. She assured him that she was equipped like him and he expressed some surprise, expecting her to possess a penis as big as that of a horse. Aged four and a half, he saw his baby sister being bathed and laughed, he said, at her 'widdler' because 'it was so lovely'. His father commented revealingly: 'Of course his answer was a disingenuous one. In reality her widdler seemed to be funny. Moreover, this was the first time he had recognized in this way the distinction between male and female genitals instead of denying it.'

On the day his phobia developed he had been asked by his mother if he had put his hand to his widdler and he admitted that he had. The following day his mother warned him to refrain from doing this. At this point, Freud provides an interpretation of Hans's behaviour and arranged with the father that he should tell Hans:

> 'that all this nonsense about horses was a piece of nonsense and nothing more. The truth was, his father was to say, that he was very fond of his mother and wanted to be taken to her bed. The reason that he was afraid of horses now was that he had taken so much interest in their widdlers.'

Freud also suggests that Hans might be given some sexual information to the effect that females 'had no widdler at all'. After this explanation there is a lull, then an influenza attack, a worsening of the phobia, a tonsillitis and a tonsillectomy, followed by more discussions between Hans and his father. Hans tells how he has seen a playmate being warned by her father to avoid a white horse lest it bite. The girl's father had said that she was not to put her finger to the white horse. Hans's father replies: 'I say, it strikes me it isn't a horse you mean but a widdler that one mustn't put a hand to.'

Hans replies, somewhat reasonably, that a widdler doesn't bite, but his father muses that perhaps it does. The following day Hans says that his fear is still bad because he still handles his widdler at which point in the narrative Freud observes that: 'doctor and patient, father and son, were therefore at one in ascribing the chief share in the pathogenesis of Hans's present condition to his habit of onanism.'

Wolpe and Rachman, on the other hand, in their behavioural dissection of this case, object that Freud implied that this unanimity is significant and disregards the fact of 'the father's indoctrination of Hans the previous day'.[15] Their account masterly re-examines the way in which Freud and the father suggest and then reinforce certain interpretations and bring about in Hans the indoctrination of the theory which Freud allegedly is supposed to be discovering. It is indeed instructive to see how the case is put together. First, there is the selection of the material. The family were known to Freud, the parents being described by him as 'among his closest adherents', a fact not exactly likely to lead to a dispassionate and unbiased account of the early development of Little Hans and sister Hanna. Second, the account depends entirely upon the father's reliability as witness and interpreter. However, the father is not above presenting his interpretations as facts. For example, when Hans is asked by him what his sister looked like shortly after her birth, Hans replied, 'All white and lovely. So pretty,' and the father adds in parenthesis 'hypocritically'. When Hans describes his sister's 'widdler' as 'lovely', this is reinterpreted by the father although no evidence is provided in support of such an alteration.

The case of Little Hans is often used to support Freud's theory of castration anxiety, although in truth what it shows is the effort of a Freudian-inclined mother to induce castration anxieties in her perfectly normal son. Freud's interpretation of the phobia is that the boy's Oedipal conflicts formed the basis of his illness which burst out when Hans underwent 'a time of privation and the intensified sexual excitement'. Hans was a little Oedipus who wanted to have his father removed so that he might sleep with his mother. At his one and only interview with the little boy, Freud told him 'that he was afraid of his father because he himself nourished jealous and hostile wishes against him'. Freud added: 'In telling him this, I had partly interpreted his fear of horses for him; the horse must be his father – whom he had good internal reasons for fearing.'

Throughout this narrative, however, there is no evidence whatever of any wish on Hans's part to copulate with his mother, no evidence either that Hans ever expressed either fear or hatred of his father save that after Freud told Hans that he did possess these emotions and after further statements to that effect by his father Hans eventually said 'yes', an affirmative which was promptly accepted as the true state of affairs, all the many denials having been ignored. The claim that the purpose of Hans's phobia was to keep him near his mother is somewhat weakened by the fact that Hans experienced anxiety even when he was out walking with his mother. The conclusion that Hans's phobia disappeared as a result of the resolution of his Oedipal conflict has to be seen in the light of the remarkably fragile evidence in support of the notion that Hans had such an Oedipal complex in the first place. Yet psychoanalysts hailed the account of Little Hans 'as the first confirmation of Freud's theory of infantile sexuality obtained by direct observation on a child'.[16] It was also the first controlled analysis on record.

It is interesting at this stage to recall Nagel's ground rules whereby psychoanalytic procedures and practices might be scientifically analysed and assessed. Nagel argued that at least some of the theoretical notions should be tied down to fairly definite and unambiguously stated observable material by way of rules of procedure variously called 'correspondence rules' and 'co-ordinating definitions'. Can conclusions be deduced from the theory prior to knowing just what consequences the theory must have if it is to be in agreement with assumed matters of fact? In the case of Little Hans, the father expounded theoretical explanations to the boy who occasionally agreed and occasionally disagreed. Agreement was invariably seized upon as evidence of the difficulty the boy was having in facing up to the truth. In classical analysis the analyst is meant to be passive, but Nagel points out:

'that in the nature of the case the full extent of the analyst's intervention is not a matter that is open to public scrutiny so that by and large one has only his testimony as to what transpires in the consulting room. . . . No matter how firmly we may resolve to make explicit our biases no human being is aware of all of them and that objectivity in science is achieved through the criticism of publicly accessible material by a community of independent inquirers.'[17]

The gradual indoctrination of the patient into the theoretical framework of psychoanalytic theory, persuasively described by Wolpe and Rachman in their analysis of the case of Little Hans, remains an obstacle to the objective assessment of the theory some eighty years on. However, there are those who insist that the true worth of the theory lies not in its objective truth so much as the fact that it provides a coherent and intelligible picture of intrapsychic life and personal relationships. Coherence there may be in the analysis of the phobia in the Little Hans case, but it is difficult to avoid the conclusion that this coherence is achieved by the ingenuity with which the reported data are made to dovetail with a preconceived psychoanalytical theoretical formulation.

What of the outcome in this case? When Freud met Hans some fourteen years later, the nineteen-year-old youth had no recollection at all of his childhood fear of horses nor of the analysis. He had negotiated puberty without trouble and survived too the break-up and divorce of his parents, each of whom had remarried. As a result, Hans lived alone and regretted that the break-up of his family had separated him from the younger sister of whom he was so fond.

The third of Freud's six major case reports concerns an eighteen-year-old girl, known as 'Dora', who entered treatment with Freud in 1900. Her treatment was in fact short-lived – it lasted three months in all. Dora is afflicted with a few classic symptoms of 'petite hysterie' – a nervous cough, periodic loss of voice, possibly migraine, together with depression and unsociability. Her parents have a close relationship with Mr and Mrs K. with whom they often spend their vacations. Dora is extremely fond of their two small children. Dora's father is frequently ill with chest infections and is nursed by Mrs K., much to Dora's annoyance. Mr K., on the other hand, overwhelms Dora with presents and flowers and Dora indignantly reveals to her mother that Mr K. has been making propositions to her, which her father refuses to believe. Mr K. for his part denies the allegations and attributes them to Dora's over-heated imagination.

Gradually, Dora tells Freud a remarkable story. Her father and Mrs K. have been having an affair for years. Four years earlier, Mr K. had kissed Dora and she had been strongly repelled. She feels herself to be delivered up to Mr K. in exchange for Mr K.'s consent to her father's adulterous affair with Mrs K. It also becomes clear that Dora is strongly attached to the K.s' children because she is deeply in love with Mr K. despite her assertions to the contrary. At the same time, Dora is extremely fond of her father and it appears that the secret aim of her hysterical neurosis is to touch the heart of her father and detach him from Mrs K.

There is more, much more. For our purposes, however, this will suffice. It is the selectivity of Freud which merits attention. Dora's mother is strangely absent from the case analysis apart from an early and dismissive reference:

> 'I never made the mother's acquaintance. From the accounts given me by the girl and her father I was led to imagine her as an uncultivated woman and above all a foolish one who had concentrated all her interests upon domestic affairs, especially since her husband's illness and the estrangement to which it led.'[18]

Freud's view of Dora's mother, therefore, is based on information received from her husband, who is actually in the midst of an adulterous affair and is scarcely unbiased, and her daughter who is preoccupied by her ambivalent feelings towards Mr K. and resentment concerning her father's lover. 'She presented a picture', adds Freud, of a woman he had never met, 'of what might be called "housewife's psychosis".'[19]

In addition to a remarkable selectivity, Freud provides further examples of his method, examples which go some way towards explaining why there is so much difficulty involved in attempting to validate or invalidate his theoretical and therapeutic claims. Whether the treatment is effective is impossible to establish because Dora breaks off treatment after a period which most contemporary analysts would consider too short to be useful. She does have symptoms on and off afterwards and Freud is left to muse over his failure to discover in time and inform Dora of her homosexual love for Mrs K., he having already revealed to her the intensity of her love for her father and the urgency of her repressed love for the repudiated Mr K.

The Dora case forms a link between *The Interpretation of Dreams* and the *Three Essays on the Theory of Sexuality* and can be seen to be an important contribution to Freud's theoretical construction. But it contributes little to the clarification of the issue of the efficaciousness of psychoanalysis as therapy.

The same can sadly be said of the fourth case.[20] This clinical account is of the psychogenesis of homosexuality in an eighteen-year-old girl whose parents allege that she is pursuing a society lady ten years her senior, that she lives with a friend, a married woman, with whom she has an intimate relationship, while at the same time she carries on promiscuous affairs with a number of men. The girl, as Freud pointed out in his report, was in no way ill, did not suffer any symptoms and did not proffer any complaints. The task facing Freud was not the resolution of a neurotic conflict but the conversion of one variety of genital organization of sexuality into another. Such an achievement, Freud conceded, is not easily attained and, in the circumstances, the unfruitful outcome of his brief intervention reveals nothing of the usefulness of psychoanalysis in more promising and more appropriate conditions.

This leaves the two remaining cases – the case of the Wolf Man and the case of the Rat Man. The Wolf Man was described by Freud as not being a particularly favourable case and is generally presented as having been an

interminable analytic case. He was indeed seen for many years by a number
of different analysts after treatment with Freud had been concluded. In the
opinion of no less a critic than James Strachey, however, the Wolf Man case
was 'the most elaborate and no doubt the most important' because at the
time it served as a formidable response to Adler and Jung and their attempt
to deny the significance of infantile sexuality, for the case appeared to
establish the potentially traumatic impact of the primal scene, the pervasive
fear of castration and the psychodynamic basis of obsessional behaviour.

It was in January, 1910 that the wealthy young Russian, Sergius P., came
to Freud for analysis. His first course of treatment, the one reported in detail
by Freud, lasted from February, 1910 to July, 1914 when Freud regarded it
as complete. Freud wrote the case history in October, 1914 but held back
publication for four years. The patient required a further period of analysis
from November, 1919 until February, 1920. In some further remarks on the
case, at the beginning of his *Analysis Terminable and Interminable*, Freud
reports that after this second course of treatment, the patient continued
living in Vienna and on the whole maintained his health, albeit with
occasional interruptions. These later episodes were dealt with by one of
Freud's pupils, Ruth Mack Brunswick, who also reported on his condition.
In 1971, Muriel Gardner published an account of the Wolf Man's difficulties
during the Second World War. More recently, some sixty-four years after
Freud published his own account of the case, the patient's own view was
published by way of a young Austrian journalist.[21]

In the Wolf Man's own account, the patient did not live out his life in
Vienna as the harmless, satisfied, almost happy pensioner portrayed by
Gardner but as a neurotic, ambivalent, and highly dependent man. In
addition to providing telling pictures of how Freud actually carried out
analysis – he apparently smoked incessantly, discussed painting, and charged
the fairly substantial sum of forty Austrian crowns a session – the Wolf Man
reflects on the therapeutic effect of his treatment and concludes, reluctantly,
that: 'In reality the whole thing looks like a catastrophe. I am in the same
state as when I first came to Freud and Freud is no more'.[22]

There seems little reason to doubt the patient's self-assessment for in the
years following his analysis with Freud he had returned again and again to
doctors. Indeed, several times during the interviews, he laments the dependency on doctors and analysts which psychoanalysis in his opinion
invariably engenders. 'Psychoanalysis', he observes mournfully at one point,
'weakens the ego.'

More serious for psychoanalytical theory and therapy, however, is the
Wolf Man's view of some crucial Freudian interpretations. Take the dream
which gave Sergius P. his psychoanalytical pseudonym. As Freud relates it,
the Wolf Man

> 'dreamt that it was night and that I was lying in my bed. . . . Suddenly the
> window opened of its own accord and I was terrified to see that some
> white wolves were sitting on the big walnut tree in front of the window.
> There were six or seven of them. The wolves were quite white and looked

more like foxes or sheep-dogs, for they had big tails like foxes and they had their ears pricked up like dogs ... in great terror, evidently of being eaten up by the wolves, I screamed and woke up'.[23]

The interpretation of this dream took several years and Freud observed that 'the patient related the dream at a very early stage in the analysis and very soon came to share my conviction that the causes of his infantile neurosis lay concealed behind it'. Freud called the illness 'a condition following an obsessional neurosis which has come to an end spontaneously but has left a defect behind it after recovery'. In fact the problems for which the Wolf Man sought Freud's help are not easy to discover from Freud's account, but Obholzer has ably summarized the details and it would appear that the Wolf Man suffered intermittent depressions, obsessional symptoms, and difficulties in his sexual life.

From the dream, then, Freud derived the cause of the neurosis. Fairy-tale material, including Red Riding Hood and the Wolf and the Seven Goats, and a story about a tailor and a tail-less wolf his grandfather had told the patient about, were identified in reworked form in the dream. Behind the dream, argued Freud, lies an experience from early childhood that provided the basis of the patient's castration fears. At the age of one-and-a-half years, the patient had fallen ill with malaria and slept in his parents' room instead of his nanny's. During the afternoon, 'he witnessed a coitus a tergo, three times repeated' where he could see 'his mother's genitals as well as his father's organ'. Step by step the different elements in the dream are elegantly woven into a striking interpretative picture. 'It was night' is a distortion of 'I was asleep'. 'Suddenly the window opened of its own accord' is translated as 'Suddenly I woke up of my own accord'. The whiteness of the wolves relates to the parents' underwear and bedclothes. The number of wolves reflects the nursery story but Freud adds that 'the fact that the number two in the primal scene is replaced (in the dream) by a large number, which would be absurd in the primal scene, is welcomed by the resistance as a means of distortion'. The wolves sitting motionless in the dream is seen as a striking, and therefore significant, contradiction of the most obvious feature of the witnessed primal scene, while the fact that the wolves had tails like foxes is a reassurance for the boy that the fearsome story of the tail-less wolf, told by his grandfather and activating castration fears, is but a story and that castration cannot occur after all. As if to answer any lingering doubts concerning this elaborate interpretation, Freud observes magisterially that 'there are more things in heaven and earth than are dreamed of in our philosophy'.

The Wolf Man, however, recalled that he did indeed dream of wolves but denied that he had ever seen his parents engage in sex and regarded the whole reconstruction by Freud as 'terribly far-fetched'. It is of course unwise to rely uncritically on a patient's recollection of analysis, especially after sixty years. After all, fourteen years after his treatment, Little Hans had no recollection whatever of his childhood phobia nor of any visit to Freud. But it may not be wise either to rely uncritically and unreservedly on an analyst's account either. What can be said with some degree of confidence is that Freud's interpretation in the case of the Wolf Man, true or false, was ineffective. The Wolf Man's subsequent life was characterized by impoverished circumstances, severe depressions, and constant attendance on doctors. His wife killed herself, as did his sister in late adolescence, and he ends his days in a Vienna psychiatric hospital, penniless, forlorn, and friendless save for his journalistic confidante. In his case history, Freud described him prior to treatment as:

> 'entirely incapacitated and completely dependent on other people . . . for a long time unassailably entrenched behind an attitude of obliging apathy. . . . his shrinking from a self-sufficient existence was so great as to outweigh all the vexations of his illness.'[24]

Muriel Gardner, in her positive account of psychoanalysis, did admit that certain of the Wolf Man's defects and deficiencies persisted after his treatment, most notably his periodic depression, ambivalence, feelings of guilt, and strong dependency needs, but she insisted that 'the positive results are impressive indeed'.[25] The picture as revealed by the Wolf Man's own recollections scarcely bears her out.

The sixth and final case is that of Paul Lorenz, the Rat Man, which, according to Fisher and Greenberg, represents Freud's only record of a complete and successful analysis. The treatment was short by later standards, lasting only eleven months in all, and Freud described it as leading to the 'complete restoration of the patient's personality and to the removal of his inhibitions'.[26] The patient was a young man who suffered from intense obsessions from childhood, the chief features of which were fears that something might happen to two people of whom he was very fond, namely his father and a lady he admired, compulsive impulses, such as the compulsive impulse to cut his throat with a razor, and prohibitions which he produced to govern his behaviour with regard to quite trivial matters. He had tried various treatments. His sexual life was stunted. He came to Freud because he had read of his theories.

Treatment began on 1 October, 1907, and Freud gave several reports of the case as it proceeded. His original record of the first third of the treatment, from day to day as the treatment unfolded, has survived and a substantial part of it is reproduced in the tenth volume of the Standard Edition of Freud's works. The pseudonym originates from an obsessional rumination which involved a fantasy of rats boring into the anus of his father, who had died some years before therapy began, and of his lady friend. On the basis of this case, Freud developed many of his psychoanalytical explanations of obsessional fears, doubts, ruminations, and compulsions. Paul Lorenz emerged from his analysis with Freud reportedly free of symptoms but details of the follow-up are sparse and the patient, in Freud's words, 'like so many other young men of value and promise . . . perished in the Great War.'[27]

For all its length, however, the account of the Rat Man's treatment is fragmentary and uneven. The first seven hours take about five minutes to read. Whatever they say about the outcome, analysts have tended to decry Freud's technique, criticizing the fact that on one occasion he gave the Rat Man a meal, on another lent him a book, and throughout the treatment made many conversational asides. More important, the problem of bias, noted in the case of Little Hans, arises again.[28]

These then are Freud's six major analytic cases. Each in its own way conforms to the assessment of Freud's writings made by Steven Marcus when, at the end of a perceptive essay, he observes:

'Freud's case histories are a new form of literature – they are creative narratives that include their own analysis and interpretations. Nevertheless, like the living works of literature that they are, the material they contain is always richer than the original analysis and interpretation that accompany it; and this means that future generations will return to these works and will find in them a language they are seeking and a story they need to be told.'[29]

Commenting on the Dora case, Marcus goes even further and notes that Freud is as much a novelist as an analyst and the case is full of 'such literary and novelistic devices or conventions as thematic analogies, double plots, reversals, inversions, variations, betrayals'. Such a comment could as easily be applied to the other case reports and raises profound difficulties for any scientific appraisal of the clinical worth of the cases as clinical cases.

Yet these six major cases, together with six more that more properly belong to the pre-analytic phase of Freud's thinking and between one hundred and two hundred fragmented references, are all that we have. About half the total were published before 1900 and the overwhelming majority before 1920. By this time Freud, as a practising analyst, was slowing down. Ernest Jones refers to the fact that from the end of the First World War onwards, Freud 'took on fewer patients, there being so many pupils'.[30] and by the end of the 1920s he was quite an ill man, in his seventies and living the life of a semi-invalid. Yet that decade also witnessed some of the most productive years of theoretical writing. As the case reporting dwindled, so the theories continued to stream forth – several key papers on dream theory, his celebrated formulation of the death instinct, his revised introductory lectures, 'Beyond the Pleasure Principle' and 'The Question of Lay Analysis'. With the final decline in his clinical practice coincided his more philosophical works including 'The Future of an Illusion', 'Civilization and Its Discontents', and 'Moses and Monoetheism'.

As cases, therefore, it is hard to contest their importance. As Brody observes:

'more than most other sciences, psychoanalysis is the creation of a single man. The clinical experience, social ideology and perhaps even the personal idiosyncrasies of Sigmund Freud, are still the cornerstones of analytical practice and theory some sixty years after his initial observations.'[31]

The selectivity of these cases is further underlined by Brody's note to the effect that about two-thirds of them involved women, the great bulk of the clinical conditions were concerned with hysteria and obsessional illnesses, the great majority of the patients were in their late teens or early twenties, and every patient was upper class.

Current psychoanalytic practice

While the theoretical complexity of psychoanalysis has developed over the years, analytic practice has, with respect to the issues of selectivity, scarcely changed. Kubie's statistics concerning the scale of analytical fees[32] make it highly unlikely that more than a few lower-class patients have been analysed for any length of time and even the low-cost service provided by institutes such as the William Alanson White Institute has failed to alter this bias. Surveys have repeatedly shown that typical private analytic patients are almost all native Americans, white, relatively young, and predominantly of Protestant or Jewish backgrounds. In addition, they tend to be well educated with only a small minority not having at least some training beyond the high-school level. One of the most extensive surveys ever conducted revealed that over half the patients in private analysis in the USA were either active as practitioners in the mental health field or were closely related to a mental health practitioner.[33]

The relatively high level of educational and professional success of most analytic patients also suggests that as a group they may give fewer indications of gross psychological disturbance than patients being treated by other therapies. Most studies reveal that analytic candidates are chosen from patients displaying a greater number of assets and less impaired functioning and this trend has affected patient selection with regard to psychoanalytically-derived psychotherapies too. The remarkable burgeoning of psychoanalytic practice and influence in the years since Freud, most particularly in the United States, cannot be separated from social, economic, and cultural factors.[34] It owed little to established efficacy. Freud's cases were received by the analytic faithful relatively uncritically – such criticisms as were expressed did not detract from the fundamental truths such cases were believed to convey nor from the assumption that the character-altering nature of psychoanalysis, in contrast to the symptom-relieving nature of all other therapies, made it infinitely superior as a treatment. The extent to which analytic ideas and influences invaded American psychiatry is a subject which has concerned others. Here it merely suffices to recall the observation of one American analyst who in 1969 commented upon the difficulty of persuading his colleagues to discuss the relationship between psychoanalysis and psychiatry:

'This is a difficult task ... for candidly, our teachers, our friends, our colleagues, our personal psychotherapists, our wives' psychotherapists, our former psychiatric residents, and many of our government's "site visitors" are all psychoanalysts.... In short, for many American psychiatrists, psychoanalytic or otherwise, it is very difficult to discuss the role of psychoanalytic organizations in American psychiatry today except in an ambivalent and over-determined manner. Indeed, it is precisely this "yes-no" simultaneously spoken, the public affirmation and private depreciation, which has chiefly characterized academic psychiatry's overall relationship to organized psychoanalysis for over a decade or more. Psychoanalytic institutions have been a tiger by the tail for American psychiatric educators.'[35]

As a consequence, questions of efficacy and applicability have languished. No great advance has been made in the years since Freud wrote his literary accounts of clinical consultations. Patient selection continues to confound judgements concerning suitability and usefulness of treatment. Research efforts to clarify the situation have foundered. Farrell[36] and Fisher and Greenberg,[37] searching the literature over the past fifty years, have found a handful of reports which suggested that psychoanalysis might be useful in varying conditions, from psychosomatic ill-health to neuroses, but in not a single one were the basic elements of a respectable study present, such as proper base-line information, a control group, independent assessment of outcome, and information concerning other treatments, interventions, and alterations occurring simultaneously with the analysis.

'Since psychoanalysis does claim to function as a therapy', remarked Sidney Hook, 'its clinical successes and failures seem to me to be highly relevant in evaluating the truth of its theories.'[38] If it has no clinical successes and if it is not confirmed by experimental findings, then it has no more scientific standing than any other coherent, consistent mythology. At the present time, it is difficult to make a case on behalf of the therapeutic achievements of psychoanalysis. Indeed, Judd Marmor, an analyst himself and sympathetic to the analytic cause, was forced to precisely this conclusion himself when he admitted of analysis that:

'In retrospect, it seems clear that it was oversold as an optimal technique, since at best it is indicated in only a small number of cases. Indeed, whether or not the classical psychoanalytic technique is truly the optimal approach for *any* specific form of psychopathology still remains to be conclusively proved. This is not to imply that it is without merit but merely that its superiority over all other psychotherapeutic approaches is presently more an article of faith than a scientifically demonstrated fact'.[39]

One might even go further. Whereas Freud was fond of comparing psychoanalysis to surgery, psychoanalysis, unlike surgery, has never been concerned to any significant extent with the severe end of the disease spectrum. Serious mental disorders, even in the USA, are currently treated

with biological treatments, social manipulations, and psychological procedures whose similarity to Freudian psychoanalysis is slight and whose
claim to be dynamic in the psychoanalytic sense is even slighter. In the case
of serious neurotic disturbances, such as crippling obsessions similar to
those which crippled the Rat Man, phobias such as affected Little Hans,
anxiety neuroses and psychosomatic symptoms akin to those of Dora,
developments in behavioural management, social skills training, and drug
therapy have rendered psychoanalytical treatment redundant. In the case of
milder psychological disturbances, including the anxieties, depressions, and
interpersonal difficulties of everyday life, there is now convincing evidence
that those which show a good prognosis respond to interventions which are
very much more straightforward, economical, and brief than classical
analysis, while those that have a poorer outcome are invariably bound
up with such variables as poor client motivation, weak ego strength,
and disorganized social and personal circumstances, factors recognized,
indeed identified by psychoanalysts themselves, as contra-indications to
psychoanalytic treatment.[40]

In the circumstances, it is difficult to avoid the conclusion that eighty
years on from Freud's initial claims on behalf of his creation its standing as a
treatment within orthodox psychiatry has never been lower. At the end of
the thirty-fourth introductory lecture, Freud provided his considered view
of analysis as treatment:

> 'I have told you that psychoanalysis began as a method of treatment; but I
> did not want to commend it to your interest as a method of treatment but
> on account of the truths it contains, on account of the information it gives
> us about what concerns human beings most of all – their own nature –
> and on account of the connections it discloses between the most different
> of their activities. As a method of treatment it is one among many, though
> to be sure, primus inter pares. If it was without therapeutic value it would
> not have been discovered, as it was, in connection with sick people and
> would not have gone on developing for more than thirty years'.[41]

Now, no one other than utterly incorrigible analytic practitioners claims
such an elevated position for psychoanalysis as a treatment. Most practitioners acknowledge its relative ineffectiveness. Not many realize, however,
that as a treatment its foundations were never as securely established as its
creator claimed and the actual clinical case-load upon which so many of its
theoretical principles rest is surprisingly flimsy.

Notes

1 E. Nagel, 'Methodological Issues in Psychoanalytic Theory', in *Psychoanalysis,
  Scientific Method and Philosophy*, ed. S. Hook (New York: New York University, 1959), pp. 38–56.
2 S. Freud, *The Question of Lay Analysis* (1926), *Standard Edition of the Complete*

Psychological Works of Sigmund Freud (hereafter abbreviated as SE), trans. J. Strachey (London: The Hogarth Press and the Institute of Psycho-analysis, 1953–74), vol. 20.

3 S. Freud, *The Future Prospects of Psychoanalytic Therapy* (1910), SE vol. 11 (1957).

4 S. Freud, *Introductory Lectures on Psychoanalysis* (1916), SE, vol. 15 (1957).

5 S. Freud, 'Turnings in the Ways of Psychoanalytic Therapy', paper delivered to the International Psychoanalytical Congress, Budapest, 1918.

6 S. Freud, *Fragment of an Analysis of a Case of Hysteria* (1905), SE, vol. 7, pp. 1–122.

7 S. Freud, *Analysis Terminable and Interminable.* (1937), SE, vol. 23 (1957).

8 S. Freud, *New Introductory Lectures on Psychoanalysis* (1933), SE, vol. 22 (1957).

9 B. Brody, 'Freud's Case-Load', *Psychotherapy: Theory, Research and Practice* 7 (1970): 8–12.

10 S. Fisher and R.P. Greenberg, *The Scientific Credibility of Freud's Theories and Therapy.* (Sussex: Harvester Press, 1977).

11 I. MacAlpine and R.A. Hunter (trans. *Memoirs of My Mental Illness*, by Daniel Schreber) (London: Dawsons, 1955), M. Schatzman, *Soul Murder* (London: Allen Lane, 1973).

12 For Hamlet, see the essay of W.F. Bynum and M.R. Neve in this volume.

13 S. Freud, *Analysis of a Phobia in a Five-Year-Old-Boy* (1909), SE, vol. 10 (1953) pp. 1–145.

14 E. Glover, *On The Early Development Of The Mind,* (1956). (London: Imago, 1956), p. 76.

15 J. Wolpe and S. Rachman, 'Psychoanalytic Evidence: A Critique Based on Freud's Case of Little Hans', *Journal of Nervous and Mental Disease* 131 (1960): 135–48.

16 H.F. Ellenberger, *The Discovery of the Unconscious* (London: Allen Lane, 1970).

17 Nagel, 'Methodological Issues'.

18 S. Freud, *Fragment of an Analysis of a Case of Hysteria* (1905), SE, vol. 7, pp. 1–122.

19 Freud, *Case of Hysteria.*

20 S. Freud, *The Psychogenesis of a Case of Homosexuality in a Woman* (1920), SE, vol. 18, pp. 145–72.

21 K. Obholzer, *The Wolf-Man Sixty Years Later* (London: Routledge and Kegan Paul, 1982).

22 Obholzer, *The Wolf-Man.*

23 S. Freud, *From the History of an Infantile Neurosis* (1918), SE, vol. 17 (1955), pp. 1–122.

24 Freud, *History of an Infantile Neurosis.*

25 M. Gardner (ed.), *The Wolf-Man: With the Case of the Wolf-Man by Sigmund Freud* (New York: Basic Books, 1971).

26 S. Freud, *Notes Upon A Case Of Obsessional Neurosis* (1909), SE, vol. 10, pp. 151–249.

27 Freud, *Case of Obsessional Neurosis.*

28 S. Marcus, 'Freud and Dora; Story, History, Case History', in *Freud: A Collection of Critical Essays*, ed. Perry Meisel (Englewood Cliffs, N.J.: Prentice-Hall, 1981), pp. 183–210.

29 Marcus, 'Freud and Dora'.

30 E. Jones, *The Life and Work of Sigmund Freud* (London: Pelican, 1953).

31 S. Brody 'Freud's Case-Load', *Psychotherapy: Theory, Research and Practice* 7 (1970): 8–12.

32 L.S. Kubie, 'A Pilot Study of Psychoanalytic Practice in the United States' *Psychiatry* 13 (1950): 227–45.

33 W. Weintraub, and H. Aronson, 'A Survey of Patients in Classical Psychoanalysis: Some Vital Statistics', *Journal of Nervous and Mental Disease* 146 (1962): 98–102.

34 N.G. Hale, Jr, *Freud and the Americans* (Oxford: Oxford University Press, 1971).

35 J. Marmor, 'Current Status of Psychoanalysis in American Psychiatry', in: *Psychoanalysis in Present-Day Psychiatry*, ed. I. Gouldstone (New York: Brunner-Mazel, 1969), ch. 1, p. 11.

36 B.A. Farrell, *The Standing of Psychoanalysis*. (Oxford: Oxford University Press, 1981).

37 Fisher and Greenberg, *Scientific Credibility*.

38 S. Hook, (ed.), *Psychoanalysis, Scientific Method and Philosophy* (New York: New York University, 1959).

39 Marmor, 'Current Status of Psychoanalysis'.

40 Menninger Clinic, *Psychotherapy and Psychoanalysis*, final report of the Menninger Foundation's Psychotherapy Research Project, *Bulletin of the Menninger Clinic*, vol. 36, (1972), nos. 1–2.

41 Freud, *New Introductory Lectures*.

CHAPTER TWELVE

Hamlet on the couch

W.F. Bynum and Michael Neve

THE HISTORY OF disease and disease concepts are aspects of medical history fraught with problems and yet full of possibilities. The history of 'consumption' before Robert Koch is only partially continuous with the history of 'tuberculosis' after him. In one sense, the history of myocardial infarction begins only about 1900, even though men and women suffered from arteriosclerosis before that date. The history of chlorosis has been conceived in terms of diet, anaemia, and other physical categories on the one hand, and in terms of social relations and repressed women on the other. 'Hysteria' has been recently written about as largely misdiagnosed epilepsy by one historian, and as a kind of alternative career for women denied adequate avenues of social expression by other historians.[1] The fascination with retrospective diagnosis so beloved by practising doctors who turn their attention to history has been castigated by historians who find the exercise distortive, Whiggish, and historically irrelevant. To ask, for example, what was 'really wrong' with Napoleon or Darwin has been seen as asking an unanswerable question, or as encouraging speculation in excess of the evidence. Those who have insisted that it is the historian's proper task to try to understand the diagnostic categories and therapeutic options available to a doctor at any particular time only within the terms of his own society are responding to a real historical problem, for our own knowledge of the afflictions of earlier generations is often limited by what they and their doctors made of it. In the end, we may well be forced to conclude that an eighteenth-century lady suffering from the vapours or a nineteenth-century maniac in a Victorian country asylum were afflicted with precisely those diseases.[2]

But such historical contextualism can be pushed too far. It is, perhaps, inevitable that we judge when we write history. We perceive good diagnosticians, and mediocre ones, in the past, just as we have variable confidence in different doctors – and historians – in our own time. And part of our historical judgement bears directly on the doctor's relationship to the realities with which he was faced. Too few historians of psychiatry have concerned themselves with these realities: with, for instance, the prevalence of neurosyphilis and other organic disorders in Victorian asylums. It is not enough to see psychiatric diagnoses simply in terms of ideologies or social control, just as it is not enough to view psychiatric, or medical, disorders as timeless, ahistorical categories which doctors in the past have groped for and which we, with the benefit of electroencephalograms and CAT scanners, have at last discovered.

To take a concrete example: the medical world of John Conolly at Hanwell Asylum can be only partially reconstructed. We are forever denied immediate access to the patients he examined, though we can know something – but only something – of their personalities, their physiognomies, their bodies.[3] We can have reasonable access to what he considered significant in his patients' life histories, psychological make-ups, and social relations; we can infer what he did not consider worth noting or eliciting. But we cannot examine his patients ourselves, order an electroencephalogram, do a mental status examination, or ask about their dreams or early childhoods.

There is, however, one psychiatric case about which dozens of psychiatrists have written and to which our own access is just as privileged as theirs: Hamlet, the Dane, about whom more has been written than about any Danish person of real historical substance. Indeed, more has been written of Hamlet than of any doctor who ever lived. He has become part of world culture, and the literature about him knows no ordinary national or linguistic barriers. The French find him fascinating and the Germans seem sometimes to believe that his original utterance was 'Sein oder nicht Sein'.[4]

It should thus not come as a surprise to learn that Hamlet has fascinated psychiatrists of the past century and a half. The roll-call of nineteenth-century psychiatrists who turned their attention to him reads almost like a *Who's Who* of British, American, and German psychiatry: Conolly himself, as well as J.C. Bucknill, Henry Maudsley, and Forbes Winslow in England; Isaac Ray, Amariah Brigham, and A.O. Kellogg in America; and from the Continent, Cesare Lombroso, A. Delbruck, Heinrich Laehr, and H. Turek. Even a Dr Jekels has contributed to the literature on psychopathology in Shakespeare.[5]

In this century, psychoanalysts since Freud himself have been eager to add their solutions, most notably Ernest Jones and Otto Rank, and more recently Kurt Eissler, W.I.D. Scott, Theodore Lidz, Irving Edgar, and Norman Holland.[6] Dr Eliot Slater, one of the most organically orientated of leading contemporary British psychiatrists, even added his mite, arguing with playfulness but with some interesting textual evidence that Hamlet's 'problem' was the discovery that he and Ophelia had actually committed incest together.[7]

The range of other diagnoses has been equally wide. Hamlet has been confidently diagnosed as a melancholic, a maniac, and both, that is a manic-depressive; he has been seen as a neurotic, most classically as one with unresolved Oedipal conflicts, but with a variety of other compulsions and obsessions; he has been pronounced a neurasthenic, an hysteric, a type of human degeneracy, and a classical case of the malingerer. He has been approached as one who was criminally insane and had the extent of his criminal responsibility assessed. Occasionally, psychiatrists have even dared suggest he was sane, although this diagnosis has largely been the province of literary critics; psychiatrists, it seems, are more prone to diagnose mental disturbance in individuals than are lay people.[8] '*Hamlet*, in particular,' writes the American psychiatrist Theodore Lidz, 'attracts the psychiatrist because it is a play that directly challenges his professional acumen.'[9] A century ago, Henry Maudsley, Conolly's son-in-law and the pre-eminent British psychiatrist of the second half of the nineteenth century, was a bit more modest:

'An artist like Shakespeare, penetrating with subtle insight the character of the individual, and the relations between him and his circumstances, discerning the order which there is amidst so much apparent disorder, and revealing the necessary mode of the evolution of the events of life – furnishes, in the work of creative art, more valuable information [about the causes of insanity] than can be obtained from the vague and general statements with which science, in its present defective state, is constrained to content itself.'[10]

Given the range of psychiatric and critical comment already offered on Hamlet's personality and psychology, in short, his 'problem', there would be little point in adding to the pile. Rather, we propose to look at the historical Hamlet, at a character – almost, it would seem, a person – who has in essence been alive these three and a half centuries and more. Analysis terminable and interminable, one might say. But analysis there has been, only a fraction, of course, by psychiatrists, but enough to give a fairly precise flavour of changing psychiatric parameters and perceptions. We can only sketch Hamlet the person and can do only a little more for Hamlet on the couch, but since Hamlet has no existence outside the boundaries of his play, since we can in theory know exactly as much about him as did Dr Johnson, or John Conolly, or Ernest Jones, we can use him as a kind of touchstone by which to measure changing opinion – psychiatric and otherwise – about normalcy and madness.

Professional psychiatric concern seems almost coincident with the psychiatric profession itself – from the middle decades of the nineteenth century. But what these psychiatrists had inherited was a prince – a person or patient, or what you will – who had undergone a complex metamorphosis over two and a third centuries. Let us mention briefly what this was. Shakespeare's Hamlet, for historical purposes, was a text: a set of words, stage directions and implied actions and interactions. But of course Shakespeare's Hamlet also related to what we know about Shakespeare himself, and to a character and plot which Shakespeare inherited from earlier sources and moulded to suit his own particular dramatic purposes. This was undoubtedly important to Shakespeare's audience, who would have been familiar with Thomas Kyd's earlier version and who would in any case have reacted in certain ways to Hamlet as a character in a revenge tragedy.[11] This earlier plot and this well-established tradition would have satisfactorily explained to Shakespeare's original audiences two of the central problems which were so much to exercise later critics and psychiatrists: first, was Hamlet *really* mad, or did he merely feign madness? Unfortunately, Hamlet doesn't help us much at this point, for he warns Horatio and Marcellus, after his encounter with the ghost, that he may have future occasion to 'put an antic disposition on'; whereas, almost at the end, when preparing to fight Laertes, he announces that it was his madness which caused him to wrong Laertes, and by extension, Polonius and Ophelia as well. What to believe, Hamlet's prediction or Hamlet's reflection? Hamlet of Act I or Hamlet of Act V? For a century and more, it was the early Hamlet who was believed, one reason at least being because Kyd's Hamlet unequivocally feigned madness.

The second problem was not unrelated to the first. If Hamlet was sane throughout, is he really the stuff of tragic stature? Can he really be a tragic hero? For he could be said to procrastinate; he jilts his true love and indirectly causes her death; he kills her father and, eventually, her brother; he sends Rosenkrantz and Guildenstern to their deaths and generally wreaks havoc wherever he goes. But this is to bring later glosses on the action, for the tragedy of revenge did not require morally blameless heroes and Shakespeare's seventeenth-century audiences probably saw Hamlet as a rather bitter, sarcastic, cynical, and often witty malcontent, and if mad, mad rather comically, in the way that all lovers are a little mad.[12] But in any case, psychological readings of Hamlet do not appear until the eighteenth century.[13]

During that century, David Garrick brought to Hamlet a new realism and naturalism, attuned to the refinements and sensibilities of the age. His Hamlet was every inch a prince, a tragic character caught in a web of intrigue and circumstance, consonant with the critic William Richardson's 1784 description of Hamlet's 'virtue and moral beauty'.[14] Garrick, said one of his contemporaries, has 'drawn this prince of a reserved cautious turn, arising from a melancholy stamped on him by his father's untimely death and some consequent misfortunes'.[15] In the eighteenth century, what were increasingly being called 'nervous' diseases were fashionable, and to have one was a sign of refinement and sensibility.[16] Given such widespread eighteenth-century fascination with the genteel, it is not surprising that Hamlet's melancholic turn of mind should strike sympathetic chords. Eighteenth-century audiences and critics discovered Hamlet's psychology, his meditative, thoughtful, contemplative self; in short, they saw melancholy, but they did not medicalize it. Eighteenth-century psychiatric writings often distinguish rather sharply between melancholy and madness, and if, as for King Lear, that way madness lies, Hamlet stayed firmly on this side of the pale.

Of course, the aesthetics of sensibility sometimes jostled uneasily with the purity of Augustan humanism, and in England, Dr Johnson was certain that Hamlet's madness was simply pretended, reserving his tears for Ophelia, 'the young, the beautiful, the harmless, and the pious'.[17] In France, Voltaire was unmoved. Writing in the 1740s, when Garrick was in his prime, Voltaire could insist:

'Englishmen believe in ghosts no more than the Romans did, yet they take pleasure in the tragedy of Hamlet, in which the ghost of a king appears on the stage. ... Far be it from me to justify everything in that tragedy; it is a vulgar and barbarous drama, which would not be tolerated by the vilest populace of France, or Italy. Hamlet becomes crazy in the second act, and his mistress becomes crazy in the third; the prince slays the father of his mistress under the pretence of killing a rat, and the heroine throws herself into the river; a grave is dug on the stage, and the grave-diggers talk quodlibets worthy of themselves, while holding skulls in their hands; Hamlet responds to their nasty vulgarities in silliness no less disgusting. In the meanwhile another of the actors conquers Poland. Hamlet, his mother, and his father-in-law, carouse on the stage; songs are sung at table; there is quarrelling, fighting, killing – one would imagine this piece to be the work of a drunken savage.'[18]

In the end, of course, sensibility won out, and Romanticism created its own version of human nature, its own Hamlet. For the Romantics, Hamlet embodied quintessentially the all-too-human dichotomy between thought and action, between exultation and despair. For Samuel Taylor Coleridge, he had 'every excellence but the power to act'.[19] He was a young Werther before his time, and it is not surprising that the creator of Werther – Goethe – should have left a description of Hamlet which embodied all the Romantic fascination with Shakespeare's character. Of Hamlet, Goethe wrote:

'Tender and nobly descended, this royal flower grew up under the direct influences of majesty; the idea of the right and of princely dignity, the feeling for the good and the graceful, with the consciousness of his high birth, were unfolded in him together. He was a prince, a born prince. Pleasing in figure, polished by nature, courteous from the heart, he was to be the model of youth and the delight of the world.'

'A beautiful, pure, and most moral nature, without the strength of nerve which makes the hero, sinks beneath a burden which it can either bear nor throw off; every duty is holy to him – his too hard. The impossible is required of him – not the impossible in itself, but the impossible to him. How he winds, turns, agonizes, advances, and recoils ever reminded, ever reminding himself, and at last almost loses his purpose from his thoughts, without ever again recovering his peace of mind.'[20]

The Romantics established once and for all what earlier critics had only hinted at: that *Hamlet* is Shakespeare's most personal play, and that Hamlet himself can be seen as an existential, universal Everyman. 'Hamlet is a name,' wrote William Hazlitt in 1818, 'his speeches and sayings but the idle coinage of the poet's brain. What then, are they not real? They are as real as our own thoughts. Their reality is in the reader's mind. It is *we* who are Hamlet'.[21]

We can see, then, that by the early nineteenth century there had been many Hamlets; from the rather bitter and cynical revenger of the seventeenth century, to the psychologically rounded, sympathetic character of Garrick in the eighteenth century, to Hazlitt's 'prince of philosophical speculators'. There had been the occasional suggestion that Hamlet actually goes mad in the play, but no more than suggestions, and for the most part, Hamlet's contemplative melancholy was simply part of his character. And the balance of theatrical opinion throughout the nineteenth century was that diagnosing madness kills the tragedy. Or as James Russell Lowell put it in the 1860s, if Hamlet were really mad he would be irresponsible, and the whole play a chaos.[22] Most of the great nineteenth-century actors, such as Henry Irving or Edwin Booth, refused to interpret a mad Hamlet. Booth was surrounded by tragedy: his brother John Wilkes Booth was Lincoln's assassin, his wife went mad, he himself was constitutionally melancholic. But he aimed to present Hamlet as consistently sane: 'I do not consider Hamlet mad,' he said, 'except in craft.'[23] Irving's Hamlet was described as 'entirely lovable'.

Thus, nineteenth-century critical and theatrical opinion continued largely to operate within the framework established by the Romantics. Of course, Hamlet was an enigma, but that was part of his fascination.

Banded against this was a body of opinion which insisted that Hamlet was insane. It derived almost entirely from the nascent psychiatric profession in America and Britain, a speciality which in its formative period can be identified with the orderly, moralistic, and initially optimistic world of the asylum.[24] We have mentioned its main protagonists: John Conolly, medical superintendent at Hanwell Asylum, near London, where he introduced the 'non-restraint' system; J.C. Bucknill, resident superintendent of the Devon County Asylum from 1844 to 1862, first editor of the *Journal of Mental Science* (1853-62) and a co-founder of the neurological journal *Brain* (1878);[25] Amariah Brigham, Bucknill's complement as first editor of the *American Journal of Insanity* (1844), and superintendent of the New York State Lunatic Asylum;[26] Isaac Ray, a key figure in the establishment of legal psychiatry in the United States, like Brigham a founder of the Association of Medical Superintendents of American Institutions for the Insane, and physician-in-chief of Butler Hospital in Providence, Rhode Island;[27] A.O. Kellogg, assistant physician of the State Hospital for the Insane in Poughkeepsie, NY; and an obscure English doctor, possibly formerly an actor, George Farren, who was described as resident director of the Asylum Foreign and Domestic Life Assurance Company in the 1830s.[28]

There are a few differences in these doctors' opinions, variously delivered in the half-century between the 1830s and the 1880s, but the differences are as nothing when compared with their points of professional agreement, and they may be treated essentially as a group. All were certain that Hamlet was of unsound mind. The problem with critics, Isaac Ray complained, was that they lacked the medical acumen 'to discern the essential distinction between real and feigned insanity'.[29] A.O. Kellogg believed it impossible to 'unlock

the profound mystery with which [Shakespeare] has surrounded the character of his hero, without the true key, which is at once furnished by the
supposition of the *real* madness of Hamlet, which, to the experienced
medical psychologist is quite . . . evident'.[30] Hamlet's first soliloquy ['O that
this too too solid flesh would melt'] already, Conolly insisted, demonstrates
his predisposition to unsoundness. Hamlet is 'constitutionally deficient in
that quality of a healthy brain or mind which may be termed its elasticity, in
virtue of which the changes and chances of the mutable world should be
sustained without damage, and in various trials steadfastness and trust still
preserved'.[31]

There were several reasons why these nineteenth-century psychiatrists
believed Hamlet to be of unsound mind. One was his suicidal tendencies. In
Shakespeare's day, suicide was a crime and unless the person who took his
own life could be proved to have been mentally deranged, he died a felon
and his property was forfeited to the state.[32] Christianity as interpreted by
sixteenth- and seventeenth-century churchmen was firm in its prohibition of
suicide – as Hamlet himself recognizes: 'Or that the Everlasting had not
fixt/His canon 'gainst self-slaughter.' Ophelia's suicide was done after overt
distraction had supervened, and her madness was never really in doubt. In
general Shakespeare and his fellow Elizabethan and Jacobean dramatists
reserved suicide for obvious villains or noble Romans, for whom suicide was
in some circumstances the only honourable way out. By the eighteenth
century, social attitudes to suicide had relaxed, but the law had not, so
coroners' juries routinely gave a verdict of temporary madness at the time of
the act (or of accidental death, if this was a possible interpretation) so that
the deceased's family could inherit his property.[33] In Garrick's version
Hamlet actually dies by running into Laertes' sword, and then joins Laertes'
(who survives) and Horatio's hands to pick up the pieces of the rotten state
of Denmark.[34] Werther of course dies by his own hand, and Hamlet's own
deliberations were in tune with the cultural preoccupations of the early
nineteenth century.

By early Victorian times, when psychiatric comment on Hamlet began,
suicide had been more or less completely medicalized, and was seen as
evidence either of excessive melancholy or of the same kind of irresistible
impulse seen in various forms of mania, such as homicidal or erotic
monomania. And Farren added a strongly religious and moral judgement to
Hamlet's 'To be or not to be' contemplation of suicide, claiming that he
there weighs the pros and cons of living so cold-bloodedly, and irreligiously,
that he must already show evidence of his madness.[35]

It was not simply Hamlet's meditations on suicide that gave nineteenth-
century psychiatrists the assurance to diagnose insanity. Ironically, it was
also his warning to Horatio and the others that he might put on an 'antic
disposition': that he might feign madness. Conolly insisted that Hamlet's
curious mixture of feigned and real madness was 'generally only known to
those who live much among the insane'; Farren triumphantly concluded that
'feigning madness is a theory with many persons who are subject to mental

aberrations'. More cautiously Bucknill pointed out that since one of Shakespeare's sources depicted another prince Hamlet feigning madness to escape the tyranny of his uncle, perhaps not too much should be construed from this twist of the plot.[36]

But Bucknill was at one with his psychiatric colleagues in seeing in Hamlet's incapacity to effect the revenge with which the ghost had charged him – his incapacity to act – the evidence of mental disease. It was a disjunction between *desire* and *will* which was construed by Victorian psychiatrists as a common feature of the lunatic.[37] Lunatics had simply lost control. It is in the 'nature of insanity to talk but not to act, to resolve but not to execute', believed Ray.[38] The Victorian concept of manliness, urged in dozens of pamphlets, sermons, and tracts aimed at the young, and built into the Victorian public school emphasis on vigorous sports and the fair play they were supposed to engender, viewed excessive introspection and preoccupation with self as a dangerous and vicious habit one step away from frank insanity.[39] Hamlet's early introspective cast of mind, Ray insisted, was but 'the precursor of [his] decided insanity'. The Romantic critic Charles Lamb, who described Hamlet as shy, negligent, and retiring, had pointed out than nine-tenths of what Hamlet says and does are 'transactions between himself and his moral sense, . . . effusions of his solitary musings'.[40] For the High Victorian psychiatrist, this was evidence of a morbid mind. A Hamlet paralysed to inaction, unable to call up the resources of will-power, unable to do his duty, is a Hamlet who is the victim of disease.

But it is not simply that Hamlet did not conform to the model product of the Victorian public schools. Insanity, for nineteenth-century psychiatrists, was a physical disease, the product of physiological dysfunction or organic changes. Nineteenth-century psychiatrists admitted the general relevance of certain psychological factors in the causation of insanity – jealousy, profound sorrow, and other strong emotions, for instance – but they resisted the impulse to formulate the idea of *primary* mental disease.[41] There were professional issues at stake here, for if insanity was a physical disease, little different in theory from tuberculosis or typhus, their own claims to being by education, knowledge, and social function obvious experts in looking after the insane logically followed.[42] A considerable amount of recent historical work has examined the professional side of Victorian psychiatry, and it was consistent with these psychiatrists' more general ideas of insanity, and their professional aspirations, that our nineteenth-century commentators on Hamlet should stress that his insanity was organically grounded. Amariah Brigham summarized this attitude as follows:

'An examination of Shakespeare's writings will show that he believed the following facts, all of which were in advance of the general opinions of the age, and are now deemed correct.
(1) That a well-formed brain, a good shaped head, is essential to a good mind.
(2) That insanity is a disease of the brain.

(3) That there is a general and partial insanity.

(4) That it is a disease which can be cured by medical means.

(5) That the causes are various, the most common of which he has particularly noticed.'[43]

Shakespeare, these nineteenth-century commentators insisted, with his intuitive genius recognized many of the physical indications of insanity. For instance when Hamlet, closeted with his mother, having just killed Polonius and having seen for the last time the ghost of his father, is urging her frantically to abstain from the incestuous bed, and is accused by his terrified mother of distraction, he replies, 'Ecstasy?/My pulse as yours doth temperately keep time/And makes as healthful music. It is not madness/That I have uttered; bring me to the test/And I the matter will re-word, which madness/Would gambol from.' A normal pulse and the ability to repeat what has been said without confusion: these, Hamlet insists, are proof of sanity. To this Bucknill replies: 'the pulse in mania averages about fifteen beats above that in health; that of the insane generally, including maniacs, only averages nine beats above the healthy standards; the pulse of melancholia and monomania is not above the average.' 'It is curious to observe', Conolly added, 'that the arguments [Hamlet] adduces to disprove his mother's supposition [of his madness] are precisely such as certain ingenious madmen delight to employ.' Put to the test, both Conolly and Bucknill imply, Hamlet would fail; his earlier bouts of feigned madness (if feigned they were) are gone, and he is physiologically deranged.[44]

In the end, however, nineteenth-century psychiatrists judged Hamlet mad on moral grounds. They found him sympathetic and moving only if mad. For, after all, in their eyes, he botches just about everything he attempts. Everything he touches turns to dross. He is in turn capricious and obscene with Ophelia; he feels no remorse after killing Polonius; contemplates killing his uncle when the latter is at fitful prayer and declines for fear that his uncle might go to heaven, thereby taking upon himself the right of judgement which God alone should possess;[45] he cold-bloodedly sends Rosenkrantz and Guildenstern to their deaths; he causes Ophelia's distraction and death; his mother and Laertes die as a result of his bungling. He is, within the moral world of Victorian psychiatry, either an unfeeling, egocentric cad or a madman, and it is only if his actions are explained by reference to his madness that our psychiatrists could view his tragedy in sympathetic terms, or could rationalize their own emotional responses to his story.

Nineteenth-century psychiatrists analysed Hamlet in terms of his actions, and their relation to his expressed states of mind and emotions. They noted, of course, his obsession with his mother's remarriage but were much more interested in his relationship with Ophelia than with Gertrude. They saw his delay as symptomatic of his melancholic disposition, his morbidly introspective personality, and his inappropriate and blunted emotional responses. They assumed his love of Ophelia to be pure and straightforward, and

attributed some of his psychological problems to her contradictory behaviour towards him.

But Hamlet changed with the coming of psychoanalysis. He acquired a
sexual identity, his introspectiveness became part of his fascination instead
of a part of his disease, his musings on suicide again, as in Romanticism,
became painful evocations of the existential human condition instead of an
indication of insanity. Freud was always drawn towards Shakespeare's plays
and it was he who first proposed what, with variations and endless
elaborations, has become a standard psychoanalytic interpretation in the
present century. For Freud, Hamlet was simply another version of the
universal Oedipal strivings which, unresolved, are the origin of much
neurotic behaviour in adults. Hamlet was Shakespeare's unique creation;
indeed, Hamlet *was* Shakespeare, created while mourning the death of his
father, and the death of his small son, named Hamnet, and reflecting
Shakespeare's own suicidal longings, his own weariness with this sterile
promontory, his own sexual fantasies and conflicts. Symbolically, the ghost
– Hamlet's father – is one of the roles Shakespeare the actor has been
thought to play. These biographical implications of Shakespeare naming his
son Hamnet, and playing the ghost, were used by James Joyce when, in
Ulysses, he wrote:

> 'Is it possible that the player Shakespeare, a ghost by absence, and in the
> vesture of buried Denmark, a ghost by death, speaking his own words to
> his own son's name (had Hamnet Shakespeare lived he would have been
> Prince Hamlet's twin) is it possible, I want to know, or probable that he
> did not foresee the logical conclusion of these premises: You are the
> dispossessed son, I am the murdered father; your mother is the guilty
> queen, Ann Shakespeare, born Hathaway.'[46]

For Freud, Hamlet cannot kill his uncle because of these Oedipal
strivings; because he identifies – unconsciously – with his uncle as having
done precisely what every male child fantasizes: killed his father and married
his own mother. By this, Freud could explain at once Hamlet's delay
(indeed, even in the final act, he can kill his uncle only after his mother is
dead) and Hamlet's intense emotional reaction to his mother's re-marriage
and sexuality. Curiously enough, Freud changed his mind: not about the
Oedipal interpretation but about the authorship of the play. He became a
keen student of the early twentieth-century suggestions that this untutored
actor from Stratford could not possibly have written such great works of art.
Freud was attracted by the possibility that England's national poet was not
even English – perhaps it was a corruption of the French name Jacques
Pierre?[47] Then, an Englishman with the appropriate name of Thomas
Looney published in 1920 a work entitled *'Shakespeare' Identified*, in which
Edward de Vere, Earl of Oxford, was confidently asserted as the author of
the plays bearing Shakespeare's name. It is, of course, in the nature of
psychoanalysis that it can explain not only Hamlet, but the reasons why
Freud could not accept Shakespeare as the author of his own plays: as

Norman Holland has written, Freud's urge to dethrone Shakespeare stemmed from his view of 'the artist as a kind of totem whom he both resented and emulated'.[48] At any rate, Freud's final pronouncement was that

'the name "William Shakespeare" is very probably a pseudonym behind which a great unknown lies concealed. Edward de Vere, Earl of Oxford, a man who has been thought to be identified with the author of Shakespeare's works, lost a beloved and admired father while he was still a boy and completely repudiated his mother, who contracted a new marriage very soon after her husband's death.'[49]

Freud's defection was a source of some embarrassment to his biographer, Ernest Jones, who earlier had extended Freud's initial brief comments on the Oedipal theme in *Hamlet* into a full essay, entitled 'A Psycho-analytic Study of Hamlet'; weaving Shakespeare's life as it is known or conjectured with the themes from the play, and finally pronouncing Hamlet a cyclo-thymic hysteric. As Jones sums it up:

'The main theme of [*Hamlet*] is a highly elaborated and disguised account of a boy's love for his mother and consequent jealousy of and hatred towards his father. ... There is ... reason to believe that the new life which Shakespeare poured into the old story was the outcome of inspirations that took their origin in the deepest and darkest regions of his mind.'[50]

Jones's discussion, couched in the language of psychoanalysis, is concerned with neurosis, not madness. Like other psychiatrists before and since, he used his own peculiar spectacles to view the world of Hamlet. For instance Theodore Lidz, concerned in research with the family dynamics of schizophrenia, has emphasized the complex series of familial and surrogate familial relationships in the play;[51] W.I.D. Scott, more interested in psychotic illness and in Jungian typologies, analysed Hamlet as a manic-depressive with a variable mental and emotional state (a 'morally orientated introverted intuitive');[52] Norman Holland, coming to psychoanalysis from literature, used the whole Shakespearean canon to attempt to illuminate many facets of Shakespeare's personality, insisting, as is common, that *Hamlet* is a uniquely personal statement by the Bard.

With the triumph of the psychoanalytical interpretation of Hamlet, we return, not necessarily to the character Shakespeare created, but to a Hamlet much closer to that of the Romantics: of Goethe, Schelling, Coleridge, Hazlitt, and Charles Lamb. While psychoanalytical readings have met with a mixed response from critics, they have at least provided a set of more flexible, culturally rooted concepts with which to join the world of art to the world of psychiatry.[53] Any reader of Henri Ellenberger's *Discovery of the Unconscious* will already have noted the Romantic roots of dynamic psychiatry.[54] And so with psychoanalysis, as he was for the Romantic critics, Hamlet has once again become for us Everyman. But with a difference, perhaps, for the psychoanalytical Everyman has been medicalized, become the modern Oedipal neurotic in need of professional help.

But in conclusion we must give Shakespeare – and Hamlet – the last word. Would Shakespeare have welcomed the coming of psychoanalysis? We cannot of course know, but there is a theme in Hamlet which suggests that, like the High Victorians, there were areas of life about which he knew but about which he might choose to remain silent. For *Hamlet* is a play not just about madness, real or feigned, but about the intrusiveness of spying. Rosenkrantz and Guildenstern are brought in to spy on Hamlet; Polonius, Gertrude, and Claudius spy on Hamlet and Ophelia; Polonius spies on Hamlet and Gertrude; Polonius sends Reynaldo to spy on Laertes in Paris. In fact, Polonius is the arch spy, masterminding a whole intricate network of intrigue. He is also, as Erik Erikson once noted, a kind of resident psychiatrist ('I have found the very cause of Hamlet's lunacy').[55] But what did Hamlet himself think of it all? Would he have enjoyed being on the couch? After the Player Scene, Hamlet and Rosenkrantz and Guildenstern are speaking.

Hamlet is fending himself from the persistent questioning and spying of his erstwhile friends. A recorder is brought on, and Hamlet challenges Guildenstern to play upon it:

Hamlet: Will you play upon this pipe?
Guildenstern: My Lord, I cannot.
Hamlet: I pray you.
Guildenstern: Believe me, I cannot.
Hamlet: I do beseech you.
Guildenstern: I know no touch of it, my Lord.
Hamlet: 'Tis as easy as lying: govern these ventages with your finger and thumb, give it breath with your mouth, and it will discourse most eloquent music. Look you, these are the stops.
Guildenstern: But these cannot I command to any utterance of harmony, I have not the skill.
Hamlet: Why look you now, how unworthy a thing you make of me: you would play upon me; you would seem to know my stops: you would pluck out the heart of my mystery; you would sound me from my lowest note, to the top of my compass: and there is much music, excellent voice, in this little organ, yet cannot you make it speak. Why do you think that I am easier to be played on, than a pipe? Call me what instrument you will, though you can fret me, you cannot play upon me.

Notes

1 For chlorosis, cf. Karl Figlio, 'Chlorosis and Chronic Disease in 19th-century Britain: the Social Constitution of Somatic Illness in a Capitalist Society', *Social History* 3 (1978): 167–97; and Irvine Loudon, 'The Disease Called Chlorosis', *Psychological Medicine* 14 (1984): 27–36. For hysteria, compare E.M. Thornton,

Hypnotism, Hysteria and Epilepsy: an Historical Synthesis (London: Heinemann, 1976) with Carroll Smith-Rosenberg and Charles Rosenberg, 'The Female Animal: Medical and Biological Views of Woman and Her Role in 19th Century America', *Journal of American History* 60 (1973); 332–56.

2 The problems of historical contextualism are considered in several of the essays in Peter Wright and Andrew Treacher (eds), *The Problem of Medical Knowledge: Examining the Social Construction of Medicine* (Edinburgh: Edinburgh University Press, 1982).

3 For Conolly, see Andrew Scull, 'John Conolly: A Victorian Psychiatric Career', in this volume. We have photographs of some of Conolly's patients: see Sander L. Gilman, *The Face of Madness: Hugh W. Diamond and the Origin of Psychiatric Photography* (New York: Brunner/Mazel, 1967).

4 For an intelligent sampling of this vast output, cf. Claude C.H. Williamson (ed.), *Readings on the Character of Hamlet, 1661–1947* (London: George Allen and Unwin, 1950); cf. A.A. Raven, *A Hamlet Bibliography and Reference Guide, 1877–1935* (Chicago: University of Chicago Press, 1936).

5 A generous bibliography of medical and psychiatric works on Shakespeare is in I.I. Edgar, *Shakespeare, Medicine and Psychiatry* (London: Vision, 1971).

6 The fullest psychoanalytical study of Hamlet is in K.R. Eissler, *Discourse on Hamlet and HAMLET* (New York: International Universities Press, 1971), which is 656 pages long.

7 Eliot Slater, 'What Happened at Elsinore: A Diversion', in Martin Roth and Valerie Cowie (eds), *Psychiatry, Genetics and Pathography* (London: Gaskell Press, 1979), pp. 104–21.

8 Cf. Thomas J. Scheff, *Being Mentally Ill: A Sociological Study* (Chicago: Aldine Publishing Company, 1966).

9 Theodore Lidz, *Hamlet's Enemy. Madness and Myth in HAMLET* (London: Vision, 1976), p. 9.

10 Henry Maudsley, 'Hamlet', in *Body and Mind*, 2nd edn (London: Macmillan, 1873), p. 145–95. Maudsley also left an essay entitled 'Shakespeare: "Testimonied in His Own Bringings forth"', in his *Heredity, Variation and Genius* (London: John Bale, 1908). We are grateful to Dr T.H. Turner for calling our attention to the latter, and for supplying us with a photocopy of it.

11 These problems are dealt with, *inter alia*, in J. Dover Wilson, *What Happens in Hamlet*, 3rd edn. (Cambridge: Cambridge University Press, 1951); and in J. Dover Wilson (ed.), *The Tragedie of Hamlet* (Weimar: Crannah Press, 1930). Cf. Roland M. Frye *The Renaissance Hamlet* (Princeton, NJ: Princeton University Press, 1984).

12 Paul S. Conklin, *A History of Hamlet Criticism* (London: Frank Cass, 1967), is extremely illuminating for seventeenth- and eighteenth-century attitudes.

13 In addition to Conklin, cf. Augustus Ralli, *A History of Shakespearian Criticism*, 2 vols (New York: Humanities Press, 1965).

14 Quoted in Ralli, *A History of Shakespearian Criticism*, p. 90.

15 Quoted in Conklin, *A History of Hamlet Criticism*, p. 40.

16 Cf. W.F. Bynum, 'The Nervous Patient in Eighteenth and Nineteenth-Century Britain', in this volume, and Roy Porter, '"The Rage of Party": A Glorious Revolution in English Psychiatry?', *Medical History* 27 (1983): 35–50.

17 Johnson's phrase is from his 'Preface' to his edition of Shakespeare (1765), quoted in Williamson, *Readings on the Character of Hamlet*, p. 14. Cf. Arthur Sherbo (ed.), *Johnson on Shakespeare*, vols 7 and 8 of the Yale Edition of the Works of

Samuel Johnson (New Haven, Conn. and London: Yale University Press, 1968).

18 Quoted in Williamson, *Readings on the Character of Hamlet*, pp. 18–19. In his adaptation of the play, David Garrick omitted the grave-digging scene. Cf. G.W. Stone, Jr. and G.M. Kahrl, *David Garrick, A Critical Biography* (Carbondale, Ill: Southern Illinois University Press, 1979), pp. 269ff.

19 Some of Coleridge's reflections on Hamlet are in Williamson, *Readings on the Character of Hamlet*, pp. 31–7, including Coleridge's confession that 'I have a smack of Hamlet myself, if I may say so.' Cf. R.A. Foakes (ed.), *Coleridge on Shakespeare* (Charlottesville, Va.: University Press of Virginia, 1971).

20 These comments are taken from Goethe's *Wilhelm Meister* (1778) and are quoted (in Carlyle's translation) in Williamson, *Readings on the Character of Hamlet*, pp. 27–8.

21 Hazlitt's comments were published in his *Characters of Shakespeare's Plays*, an extract of which is in Williamson, *Readings on the Character of Hamlet*, pp. 45–9.

22 For an extract of Lowell's comments, cf. Williamson, *Readings on the Character of Hamlet*, pp. 90–5.

23 For Irving's Hamlet, see George C.D. Odell, *Shakespeare – From Betterton to Irving*, 2 vols (New York: Benjamin Bloom, 1963,) vol. 2, p. 418; and William Winter, *Shakespeare on the Stage* (New York: Benjamin Bloom, 1969, p. 348, where the quotation appears.

24 Aspects of nineteenth-century asylums are discussed in Andrew T. Scull, *Museums of Madness* (London: Allen Lane, 1979); Nancy Tomes, *A Generous Confidence: Thomas Story Kirkbride and the Art of Asylum-keeping, 1840–1883* (Cambridge: Cambridge University Press, 1984); and Gerald Grob, *Mental Illness and American Society, 1875–1940* (Princeton, NJ: Princeton University Press, 1983).

25 For Bucknill, cf. W.F. Bynum, 'The Nervous Patient in Eighteenth- and Nineteenth-Century Britain', in this volume; and W.F. Bynum, 'Themes in British Psychiatry, J.C. Prichard (1786–1848) to Henry Maudsley (1835–1918)', in Michael Ruse (ed.), *Nature Animated* (Dordrecht and Boston: D. Reidel, 1983), pp. 225–42.

26 On the formation of a psychiatric profession in the United States, cf. John A. Pitts, 'The Association of Medical Superintendents of American Institutions for the Insane, 1844–1892: A Case Study of Specialism in American Medicine' (unpublished PhD thesis, University of Pennsylvania, 1978).

27 For Ray, see Jacques Quen, 'Issac Ray and Mental Hygiene in America', *Annals of the New York Academy of Science* 291 (1977): 83–93.

28 George Farren, *Essays on the Varieties in Mania, Exhibited by the Characters of Hamlet, Ophehia, Lear, and Edgar* (London: Dean and Munday, 1833; facsimile reprint, New York: AMS Press, n.d.). The position Farren held is given on the title page. Our supposition that he might have been an actor comes from Isaac Ray's (below, note 29) statement that an actor named William Farren published in 1824 some articles elaborating on the reality of Hamlet's madness.

29 Isaac Ray, 'Shakespeare's Delineations of Insanity', in his *Contributions to Mental Pathology* (Boston, Mass.: Little, Brown, 1873), p. 505.

30 A.O. Kellogg, *Shakespeare's Delineations of Insanity, Imbecility and Suicide* (New York: Hurd and Houghton, 1866), p. 32. Italics in original.

31 John Conolly, *A Study of Hamlet* (London: Edward Moxon, 1863), p. 24.

32 Michael MacDonald, 'The Inner Side of Wisdom: Suicide in Early Modern

England', *Psychological Medicine* 7 (1977): pp. 565–82; Roland Bartel, 'Suicide in Eighteenth-century England: the Myth of a Reputation', *Huntington Library Quarterly* 22 (1960): 145–58.

33 A treatise which shows particularly well the medicalization of suicide is Forbes Winslow, *The Anatomy of Suicide* (London: Henry Renshaw, 1840); cf. Barbara T. Gates, 'Suicide and the Victorian Psychiatrists', *Journal of the History of the Behavioral Sciences* 16 (1980): 164–74.

34 Garrick's Hamlet is discussed in Odell, *Shakespeare* vol. 1, pp. 385–89; and Stone and Kahrl, *David Garrick*, pp. 269ff.

35 Farren, *Varieties in Mania*, pp. 40ff.

36 Conolly, *A Study of Hamlet*, p. 52; Farren, *Varieties in Mania*, p. 30; J.C. Bucknill, *The Psychology of Shakespeare* (London: Longman, 1859), pp. 51ff.

37 Roger Smith, *Trial by Medicine* (Edinburgh: Edinburgh University Press, 1981), explores the medico-legal ramifications of the concepts of will and responsibility.

38 Issac Ray, 'Shakespeare's Delineations of Insanity' p. 510.

39 Victorian attitudes towards introspection have been examined by Michael J. Clark in a paper entitled 'Morbid Introspection', delivered at a seminar at University College, London. More general aspects of Victorian notions of manly health may be found in J.A. Mangan, *Athleticism in the Victorian and Edwardian Public School* (Cambridge: Cambridge University Press, 1981); and Bruce Haley, *The Healthy Body and Victorian Culture* (Cambridge, Mass.: Harvard University Press, 1978).

40 Williamson, *Readings on the Character of Hamlet*, pp. 41–3, contains some of Lamb's comments on Hamlet.

41 Michael J. Clark, 'The Rejection of Psychological Approaches to Mental Disorder in Late Nineteenth-century British Psychiatry', in Andrew Scull (ed.), *Madhouses, Mad-Doctors and Madmen* (Philadelphia, Pa.: University of Pennsylvania Press and London: Athlone Press, 1981), pp. 271–312.

42 These professional dimensions have been often explored, e.g. in Andrew Scull, *Museums of Madness* (London: Allen Lane, 1979); and W.F. Bynum, 'Rationales for Therapy in British Psychiatry, 1780–1835', *Medical History* 18 (1974): 317–34, reprinted, with other essays which examine aspects of the nineteenth-century psychiatric profession, in Scull, *Madhouses, Mad-doctors and Madmen*.

43 Amariah Brigham, 'Shakespeare's Illustrations of Insanity', *American Journal of Insanity* 1 (1844).

44 Conolly, *A Study of Hamlet*, p. 155, Bucknill, *The Psychology of Shakespeare* p. 88; and Henry Halford, 'Popular and Classical Illustrations of Insanity', in *Essays and Observations*, 3rd edn (London: J. Murray, 1842).

45 Dr Johnson commented on Hamlet's cold-blooded speech behind his uncle at prayer, 'This speech, in which *Hamlet*, represented as a virtuous character, is not content with taking blood for blood, but contrives damnation for the man that he would punish, is too horrible to be read or to be uttered.' In Mona Wilson (ed.), *Dr Johnson. Prose and Poetry* (London: Rupert Hart-Davis, 1970), p. 616.

46 James Joyce, *Ulysses* (Harmondsworth: Penguin Books, 1966).

47 A suggestion first made by an Italian, Professor Gentilli. For concise discussions of this, and Freud's attitudes to 'the man from Stratford', cf. S. Schoenbaum, *Shakespeare's Lives* (Oxford: Clarendon Press, 1970), pp. 608–13, and Ernest Jones, *Sigmund Freud: Life and Work*, 3 vols (London: Hogarth Press, 1956–57), vol. 3, pp. 459–62.

48 Norman Holland, *Psychoanalysis and Shakespeare* (New York: McGraw-Hill,

1966), p. 59; on pp. 35–6, Holland gives a full list of Freud's references and allusions to *Hamlet*.

49 Quoted, from the final edition (1940) of Freud's *Outline of Psychoanalysis*, by Schoenbaum, *Shakespeare's Lives*, p. 611.

50 Ernest Jones, 'A Psycho-analytic Study of Hamlet', in his *Essays in Applied Psycho-Analysis* (London: International Psycho-analytical Press, 1923), pp. 86, 98.

51 Lidz, *Hamlet's Enemy*; T. Lidz, *The Family and Human Adaptation* (New York: International Universities Press, 1963).

52 W.I.D. Scott, *Shakespeare's Melancholics* (London: Mills and Boon, 1962). Scott runs through much of the Shakespearean canon, liberally sprinkling psychiatric diagnoses on his major characters. Thus, Don John is a psychopath, Timon a general paralytic, Pericles a schizophrenic and Leontes a paranoid.

53 Holland's monograph *Psychoanalysis and Shakespeare* is particularly rich bibliographically.

54 Henri F. Ellenberger, *The Discovery of the Unconscious* (New York: Basic Books, 1970).

55 Noted by Holland, *Psychoanalysis and Shakespeare*, p. 175.

Name index

Ackerknecht, E. 208, 210
Adams, Dr 66, 79
Addison, J. 73
Adler, A. 280
Agrippa, King 31, 37
Albemarle, Earl of 105
Albertini, H. 42
Alexander, F. 2, 9, 40
Alexander, M. 202
Allbutt, T.C. 96
Allderidge, P. 5
Ambrose, Saint 31
Amos, Mr 117
Andersson, O. 199
Aquinas, Saint Thomas 30
Aristotle 8, 35, 36
Arnold, T. 16
Athanasius, Saint 32
Auckland, Lord 115
Austin, J.L. 266
Avicenna 37
Azam, E. 240, 244

Bacon, F. 92
Baillarger, J. 191, 192, 193, 196
Bakewell, T. 121
Balderston, K. 71
Barnett, Dr R. 130
Barrett, W. 237
Baruk, H. 172
Bate, W.J. 71
Bateson, G. 13
Battie, W. 12
Beard, G. 14, 90, 97
Bell, C. 94, 151–54, 155, 157
Bennett, J.R. 115–16
Benzoni 123
Berman, M. 40
Bernard, C. 212, 213

Bernheim, H. 240, 243, 257–58
Berrios, G.E. 17
Bertalanffy 54
Bianchi, L. 174
Bichat, M.F.X. 203
Birkbeck, Dr G. 107
Blackmore, Sir R. 73
Bleuler, E. 174
Blustein, B. 12, 90
Bodin 37
Bohme, C.C. 156
Bonaparte, M. 273
Bonnet, H. 209, 216
Booth, E. 294
Booth, J.W. 294
Boswell, J. 66–7, 68, 69, 71, 72, 74, 77,
  91
Braid, J. 239
Brain, Lord W.R. 71
Bramwell, J.M. 244
Breuer, A.O. 258, 260, 274
Brigham, A. 290, 294, 296–97
Brochin, R.H. 210, 219
Brocklesby, Dr 81
Brody, S. 283–84
Brougham, Lord 107, 115, 132
Broussais, F.J.V. 203
Brown, T. 11-12
Brown-Séquard, C.E. 211
Browne, J. 6, 15
Brunswick, R.M. 280
Brunton, T.L. 96
Brushfield, T. 157–58
Buchez, P. 214–16, 219–20
Bucknill, J.C. 96, 133, 135, 290, 294, 296,
  297
Burdon-Sanderson, J.S. 97
Burney, F. 67, 69, 72
Burton, R. 8, 37, 42, 43, 80

Subject index